"There are two features that are especially noteworthy. First, each chapter presents a nomological network which allows the reader to see how the focal construct relates to both antecedents and outcomes. Second, each chapter also includes some sample measures which is a great addition that gets right to what these constructs mean and how to tap them. This book belongs on the shelves of practitioners and researchers alike – an important reference for the 21st century."

—*Paul E. Levy, The University of Akron, USA*

# ESSENTIALS OF JOB ATTITUDES AND OTHER WORKPLACE PSYCHOLOGICAL CONSTRUCTS

Although the topic of job attitudes and other workplace psychological constructs such as perceptions, identity, bonds, and motivational states is important, there are no books addressing the topic as a whole. *Essentials of Job Attitudes and Other Workplace Psychological Constructs* seeks to fill that void in a comprehensive edited volume that compiles chapters by experts on each construct.

*Essentials of Job Attitudes and Other Workplace Psychological Constructs* begins with a review of the concept of job attitudes and other workplace psychological constructs, then devotes a single chapter to each construct. These chapters focus on organizational justice, perceived organizational support, organizational identification, job involvement, workplace commitments, job embeddedness, job satisfaction, employee engagement, and team-related work attitudes. Each of these chapters addresses parallel content including definitions, history, theory, a critique of the field to date with future research recommendations, and how the given construct can be used in practice. There are two additional features that make this book unique: first, each chapter provides a nomological network figure of the workplace psychological construct addressed; and second, each chapter provides one or more of the current measures used to assess the construct of interest.

*Essentials of Job Attitudes and Other Workplace Psychological Constructs* is an ideal text for students and professionals in industrial-organizational psychology, organizational behavior, and human resource management.

**Valerie I. Sessa** is professor of psychology at Montclair State University in Montclair, NJ, USA, where she teaches industrial-organizational psychology at the undergraduate, masters, and PhD levels.

**Nathan A. Bowling** is professor of psychology at Wright State University in Dayton, Ohio, USA, where he teaches within the industrial-organizational psychology PhD concentration.

# ESSENTIALS OF INDUSTRIAL AND ORGANIZATIONAL PSYCHOLOGY
Series Editor: Scott Highhouse

## ESSENTIALS OF JOB ATTITUDES AND OTHER WORKPLACE PSYCHOLOGICAL CONSTRUCTS
*Edited by Valerie I. Sessa and Nathan A. Bowling*

For more information about this series, please visit:
www.routledge.com/Essentials-of-Industrial-and-Organizational-Psychology/book-series/EIOP

# ESSENTIALS OF JOB ATTITUDES AND OTHER WORKPLACE PSYCHOLOGICAL CONSTRUCTS

*Edited by Valerie I. Sessa and Nathan A. Bowling*

Routledge
Taylor & Francis Group

NEW YORK AND LONDON

First published 2021
by Routledge
52 Vanderbilt Avenue, New York, NY 10017

and by Routledge
2 Park Square, Milton Park, Abingdon, Oxon OX14 4RN

*Routledge is an imprint of the Taylor & Francis Group, an informa business*

*Library of Congress Cataloging-in-Publication Data*
Names: Sessa, Valerie I., editor. | Bowling, Nathan A., editor.
Title: Essentials of job attitudes and other workplace psychological constructs /
edited by Valerie I. Sessa and Nathan A. Bowling.
Description: New York, NY: Routledge, 2021. |
Includes bibliographical references and index. Identifiers: LCCN 2020029513 (print) |
LCCN 2020029514 (ebook) | ISBN 9780367344276 (hardback) |
ISBN 9780367344283 (paperback) | ISBN 9780429325755 (ebook)
Subjects: LCSH: Employees–Attitudes | Work Psychological aspects. |
Psychology, Industrial. Classification: LCC HF5548.8 .E785 2021 (print) |
LCC HF5548.8 (ebook) | DDC 158.7 dc23
LC record available at https://lccn.loc.gov/2020029513
LC ebook record available at https://lccn.loc.gov/2020029514

ISBN: 978-0-367-34427-6 (hbk)
ISBN: 978-0-367-34428-3 (pbk)
ISBN: 978-0-429-32575-5 (ebk)

Typeset in Baskerville
by Newgen Publishing UK

We Dedicate this Book to the Grocery Store, Healthcare, Law Enforcement, Restaurant, and Transportation Workers and Others who have Braved the Front Lines During the COVID-19 Pandemic.

# CONTENTS

# CONTENTS

# FIGURES

# TABLES

# APPENDICES

# CONTRIBUTORS

**Editors:**

**Valerie I. Sessa** is a professor of psychology at Montclair State University in Montclair, NJ, USA, where she teaches industrial-organizational psychology at the undergraduate, masters, and PhD levels. Prior to MSU, she worked as a research scientist and director at the Center for Creative Leadership. Valerie has also worked as a consultant in a variety of areas, including high potential manager assessment. Her research appears in top scholarly journals, including *Journal of Applied Psychology*, *Human Resource Development Review*, *Human Resource Management*, and *Journal of Management Development*. Her books include *Executive Selection: Strategies for Success* (with Jodi Taylor), *Continuous Learning in Organizations: Individual, Group, and Organizational Perspectives* and *Work group learning: Understanding, improving, and assessing how groups learn in organizations* (both with Manny London), and *College Student Leadership Development*.

**Nathan A. Bowling** is a professor of psychology at Wright State University in Dayton, Ohio, USA, where he teaches within the industrial-organizational psychology PhD concentration. He has authored over 50 peer-reviewed articles, many of which have appeared in top-tier journals, including the *Journal of Applied Psychology*, the *Journal of Personality and Social Psychology*, and the *Journal of Occupational Health Psychology*. His research was featured in Joireman and Van Lange's (2015) American Psychological Association book *How to Publish High-Quality Research* and in 2017 he was listed among the top 2% of most cited authors in I-O psychology textbooks. Nathan is a Fellow of the Society for Industrial and Organizational Psychology (SIOP).

**Chapter Authors:**

**Natalie J. Allen** is a professor of Psychology at Western University, London, Canada. She is a fellow of the Society for Industrial & Organizational Psychology and the Canadian Psychological Association and former Associate Editor of the *Journal of Occupational and Organizational Psychology*.

Her current research focuses on the psychology of teams/teamwork and work attitudes.

**Gaëtane Caesens** is an assistant professor in Personnel Psychology and Human Resource Management at the Université catholique de Louvain, Belgium. Her research interests include perceived organizational support, work engagement, and organizational dehumanization. She is the (co-) author of a number of peer-reviewed articles published in international journals such as Journal of Business and Psychology.

**Geoffrey Chapman** is employed at CQUniversity, Australia as part of the Work and Employment Research Group. He completed his PhD at Western Sydney University where he focused on personality profiling and positive organizational behavior. His current research aims to improve Human Resource Management in organizations through positive psychology and effective team communication.

**James M. Diefendorff** is a professor of psychology in the Industrial/Organizational Psychology program at the University of Akron, USA. His research interests include self-regulatory processes, work motivation, and emotional labor. Dr. Diefendorff served as associate editor at *Personnel Psychology* and *Journal of Business and Psychology*.

**Nicole L. Fiorentino** is an undergraduate student at West Chester University of Pennsylvania, USA, interested in the field of Industrial/Organizational (I/O) Psychology. She has been awarded a grant for mentored research and has experience consulting with non-profit organizations. She enjoys her coursework in I/O Psychology and looks forward to pursuing a graduate degree in the field.

**David R. Glerum** is a research scientist at the Fisher Leadership Initiative at the Ohio State University, USA. He is also a leadership development consultant at Pangloss Industries. His research focuses on job attitudes, training & development, leadership, organizational justice, and emotional intelligence.

**Jamie A. Gruman** is a professor and Senior Research Fellow in the Gordon S. Lang School of Business and Economics at the University of Guelph, Canada. His current research interests include organizational socialization and positive organizational psychology with particular emphasis on employee engagement.

**Beni Halvorsen** is a lecturer at RMIT University's School of Management in Melbourne, Australia. He completed his PhD in Human Resource Management at the University of South Australia Business School. His research focuses on migrant, minority, refugee, and underrepresented employees' experiences in the workplace, job embeddedness, employee turnover and retention, and diversity.

**Timothy A. Judge** is the Joseph A. Alutto Chair in Leadership Effectiveness and the Executive Director of the Leadership Initiative within the Max M. Fisher College of Business at The Ohio State University, USA. His primary areas of research are leadership, job attitudes, personality, emotions, and performance.

**Megan E. Kenworthy** is a doctoral student in the Industrial/Organizational Psychology program at The University of Akron. She received her BA in Psychology with honors from The University of Akron, USA in 2018. A few of her research interests include emotional labor, employee well-being, and motivation.

**Howard J. Klein** is a professor of management and human resources in the Fisher College of Business at The Ohio State University, USA. He received his PhD from Michigan State University. His research centers on the study of workplace commitments, socialization, goal setting, training, and performance management. Professor Klein is a fellow of the Society for Industrial and Organizational Psychology.

**Hyun-Jung Lee** (PhD, LSE) is an assistant professor in Management at the London School of Economics, England. Her research focuses on "being different" and its implications in the workplace in an increasingly globalized yet fragmented world. Her work appears in leading academic journals including *Journal of Management, Journal of Management Studies,* and *Journal of Applied Psychology.*

**Alice Maniezki** is doing her PhD in the Department of Social Psychology at the University of Valencia, Spain. She is a predoctoral researcher and assistant lecturer at the Research Institute IDOCAL. Her research interest focuses on organizational justice, trust, service quality, and quality of life.

**Vicente Martínez-Tur,** PhD, is a professor in Organizational Psychology at the University of Valencia, Spain. He has published numerous studies in the discipline in books and scientific journals. He coordinates several projects about the impact of organizational processes (justice, quality, climate, emotional labor) on service users (satisfaction, quality of life).

**Carolina Moliner,** PhD, is an associate professor in Organizational Psychology at the University of Valencia, Spain. As a researcher she has participate in more than 10 research projects. She has published more than 45 research articles in national and high-impact international journals such as *European Journal of Work and Organizational Psychology, Journal of Behavioral Decision Making, Personnel Review or Research in Developmental Disabilities.* She has presented more than 80 papers in international congresses. Her primary research interests include organizational justice and trust, as well as service quality, well-being at work, and intergroups relations.

**Brad Nikolic** is a strategy expert providing advice to clients in industry on change management and organizational transformation. He completed his PhD in Organizational Behavior at RMIT University in Melbourne, Australia. His research on organizational leadership and its impact on workplace attitudes and behaviors has been presented nationally and internationally.

**Megan T. Nolan** is an Assistant Professor of Psychology at West Chester University of Pennsylvania, USA. She received her B.S. in Psychology with honors from Penn State University in 2012 and her PhD in I/O Psychology from The University of Akron in 2019. She studies motivation, coping, emotions, and employee well-being.

**Catrina Notari** is in the PhD program in the Department of Industrial/Organizational Psychology at Montclair State University in Montclair, New Jersey, USA. She is a graduate research assistant, and her research interest focuses on shared leadership and leadership development.

**Hee Man Park** is an assistant professor of Human Resource Management at the Pennsylvania State University, USA. He currently conducts research on social environments and HRM practices that facilitate employee well-being, commitment, and performance by focusing on leader behaviors (e.g., abusive supervision) and benefits and costs of interpersonal relationships.

**Katrina Radford** is a senior lecturer within Griffith University Business School, Australia. Her research interests include HRM, employee turnover and retention, and aging.

**Alan M. Saks** is a professor of Human Resources Management in the Centre for Industrial Relations and Human Resources at the University of Toronto, Canada. His main areas of research include employee engagement, organizational socialization, transfer of training, and job search.

**Florence Stinglhamber** is a professor of Organizational Psychology and Human Resource Management at the Université catholique de Louvain, Belgium. Her main research interests include perceived organizational/supervisor support and organizational dehumanization. She is the (co-)author of a number of peer-reviewed articles published in international journals such as Journal of Applied Psychology.

**Steven T. Tseng** is a PhD candidate in the Industrial/Organizational Psychology program at the University of Akron, USA. He received his MA in Industrial/Organizational Psychology at the University of Akron and his BA in Psychology at the University of California, Berkeley. His research interests include performance management, leadership, motivation, and human resource management.

**Stephen H. Wagner** is a professor of management at Governors State University, USA. He received his PhD in social and organizational psychology from Northern Illinois University and held HR positions in corporate and public sector settings. He has published in various scholarly journals, including *Journal of Applied Psychology*, *Personnel Psychology*, and *Journal of Personality and Social Psychology*.

**Hannah Weisman** is a PhD candidate in Management at the London School of Economics, England. Her research focuses on meaningful work and proactivity. In 2019, she was a finalist in the INFORMS/Organization Science Best Dissertation Proposal Competition. She was also awarded "Best Overall Paper" by the Academy of Management Careers Division.

**Chia-Huei Wu** is a professor at the University of Leeds, United Kingdom. He studies proactive behavior, personality development, work design, and subjective well-being. His work has been published in *Academy of Management Journal*, *Journal of Applied Psychology*, and *Journal of Management*, among others. He is also the author of the book *Employee Proactivity in Organizations: An Attachment Perspective*.

**Katsuhiko Yoshikawa** is an associate professor at Shizenkan University and visiting researcher at Waseda University, Japan. He conducts research on prosocial and proactive behaviors among a diverse workforce and on human resource management at multinational corporations. He received his BA in Economics from Kyoto University and his MSc and PhD in Management from London School of Economics and Political Science.

**Shuxia (Carrie) Zhang** is a PhD candidate at Fisher College of Business, the Ohio State University, USA. Her research focuses primarily on empowering leadership, leader humility, leader-employee interaction within teams, and employee well-being.

# SERIES FOREWORD

At Bowling Green State University, we recently asked our Industrial-Organizational (I-O) doctoral students a preliminary (a.k.a. comprehensive) examination question about contemporary research on job attitudes. We specifically asked them to identify chapters and authors for a hypothetical book on job attitudes. I was surprised at how hard this was for them. Upon reflection, however, I believe this demonstrates more than merely a shortcoming in our doctoral training. The area of job attitudes is more complex than it used to be, and its boundaries are more fluid than they were in the past.

To the rescue is the current edited volume by Nathan A. Bowling and Valerie I. Sessa entitled *Essentials of Job Attitudes and Other Workplace Psychological Constructs*. Valerie and Nathan succeeded in pulling together important workplace constructs to provide a reference that updates our thinking in terms of what constitutes the field of work attitudes, a field that used to have more defined boundaries and more obvious foci. The editors have assembled an impressive group of scholars who are world-renowned experts on specific attitude-related constructs relevant to work.

At a time when various areas of I-O expertise are being encroached upon by interlopers, it is important to plant a flag and take the lead in defining workplace attitudes and beliefs. Some of us love our jobs, some of us do not. Our relationship with our work impacts every part of our lives. How we respond to our jobs has enormous consequences for life meaning, mental well-being, and physical health – not to mention our contributions to society. It is time to get back to the business of studying and following developments on attitudes and related constructs at work.

The goal of the *Essentials of Industrial and Organizational Psychology Series* is to produce accessible guides that cover basic and advanced concepts in a straightforward, readable style. Each book in the series covers a specific topic, providing essentials that managers, practitioners, and other well-educated people should know. Although the presentation may range from traditional textbook format to edited volumes, they are all brief books that could be used as source texts in master's and doctoral programs in I-O, and perhaps even for specialty undergraduate courses.

I am truly grateful to the authors and editors for undertaking the daunting task of producing these important contributions to our science and practice.

*Scott Highhouse*
*Series Editor*
*Bowling Green State University*

# FOREWORD

There are two fundamental questions for the organizational sciences having to do with employees:

- How well do employees perform?
- How do employees feel about their jobs?

Most research articles in this domain will deal with one or both of these questions in some form, asking about potential antecedents, consequences, and boundary conditions. Practicing managers pay attention to both of these questions as well since employee feelings and performance represent important benchmarks that contribute to organizational success. Thus it is important that we understand both feelings and performance, and how they relate to one another.

This book provides a comprehensive overview of what is currently known about the second question—how employees feel about work. Its focus is on job attitudes broadly considered. That is, how do employees evaluate and feel about work and different aspects of their jobs? The book is highly relevant to the first question as well since job attitudes have important links to job performance—especially negative behaviors at work, that is, counterproductive work behaviors.

Researchers have developed a number of distinct but overlapping constructs that reflect job attitudes, and each has a rich literature with many sources from which to draw. The most basic job attitude is job satisfaction, which reflects how an employee feels about the job and various aspects of the job, such as pay, coworkers, nature of work, and their supervisor. This might be considered a universal outcome variable since it is included in so many research studies, linking it to hundreds of other variables. A check of PsycInfo on March 24, 2020 using the keywords "job satisfaction" or "work satisfaction" found nearly 32,000 academic sources including articles, books, chapters, and dissertations.

Job satisfaction is not the only important job attitude. Some attitudes deal with the connection of the employee to the current employer. The most often studied is organizational commitment, which reflects the attachment of an individual to the job. It includes not only the attitude toward the current employer, but the forces that keep the individual from leaving. Others are employee engagement, job embeddedness, and organizational identification. Job involvement is a similar attitude, but focuses not on the current employer, but rather on the occupation.

Some attitudes reflect specific aspects of the job rather than the overall experience. Organizational justice concerns feelings of fair treatment by the immediate supervisor or the organization itself. Perceived organizational support has to do with feelings that the employee is supported and valued.

This book has individual chapters on each of these eight attitude variables written by an impressive panel of expert researchers. Managers, researchers, students, and others interested in the topic of job attitudes will find this an invaluable resource that integrates and synthesizes a vast literature into a manageable single volume. Job attitudes are central to the understanding of how people behave in the workplace. This book provides a good introduction to the different attitudes that have been identified and studied.

*Paul E. Spector*
*University of South Florida*

# PREFACE

Job attitudes are among one of the most enduring and widely studied topics in organizational research (Dalal, 2012). Drawing from the wider social psychological research, job attitudes are fundamental evaluations of one's job experiences which potentially influence important employee behaviors and organizational outcomes. In addition, job attitude theory, measurement, and change is considered a core content competency that I-O psychology graduate students should master during the course of their graduate education. Although the topic of job attitudes is important to the research and practice of I-O psychology as well as the education of I-O students, there are no recent books addressing the topic as a whole (although there are specific books and review articles that address each construct separately, see for a few examples, Bakker & Leiter, 2015, Eisenberger & Stinglhamber, 2011, Klein, Becker, & Meyer, 2009, Moliner, Cropanzano, & Martinez-Tur, 2017, Spector, 1997). The current edited book seeks to fill this void by providing a summary of the state of the knowledge regarding job attitudes.

When deciding on which job attitudes to include in this book, we used the SIOP Guidelines for Education and Training (Society for Industrial and Organizational Psychology, Inc. 2016) as a starting point. The Guidelines suggest that job attitudes include perceptions of justice and support, job involvement, organizational commitment, job satisfaction, and engagement. Based on reviewer feedback, we added organizational identification and job embeddedness to the list. The guidelines further suggest that I-O psychologists must know how attitudes are formed and changed and how they relate to behaviors; as a result, we include a chapter covering the basics of attitude theory (Chapter 2).

The current book includes three sections. The first section includes two chapters. Chapter 1, guided by the SIOP Guidelines, reviews the concept of job attitudes and covers such topics as why attitudes are important to consider at work. It also describes organizational behaviors and other criteria associated with various job attitudes. The second chapter is a primer on the wider social psychological knowledge regarding how attitudes are formed and changed, and how they relate to behaviors. Each chapter in the second section covers a single job attitude in depth including definitions, history, theory, nomological network, and common instruments that are used to measure it (see Chapters 3 through 11). Each chapter also offers a critique of the field to date as well as "given what we know now," how it can be used in practice. Finally, each chapter addresses how future research might "push the topic forward." Authors of these chapters are experts in that particular job attitude. Thus, although these chapters differ by author writing style, each addresses parallel content. The parallel content will aid readers in comparing and contrasting different job attitude constructs as well as aid in identifying themes that cut across the job attitude literature. The final section includes a concluding chapter that pulls together themes and makes suggestions on how to move the field forward from a higher perspective.

This book also includes two big "ahas" that emerged as we pulled this book together. First, what we, as I-O psychologists, refer to as "job *attitudes*" are not all attitudes as understood within the social psychological literature. Attitudes in social psychology are generally understood as "evaluating a particular entity with some degree of favor or disfavor" (Eagly & Chaiken, 1993, p. 1). What we call "job *attitudes*" actually includes perceptions (justice and support), identity (organizational identification and job involvement), bonds (organizational commitment and job embeddedness), motivational states (engagement), and one attitude (job satisfaction). Second, what we refer to as "*job* attitudes" are also not necessarily associated with jobs, *per se*, but include work, organizations, and employees as well. Thus when we say "job attitudes" as I-O psychologists, we are really using it as a catch-all phrase for a number of work-related psychological constructs. We have chosen to retain the term "job attitudes," although we suggest in the final chapter that it might be useful to expand the term to be "workplace psychological constructs" to be more inclusive of the different constructs.

## Roots of the Book

I (Professor Valerie Sessa) have been teaching a graduate I-O psychology course for many years on job attitudes. I have patched together a reading list using chapters, review articles, primary journal articles, and measures for each topic. My students are often frustrated by the lack of a primer that would introduce them to the basics of each topic. I have been frustrated by the lack of written materials that integrate the job attitudes together (and one of my class exercises every year is for the students to tell me how the constructs fit together). Both my students and I have been curious about the instruments used to measure constructs. We have found completing and evaluating different measures to be an eye-opening experience. Every year, as I updated the course materials, I would look to see if anyone had yet written such a book. I would have been thankful for any book, but really wanted one that included basics, measures, and integration. I would complain to various publishers about the lack of such a book.

Taylor and Francis suggested that if I wanted one so badly, perhaps I should write it. Several years later, I finally relented and agreed to edit a book. I can edit a book, but I needed someone who is an expert in the field of job attitudes to co-edit it with me. The publisher introduced me to the perfect person to fit the bill: Professor Nathan Bowling who happens to have many peer-reviewed articles and book chapters on the topics in this book.

## Audience

The primary use of this book is as a main text in a job attitudes course in a graduate I-O psychology program, organizational behavior program, human resource management program, or an MBA program. Many I-O masters and PhD programs, as well as business programs have a required course on this topic. Those courses often include basics, measurement, and integration. As it is an "essentials" book, it would also serve as a resource for I-O practitioners to become familiarized with the current thinking in the field as well as some ideas for how to implement research findings within their own organizations. Finally, we think this will also serve as an important book for I-O psychology research-ers who are interested in job attitudes. Many researchers are experts in a par-ticular job attitude, but know less about other job attitudes. This book would allow them to familiarize themselves with other topics that they might like to include in their own research. It includes measures (and where to find them) to allow researchers to expand their personal tool box. Finally it includes ideas for how to move the individual topics forward (see the end of each chapter) as well as how to move the field as a whole forward (see Chapter 12).

# ACKNOWLEDGMENTS

We are indebted to our chapter authors. When we reached out to them, we were concerned only with convincing topic experts to write a chapter for us. We were pleasantly surprised when we looked more closely at their affiliations and realized that we have the best in the whole world, with authors hailing from Australia, Belgium, Canada, Japan, Spain, the United Kingdom, and the United States. Editing a book involves many people, beyond chapter authors. Thank you to the anonymous reviewers for reading and commenting on the book prospectus (and suggesting we add Organizational Identity and Job Embeddedness), our book is different and much better as a result. Thank you to Doug Klein, Small Cap Survey and Consulting for your assistance in writing the Practical Implications section of the final chapter. Thank you to Montclair State University graduate I-O students: Samantha Biggs and Taylor Jones for helping us get Chapter 1 off the ground and Christine Griffith and Dana Sobel for helping us research the development of all the instruments. A special big thank you to MSU graduate student Catrina Notari for heavily assisting us in the writing of the final chapter, and for reading and providing final editing for all the chapters. Thank you to Christina Chronister, Editor at Taylor & Francis and Danielle Dyal, her Editorial Assistant for helping us keep our book on track.

## References

Bakker, A.B. & Leiter, M.P. (2015). *Work Engagement: A Handbook of Essential Theory and Research*. New York: Psychology Press.

Dalal, R.S. (2012). Job attitudes: Cognition and affect. In I.B. Weiner, N.W. Schmitt, & S. Highhouse, (Eds). *Handbook of Psychology*, Second Edition. *Handbook of Psychology*, volume 12. Hoboken, NJ: Wiley.

Eagly, A.H. & Chaiken, S. (1993). *The Psychology of Attitudes*. Fort Worth, TX: Harcourt Brace Jovanovich.

Eisenberger, R. & Stinglhamber, F. (2011). *Perceived Organizational Support: Fostering Enthusiastic and Productive Employees*. Washington, DC: American Psychological Association.

Klein, H.J., Becker, T.E., & Meyer, J.P. (Editors) (2009): *Commitment in Organizations: Accumulated Wisdom and New Directions*. New York: Routledge.

Moliner, C., Cropanzano, R., & Martinez-Tur, V. (2017). *Organizational Justice: International Perspectives and Conceptual Advances*. New York, NY: Routledge.

Society for Industrial and Organizational Psychology, Inc. (2016). *Guidelines for education and training in industrial-organizational psychology*. Bowling Green, OH: Author. (www.siop.org/Events-Education/Graduate-Training-Program/Guidelines-for-Education-and-Training)

Spector, P. (1997). *Job Satisfaction: Application, Assessment, Causes and Consequences*. Thousand Oaks, CA. Sage Publications.

# Part I

# WHY STUDY JOB ATTITUDES AND OTHER WORKPLACE PSYCHOLOGICAL CONSTRUCTS

# 1

# ESSENTIALS OF JOB ATTITUDES AND OTHER WORKPLACE PSYCHOLOGICAL CONSTRUCTS

## An Introductory Chapter

*Nathan A. Bowling and Valerie I. Sessa*

This book takes on the audacious task of reviewing the literature on one of the core content areas within the Society for Industrial and Organizational Psychology's (SIOP, 2016) *Guidelines for Education and Training in Industrial-Organizational Psychology:* Attitude Theory, Measurement, and Change (see Competency 7 from the Guidelines):

> Attitudes, opinions, and beliefs are important for quality of work life, for diagnosing problems in organizations, and in regards to their relation to behavioral intentions and behaviors at work. Some of the job attitudes typically studied by I-O psychologists include, but are not limited to, engagement, job satisfaction (general and facets), job involvement, organizational commitment, and perceptions of support and fairness.
>
> I-O psychologists should also be aware of the extensive literature on attitude theory, measurement, and change. In particular, I-O psychologists must know how attitudes are formed and changed and how they relate to behaviors. With respect to the latter, knowledge of the literature on the relationship between attitudes and behavior is important if for no other reason than to know the limitations of the connections between these two sets of constructs.

Providing a thorough review of this literature is challenging for three reasons. First, as the SIOP Guidelines note, the term "job attitude" subsumes several ostensibly distinct constructs—for example, perceptions of fairness and support, job satisfaction, job involvement, organizational commitment, and work engagement (for further discussion of the many variables described as "job attitudes," see Brief, 1998; Harrison, Newman, & Roth, 2006). Because of their large number, it is difficult for one person to develop expertise in every type of job attitude (or expertise in the relationships among these attitudes). And in many instances, an individual researcher may have developed expertise in one attitude while generally neglecting the others.

To address this challenge, Chapters 3 through 10 each focus on an individual job attitude. We include the following as suggested by the competency: perceptions of justice, perceptions of organizational support, job involvement, commitment, job satisfaction, and engagement. And, based on reviewer suggestions, we also include chapters on organizational identification and job embeddedness. We included an additional chapter focusing on team-based attitudes—a timely topic, given that work in modern organizations often occurs within a team context (Devaraj & Jiang, 2019; Shuffler et al., 2018). Each chapter was authored by experts on that particular job attitude. And in the closing chapter we critically evaluate the state of the job attitude literature, noting themes and limitations that cut across the various attitudes. We suggest future directions for job attitude research. And based on what we know as a result of this book, we made some practical implications for organizations to consider.

Second, the inconsistencies in how researchers have used the term "attitudes" has added to the difficulty in organizing this book. When we questioned past and present members of SIOP's Education and Training Committee (e.g., Janet Barnes-Farrell, Jeannette Cleveland, Whitney Botsford Morgan, Stephanie Payne, personal communications, 2019), they affirmed something that we suspected from the outset—that researchers often use the term "job attitudes" as a catch-all phrase for several workplace psychological constructs. Our experience editing this book reinforces this suspicion. The chapters in this book define such terms as perceptions, identities, bonds, and motivational states with only the job satisfaction chapter clearly reflecting a "job attitude." However, because the SIOP competency considers them together, we include them in the current book. Again, in the final chapter, we attempt to untangle these constructs and then organize them in a more coherent way.

The sheer volume of job attitude research presents a final challenge to reviewing the literature. A recent Google Scholar search using the term "job satisfaction," for example, yielded over 1.7 million references (see Table 1.1). Although less widely studied than job satisfaction, the remaining job attitudes examined in the current book have each been referenced several thousand times. Needless to say, we have a lot of ground to cover. Our goal in this opening chapter is to clear a path for the subsequent chapters. We first define the term "job attitude." We then discuss why job attitudes (and the other workplace psychological constructs) are important—what, in other words, are their theoretical and practical significance? Finally, we present an overview of the subsequent chapters.

4

*Table 1.1* Number of Google Scholar References in Various Job Attitude Constructs

| Job Attitude | Number of Google Scholar References | Chapter |
|---|---|---|
| Organizational Justice | > 91,000 | 3 |
| Perceived Organizational Support | ~ 58,000 | 4 |
| Organizational Identification | > 42,000 | 5 |
| Job involvement | > 49,000 | 6 |
| Organizational Commitment | ~ 476,000 | 7 |
| Job Embeddedness | > 10,000 | 8 |
| Job Satisfaction | > 1,700,000 | 9 |
| Employee Engagement | ~ 110,000 | 10 |

*Note:* These results were based on a Google Scholar search conducted on April 30, 2020.

## Defining Job Attitudes and Other Workplace Psychological Constructs

In describing the nature of job attitudes, I-O psychologists draw heavily from the social psychological definition of the term "attitude." Social psychologists describe attitudes as representing a person's evaluative response toward an attitude object (Eagly & Chaiken, 1993). As Wagner notes in Chapter 2, attitudes have valence—a positive or negative direction (e.g., good vs. bad)—and they differ in the intensity associated with that valence (e.g., extremely good vs. moderately bad; Wagner, Chapter 2, [page 14]). Attitudes, in other words, are directed toward something, such as a group of people (e.g., immigrants), a specific person (e.g., Dr. Martin Luther King Jr.), an idea (e.g., capitalism), or a physical object (e.g., blue jeans). In the case of job attitudes, the attitude object is workplace-related. Commonly studied workplace-related attitude objects include one's job, employer, or the concept of being employed. Note that job attitude objects may vary in their level of abstraction. The most general conceptualization of job satisfaction, for instance, is global satisfaction—a person's overall level of satisfaction with his or her job (Spector, 1997). More specific facets of job satisfaction include satisfaction with (a) work tasks, (b) supervision, (c) coworkers, (d) pay, and (e) promotional opportunities (Bowling, Wagner, & Beehr, 2018; Smith, Kendall, & Hulin, 1969). These facets can be further divided into more specific dimensions. Pay satisfaction, for instance, comprises several dimensions, including satisfaction with pay level, pay raises, and pay administration (Heneman & Schwab, 1985).

Social psychologists have further describe attitudes as having both affective and cognitive components (see Brief, 1998). The former reflects how a person feels toward the attitude object; the latter reflects what a person thinks or believes about the attitude object. Indeed, the distinction between affect and cognition is reflected in the content of job attitude measures (see Brief & Roberson, 1989; Moorman, 1993; Schleicher et al., 2015). To understand this distinction, consider the difference between the hypothetical items "I like my supervisor" and "My supervisor is competent." The first item clearly contains affect (note the word "like"), whereas the second item is more cognitive—it reflects a "cold," ostensibly factual description of one's supervisor.

Although social psychologists often define attitudes as also including a behavioral component, most I-O psychologists consider behaviors to be a consequence of job attitudes and not part of the job attitude construct *per se* (see Judge et al., 2001). Attitudes and behavior, in other words, are conceptually different; the former reflect internal psychological states, whereas the latter reflect outwardly observable actions. This distinction is also borne out of the end of the SIOP competency, 7: "…knowledge of the literature on the relationship between attitudes and behavior is important if for no other reason than to know the limitations of the connections between these two sets of constructs" (Society for Industrial and Organizational Psychology, Inc. 2016).

The SIOP competency also includes the words "beliefs" and "opinions," although in our conversations with members of the SIOP Guidelines committee, no one could recall why those particular terms were used, other than to acknowledge the fact that some of the constructs/measures might not technically be classified as attitudes. What is more interesting to note, though, is that the authors in many of the subsequent chapters do not use the terms "beliefs" or "opinions" either; rather, as noted above, they use "perceptions," "identity," "bonds," and "motivational states" which are all distinct from attitudes and have their own social psychological bases. We will address these terms later in this chapter, throughout the subsequent chapters, then again in more detail in the final chapter. But because I-O psychologists refer to these job-related psychological constructs as "job attitudes," we continue to use that term for this chapter.

## *The Importance of Job Attitudes*

The size of its research literature attests to the importance of job attitudes (see Table 1.1). But what's with all the fuss? Why do I-O psychologists seem to care so much about job attitudes? There are four primary answers to this question: (a) job attitudes are inherently valuable, (b) they provide organizations with diagnostic information, (c) they can be used for assessing the effectiveness of organizational interventions, and (d) they are potential causes of key organizational outcomes (see Spector, 1997). We review each of these in the following subsections.

### *Job Attitudes are Inherently Valuable*

The professional associations that I-O psychologists typically belong to— including the American Psychological Association, the Association for Psychological Science, Academy of Management, and SIOP—encourage their members to use their skills for the betterment of society. Principle A of the APA's Ethical Principles of Psychologists and Code of Conduct, for instance, states that "Psychologists strive to benefit those with whom they work . . ." One way that I-O psychologists can satisfy this mandate is through research and practice aimed at improving workers' job attitudes. And indeed, there are good reasons to believe that improved job attitudes contribute to a better society—job attitudes (particularly job satisfaction) may contribute to more general forms of well-being (e.g., overall life satisfaction; Bowling, Eschleman, & Wang, 2010), they may relate to psychological distress (Lee & Ashforth, 1996 ), and they may themselves be considered indicators of employee well-being (see Jex, Beehr, & Roberts, 1992).

### *Job Attitudes Provide Diagnostic Information*

Job attitudes are also important because of the diagnostic information they provide to organizations (Spector, 1997). Knowing that a particular subgroup of employees has negative attitudes, for example, or knowing which aspects of the work environment workers generally dislike (e.g., the organization's sick leave policy) can help management pinpoint the source of organizational dysfunction. The widespread use of job attitude questionnaires by organizations suggests that business leaders recognize the diagnostic value of job attitude data.

### *Job Attitudes Can Be Used to Assess the Effectiveness of Interventions*

Organizations often implement interventions intended to improve organizational functioning. In many cases, organizations hope that such interventions will improve employees' job attitudes. Because it is important to document that such interventions have produced their intended effect, I-O psychologists often use job attitudes as criterion measures to assess the effectiveness of interventions (see Neuman, Edwards, & Raju, 1989).

### *Job Attitudes May Cause Key Outcomes*

Finally, job attitudes are important because of their potential to predict several criteria that are important to organizations. We briefly discuss two types of criteria here—job performance and organizational withdrawal. Subsequent chapters consider the relationships between job attitudes and various criteria.

#### JOB PERFORMANCE

Job performance is perhaps the most widely studied criterion variable in job attitude research. There are three primary dimensions of job performance: (a) task performance, (b) organizational citizenship behavior (OCB), and (c) counterproductive work behavior (CWB; for a discussion of this three-factor model of job performance, see Dalal, 2005; Rotundo & Sackett, 2002). Task performance, which is often referred to as "in-role performance," reflects the extent to which an employee effectively performs his or her official job duties (Borman & Motowidlo, 1997; Viswesvaran & Ones, 2000; Williams & Anderson, 1991). This form of job performance is non-discretionary and is often used as a basis for making administrative decisions about individual employees (e.g., deciding which employees to hire and which to fire).

OCBs, on the other hand, comprise discretionary helping behaviors performed while at work (Organ & Ryan, 1995; Smith, Organ, & Near, 1983). Researchers often distinguish between OCBs targeting individual organizational members (OCB-Is) and OCBs targeting the organization as a whole (OCB-Os; see Lee & Allen, 2002). Examples of the former include assisting a coworker with a personnel problem or helping to orient a new employee; examples of the latter include volunteering to perform an undesirable work task or talking positively about the organization to outsiders.

Finally, CWBs are discretionary behaviors that harm either individual organizational members (CWB-Is) or the organization as a whole (CWB-Os; see Bennett & Robinson, 2000; Robinson & Bennett, 1995). Examples of CWB-Is include yelling at or playing a mean prank on a coworker; examples of CWB-Os include arriving late to work without permission or stealing money from one's employer (see Spector et al., 2006). Although OCB and CWB share some similarities—both are discretionary and are largely a function of motivation rather than ability—the two types of behavior are empirically distinct (Dalal, 2005).

ORGANIZATIONAL WITHDRAWAL

Organizational withdrawal is a diverse set of behaviors that share a common theme: They are each strategies that employees use to distance themselves from an undesirable work environment (Hanisch & Hulin, 1990, 1991). Three types of organizational withdrawal behaviors have been widely studied by job attitude researchers: (a) arriving to work after one's shift is scheduled to begin (lateness), (b) failing to report for work (absenteeism), and (c) permanently quitting one's job (turnover).

## Overview of Subsequent Chapters

As we discussed earlier, as emphasized in the SIOP competency, research on job attitudes can and should be informed by social psychological research on attitudes and other related constructs. Accordingly, Chapter 2 provides a social psychological foundation on attitudes, which helps inform the subsequent chapters of this book. We do not include the social psychological foundations of other constructs (perceptions, identity, psychological bonds, and motivational states) but in our final chapter we will emphasize the need to do so.

Drawing from the literature on general attitudes, Chapter 2 describes (a) how attitudes are typically conceptualized and measured, (b) the concept of "attitude strength," (c) how attitudes develop and change, and (d) the potential effects of attitudes on behavior.

Chapters 3 through 10 each focus on a single job attitude, with Chapter 11 suggesting a new focus on teams rather than on jobs or organizations. To guide the writing of each chapter, we asked the authors to grapple with a series of questions: "What is this construct; what is its nature or definition? Is this an attitude, opinion, belief, or even something else?" As we noted earlier, the authors used a variety of different terms to describe their constructs. The chapters on Organizational Justice (Chapter 3) and Organizational Support (Chapter 4) note that their constructs are perceptions. The chapters on Organizational Identity (Chapter 5) and Job Involvement (Chapter 6) emphasize social identities. The Workplace Commitments chapter (Chapter 7) uses the term "psychological bond," while the Job Embeddedness chapter (Chapter 8) invokes instrumental bonds. The Employee Engagement chapter (Chapter 10), on the other hand, describes engagement as a "motivational state." Finally, the chapter on Job Satisfaction (Chapter 9) uses the term "attitude." Perceptions, social identities, psychological bonds, and psychological states each have their own definitions, histories, theories, and measurements in the field of psychology (see for example, Barrett & Bliss-Moreau, 2009, Ellemers, Spears, & Doosje, 2002, Mikulincer & Shaver, 2003, Zacks et al., 2007). As in the attitude literature, social psychologists generally assume that these constructs affect behavior.

Next we asked the authors to include a brief summary of their construct's history. When was the construct first studied (and where), and what is its story from then until now? The constructs span a wide range of years, beginning with job satisfaction in the 1920s to employee engagement in the early 2000s. While most constructs began in the field of Industrial and Organizational Psychology or Organizational Behavior, some did originate elsewhere. Commitment, for example, originated in sociology and economics. And although Kahn (1990) conducted the first major study on employee engagement and published it in a business journal, the concept was popularized in the early 2000s by consulting firms (and the term was not, at that time, associated with Kahn's work).

It is important to understand the theoretical underpinnings of the various job attitudes examined in this book. As a result, we asked our authors to identify theories associated with the construct. Collectively, they mentioned several theories, including Social Exchange Theory (Blau, 1964), Social Identity Theory (Tajfel, 1978), and Affective Events theory (Weiss & Cropanzano, 1996). In addition, we asked the authors to provide a nomological network of antecedents and consequences for their respective attitude. Authors outlined them in the text of the chapters and developed these into figures, allowing readers to easily compare the different constructs. We used the nomological networks provided by the authors to order the chapters (see below).

The authors also provide examples of typical scales used to assess each construct. It is one thing to read about each construct at a theoretical and definitional level, but seeing the actual scale items provides a more concrete understanding of the nature of each construct. In addition, having the items in easily accessible tables allows the readers to understand and critique the measurement of these constructs as well as compare them to their construct definition. Reviewing the content of instruments, and determining if it measures what you think it should measure (i.e., has face validity) adds an additional layer of understanding.

We also asked our authors to address practical implications: How, specifically, might organizations use what is known about your construct? And finally, we asked our authors to critique the existing literature and to describe future research directions for their respective constructs.

Based on the information in the chapters—in particular the nomological network figures—we ordered Chapters 3 through 10 in the following way. Most of the nomological networks in this book include organizational factors or perceptions of organizational factors on the antecedent side of their models. We begin the next section with those chapters: Chapters 3 (Perceived Organizational Justice) and Chapter 4 (Perceived Organizational Support). According to Klein, Molloy, and Brinsfield (2012), identity, commitment, and instrumental bonds are on a continuum of types of bonds from self-defining oneself in terms of the job or organization (identity) to embracement of the bond (commitment) to acceptance of the bond (job embeddedness). According to the nomological networks, these bonds are stimulated by perceptions. Thus Chapter 5 (Organizational Identity), Chapter 6 (Job Involvement), Chapter 7 (Workplace Commitment), and Chapter 8 (Job Embeddedness) are placed one after another ranging from more psychological involvement to less psychological involvement. Many of the nomological networks place job satisfaction (an attitude, Chapter 9) and employee engagement (a motivational state, Chapter 10) on the consequence side of their models, thus their placement in the book. Finally, Chapter 11 addresses a related and growing area of interest, team-based attitudes.

Finally, in Chapter 12 we focus our attention on themes that cut across the many constructs examined in this book including: (a) When we say job attitudes, what exactly are we measuring, (b) How are we measuring it, (c) Generally ignored questions across areas, and (d) Organizational uses and interventions.

## References

Barrett, L.F. & Bliss-Moreau, E. (2009). Affect as a psychological primitive. *Advances in Experimental Social Psychology, 41,* 167–218. doi: 10.1016/S0065-2601(08)00404-8.

Bennett, R.J. & Robinson, S.L. (2000). Development of a measure of workplace deviance. *Journal of Applied Psychology, 85,* 349–360.

Borman, W.C. & Motowidlo, S.J. (1997). Task performance and contextual performance: The meaning for personnel selection research. *Human performance, 10*, 99–109.

Bowling, N.A., Eschleman, K.J., & Wang, Q. (2010). A meta-analytic examination of the relationship between job satisfaction and subjective well-being. *Journal of Occupational and Organizational Psychology, 83*, 915–934.

Bowling, N.A., Wagner, S.H., & Beehr, T.A. (2018). The Facet Satisfaction Scale: An Effective Affective Measure of Job Satisfaction Facets. *Journal of Business and Psychology, 33*, 383–403.

Blau, P.M. (1964). *Exchange and power in social life*. New York, NY: Wiley.

Brief, A.P. (1998). *Attitudes in and around organizations*. Thousand Oaks, CA: Sage.

Brief, A.P. & Roberson, L. (1989). Job Attitude Organization: An Exploratory Study. *Journal of Applied Social Psychology, 19*, 717–727.

Dalal, R.S. (2005). A meta-analysis of the relationship between organizational citizenship behavior and counterproductive work behavior. *Journal of Applied Psychology, 90*, 1241–1255.

Devaraj, S. & Jiang, K. (2019). It's about time: A longitudinal adaptation model of high-performance work teams. *Journal of Applied Psychology, 104*, 433–447.

Eagly, A. H. & Chaiken, S. (1993). *The psychology of attitudes*. Fort Worth, TX: Harcourt Brace Jovanovich.

Ellemers, N., Spears, R., & Doosje, B. (2002). Self and social identity. *Annual Review of Psychology, 53*, 161–186.

Hanisch, K.A. & Hulin, C.L. (1990). Job attitudes and organizational withdrawal: An examination of retirement and other voluntary withdrawal behaviors. *Journal of Vocational Behavior, 37*, 60–78.

Hanisch, K.A. & Hulin, C.L. (1991). General attitudes and organizational withdrawal: An evaluation of a causal model. *Journal of Vocational Behavior, 39*, 110–128.

Harrison, D.A., Newman, D.A. & Roth, P.L. (2006). How important are job attitudes? Meta-analytic comparisons of integrative behavioral outcomes and time sequences. *Academy of Management Journal, 49*, 305–325.

Heneman III, H.G. & Schwab, D.P. (1985). Pay satisfaction: Its multidimensional nature and measurement. *International Journal of Psychology, 20*, 129–141.

Jex, S.M., Beehr, T.A., & Roberts, C.K. (1992). The meaning of occupational stress items to survey respondents. *Journal of Applied Psychology, 77*, 623–628.

Judge, T.A., Thoresen, C.J., Bono, J.E., & Patton, G.K. (2001). The job satisfaction-job performance relationship: A qualitative and quantitative review. *Psychological Bulletin, 127*, 376–407.

Kahn, W.A. (1990). Psychological conditions of personal engagement and disengagement at work, *Academy of Management Journal, 33*, 692–724.

Klein, H.J., Molloy, J.C., & Brinsfield, C.T. (2012). Reconceptualizing workplace commitment to redress a stretched construct: revisiting assumptions and removing confounds. *Academy of Management Review, 37(1)*, 130–151.

Lee, K. & Allen, N.J. (2002). Organizational citizenship behavior and workplace deviance: The role of affect and cognitions. *Journal of Applied Psychology, 87*, 131–142.

Lee, R.T. & Ashforth, B.E. (1996). A meta-analytic examination of the correlates of the three dimensions of job burnout. *Journal of Applied Psychology, 81*, 123–133.

Mikulincer, M. & Shaver, P.R. (2003). The attachment behavioral system in adulthood: Activation, psychodynamics, and interpersonal processes. *Advances in Experimental Social Psychology, 35*, 53–150.

Moorman, R.H. (1993). The influence of cognitive and affective based job satisfaction measures on the relationship between satisfaction and organizational citizenship behavior. *Human Relations, 46*, 759–776.

Neuman, G.A., Edwards, J.E., & Raju, N.S. (1989). Organizational development interventions: A meta-analysis of their effects on satisfaction and other attitudes. *Personnel Psychology, 42*, 461–489.

Organ, D.W. & Ryan, K. (1995). A meta-analytic review of attitudinal and dispositional predictors of organizational citizenship behavior. *Personnel Psychology, 48*, 775–802.

Robinson, S.L. & Bennett, R.J. (1995). A typology of deviant workplace behaviors: A multidimensional scaling study. *Academy of Management Journal, 38*, 555–572.

Rotundo, M. & Sackett, P.R. (2002). The relative importance of task, citizenship, and counterproductive performance to global ratings of job performance: A policy-capturing approach. *Journal of Applied Psychology, 87*, 66–80.

Schleicher, D.J., Smith, T.A., Casper, W.J., Watt, J.D., & Greguras, G.J. (2015). It's all in the attitude: The role of job attitude strength in job attitude–outcome relationships. *Journal of Applied Psychology, 100*, 1259–1274.

Shuffler, M.L., Diazgranados, D., Maynard, M.T., & Salas, E. (2018). Developing, sustaining, and maximizing team effectiveness: An integrative, dynamic perspective of team development interventions. *Academy of Management Annals, 12*, 688–724.

Smith, P.C., Kendall, L.M., & Hulin, C.L. (1969). *Measurement of satisfaction in work and retirement.* Chicago, IL: Rand-McNally.

Smith, C.A., Organ, D.W., & Near, J.P. (1983). Organizational citizenship behavior: Its nature and antecedents. *Journal of Applied Psychology, 68*, 653–663.

Society for Industrial and Organizational Psychology, Inc. (2016). *Guidelines for education and training in industrial-organizational psychology.* Bowling Green, OH (www.siop.org/Events-Education/Graduate-Training-Program/Guidelines-for-Education-and-Training).

Spector, P.E. (1997). *Job Satisfaction: Applications, Assessment, Causes and Consequences.* Thousand Oaks, CA: Sage.

Spector, P.E., Fox, S., Penney, L.M., Bruursema, K., Goh, A., & Kessler, S. (2006). The dimensionality of counterproductivity: Are all counterproductive behaviors created equal? *Journal of Vocational Behavior, 68*, 446–460.

Tajfel, H. (1978). Social categorization, social identity and social comparison. In H. Tajfel (Ed.), *Differentiation between social groups: Studies in the social psychology of intergroup relations* (pp. 61–76). London: Academic Press.

Viswesvaran, C. & Ones, D.S. (2000). Perspectives on models of job performance. *International Journal of Selection and Assessment, 8*, 216–226.

Weiss, H.M. & Cropanzano, R. (1996). Affective events theory: A theoretical discussion of the structure, causes and consequences of affective experiences at work. *Research in Organizational Behavior, 18*, 1–74.

Williams, L.J. & Anderson, S.E. (1991). Job satisfaction and organizational commitment as predictors of organizational citizenship and in-role behaviors. *Journal of Management, 17*, 601–617.

Zacks, J.M., Speer, N.K., Swallow, K.H., Braver, T.S., & Reynolds, J.R. (2007). Event perception: A mind/brain perspective. *Psychological Bulletin, 133*(2), 273–293. doi: 10.1037/0033-2909.133.2.273.

# 2

# ATTITUDE THEORY AND JOB ATTITUDES

## On the Value of Intersections between Basic and Applied Psychology

*Stephen H. Wagner*

Attitudes are a vital construct for understanding human behavior because they describe a person's inclination to experience a stimulus object as "good" or "bad." This evaluative tendency is a persistent aspect of the human experience that can both be accessed through memory and produced instantaneously and unconsciously. The perception and processing of information is influenced by attitudes and they are connected to other central elements of the human experience, like behaviors, emotions, and beliefs. The social implications of attitudes are substantial as they can serve as a source of affinity or antipathy with others. One's identity can be largely characterized by attitudes, as they are connected to one's values and thus can serve to guard or bolster one's self-image. Given the wide-ranging implications of attitudes (Maio, Haddock, & Verplanken, 2019), it is not surprising that they have been an important focus of psychological research for more than a century. Theory and research on attitudes have been a prominent, and at times a central, focal point for the discipline of social psychology with research often addressing basic theoretical questions with experimental designs. At the same time, the term "attitude" has also been used in many other applied disciplines of psychology, perhaps most prominently in industrial-organizational (I-O) psychology. Recent reviews of the job attitude literature in I-O psychology have emphasized the usefulness of using basic concepts and theories established in social psychology literature on attitudes (Brief, 1998; Judge et al., 2017; Pratkanis & Turner, 1994; Weiss, 2002).

The purpose of this chapter is to examine the intersection between basic concepts and theories on attitudes and the applied research on job attitudes. There are a number of advantages to framing research on job attitudes with the concepts and theories used in social psychology. Social psychology research on attitudes has addressed fundamental issues about construct validity, measurement, and theoretical connections with behaviors, situations, and dispositional effects that inform research in many applied settings, including organizations.

In turn, examination of attitudes in organizational settings expands the under-standing of the nature of attitudes by examining it in different contexts, with new measurement challenges, and investigating a wide range of different atti-tude objects. One goal of this chapter is to review concepts and theories that are central to understanding attitudes in general and job attitudes in particu-lar. A second goal is to examine how research on job attitudes has addressed unique challenges to studying attitudes in organizational contexts.

## Conceptualizing Attitudes

### *Definitions of Attitudes*

Use of the term "attitude" in the vernacular is not synonymous with its mean-ing in a scholarly context. In informal conversations, when it is said that a person has "a good attitude" or "a bad attitude" this connotes an individual difference associated with one's emotional reactions to and beliefs about the world at large and all things in it. However, when the term "attitude" is used in scholarly communications, it is referring to an attitude about something in particular and not all things in general. Within the literature of social psychol-ogy, definitions of the term "attitude" have taken various forms. Zanna and Rempel (1988, p. 319) defined an attitude as "the categorization of a stimulus object along an evaluative dimension" which is based on information that is cognitive, emotional, and/or pertaining to past behaviors or behavioral ten-dencies. This  tripartite approach to conceptualizing attitudes has been, and continues to be, prominently used in social psychological literature on attitudes (Maio et al., 2019). Eagly and Chaiken (1993, p. 1), stated that an "attitude is a psychological tendency that is expressed by evaluating a particular entity with some degree of favor or disfavor." Fazio (1995, p. 247) defined an attitude as "an association in memory between a given object and a given summary evalu-ation of the object."

Central to each of these academic definitions of the term "attitude" is the evaluation of a particular object. Attitudes have valence, a positive or nega-tive direction (e.g., good vs. bad), and differ in the intensity associated with the valence (e.g., extremely good vs. moderately bad). Zanna and Rempel's (1988) definition mentions beliefs, emotions, and aspects of behavior with the purpose of clarifying that these mental processes are related to an attitude but distinct from the evaluation. Fazio (1995) highlights that this is a summary evaluation, meaning that the evaluation is rapid or immediate. Eagly and Chaiken (1993) stated that an attitude involves a psychological tendency which implies a degree of stability in the evaluation but also a potential for malleability.

Although there seems to be convergence in social psychology on the critical elements for the definition of an attitude, there are also conceptual disagree-ments that persist. In opposition to the view that an attitude is stored in mem-ory, Schwarz (2007, p. 639) defined an attitude as "an evaluative judgment, formed when needed." The definitions offered by Eagly and Chaiken (1993) and Schwarz stand relatively opposed, with the former suggesting attitudes are based in memory whereas the latter asserts that attitudes are constructed "on the spot." However, it is plausible that attitudes can emerge from either of these processes (Nayakankuppam et al., 2018). For the purpose of the current review, it was concluded that both memory-based and online processes contribute to the use of attitudes. Also, the use of the word "opinion" within attitude literature seems somewhat inconsistent, with some referring to the term opinion as a belief, that is a thought or idea about something (Eagly & Chaiken, 1993), and others using the term synonymously with the word attitude, that is an evaluation of something (Maio et al., 2019). Bergman, (1998) compared the uses of the terms "attitude" and "opinion" and concluded these terms are, for most purposes, synonymous – and in the current review they shall be considered as such.

## *Definitions of Job Attitudes*

The accepted definition of job attitudes and the various terms by which we identify job attitudes have changed substantially throughout the century of studying work-related attitudes (Judge et al., 2017). In the current era of research on job attitudes, described by Judge et al. as the "Affective Era," definitions of job satisfaction have referred to it clearly as an attitude and often make explicit connections to literature on attitudes from social psychology. Inconsistencies between conceptualizations and operationalizations of job satisfaction were identified by Organ and Near (1985). In particular, their review identified the tendency of measures of job satisfaction to rely mainly on items that were cognitive in nature but to refer mainly to affect when describing the concept of job satisfaction. Brief and Roberson (1989) found that measures of job cognitions and job affect had different patterns of association with widely-used measures of job satisfaction, with some having much greater connection with job cognition than job affect. Recognition of the confounded use of the terms attitude, belief, and affect in the literature on job satisfaction has resulted in scholars calling for greater alignment between research on job satisfaction and basic social attitudes (Brief, 1998; Motowidlo, 1996; Pratkanis & Turner, 1994). Congruent with these concerns, Weiss (2002) defined job satisfaction as an attitude and stated that it's "a positive (or negative) evaluative judgment one makes about one's job or job situation" (p. 175). Furthermore, Judge et al. (2017) identified job attitudes as including overall job satisfaction, organizational commitment, job involvement, and other evaluations of features of a job, including specific job satisfaction facets. Further, job attitudes are distinct from information associated with them that is cognitive (e.g., organizational justice perceptions), affective (e.g., emotions associated with the attitude object), or behavioral (e.g., behavioral intentions connected to the attitude object) (Judge et al., 2017; Weiss, 2002). Table 2.1 displays a summary of basic terms

*Table 2.1* Key Concepts of Attitude Theory Applied to a Job Attitude

| Concept | Definition / Considerations | Job-Related Example |
|---|---|---|
| **Attitude** | An evaluative tendency toward an object based on affective, cognitive, and/or behavioral information | Satisfaction with performance review process |
| **Affective Information** | Emotions or feelings associated with the attitude object | Emotions experiences during your most recent performance feedback |
| **Cognitive Information** | Beliefs, thoughts, and attributes linked with the attitude object | Fairness perceptions for performance feedback |
| **Behavioral Information** | Past behaviors or experiences with the attitude object | Your history of job performance and performance feedback |
| **Explicit Measures** | A measure that asks directly about one's attitude | An annual organizational survey that asks about satisfaction with performance reviews |
| **Implicit Measures** | Indirect tests of an attitude, attitude measurements made without the awareness of the respondent | An IAT test designed assess attitudes toward performance feedback |

used in the psychology of attitudes and provides an example of their use in a job-related context.

The organizational context of job attitudes presents a rich environment that has contributed to distinctive innovations in and presented some unique challenges for the study of attitudes. The number of attitude objects worth consideration and study is substantial and, in the case of job satisfaction, both overall evaluations of job satisfaction (e.g., Wanous, Reichers, & Hudy, 1997) and attitudes about particular aspects of a job – typically referred to as facets (e.g., the work itself, supervisor, co-workers, pay, development opportunities) provide unique information about one's job attitude. (Highhouse & Becker, 1993; Scarpello & Campbell, 1983); In comparisons of overall job satisfaction attitudes and facet satisfaction attitudes, Ironson et al. (1989) concluded that each provides useful information for both theoretical and practical problems. Certain facets of job satisfaction have received a considerable amount of study, such as satisfaction with pay (see meta-analysis by Judge et al., 2010) and as the nature of work evolves, new facets of job satisfaction appear in the literature, such as job satisfaction with meetings (Rogelberg et al., 2010).

Job attitudes include not only aspects of an individual's job but also features of the organizational context surrounding that job. Job attitudes might pertain to other social units within the organization (e.g., group or team) or evaluations of particular policies (e.g., retirement benefits). Judge et al. (2017) tracked the historic usage of various job attitudes and found that job satisfaction was the most frequently studied variable across all eras, and research on organizational commitment was increasingly frequent since the 1970s. Job satisfaction and organizational commitment both involve an evaluation of a specific attitude object in a work-related context, and therefore both are job attitudes. Like job satisfaction, organizational commitment (and other work-related attitudes) can be conceptualized along a continuum of more general (i.e., overall) to more specific (i.e., multi-dimensional). However, the function served by each job attitude is distinct, with evaluations of organizational commitment being more values-based and job satisfaction being more utilitarian in its purpose (concepts of attitude function are described in more depth later in this chapter).

The multi-level nature of the organizational context has also led to attitude objects conceptualized at different levels. Research on job attitudes has addressed levels of analysis beyond the individual job attitude and individual outcomes and new meso- and macro-level perspectives for investigating job attitudes have been established. Research on job attitudes used innovative approaches to analysis and data collection to address the multi-level nature of organizations. Schneider et al. (2003) examined, at the organizational level, attitude data from 35 companies over eight years and found that there were stronger patterns of prediction of overall job satisfaction by organizational financial performance than vice versa; however there was also some support for the longstanding hypothesis that greater job satisfaction leads to better performance. Diestel, Wegge, and Schmidt (2014) conducted cross-level analyses to determine that individual absenteeism, measured over time, was best predicted by internally-focused job satisfaction facets and a work group characterized by low levels of absenteeism. The use of repeated measures of data to examine job attitudes has also enhanced micro-level analyses through the use of event sampling as a method to better understand the interplay between job attitudes and related events, beliefs and emotions (e.g., Weiss, Nicholas, & Daus, 1999).

## Operationalizing Attitudes

Like many mental phenomena studied in psychology, attitudes are not directly observable and are studied as constructs that are inferred through indicators that can be measured through various processes. The development of techniques for measuring attitudes has been a central feature in advancing knowledge of this phenomenon. An adequate conception of attitude measurement requires an understanding of psychometric procedures to assess reliability and validity (see Irwing, Hughes, & Booth, 2018) that is beyond the scope of this chapter. Instead, the focus of this section is to describe techniques that represent the foundation for measuring attitudes as well as contemporary developments in attitude measurement that have introduced interesting nuances to our understanding of this pervasive evaluative tendency. Uses of these different techniques to measure job attitudes are also highlighted, along with challenges of using these methods in organizational settings.

### Rating Scale Methods

In an article entitled "Attitudes Can Be Measured," Thurstone (1928) inaugurated the close relationship between the study of attitudes and advancements in psychological measurement. This paper described a process, based on techniques used in psychophysical scaling, wherein the scale developer first created belief statements meant to characterize different levels of favorability within the evaluation of the attitude object. Through multiple stages of scale development involving paired comparisons of items by judges, analysis of item statistics, and item selection (see Himmelfarb, 1993), this technique can generate a unidimensional assessment with equal intervals between the levels of an attitude. The primary advantage of Thurstone's approach is that it results in a fairly descriptive self-reported gauge of one's attitude and thus can be especially useful when practical communications of the attitude are a goal of measurement. However, this approach has been criticized for failing to accurately measure extremely favorable attitudes (Himmelfarb, 1993) and involving a prohibitively time-consuming scale development process (Maio et al., 2019). Despite these criticisms, there are strong proponents of Thurstone's techniques (Drasgow, Cheryshenko, & Stark, 2010) and they are still utilized in contemporary applied psychology research (e.g., Kan Ma et al., 2013).

Likert (1932) described a summated rating method of measuring attitudes that is less labor intensive to develop than Thurstone's technique. In this approach, the researcher develops statements that are indicative of a favorable or unfavorable evaluation of the stimulus object. Respondents then rate the statements in terms of the degree that they agree or disagree with each statement. Item analysis determining the reliability, factor structure, and validity of the items should be used to refine the psychometric quality of the attitude measure (see Spector, 1991). When this method is used in research, the ratings of the items are summed to represent each respondent's favorability level of their attitude toward the stimulus object (e.g., Spector, 1997). The Brayfield and Rothe (1951) Index of Job Satisfaction uses a combination of scale development techniques, including those of Likert (1932) and Thurstone (1928). One disadvantage of Likert's approach is that it can be difficult to compare attitudes of different stimulus objects because statements rated for different objects rarely have parallel construction and thus it is unlikely that scores reflect similar magnitudes of favorability (Maio et al., 2019).

The semantic differential scale, developed by Osgood, Suci, and Tannenbaum (1957), provides an even more efficient method for measuring self-reported attitudes than the Likert (1932) technique. With this method, the stimulus object is identified and followed by a series of paired evaluative adjectives that are antonyms of one another. Between the adjectives is a non-descript, horizontal line that is segmented in six sections. Respondents are instructed to place a mark on one of the six sections to indicate their evaluations of the stimulus object and ratings are typically summed into one score that represents the level of the attitude. The ease of constructing parallel rating scales for different stimulus objects makes semantic differential scales useful for comparing attitudes toward different things (Himmelfarb, 1993), such as different policies or consumer products. By serving as generalized attitudes scales, semantic differential scales may be the most frequently used method for measuring attitudes (Krosnick, Judd, & Wittenbrink, 2005). Hatfield, Robinson, and Huseman (1985) developed a job satisfaction measure of five different facets evaluated with semantic differential pairings.

## Qualitative Methods

Open-ended questions are often used in application of attitude surveys to give respondents the opportunity to address aspects of their attitudes that may not have been addressed in closed-ended questions. However, scholarly research has also found open-ended attitude assessments to be a useful method for measuring various aspects of attitudes. Open-ended questions can be framed to assess the aspects of one's attitude that are most relevant and salient (Maio et al., 2019). Furthermore, they can also be particularly useful for measuring the multiple components associated with attitudes, including beliefs, emotions, and cognition (see Esses & Maio, 2002). One disadvantage of open-ended questions for attitude measures is the complexity of coding responses; however, many software solutions now exist for assisting in content coding (Kulesa & Bishop, 2006). Open-ended attitude questions have been criticized because respondents may find it difficult to articulate responses but some research suggests that this criticism may be overstated (Geer, 1988). It has also been suggested that open-ended questions might oversample salient information over more relevant responses; however, research has also provided evidence that contradicts this concern (Shuman, Ludwig, & Krosnick, 1986). Use of open-ended questions in research on job attitudes provides a good method of obtaining highly descriptive data on areas that may have not previously received extensive research attention. For instance, Rabelo and Mahalingam (2017) used open-ended questions to explore the perceptions of workers in cleaning positions and describe specific emotions and beliefs associated with a sense of invisibility at work, along with their connections to job attitudes.

### *Implicit Attitudes*

All the aforementioned techniques for measuring attitudes assess explicit attitudes, that is, they inquire about a person's overt evaluation of a stimulus object. Attitudes for certain stimulus objects, like a different racial group or a polarizing political policy, may be associated with perceived social pressure to express an attitude that is different than the attitude one actually holds. This is referred to as socially desirable responding. Implicit measures of attitudes that assess an individual's evaluation of a stimulus object more covertly were developed as means to overcome the distorting effects of socially desirable responses that are sometimes observed in research on attitudes. Contemporary approaches to assessing implicit attitudes use computers as part of the measurement procedure to introduce stimuli and gauge response latencies to making judgments of those stimuli. The most popular modern implicit attitude measure is called the Implicit Association Test (IAT; Greenwald, McGhee, & Schwartz, 1998). The IAT uses a response competition technique that requires the respondent to indicate whether various stimuli should be classified into one of two different categories. In some trials, the task involves assigning the stimuli based on category membership (attitude object category or other category) and on other trials the task involves assigning the stimuli based on evaluative category (good or bad). Categorizing target stimulus objects at a relatively faster pace during the evaluation phase in comparison to the category membership phase indicates a more automatic preference for attitude object category or the other category.

When the IAT was initially developed, there was intense enthusiasm about this approach that led to exaggerated predictions about the capacity of this approach to control response bias and reveal attitudes that are completely unconscious to the respondent; however, extensive research on the IAT has supported it as an effective method of measuring attitudes that provides information that is distinct from explicit measures of attitudes (Maio et al., 2019). Research on implicit attitudes in organizations has focused on job attitudes, stereotypes in organizations, and work-related self-concept. (Haines & Sumner, 2006; Uhlmann et al., 2012). Leavitt, Fong, and Greenwald (2011) found job behaviors (i.e., job performance and organizational citizenship) were best predicted by the combination of implicit and explicit job attitudes.

## Characteristic Features of Attitudes

As described in Table 2.2, characteristic features of attitudes include the attitude structure, strength, and function. Although these characteristic features have been studied within the research on attitudes for some time, understanding of these concepts continues to develop. Each of these characteristic features of attitudes is described below, as are important developments within the social psychology research on these concepts. Furthermore, the growing body

*Table 2.2* Characteristic Features of Attitudes Applied to a Job Attitude

| Concept | Definition / Considerations | Job-Related Example |
| --- | --- | --- |
| **Attitude Object** | Some particular entity that is evaluated by the attitude | The performance management system at one's job |
| **Attitude Structure** | Evaluative consistency between information associated with an attitude | Consistency between one's overall satisfaction with performance reviews, your emotional response to performance feedback, and your perceptions of fairness of the performance review system |
| **Attitude Strength** | The extent to which an attitude is persistent and resistance to change. The degree to which an attitude influences behavior | The degree to which one's satisfaction with the performance review system changes from one year to the next. |
| **Attitude Certainty** | Confidence with the evaluation of an attitude object | One's confidence with their evaluation of the performance review system |
| **Attitude Importance** | How personally important one's attitude is | How personally important one's attitude toward the performance appraisal system is |
| **Attitude Accessibility** | The ease with which one's attitude can be accessed from memory | How quickly one responds when rating the performance review system |
| **Attitude Function** | The reason for holding an attitude | One holds an attitude toward the performance review system because the information helps to maximize success experienced at work and minimize failure experienced at work |
| **Objective Appraisal Function** | One's attitude helps to organize favorable and unfavorable experiences and circumstances | One wants to have an accurate yet simple understanding of the favorable and unfavorable aspects of one's performance review system |

*(continued)*

*Table 2.2* (Cont.)

| Concept | Definition / Considerations | Job-Related Example |
| --- | --- | --- |
| **Social Adjustive Function** | One's attitude helps one fit in with others | Expressing one's dissatisfaction with the performance review system makes one fit in with others with similar views |
| **Value Expressive Function** | Your attitude is connected to deeply-held values that you believe are important to express | You strongly believe that hard work should be recognized and rewarded and that is why you evaluate the performance review system |
| **Ego Defensive Function** | Externalizing an expression of attitude to relieve some inner conflict | You are defensive about your lapsed performance and express dissatisfaction with the performance review system to shield yourself from that anxiety |

of research studying these characteristic features with respect to job attitudes is also explored below.

### Attitude Content and Structure

The tripartite approach to attitudes suggests that the overall evaluations of objects are closely associated with a structure of knowledge representing beliefs, emotions, and/or behaviors pertinent to the attitude object (see Zanna & Rempell, 1988). The cognitive component describes the attitude object in terms of its attributes or characteristics. For example, one's unfavorable attitude toward a coworker may be associated with a belief that the person is inconsiderate, whereas one's favorable attitude toward a software application may be associated with a belief that it is uncomplicated. The affective component describes emotions experienced in association with the attitude object. For example, one's favorable attitude toward classical music from the Baroque era may be associated with a feeling of serenity, whereas one's unfavorable attitude toward modern books of fiction written in a transgressive style might be a feeling of disgust. The behavioral component represents behavior intentions or past experiences associated with the attitude object. For example, a favorable attitude toward golf may be supported by the intention to engage in a past time that would make one relatable to powerful people at work, whereas an unfavorable attitude toward gardening may be associated with the memory of the past difficulty of pulling weeds.

The structure of an attitude can take various forms. The idea that components of an attitude tend to be congruent but may also exhibit inconsistency can be traced back to Heider's (1946) balance theory and Festinger's (1957) cognitive dissonance theory. The consideration of a single attitude object and the corresponding knowledge structure of beliefs, emotions, and/or behaviors is referred to as intra-attitudinal structure (Fabrigar, Macdonald, & Wegener, 2005). The valence of an attitude may influence which element has the greatest influence on the overall evaluation. Esses, Haddock, and Zanna (1993) found that unfavorable attitudes toward a group of people (i.e., prejudice) were predicted better by the beliefs about that group than emotions associated with it, whereas favorable attitudes toward a group were predicted better by emotions associated with that group than by beliefs about the liked group. The nature of the attitude object may also be related to the importance of particular components of attitude structure in predicting the overall evaluation (Eagly, Mladinic, & Otto, 1994). The salience of a particular type of content within the attitude structure has been shown to be associated with individual trait differences associated with cognitively-driven and affectively-driven thinking (Huskinson & Haddock, 2004).

The tripartite approach to attitudes has received considerable attention in empirical research and continues to be a source for developing new theories about attitudes. Maio, Esses, and Belle (2000) demonstrated the distinction between inter-component ambivalence (e.g., inconsistency between the cognitive and affective component could involve the belief that an attitude object has positive attributes but also has negative emotions associated with the attitude object), intra-component ambivalence (e.g., inconsistent cognitions associated with the attitude would be comprised of beliefs that an attitude object has both positive and negative attributes), and inconsistency between the overall evaluation and attitude components (i.e., evaluative-cognitive inconsistency and evaluative-affective inconsistency). Dalege et al. (2016) described the use of a network analysis technique used in physics that has recently been applied to psychological models as a method for investigating interactions between the structural components of an attitude in the development of their Causal Attitude Network (CAN) Model. This model provides many testable hypotheses for extending the understanding of the relative stability of attitudes and the processes by which attitudes can change.

Research that examines intra-attitudinal structure of job satisfaction in ways that are congruent with basic attitude theory has begun to accumulate. Schleicher, Watt, and Greguras (2004) found that in-role job performance was predicted better by the cognitive component of job satisfaction when it had greater consistency with the affective component of job satisfaction. Furthermore, Schleicher et al. (2015) found relations between job satisfaction and various organizational behaviors (i.e., performance, organizational citizenship behavior, and turnover intentions) were stronger when there was an increase in the structural consistency of job satisfaction (as defined by a composite of consistency between overall evaluation, cognitive satisfaction, and affective satisfaction). These findings suggest that relations between job satisfaction and organizational behaviors are stronger when there is greater structural consistency in the elements of job satisfaction. This pattern of findings was recently partially replicated with respect to organizational citizenship behaviors by Wagner (2017).

The structure associated with multiple attitudes objects is referred to as inter-attitudinal structure (Fabrigar et al., 2005) and has also been a focus of study within the field of political science and research on political ideology (e.g., Judd et al., 1995). Although inter-attitudinal research has not received much application in the area of job attitudes, it might be useful for research extending past investigations of relations between overall job satisfaction and job satisfaction facets (see Highhouse & Becker, 1993).

## *Attitude Strength*

An attitude's strength refers to its durability and influence on other psychological processes. Outcomes associated with attitude strength include attitude stability, resistance to change, and influence over information processing and behavior (Krosnick & Petty, 1995). Many different measures of attitude strength have been identified and studied. For instance, attitude ambivalence has been shown to be negatively correlated with attitude strength (Eagly & Chaiken, 1993). Table 2.2 summarizes characteristic features of attitudes and applies those concepts to an example job attitude. Included in Table 2.2 are definitions for many other dimensions of attitude strength that have been developed and used in research: *attitude certainty* (Krosnick et al., 1993), *attitude importance* (Boninger et al., 1995), and *attitude accessibility* (Fazio, 1995).

The construct validity of the various measures of attitude strength has been a recurring focal point of research. Outcomes of attitude strength have been shown to be associated with different measures of attitude strength. For example, an attitude's resistance to change has been found to be associated with attitude importance (Borgida & Howard-Pitney, 1983), attitude certainty (Swann & Ely, 1984), attitude accessibility (Bassili & Fletcher, 1991), and inter-component ambivalence (Chaiken, Pomerantz, & Giner-Sorolla, 1995). Similar patterns of relations between measures of attitude strength and outcomes of attitudes strength have raised the question of whether the various indicators of attitude strength represent one underlying construct. However, in a series of studies examining the latent factor structure underlying indicators of attitude strength, Krosnick et al. (1993) concluded that one factor could not account for the covariance between the multiple dimensions of attitude strength. Using a different approach to this question, Luttrell et al. (2016) used functional MRI to examine whether attitude ambivalence and attitude certainty have common underlying neural foundations but found that responses to each dimension of attitude strength resulted in activation of distinct brain regions. Thus, research using very different methodologies suggests that the dimensions of attitude strength are distinct. Moreover, some research suggests that dimensions of attitude strength may work best in combination to predict strength-related outcomes. For example, Lavine et al. (1998) found that attitude strength buffered context effects in surveys when attitude strength was comprised of multiple related measures but not when attitude strength was represented by a single measure.

Research suggests that job satisfaction is highly stable. A meta-analysis by Dormann and Zapf (2001) calculated a test-retest correlation corrected for unreliability of $\rho = .50$. As stability is one of the main categories of attitude strength, it appears as if job attitudes tend to be strong attitudes. The research on job attitude structure, as previously discussed, confirmed predictions that greater intra-attitudinal consistency has the strength-related consequence of job attitudes being more predictive of job behaviors (Schleicher et al. 2015). Other indicators of attitude strength have also been investigated by job attitude research conducted by Ziegler and colleagues, including job ambiguity (Ziegler, Hagen, & Diehl, 2012) and work centrality (Zeigler & Schlett, 2016).

### *Attitude Functions*

Given that attitudes are such a prevalent aspect of the human experience, they must serve important purposes for the individuals possessing these attitudes. The various reasons for a person to hold an attitude have been described as attitude functions. Taxonomies for various attitude functions were developed by different researchers, including Smith, Bruner, and White (1956) and Katz (1960). Although these taxonomies identify some common attitude functions, they also complement one another by identifying functions that are unique from the other taxonomy. Elements of both taxonomies remain relevant in contemporary discussions of attitude function.

Descriptions of the various attitude functions are displayed in Table 2.2, along with an example of each framed as a job attitude. The object appraisal function is the essential function of an attitude and thus notwithstanding other functions served by an attitude, every attitude serves an object appraisal function (Fazio, 2000). Katz (1960) described two attitude functions, the knowledge and utilitarian functions, which correspond to Smith et al.'s object appraisal function. The knowledge function addresses the role of attitudes in organizing information and the utilitarian function addresses the use of attitude information to maximize rewarding experiences and minimize experiences perceived to be detrimental. Thus, attitudes provide an experiential schematic (Herek, 1986) and serve the function of quickly informing a person what to approach and what to avoid (Fazio, 2000). Attitudes are also useful by means of their expression (Herek, 1986), including the social-adjustive function (Smith et al., 1956) and value-expressive function (Katz, 1960) that are described in Table 2.2. Finally, the experience of internal conflicts, such as conflicting beliefs and emotions, can be a source of anxiety which can be eliminated by expressing one's attitude. This attitude function was called the ego-defensive function by Katz (1960) and the externalization function by Smith et al. (1956), it and suggests that the expression of an attitude can serve as a summary judgment that alleviates the tension of internal conflict.

Contemporary research on attitudes has used the concepts of attitude functions to study different phenomena, including political persuasion (e.g. Lavine et al., 1999), consumer behavior (e.g., Shavitt, 1990), and racial prejudice (e.g., Khan & Pedersen, 2010). The execution of research on attitude functions was facilitated by Herek's (1987) development and validation of the Attitude Functions Inventory, a self-report questionnaire measuring functions of attitudes toward lesbians and gay men and toward individuals with stigmatizing illnesses. This scale can be modified for use with other attitude objects. A new approach to measuring the social-adjustive and value-expressive functions of attitudes was provided by Zunick, Teeny, and Fazio (2017) who combined these attitude functions into what is termed the self-definition function of attitudes. Their research found that attitudes toward environmentalism that rated as high for the self-definition function were negatively related to attitude ambivalence and positively related to attitude extremity and intentions to spontaneously advocate for one's attitude.

Reviews on job attitudes that invoke basic attitude theory have discussed the relevance of attitude functions to work-related contexts (Brief, 1998; Judge et al., 2017; Lee et al. 2015; Pratkanis & Turner, 1994). Research applying the functional approach to job attitudes is sparse, though. Houle, Sagarin, and Kaplan (2005) found that volunteers identified different attitude functions for their participation and attitude functions predicted the tasks chosen by volunteers. Pryor, Reeder, and McManus (1991) used an experimental design to examine attitudes toward interacting with a co-worker with AIDS and concluded that AIDS education training was more effective for individuals with attitudes toward AIDS based on utilitarian functions but not effective for those with attitudes based on more symbolic functions, like the value expressive function or ego defensive function.

## Attitude Development and Change

Connections between attitudes and their characteristic features (structure, strength, and function) have been a recurring theme in this chapter, and these characteristics of attitudes are also central to understanding how attitudes are formed and changed. An individual's summary evaluation of an object may be deliberative or automatic but, in either circumstance, it is also connected to processes that are cognitive, affective, and/or behavioral. The process of establishing this summary evaluation can result in an attitude that is strong or weak and, in turn, influence how resistant the attitude is to persuasive appeals. The resulting attitudes will serve some function, and persuasive appeals to that attitude will be more effective to the extent that they match that function. Many theories on attitude formation and change exist but the discussion below highlights selected theories and recent research associated with them. Special attention is also provided to how these theories are used in organizational contexts and how research on job attitudes contributes to the broader understanding of attitude formation and change.

## Dual Process Models

Perhaps the most influential theories of attitude formation and change are described as "dual-process" models and include the Elaboration-Likelihood Model (ELM; Petty & Cacioppo, 1996) and the Heuristic-Systematic Model (HSM; Chaiken, 1980). Both ELM and HSM suggest that persuasive messages are processed in one of two ways: (1) a relatively deliberative fashion involving effortful thought or (2) with relatively little effort and reliance on peripheral cues about the quality of the information. The more effortful path is used when an individual is motivated and has adequate cognitive resources for active processing, whereas the less effortful path is used when an individual lacks either the motivation or resources demanded by more active thinking. Although ELM and HSM appear very similar, there are some important distinctions between the two theories. For instance, the amount of focus on attitude strength within each dual process model is an important point of distinction within these theories with ELM asserting that attitude strength is developed through effortful processing of persuasive messages in a manner that is more overt and detailed than HSM. The dual process models also differ in how they integrate attitude functions and motivation to think about persuasive information. ELM assumes that individuals are motivated to have an accurate attitude, a drive that is reminiscent of the object appraisal function of attitudes. In contrast, HSM asserts that individuals can be influenced by multiple motivations, including drives like the object appraisal, value expressive, and social adjustive functions of attitudes. Research in organizational settings has used ELM to explore a variety of research topics. Douglas et al. (2008) developed an ELM-based theory for predicting workplace aggression. They suggest that cognition-, attitude-, and affect-initiated elaborative processing mediates the relationship between triggering events and workplace aggression. Li (2013) adapted ELM to test different approaches for structuring persuasive messages within training for workplace information systems.

## Evaluative Conditioning

Evaluation conditioning (EC) suggests that attitudes develop as an attitude object is repeatedly associated with another stimulus object that evokes positively- or negatively-valenced reactions, such as a positive or negative emotion (De Houwer, Thomas, & Baeyens, 2001). The concepts of classical conditioning are closely aligned with EC, in that a conditioned stimulus is repeatedly paired with an unconditioned stimulus and, over time, the response associated with the unconditioned stimulus is also associated with the conditioned stimulus. One important distinction between these approaches to conditioning is that EC presumes that the unconditioned stimulus evokes an internal reaction (e.g., happiness) that is not directly observed whereas classical conditioning uses an unconditioned stimulus that evokes a physical reaction that can be directly observed (e.g., salivating). Research suggests that EC can influence both attitude formation and attitude change (Olson & Fazio, 2006) and is resistant to change due to extinction (DeHouwer et al., 2001). A meta-analysis conducted by Hofmann et al. (2010) found that studies of EC tend to confirm their hypotheses with moderate-level effect sizes; however, the effects of EC tend to be smaller when using children as research participants and when implicit measures are used to assess attitudes. Lai et al. (2016) conducted a meta-analysis of interventions associated with reducing implicit racial preferences, including the use of EC, and found that the effectiveness of EC interventions were substantially higher when a "Go-Not Go" task was used for conditioning new associations.

### Self-Perception

Bem's (1972) Self-Perception Theory suggests that attitudes can develop and change as a consequence of observing one's own behavior and the situation in which that behavior takes place. A central premise of this theory is that individuals make attributions of their internal states by observing their own behavior, much in the same fashion that one infers the internal states of others by observing their actions. Furthermore, Bem proposed that self-perceptions are most likely to occur when an individual's existing attitude is weak and/or ambivalent and there are not situational constraints that provide an explanation for the behavior. Self-perception effects have also been demonstrated to occur vicariously when an individual is observing another person with whom they identify personally and intensely and when the behavior observed is perceived as freely chosen (Goldstein & Cialdini, 2007). Research on techniques of persuasion has often used Self-Perception Theory as an explanation for persuasion processes. For example, the lowball technique involves asking an individual to agree to a price for some product or service and then later raising that price slightly. Individuals who first agree to pay the initial price are more likely to pay the slightly higher price than individuals only presented the higher price (Cialdini et al., 1978). In a meta-analytic review of the lowball technique, Burger and Caputo (2015) found support for Self-Presentation Theory as an explanatory mechanism for the phenomenon because studies that did not have participants publicly state their initial agreement resulted in low effect sizes for lowball compliance than studies that involved public commitment to the initial price.

The relations between attitudes and behaviors can sometimes seem like a "chicken and egg" situation with some theories asserting that attitudes influence behavior, such as Fazio's (1986) MODE Model, and other theories asserting that behaviors influence attitude, such as Bem's (1972) Self-Perception theory. This dilemma has been highlighted with research examining the relations between job satisfaction and job performance. However, research is increasingly supporting the conclusion that job satisfaction and job performance have reciprocal relations and influence one another over time. For example, Alessandri, Borgogni, and Latham (2017) used longitudinal data of job satisfaction and job performance to compare unidirectional causal models (job satisfaction influencing job performance or job performance leading to job satisfaction), a bidirectional causal model (reciprocal relations between job satisfaction and job performance), and a model that specified correlation between the variables but no causal links. Their analyses provided the best support for a model suggesting that there was reciprocity over time in the relations between job satisfaction and job performance.

## The Dispositional Approach to Attitudes

Social psychological research pertaining to dispositional influences on attitude development and change has involved a variety of dispositional concepts and research methods to examine their influence on attitudes. Eaves, Eysenck, and Martin (1989) used a twins methodology to examine the heritability of a number of different social attitudes including race, religion, and life style. Their results indicated that the heritability of attitudes varied widely across social attitudes and ranged from being practically insignificant to large in effect size. Using similar methodologies, Arvey et al. (1989) reported that approximately 30% of the variance in job satisfaction was attributable to genetic factors. These findings suggest that stability of job satisfaction is attributable to a substantial degree to individual disposition.

Research on dispositions associated with attitudes has identified a number of different personality traits that influence attitudes. For instance, the personality trait of self-monitoring has been used in research examining attitude function and persuasion to differentiate between individuals with attitudes motivated by the social adjustive function (i.e., high self-monitors) or the value-expressive function (i.e., low self-monitors) (see Snyder & DeBono, 1987). Relations between attitudes and behaviors have also been shown to be moderated by personality traits, including self-monitoring (Snyder & Kendzierski, 1982) and need for cognition (Cacioppo et al., 1986). Research on job attitudes has examined the influence of various self-concept traits on job satisfaction. Judge and Bono's (2001) meta-analysis described the relationship between job satisfaction and four core self-evaluations: self-esteem ($\rho = .26$), generalized self-efficacy ($\rho = .45$), internal locus of control ($\rho = .32$), and emotional stability ($\rho = .24$). Trait affectivity, including positive affectivity and negative affectivity, has also been examined with meta-analyses in relation to overall job satisfaction and organizational commitment (Thoresen et al., 2003) and facet satisfaction (Bowling, Hendricks, & Wagner, 2008).

## *Affective Events Theory*

The recognition that job attitudes should correspond more to concepts and theories used to study attitudes in social psychology resulted in large part from the recognition that there was value in differentiating between attitudes, affective information, and cognitive information to understand the formation and development of job attitudes. The development of Affective Events Theory (AET; Weiss & Cropanzano, 1996) marked the turning point into what Judge et al.'s (2017) historical analysis characterized the Affective Era of job attitudes, starting in 1995 and spanning to the present. AET suggests job attitudes are influenced beliefs about one's job and emotional reactions to events one experiences at work. AET also posits that personality traits (e.g., negative affectivity) directly influence job satisfaction and moderate relations between emotional reactions to work experiences and job satisfaction. Furthermore, AET suggests that contextual factors (e.g., customer service context) moderate relations between perceptions of the work environment and job satisfaction. Carlson et al. (2011) used AET to explain relations between work-family enrichment programs and improved job performance. Ohly and Schmitt (2013) used a diary study with open-ended assessments of reactions of work events to develop a taxonomy of affective events that included four clusters of events associated with positive events and seven clusters of events associated with negative events.

# Consequences of Attitudes

Strong attitudes have consequences through influencing information processing and behavior. Social psychology has developed numerous theories to aid in understanding these attitudinal processes and research continues to modify and extend these theories. This section describes theories central to understanding the consequences of attitudes and new research developments associated with these theories. Connections are also made to job attitude literature that is relevant to appreciating the consequences of attitudes.

## *Effects of Attitudes on Information Processing*

The influence of attitudes on various aspects of information processing, including attention, perception, and memory, has long been a central theme of theories and research on attitudes. In general, it is believed that there is a confirmation bias that exists with information that is consistent with one's existing attitude receiving greater attention, being judged more favorably during perception, and being retrieved more readily from memory. Another term used for this confirmation bias for attitude-consistent information is the congeniality effect (Eagly & Chaiken, 1993).

Research on selective exposure, the tendency to seek out information congruent with one's attitude and avoid information that is incongruent with one's attitude (Festinger, 1957), has played a major role in understanding the effects of attitudes on attention and has been validated with meta-analytic analysis (Hart et al., 2009). Both explicit and implicit attitudes have been shown to produce selective exposure effects (Arendt, Steindl, & Kümpel, 2016). Furthermore, aspects of attitude structure, attitude function, and attitude strength have been shown to moderate the selective exposure effect. Brannon, Tagler, and Eagly (2007) found that aspects of attitude strength (i.e., attitude importance and attitude certainty) amplified the selective exposure effect. Research also suggests that the selective exposure effect is more pronounced with attitudes that are low in evaluative-cognitive ambivalence or in evaluative-affective ambivalence than high in both evaluative-cognitive and evaluative-affective ambivalence (Wagner, Lavine, & McBride, 1997). Stronger selective exposure effects have also been observed when attitude objects were relatively high in value relevance and respondents were relatively low in self-esteem (Wiersema, van Harreveld, & van der Pligt, 2012), which suggests an interactive effect of value-expressive and ego-defensive attitude functions (Maio et al., 2019).

The perception and judgment of information is also influenced by attitudes. According to Sherif and Hovland's (1961) social judgment theory, an attitude provides a judgmental anchor that results in assimilation of perceived information similar to the attitude and contrasting with perceived information dissimilar to the attitude. Bothwell and Brigham (1983) had students watch a presidential debate between Ronald Reagan and Jimmy Carter and found that their perceptions of who won the debate tended to be consistent with their pre-existing explicit attitudes toward the candidates. Research has also demonstrated the selective perception effect with implicit attitudes (Knowles, Lowery, & Schaumberg, 2010). Moreover, research suggests that attitude strength, when measured by attitude accessibility, amplifies selective perception effects (Houston & Fazio, 1989). An important implication of selective perception and judgment is in-group favoritism (Tajfel & Turner, 1986), that is, judging people within one's own social group more favorably than those in a group to which one does not belong (i.e., an out-group). Research on perception of faces has demonstrated this phenomenon across different racial groups (Blair et al., 2002) and technological advancements in facial perception methodologies, such as those associated with reverse correlation data reduction, have advanced understanding of the processes underlying this aspect of social cognition (Ratner et al., 2014).

Many studies have investigated whether there is selective memory of attitude-congruent information. In a meta-analysis, Eagly et al. (1999) found that results of studies were highly inconsistent and, when averaged, resulted in a small average effect size that was consistent with the congeniality effect. Given the variability of the findings, however, the moderators examined by Eagly et al. were particularly relevant to understanding what research says about selective memory. One moderator investigated was the value relevance of the attitude object, that is, the extent to which the attitude was linked to important values, such as ethical issues. For both recall and recognition measures of memory, high value relevant attitudes exhibit larger selective memory effects than low value relevant attitudes. Thus, attitudes that fulfill a value expressive function may be especially likely to exhibit selective memory effects. The Eagly et al. meta-analysis also described unpublished research by Chaiken and colleagues that suggested that attitude structure moderated memory-based congeniality effects with evaluative-affective ambiguity resulting in less selective memory and evaluative-cognitive ambiguity resulting in more selective memory effects. These findings suggest that different patterns of attitude structure may result in distinct retrieval processes for attitude congruent information; however, more research on this subject is needed to confirm these findings and further explore the processes that may explain them.

The selective informational processing effects of job attitudes has implications for resistance to organizational change. Brief (1998) discussed how application of inoculation theory (McGuire, 1964), which suggests presentation of weak arguments against a position encourages individuals to elaborate on stronger arguments, would be useful for persuasion in organizational contexts. Furthermore, Aguinis (2019) suggests a number of methods to address informational processing biases to overcome resistance, including involving employees, pro-actively creating a positive attitude, providing clear facts that support the change, using credible sources, and repeating the message through multiple channels of communication.

### *Effects of Attitudes on Behavior*

If attitudes guide one's interpretation of stimuli, then it seems logical that they should also direct one's behavior. The functional theory of attitudes suggests that a primary purpose of attitudes, object appraisal, guides an individual's tendency to approach or avoid the attitude object. Meta-analytic research has demonstrated that multiple aspects of attitude strength amplify the attitude-behavior relationship (Glasman & Albarracín, 2006). However, the link between an attitude and behavior is not simple or certain. Ajzen and Fishbein (1977) described conditions under which attitude-behavior relations were more likely to be observed. Called the principle of correspondence, these conditions include an alignment in the specificity of the attitude and behavior in terms of target (i.e., the entity toward which behavior is directed), action (i.e., the nature of the behavior), context (i.e., the place behavior occurs), and time (i.e., the timeframe of behavior). Subsequent theories of the effects of attitudes on behaviors have elaborated on the underlying processes for this relationship and expanded our understanding of the network of variables that connects attitudes to behavior.

The Theory of Reasoned Action (Fishbein & Ajzen, 1975) posits that volitional behavior (i.e., behavior fully under one's control) is influenced by behavioral intentions which are caused by one's attitude toward a behavior and subjective norms (i.e., social pressure pertaining to the behavior). An important assumption of this theory is that specific behaviors are best predicted by attitude measures that correspond in specificity. Thus, this theory examines attitudes toward behaviors rather than attitudes toward objects. Furthermore, the attitude associated with the behavioral intention may not result in such intentions when social customs or peer pressure oppose the behavior in question. Thus, this theory describes a detailed attitude structure (Fabrigar et al., 2005) that has been applied extensively to predict voluntary behaviors (Eagly & Chaiken, 1993). The Theory of Planned Behavior (Ajzen, 1991) was developed as an extension of the Theory of Reasoned Action to expand consideration of behaviors that require some competence and/or contextual opportunity and added the construct of perceived behavioral control as a predictor of both behavioral intentions and execution of the behavior. The implication of this model is that attitudes consistent with having a behavior intention are more likely to result in the execution of that behavior when it is consistent with social norms and perceived to be an action one can execute. A meta-analysis examining the effectiveness of behavior change interventions based on the Theory of Planned Behavior found that they tended to be valid and, on average, resulted in moderate-sized effects (Steinmetz et al., 2016). Moderator analysis of the behavior change interventions studied in this meta-analysis suggested that greater effectiveness was observed when the interventions were focused on groups and conducted in public than when the interventions were directed toward an individual and conducted in privacy.

The relationship between general attitudes (i.e., attitudes toward objects) and behavior has been addressed by the MODE model (Fazio, 1986) which stands for motivations and opportunities as determinants of behavior. This model makes predictions for behavior that is both deliberate and spontaneous. The model suggests that when an individual is adequately motivated and has the opportunity to process information associated with their attitude, then his or her deliberate behavior will be relatively consistent with their attitude. When an individual is not sufficiently motivated and/or lacks the opportunity to process attitude-relevant information, then the strength of one's attitude (i.e., its accessibility in memory) will determine whether it is automatically activated and lead to spontaneous behavior that is attitude consistent. However, attitudes that lack strength are not automatically activated and thus do not result in spontaneous behavior consistent with one's attitude. The MODE model has become an increasingly important theory for understanding attitude-behavior relations and has been applied across a variety of contexts (Maio et al., 2019). For example, Kumar, Karabenick, and Burgoon (2015), used the MODE model to explain how teachers' implicit and explicit attitudes toward non-white students were associated with classroom teaching practices. Their findings supported elements of the MODE model as factors explaining when teaching practices were associated with deliberative processes through their explicit attitudes toward non-white students and automatically activated processes associated with their implicit attitudes toward non-white students.

The relationship between job attitudes and job behaviors has received extensive research attention and many meta-analyses have been conducted to synthesize and describe the results of this research. Judge et al.'s (2001) meta-analysis estimated a mean correlation of $\rho = .30$. Higher relationships between job satisfaction and job performance were observed when jobs had higher complexity. Dalal's (2005) meta-analysis examined relations between job attitudes and extra-role behaviors. Organizational citizenship behaviors were positively related to job satisfaction $\rho = .16$ and organizational commitment $\rho = .28$; whereas counterproductive work behaviors were negatively related to job satisfaction $\rho = -.37$ and organizational commitment $\rho = -.36$. Rubenstein et al.'s (2017) meta-analysis examined relations between job attitudes and voluntary turnover, finding a corrected correlation of $\rho = -.28$ for job satisfaction and $\rho = -.29$ for organizational commitment. An interesting moderator effect of the relations between job attitudes and voluntary turnover was personal fit (i.e., similarity to workgroup) with stronger relations between job attitudes (both job satisfaction and organizational commitment) and voluntary turnover being observed in groups where employees were more satisfied and committed. Attitude-behavior relations have also been shown to be moderated by situational strength, that is, the extent to which a situation dictates how one should behave in it. Using meta-analysis, Bowling et al., (2015) found that situation strength buffered relations between job satisfaction and job performance.

## Conclusion

Understanding attitudes has long been an integral aspect of appreciating and using the science of psychology. Gordon Allport (1935, p. 798) is often quoted for saying "the concept of attitude is probably the most distinctive and indispensable concept in contemporary American social psychology." Over generations, theories and research on attitudes have evolved. In this time, interest in attitudes as a topic worth studying has waxed and waned and waxed again. One goal of this chapter was to introduce theories and research findings that provide the foundation for understanding attitudes. Although many of the most important attitude concepts were addressed by this chapter, some were left out due to necessary constraints. Readers are encouraged to seek out textbooks on the science of attitudes to pursue greater depth and breadth of knowledge of this field, including texts by Eagly and Chaiken (1993) and Maio et al., (2019). A second goal of this chapter was to examine how research on job attitudes has applied basic attitude concepts and addressed unique challenges to studying attitudes in organizational contexts. Looking at the intersection of the basic social psychology of attitudes and the applied psychology of job attitudes is especially interesting with the growing recognition that job attitude research benefits from conceptual congruence with the literature on attitudes from social psychology. Many opportunities for research within the terrain between general attitude theory and job attitudes remain, and the ultimate aim of this chapter was to encourage ideas that lead to such research.

# References

Aguinis, H. (2019). *Performance management* (4rd Ed.). Chicago, IL: Chicago Business Press.

Ajzen, I. (1991). The theory of planned behavior. *Organizational Behavior and Human Decision Processes, 50*, 179–211.

Ajzen, I. & Fishbein, M. (1977). Attitude–behavior relations: A theoretical analysis and review of empirical research. *Psychological Bulletin, 84*, 888–918.Alessandri, G., Borgogni, L., & Latham, G.P. (2017). A dynamic model of the longitudinal relationship between job satisfaction and supervisor-rated job performance. *Applied Psychology: An International Review, 66*(2), 207–232.

Allport, G.W. (1935). Attitudes. In: C. Murchison (Ed.), *A Handbook of Social Psychology* (pp. 798–844). Worcester, MA: Clark University Press.

Arendt, F., Steindl, N., & Kümpel, A. (2016). Implicit and explicit attitudes as predictors of gatekeeping, selective exposure, and news sharing: Testing a general model of media-related selection. *Journal of Communication, 66*, 717–740.

Arvey, R.D., Bouchard, T.J., Segal, N.L., & Abraham, L.M. (1989). Job satisfaction: Environmental and genetic components. *Journal of Applied Psychology, 74*(2), 187–192.

Bassili, J.N. & Fletcher, J.F. (1991). Response-time measurement in survey research: A method for CATI and a new look at nonattitudes. *Public Opinion Quarterly, 55*, 331–346.

Bem, D.J. (1972). Self-perception theory. In L. Berkowitz (ed.), *Advances in experimental social psychology* (Vol. 6, pp. 1–62). San Diego, CA: Academic Press.

Bergman, M.M. (1998). A theoretical note on the differences between attitudes, opinions, and values. *Swiss Political Science Review, 4*, 81–93.

Blair, L., Judd, C.M., Sadler, M.S., & Jenkins, C. (2002). The role of afro-centric features in person perception: Judging by features and categories. *Journal of Personality and Social Psychology, 83*, 5–25.

Boninger, D.S., Krosnick, J.A., Berent, M.K., & Fabrigar, L.R. (1995). The causes and consequences of attitudinal involvement. In R.E. Petty & J.A. Krosnick (Eds.) *Attitude strength: Antecedents and consequences* (pp. 159–190). Mahwah, NJ: Erlbaum.

Borgida, E. & Howard-Pitney, B. (1983). Personal involvement and the robustness of perceptual salience effects. *Journal of Personality and Social Psychology, 45*, 560–570.

Bothwell, R.K. & Brigham, J.C. (1983). Selective evaluation and recall during the 1980 Reagan-Carter debate. *Journal of Applied Social Psychology, 13*, 427–442.

Bowling, N.A., Hendricks, E.A., & Wagner, S.H. (2008). Positive and negative affectivity and facet satisfaction: A meta-analysis. *Journal of Business and Psychology, 23*(3–4), 115–125.

Bowling, N.A., Khazon, S., Meyer, R.D., & Burrus, C.J. (2015). Situation strength as a moderator of the relationship between job satisfaction and job performance: A meta-analytic examination. *Journal of Business and Psychology, 30*, 89–104.

Brannon, L.A., Tagler, M.J., & Eagly, A.H. (2007). The moderating role of attitude strength in selective exposure to information. *Journal of Experimental Social Psychology, 43*, 611–617.

Brayfield, A.H. & Rothe, H.F. (1951). An index of job satisfaction. *Journal of Applied Psychology*, *35*(5), 307–311.

Brief, A. (1998). *Attitudes in and around organizations*. Thousand Oaks, CA: Sage.

Brief, A.P. & Roberson, L. (1989). Job attitude organization: An exploratory study. *Journal of Applied Social Psychology*, *19*, 717–727.

Burger, J.M. & Caputo, D. (2015). The low-ball compliance procedure: A meta-analysis. *Social Influence*, *10*(4), 214–220.

Cacioppo, J.T., Petty, R.E., Kao, C.F., & Rodriguez, R. (1986). Central and peripheral routes to persuasion: An individual difference perspective. *Journal of Personality and Social Psychology*, *51*, 1032–1043.

Carlson, D., Kacmar, K.M., Zivnuska, S., Ferguson, M., & Whitten, D. (2011). Work-family enrichment and job performance: A constructive replication of affective events theory. *Journal of Occupational Health Psychology*, *16*(3), 297–312.

Chaiken, S. (1980). Heuristic versus systematic information processing and the use of source versus message cues in persuasion. *Journal of Personality and Social Psychology*, *39*, 752–766.

Chaiken, S., Pomerantz, E.M., & Giner-Sorolla, R. (1995). Structural consistency and attitude strength. In R.E. Petty & J.A. Krosnick (Eds.), *Attitude strength: Antecedents and consequences* (pp. 387–412). Mahwah, NJ: Lawrence Erlbaum Associates.

Cialdini, R.B., Cacioppo, J.T., Bassett, R., & Miller, J.A. (1978). Low-ball procedure for producing compliance: Commitment then cost. *Journal of Personality and Social Psychology*, *36*, 463–476.

Dalal, R.S. (2005). A meta-analysis of the relationship between organizational citizenship behavior and counterproductive work behavior. *Journal of Applied Psychology*, *90*(6), 1241–1255.

Dalege, J., Borsboom, D., van Harreveld, F., van den Berg, H., Conner, M., & van der Mass, H.L.J. (2016). Toward a formalized account of attitudes. *Psychological Review*, *123*, 2–22.

De Houwer, J., Thomas, S., & Baeyens, F. (2001). Associative learning of likes and dislikes: A review of 25 years of research on human evaluative conditioning. *Psychological Bulletin*, *127*, 853–869.

Diestel, S., Wegge, J., & Schmidt, K.-H. (2014). The impact of social context on the relationship between individual job satisfaction and absenteeism: The roles of different foci of job satisfaction and work-unit absenteeism. *Academy of Management Journal*, *57*(2), 353–382.

Dormann, C. & Zapf, D. (2001). Job satisfaction: A meta-analysis of stabilities. *Journal of Organizational Behavior*, *22*(5), 483–504.

Douglas, S.C., Kiewitz, C., Martinko, M.J., Harvey, P., Kim, Y., & Chun, J.U. (2008). Cognitions, emotions, and evaluations: An elaboration likelihood model for workplace aggression. *The Academy of Management Review*, *33*(2), 425–451.

Drasgow, F., Chernyshenko, O.S., & Stark, S. (2010). 75 years after Likert: Thurstone was right! *Industrial and Organizational Psychology: Perspectives on Science and Practice*, *3*(4), 465–476

Eagly, A.H. & Chaiken, S. (1993). *The psychology of attitudes*. Fort Worth, TX: Harcourt Brace Jovanovich.

Eagly, A.H., Mladinic, A., & Otto, S. (1994). Cognitive and affective bases of attitudes toward social groups and social policies. *Journal of Experimental Social Psychology*, *30*, 113–137.

Eagly, A.H., Chen, S., Chaiken, S., & Shaw-Barnes, K. (1999). The impact of attitudes on memory: An affair to remember. *Psychological Bulletin, 125,* 64–89.

Eaves, L.J., Eysenck, H.J., & Martin, N.G. (1989). *Genes, culture and personality: An empirical approach.* San Diego, CA: Academic Press.

Esses, V.M. & Maio, G.R. (2002). Expanding the assessment of attitude components and structure: The benefits of open-ended measures. In W. Stroebe & M. Hewstone (eds.), *European review of social psychology* (Vol. 12, pp. 71–102). Chichester: Wiley.

Esses, V.M., Haddock, G., & Zanna, M.P. (1993). Values, stereotypes and emotions as determinants of intergroup attitudes. In D.M. Mackie & D.L. Hamilton (eds.), *Affect, cognition and stereotyping: Interactive processes in group perception* (pp. 137–166). New York: Academic Press.

Fabrigar, L.R., MacDonald, T.K., & Wegener, D.T. (2005). The structure of attitudes. In D. Albarracín, B.T. Johnson, & M.P. Zanna (Eds.), *Handbook of attitudes and attitude change.* Mahwah, NJ: Erlbaum.

Fazio, R.H. (1986). How do attitudes guide behavior? In R.M. Sorrentino & E. Tory (Eds.), *Handbook of motivation and cognition: Foundations of social behavior* (pp. 204–243). New York, NY: Guilford Press.

Fazio, R.H. (1995). Attitudes as object-evaluation associations: Determinants, consequences and correlates of attitude accessibility. In R.E. Petty & J.A. Krosnick (eds.), *Attitude strength: Antecedents and consequences* (pp. 247–282). Hillsdale, NJ: Erlbaum.

Fazio, R.H. (2000). Accessible attitudes as tools for object appraisal: Their costs and benefits. In G.R. Maio & J.M. Olson (Eds.), *Why we evaluate: Functions of attitudes* (pp. 1–36). Mahwah, NJ: Lawrence Erlbaum Associates.

Festinger, L. (1957). *A theory of cognitive dissonance.* Evanston, IL: Row, Peterson.

Fishbein, M. & Ajzen, I. (1975). *Belief, attitude, intention and behavior: An introduction to theory and research.* Reading, MA: Addison-Wesley.

Geer, J.G. (1988). What do open-ended questions measure? *Public Opinion Quarterly, 52,* 365–371.

Glasman, L.R. & Albarracín, D. (2006). Forming attitudes that predict future behavior: A meta-analysis of the attitude–behavior relation. *Psychological Bulletin, 132,* 778–822.

Goldstein, N.J. & Cialdini, R.B. (2007). The spyglass self: A model of vicarious self-perception. *Journal of Personality and Social Psychology, 92,* 402–417.

Greenwald, A.G., McGhee, D., & Schwartz, J. (1998). Measuring individual differences in implicit cognition: The Implicit Association Test. *Journal of Personality and Social Psychology, 74,* 1464–1480.

Haines, E.L. & Sumner, K.E. (2006). Implicit measurement of attitudes, stereotypes, and self-concepts in organizations: Teaching old dogmas new tricks. *Organizational Research Methods, 9*(4), 536–553.

Hart, W., Albarracín, D., Eagly, A.H., Brechan, I., Lindberg, M.J., & Merrill, L. (2009). Feeling validated versus being correct: A meta-analysis of selective exposure to information. *Psychological Bulletin, 135,* 555–588.

Hatfield, J.D., Robinson, R.B., & Huseman, R.C. (1985). An empirical evaluation of a test for assessing job satisfaction. *Psychological Reports, 56*(1), 39–45.

Heider, F. (1946). Attitudes and cognitive organization. *Journal of Psychology, 21,* 107–112.

Herek, G.M. (1986). The instrumentality of attitudes: Toward a neofunctional theory. *Journal of Social Issues, 42,* 99–114.

Herek, G.M. (1987). Can functions be measured? A new perspective on the functional approach to attitudes. *Social Psychology Quarterly, 50*, 285–303.

Highhouse, S. & Becker, A.S. (1993). Facet measures and global job satisfaction. *Journal of Business and Psychology, 8*, 117–127.

Himmelfarb, S. (1993). The measurement of attitudes. In A.H. Eagly & S. Chaiken, *The psychology of attitudes*. Fort Worth, TX: Harcourt Brace Jovanovich.

Hofmann, W., De Houwer, J., Perugini, M., Baeyens, F., & Crombez, G. (2010). Evaluative conditioning in humans: A meta-analysis. *Psychological Bulletin, 136*, 390–421.

Houle, B.J., Sagarin, B.J., & Kaplan, M.F. (2005) A functional approach to volunteerism: Do volunteer motives predict task preference? *Basic and Applied Social Psychology, 27*(4), 337–344.

Houston, D.A. & Fazio, R.H. (1989). Biased processing as a function of attitude accessibility: Making objective judgments subjectively. *Social Cognition, 7*, 51–66.

Huskinson, T.L. & Haddock, G. (2004). Individual differences in attitude structure: Variance in the chronic reliance on affective and cognitive information. *Journal of Experimental Social Psychology, 40*, 83–90.

Ironson, G.H., Smith, P.C., Brannick, M.T., Gibson, W.M., & Paul, K.B. (1989). Construction of a job in general scale: A comparison of global, composite, and specific measures. *Journal of Applied Psychology, 74*(2), 193–200.

Irwing, P., Hughes, D., & Booth, T. (2018). *The Wiley handbook of psychometric testing, 2 volume set: A multidisciplinary reference on survey, scale and test development*. New York: Wiley.

Judd, C.M., Drake, R.A., Downing, J.W., & Krosnick, J.A. (1991). Some dynamic properties to attitude structure: Context-induced response facilitation and polarization. *Journal of Personality and Social Psychology, 60*, 193–202.

Judge, T.A. & Bono, J.E. (2001). Relationship of core self-evaluations traits—self-esteem, generalized self-efficacy, locus of control, and emotional stability – with job satisfaction and job performance: A meta-analysis. *Journal of Applied Psychology, 86*, 80–92.

Judge, T.A., Thoresen, C.J., Bono, J.E., & Patton, G.K. (2001). The job satisfaction–job performance relationship: A qualitative and quantitative review. *Psychological Bulletin, 127*(3), 376–407.

Judge, T.A., Weiss, H.M., Kammeyer-Mueller, J.D., & Hulin, C.L. (2017). Job attitudes, job satisfaction, and job affect: A century of continuity and of change. *Journal of Applied Psychology, 102*(3), 356–374.

Judge, T.A., Piccolo, R.F., Podsakoff, N.P., Shaw, J.C., & Rich, B.L. (2010). The relationship between pay and job satisfaction: A meta-analysis of the literature. *Journal of Vocational Behavior, 77*(2), 157–167.

Kan Ma, H., Min, C., Neville, A., & Eva, K. (2013). How good is good? Students and assessors' perceptions of qualitative markers of performance. *Teaching and Learning in Medicine, 25*(1), 15–23.

Katz, D. (1960). The functional approach to the study of attitudes. *Public Opinion Quarterly, 24*, 163–204.

Khan, S. & Pedersen, A. (2010). Black African immigrants to Australia: Prejudice and the function of attitudes. *Journal of Pacific Rim Psychology, 4*, 116–129.

Knowles, E.D., Lowery, B.S., & Schaumberg, R.L. (2010). Racial prejudice predicts opposition to Obama and his health care reform plan. *Journal of Experimental Social Psychology, 46*, 420–423.

Krosnick, J.A. & Petty, R.E. (1995). Attitude strength: An overview. In R.E. Petty & J.A. Krosnick (Eds.), *Attitude strength: Antecedents and consequences* (pp. 1–24). Hillsdale, NJ: Erlbaum.

Krosnick, J.A., Judd, C.M., & Wittenbrink, B. (2005). Attitude measurement. In D. Albarracín, B.T. Johnson, & M.P. Zanna (eds.), *Handbook of attitudes and attitude change*. Mahwah, NJ: Erlbaum.

Krosnick, J.A., Boninger, D.S., Chuang, Y.C., Berent, M.K., & Carnot, C.G. (1993). Attitude strength: One construct or many related constructs? *Journal of Personality and Social Psychology, 65*, 1132–1151.

Kulesa, P. & Bishop, R.J. (2006). What did they really mean? New and emerging methods for analyzing themes in open-ended comments. In A.I. Kraut (Ed.), *Getting action from organizational surveys: New concepts, technologies, and applications*. San Francisco, CA: Jossey-Bass.

Kumar, R., Karabenick, S.A., & Burgoon, J.N. (2015). Teachers' implicit attitudes, explicit beliefs, and the mediating role of respect and cultural responsibility on mastery and performance-focused instructional practices. *Journal of Educational Psychology, 107*, 533–545.

Lai CK, Skinner AL, Cooley E, et al. (2016) Reducing implicit racial preferences: II. Intervention effectiveness across time. *Journal of Experimental Psychology: General, 145*(8), 1001–1016.

Lavine, H., Huff, J.W., Wagner, S.H., & Sweeney, D. (1998). The moderating influence of attitude strength on the susceptibility to context effects in attitude surveys. *Journal of Personality and Social Psychology, 75*, 359–373.

Lavine, H., Burgess, D., Snyder, M., Transue, J., Sullivan, J.L., Haney, B., & Wagner, S.H. (1999). Threat, authoritarianism, and voting: An investigation of personality and persuasion. *Personality and Social Psychology Bulletin, 25*, 337–347.

Leavitt, K., Fong, C.T., & Greenwald, A.G. (2011). Asking about well-being gets you half an answer: Intra-individual processes of implicit and explicit job attitudes. *Journal of Organizational Behavior, 32*(4), 672–681.

Lee, E.-S., Park, T.-Y., & Koo, B. (2015). Identifying organizational identification as abasis for attitudes and behaviors: A meta-analytic review. *Psychological Bulletin, 141*(5), 1–32.

Li, C.-Y. (2013). Persuasive messages on information system acceptance: A theoretical extension of elaboration likelihood model and social influence theory. *Computers in Human Behavior, 29*(1), 264–275.

Likert, R. (1932). A technique for the measurement of attitudes. *Archives of Psychology, 140*, 5–53.

Luttrell, A., Stillman, P.E., Hasinski, A., & Cunningham, W.A. (2016). Neural dissociations in attitude strength: Distinct regions of cingulate cortex track ambivalence and certainty. *Journal of Experimental Psychology: General, 145*, 419–433.

Maio, G.R., Esses, V.M., & Bell, D.W. (2000). Examining conflict between components of attitudes: Ambivalence and inconsistency are distinct constructs. *Canadian Journal of Behavioural Science, 32*, 71–83.

Maio, G.R., Haddock, G., & Verplanken, B. (2019). *The psychology of attitudes and attitude change* (3rd Ed.). Thousand Oaks, CA: SAGE Publication.

McGuire, W. J. (1964). Inducing resistance to persuasion: Some contemporary approaches. *Advances in Experimental Social Psychology, 1*, 191–229.

Motowidlo, S.J. (1996). Orientation toward the job and organization. In K.R. Murphy (Ed.), *Individual differences in behavior in organizations*. San Francisco: Jossey-Bass.

Nayakankuppam, D.J., Priester, J.R., Kwon, J.H., Donovan, L.A., & Petty, R.E. (2018). Construction and retrieval of evaluative judgments: The attitude strength moderation model. *Journal of Experimental Social Psychology, 76*, 54–66.

Ohly, S., Schmitt, A. (2015). What makes us enthusiastic, angry, feeling at rest or worried? Development and validation of an affective work events taxonomy using concept mapping methodology. *Journal of Business and Psychology, 30*, 15–35.

Olson, M.A. & Fazio, R.H. (2006). Reducing automatically activated prejudice through implicit evaluative conditioning. *Personality and Social Psychology Bulletin, 32*, 421–433.

Organ, D.W. & Near, J.P. (1985). Cognition vs affect in measures of job satisfaction. *International Journal of Psychology, 20*(2), 241–253.

Osgood, C.E., Suci, G.J., & Tannenbaum, P.H. (1957). *The measurement of meaning.* Urbana, IL: University of Illinois Press.

Petty, R.E. & Cacioppo, J.T. (1996). *Attitudes and persuasion: Classic and contemporary approaches.* Dubuque, IA: Brown.

Pratkanis, A.R. & Turner, M.E. (1994). Of what value is a job attitude? A Socio-cognitive analysis. *Human Relations, 47*, 1545–1577.

Pryor, J. B., Reeder, G. D., & McManus, J. (1991). Fear and loathing in the workplace: Reactions to AIDS infected co-workers. *Personality and Social Psychology Bulletin, 17*, 133–140.

Rabelo, V.C. & Mahalingam, R. (2019). "They really don't want to see us": How cleaners experience invisible "dirty" work. *Journal of Vocational Behavior, 113*, 103–114.

Ratner, K.G., Dotsch, R., Wigboldus, D.H.J., van Knippenberg, A., & Amodio, D.M. (2014). Visualizing minimal ingroup and outgroup faces: Implications for impressions, attitudes, and behaviors. *Journal of Personality and Social Psychology, 106*, 897–911.

Rogelberg, S.G., Allen, J.A., Shanock, L., Scott, C., & Shuffler, M. (2010). Employee satisfaction with meetings: A contemporary facet of job satisfaction. *Human Resource Management, 49*(2), 149–172.

Rubenstein, A.L., Eberly, M.B., Lee, T.W., & Mitchell, T.R. (2017). Surveying the forest: A meta-analysis, moderator investigation, and future-oriented discussion of the antecedents of voluntary employee turnover. *Personnel Psychology, 71*(1), 23–65.

Scarpello, V. & Campbell, J.P. (1983). Job satisfaction: Are all the parts there? *Personnel Psychology, 36*, 577–600.

Schwarz, N. (2007). Attitude construction: Evaluation in context. *Social Cognition, 25*, 638–656.

Schleicher, D.J., Watt, J.D., & Greguras, G.J. (2004). Reexamining the Job Satisfaction-Performance Relationship: The Complexity of Attitudes. *Journal of Applied Psychology, 89*(1), 165–177.

Schleicher, D.J., Smith, T.A., Casper, W.J., Watt, J.D., & Greguras, G.J. (2015). It's all in the attitude: The role of job attitude strength in job attitude–outcome relationships. *Journal of Applied Psychology, 100*(4), 1259–1274.

Schneider, B., Hanges, P.J., Smith, D.B., & Salvaggio, A.N. (2003). Which comes first: Employee attitudes or organizational financial and market performance? *Journal of Applied Psychology, 88*(5), 836–851.

Shavitt, S. (1990). The role of attitude objects in attitude functions. *Journal of Experimental Social Psychology, 26*, 124–148.

Sherif, M. & Hovland, C.I. (1961). *Social judgment: Assimilation and contrast effects in communication and attitude change.* New Haven CT: Yale University Press.

Shuman, H., Ludwig, J., & Krosnick, J.A. (1986). The perceived threat of nuclear war, salience, and open-ended questions. *Public Opinion Quarterly, 35,* 44–68.

Smith, M.B., Bruner, J.S., & White, R.W. (1956). *Opinions and personality.* New York: Wiley.

Snyder, M. & DeBono, K.G., (1987). A functional approach to attitudes and persuasion. In M.P. Zanna, J.M. Olsen, & C.P. Herman (Eds.), *Social influence: The Ontario symposium* (Vol. 5, pp. 107–125*).* Hillsdale, NJ: Lawrence Erlbaum Associates.

Snyder, M. & Kendzierski, D. (1982). Acting on one's attitudes: Procedures for linking attitudes and behavior. *Journal of Experimental Social Psychology, 18,* 165–183.

Spector, P.E. (1991). *Summated rating scale construction: An introduction.* Thousand Oaks, CA: Sage Publication.

Spector, P.E. (1997). *Job satisfaction: Application, assessment, causes, and consequences.* Thousand Oaks, CA: Sage.

Steinmetz, H., Knappstein, M., Ajzen, I., Schmidt, P., & Kabst, R. (2016). How effective are behavior change interventions based on the theory of planned behavior? A three-level meta-analysis. *Zeitschrift Für Psychologie, 224*(3), 216–233.

Swann, W.B., Jr. & Ely, R.J. (1984). A battle of wills: Self-verification versus behavioral confirmation. *Journal of Personality and Social Psychology, 46,* 1287–1302.

Tajfel, H. & Turner, J.C. (1986). The social identity theory of intergroup behavior. In S. Worchel & W.G. Austin (Eds.), *Psychology of intergroup relations* (2nd Ed., pp. 7–24). Chicago, IL: Nelson-Hall.

Thoresen, C.J., Kaplan, S.A., Barsky, A.P., Warren, C.R., & de Chermont, K. (2003). The affective underpinnings of job perceptions and attitudes: A meta-analytic review and integration. *Psychological Bulletin, 129*(6), 914–945.

Thurstone, L.L. (1928). Attitudes can be measured. *American Journal of Sociology, 33,* 529–554.

Uhlmann, E.L., Leavitt, K., Menges, J.I., Koopman, J., Howe, M., & Johnson, R.E. (2012). Getting explicit about the implicit: A taxonomy of implicit measures and guide for their use in organizational research. *Organizational Research Methods, 15*(4), 553–601.

Wagner, S.H. (2017). Exploring the structure of job satisfaction and its impact on the satisfaction-performance relationship. *Journal of Organizational Psychology, 17,* 90–101.

Wagner, S.H., Lavine, H., & McBride, T. (1997). *Intra-attitudinal structure and selective exposure to attitude-congruent information.* Presented at the annual conference of the American Psychological Association, Chicago, IL.

Wanous, J.P., Reichers, A.E., & Hudy, M.J. (1997). Overall job satisfaction: How good are single item measures. *Journal of Applied Psychology, 82,* 247–252.

Weiss, H.M. (2002). Deconstructing job satisfaction: Separating evaluations, beliefs and affective experiences. *Human Resource Management Review, 12*(2), 173–194.

Weiss, H.M. & Cropanzano, R. (1996). Affective events theory: A theoretical discussion of the structure, causes and consequences of affective experiences at work. *Research in Organizational Behavior, 18,* 1–74.

Weiss, H.M., Nicholas, J.P., & Daus, C.S. (1999). An examination of the joint effects of affective experiences and job beliefs on job satisfaction and variations in affective experiences over time. *Organizational Behavior and Human Decision Processes, 78*(1), 1–24.

Wiersema, D.V., van Harreveld, F., & van der Pligt, J. (2012). Shut your eyes and think of something else: Self-esteem and avoidance when dealing with counter-attitudinal information. *Social Cognition, 30*, 323–334.

Zanna, M.P. & Rempel, J.K. (1988). Attitudes: A new look at an old concept. In D. BarTal & A.W. Kruglanski (eds.), *The social psychology of knowledge* (pp. 315–334). Cambridge: Cambridge University Press.

Ziegler, R. & Schlett, C. (2016). An attitude strength and self-perception framework regarding the Bi-directional relationship of job satisfaction with extra-role and in-role behavior: The doubly moderating role of work centrality. *Frontiers in Psychology, 7.* Retrieved from search.ebscohost.com/login.aspx?direct=true&db=psyh&AN=2016-18696-001&site=ehost-live

Ziegler, R., Hagen, B., & Diehl, M. (2012). Relationship between job satisfaction and job performance: Job ambivalence as a moderator. *Journal of Applied Social Psychology, 42*(8), 2019–2040.

Zunick, P.V., Teeny, J.D., & Fazio, R.H. (2017). Are some attitudes more self-defining than others? Assessing self-related attitude functions and their consequences. *Personality and Social Psychology Bulletin, 43*, 1136–1149.

# Part II

# JOB ATTITUDES AND OTHER WORKPLACE PSYCHOLOGICAL CONSTRUCTS

# 3

# ORGANIZATIONAL JUSTICE

*Vicente Martínez-Tur, Carolina Moliner, and Alice Maniezki*

People want to be treated fairly in every area of their lives, including the work-place. More than 50 years ago, Adams (1965) published his seminal paper on equity theory, facilitating the extension of justice research to organizational contexts. Research in the past five decades has made relevant progress. Over time, conceptual debates and consideration of different theoretical approaches have provided a rich picture of the nature of organizational justice and the mechanisms involved. Scholars have also identified relevant antecedents and consequences of organizational justice. Although there is agreement about the relevance of this progress, some important questions remain unanswered. The current chapter presents the state of the art in the study of organizational jus-tice, including conceptual issues, theories, antecedents, and consequences. We also discuss future initiatives for research and practice.

## Organizational Justice: Its Nature and Conceptualization

There are relevant debates about different facets of the justice concept, such as its dimensionality, the theoretical approaches involved, the sources, and the levels of construct and analysis. We describe them in the following paragraphs.

### Definition and Dimensions

Greenberg (1990) used *organizational justice* as a general concept to refer to whether employees perceive they are treated in a just, fair, and ethical man-ner. Scholars agree that it is a multidimensional phenomenon, and they iden-tify four different types of organizational justice (Colquitt, Zapata-Phelan, & Greenberg, 2005; Colquitt, 2001; Greenberg, 1993): distributive, procedural, and interactional justice, which is divided into informational justice and imper-sonal justice.

In the early literature on justice in the workplace, scholars focused on the fairness of outcomes, referred to as *distributive justice*. This dimension deals with the distribution of resources, including equity (Adams, 1965), equality, and need (Leventhal, 1976), as the rules that individuals use to evaluate an out-come as fair. According to Adam's equity theory (1965), people compare the effort they put into their interactions with other actors (e.g., supervisor) with the benefits they receive in return. In addition, the individual compares this ratio of costs/benefits with those of other significant people (e.g., co-workers) in order to evaluate fairness. If, as a result of this comparison process, these ratios match, the person feels a sense of equity. Although equity is typically viewed as the most appropriate allocation norm to define justice, other norms can be considered in different situations, contexts, or cultures. For example, allocating outcomes according to equality (all employees receive the same benefits) and need (employees receive benefits according to their needs) norms could be relevant when personal welfare is a relevant goal (Deutsch, 1975; Leventhal, 1976).

Employees consider not only the fair allocation of outcomes but also the procedures used for the distribution of outcomes. Accordingly, *procedural justice* reflects the degree to which the procedures through which the resources are allocated are fair (Leventhal, 1980; Thibaut & Walker, 1975). Scholars have proposed different rules to understand the fairness of procedures. Thibaut and Walker (1975) referred to process control, whereas Leventhal (1980) proposed six procedural justice rules including consistency (a procedure should be applied consistently across persons and time), bias suppression (both self-interest and personal biases should be avoided), the accuracy of information (decisions on procedures should be based on correct and appropriate information), correctability (including the possibility of modifying a decision or correcting an error), representativeness (all affected parties should be considered in the decision-making), and ethicality (procedures should be based on fundamental moral and ethical values).

In addition to distributive and procedural fairness, scholars have identified one more dimension, *interactional justice*. This dimension of justice was first introduced by Bies and Moag (1986). Whereas procedural justice refers to the more structural facet of procedures, interactional justice focuses on the more interpersonal aspects because it concentrates on the fairness of interpersonal treatment (Colquitt, 2001). Later on, Greenberg (1993) argued that interactional justice is composed of two facets: *interpersonal* (adequate treatment from supervisors in terms of dignity, respect, etc.) and *informational* (the degree to which the supervisor shares information with transparency and truthfulness) justice. Empirical evidence has supported the distinctiveness of the four dimensions of justice (e.g., Alkhadher & Gadelrab, 2016; Colquitt, 2001).

## *Overall Justice*

Despite the general acknowledgment that the aforementioned justice dimensions are conceptually distinct, scholars have begun to consider an overall approach in order to achieve better knowledge about the nature of organizational justice (e.g., Ambrose & Schminke, 2009; Barclay & Kiefer, 2014). Some scholars argue that people's experiences of justice are better captured by overall fairness than by specific types of justice (e.g., Lind, 2001; Shapiro, 2001) because it may be unrealistic to assume that a clear distinction between

46

justice dimensions always occurs in real organizational life. Therefore, people may holistically experience justice, providing a more parsimonious perspective (Ambrose & Schminke, 2009; Jones & Martens, 2009). In fact, meta-analytic evidence suggests that overall fairness accounts for more unique variance in different dimensions of organizational citizenship behavior than the sum of the unique effects of types of justice (Fassina, Jones, and Uggerslev, 2008). Additionally, Ambrose and Schminke (2009) observed that overall fairness mediates the link from justice dimensions to employee attitudes and behaviors, supporting overall fairness as a more proximal predictor of justice-based responses than the specific facets of justice (Lind, 2001). In sum, although specific dimensions of justice exist, there is increasing evidence that employees develop an overall justice perception that has a more direct and stronger influence on their attitudes and behaviors.

## *Justice Assessment*

This differentiation between dimensions of justice, on the one hand, and overall justice perception, on the other, influences the way organizational justice is measured. When dimensions are considered, a specific scale is traditionally used for each facet of justice. For example, Colquitt (2001) validated a well-recognized scale. See Table 3.1 for the items.

In contrast, the measure of overall justice is about the general perception about the treatment received. Ambrose and Schminke (2009), based on Lind's (2001) and Colquitt and Shaw's (2005) suggestions, developed a six-item measure called the Perceived Overall Justice (POJ) scale (see Table 3.2 for the items).

## *Justice-Related Theories*

In this section, we differentiate between three types of justice-related theories. The first group of theories was developed from other fields but has been applied to understand organizational justice. The second group of theories was generated within the justice literature. Finally, the third group of theories focuses on the justice process.

### *Social Exchange and Affective Events Theories*

Scholars have considered different theories to understand why justice is relevant for employees and how (un)justice perceptions emerge. Two general frameworks formulated outside the specific fairness literature have been considered in the investigation of organizational justice: social exchange (Blau, 1964) and affective events theories (Weiss & Cropanzano 1996). *Social exchange theory* refers to the way multiple varieties of resources are exchanged following specific rules, and how such exchanges can foster high-quality relationships. Based on the social norm of reciprocity, a person's experiences are related to

*Table 3.1* Justice Measure Items

Procedural Justice. *The following items refer to the procedures used to arrive at your (outcome).
To what extent:*
1. Have you been able to express your views and feelings during those procedures?
2. Have you had influence over the (outcome) arrived at by those procedures?
3. Have those procedures been applied consistently?
4. Have those procedures been free of bias?
5. Have those procedures been based on accurate information?
6. Have you been able to appeal the (outcome) arrived at by those procedures?
7. Have those procedures upheld ethical and moral standards?

Distributive Justice. *The following items refer to your (outcome). To what extent:*
1. Does your (outcome) reflect the effort you have put into your work?
2. Is your (outcome) appropriate for the work you have completed?
3. Does your (outcome) reflect what you have contributed to the organization?
4. Is your (outcome) justified, given your performance?

Interpersonal Justice. *The following items refer to (the authority figure who enacted the procedure).
To what extent:*
1. Has (he/she) treated you in a polite manner?
2. Has (he/she) treated you with dignity?
3. Has (he/she) treated you with respect?
4. Has (he/she) refrained from improper remarks or comments?

Informational Justice. *The following items refer to (the authority figure who enacted the
procedure). To what extent:*
1. Has (he/she) been candid in (his/her) communication with you?
2. Has (he/she) explained the procedures thoroughly?
3. Were (his/her) explanations regarding the procedures reasonable?
4. Has (he/she) communicated details in a timely manner?
5. Has (he/she) seemed to tailor (his/her) communication to individuals' specific needs?

*Source:* Reprinted with permission from Colquitt (2001).
*Note:* All items use a 5-point scale with anchors of 1 = to a small extent and 5 = to a large extent.

*Table 3.2* Perceived Overall Justice Scale

POJ1. Overall, I'm treated fairly by my organization.
POJ2. Usually, the way things work in this organization are not fair. (R)
POJ3. In general, I can count on this organization to be fair.
POJ4. In general, the treatment I receive around here is fair.
POJ5. For the most part, this organization treats its employees fairly.
POJ6. Most of the people who work here would say they are often treated unfairly (R)

*Source:* Items retrieved from Ambrose and Schimke, (2009).

*Notes:* All items use a 7-point scale ranging from 1 (strongly disagree) to 7 (strongly agree).
(R) indicates the item is reverse scored. POJ1, POJ3, POJ4, evaluate the individual experience,
whereas POJ2, POJ5, and POJ6 provide a general evaluation on how fair is an organization. Higher
ratings reflect greater perceptions of fairness.

the extent to which their efforts are reciprocated by significant others (e.g., the supervisor) in social exchanges, facilitating (or hindering) a positive relationship characterized by justice perceptions and trust. By contrast, *affective events theory* focuses on how events are appraised in terms of their effects on the achievement of important personal goals. If an event facilitates goal achievement, positive emotions emerge. However, if the event hinders the progress toward a goal, negative emotions are likely to arise. Justice is part of the appraisal process because just and unjust events are relevant for the achievement of goals (e.g., Volmer, 2015).

### Justice Models: Multiple Needs, Instrumental, Relational, and Deontic Models

Other theories have originated within specific justice literature. Some of them emphasize the satisfaction of psychological needs as a way to understand why persons attribute importance to justice. Building on Williams's (1997) multiple needs model, it is reasonable to propose that humans care about being fairly treated because justice fulfills important psychological needs, including control, belonging, self-esteem, and meaningful existence. The instrumental model (Tyler, 1987; Lind & Tyler, 1988) stresses the need for control. Justice is valued because it provides a sense of control and predictability of outcomes in the long run. The relational (or group-value) model (Lind & Tyler, 1988) emphasizes the satisfaction of both belongingness and self-esteem. Because humans are socially motivated to belong to groups, they will look for clues and signals containing information about how much these groups value them. Fair treatment informs the employee that she/he is respected and belongs to the group and/or organization, thus enhancing her/his self-esteem. Finally, the deontic model suggests that persons care about fairness to satisfy their need for a meaningful existence associated with the search for a life in accordance with moral standards (Cropanzano, Goldman, & Folger, 2003; Folger, 1998).

### Theories on How Fairness Process Takes Place

Another group of theories has focused more on how the fairness process takes place, although human needs and psychological functions are also considered in order to understand why persons think about justice. The *fairness theory* proposes deliberative cognitive processing based on counterfactuals. When employees evaluate the authority figure (e.g., the supervisor), they compare his/her behavior with the prevailing ethical standards. Therefore, other alternative scenarios are considered (e.g., the degree to which another action would improve well-being). Deviation from ethical standards hinders justice perceptions in the workplace. The fairness theory focuses on the authority figure as a relevant source of justice who can satisfy important personal needs related to control (e.g., predictability in the distribution of outcomes), belonging, and morality. The *fairness heuristic theory* argues that justice-relevant information is quickly aggregated into a fairness heuristic that is used as a shortcut to guide attitudes and behaviors (Van den Bos, 2001). Workers usually do not have time for deliberative cognitive processing in the workplace. Employees create their overall fairness perceptions based on a brief initial processing phase that considers the information that is accessible and understandable during early justice experiences. The initial judgment is persistent and explains overall justice perceptions over time unless an unexpected and relevant event occurs. Grounded in the fairness heuristic theory, the *uncertainty management theory* (Lind & Van den Bos, 2002) proposes that people seek fairness information in order to confront uncertain situations existing in the workplace. Both fairness heuristic theory and uncertainty management theory suggest that fairness beliefs have a psychological function because they help employees to manage feelings of uncertainty.

## Sources of Justice

Organizational justice research has mainly focused on authorities (i.e., the supervisor and the organization as a whole) as sources of justice. However, more and more scholars argue (Rupp et al., 2017) that other sources of justice (e.g., co-workers, clients) are highly relevant. Accordingly, the *multi-foci perspective* proposes asking about justice by indicating whom the source is and considering the different agents with whom the employee interacts. From this perspective, research offers a more holistic view of prospective justice sources and affirms that employees can evaluate any justice source as long as it is the actual cause of the (un)fair treatment (Cropanzano et al., 2001; Byrne & Cropanzano, 2000; Rupp & Cropanzano, 2002). More specifically, justice perceptions about a particular party are related to attitudinal and behavioral reactions explicitly directed at that party. The alignment of the justice source with the response target has been termed *target similarity* (Lavelle, Rupp, & Brockner, 2007).

Beyond authorities, co-workers are a relevant source of justice. Modern organizations often have a network structure with employees working together in teams to reach common goals (Bosch-Sijtsema et al., 2011). The employees in these teams are concerned with what can facilitate or hinder the achievement of common goals, including the treatment received by other team members. To capture justice within teams, Cropanzano, Bowen, and Gilliland (2007) referred to *peer justice* (or intra-unit justice) as the perception of the way the employee is treated when the source of justice comes from inside the team. Some empirical evidence has suggested that peer justice is significantly related to performance (Cropanzano et al., 2011; Molina et al., 2015). Other relevant sources of justice are present in service encounters. Employees are relevant sources of justice for the customer because she/he is sensitive to their interpersonal treatment (Martínez-Tur et al., 2006). Similarly, the customer's behavior also informs about justice directed toward the employee. In fact, Koopmann and colleagues (2015) conceptualized customer mistreatment of employees as a type of interactional injustice with relevant consequences, such as employee sabotage.

## *Justice Climate*

Most of the research on organizational justice has been conceptualized at the individual level of construct and analysis, but scholars increasingly recognize that justice may be conceptualized at higher levels than the individual (Martínez-Tur & Moliner, 2017; Moliner et al., 2005; Morgeson & Hofmann, 1999). The seminal research study by Naumann and Bennett (2000) referred to the collective fairness approach as *justice climate*, defined as "a distinct group-level cognition about how a workgroup as a whole is treated" (p. 882). During the past 20 years, research has consolidated justice climate as a relevant construct to understand fairness in the workplace, with significant effects on effectiveness in organizations (Whitman et al., 2012).

Building on the proposal by Schneider and Reichers (1983), Naumann and Bennett (2000) proposed three types of mechanisms to explain how shared justice perceptions emerge. First, according to the *symbolic interaction* mechanism, a work-unit is an adequate context for frequent social interactions and mutual influence, facilitating the emergence of shared perceptions. The exchange of information underlying symbolic interaction is also present in other proposals, such as *contagion processes* (members of a work-unit tend to interact and develop shared interpretations to deal with ambiguity) (Degoey, 2000); *social information processing* (justice events are relevant for work-unit members, and they discuss these events, creating shared perceptions) (Whitman et al., 2012); and *sense-making* (working as a collective heuristic or shortcut, members try to create consensual views to rationalize and interpret the reality due to the frequent absence of objective indicators) (Roberson, 2006; Whitman et al., 2012). All these models share the argument that interactions and discussions about justice are likely to occur within work-units, thus creating a justice climate. Some empirical evidence has confirmed this proposal (Naumann & Bennett, 2000; Roberson, 2006). Second, the *attraction/selection/attrition* (ASA) *model* (Schneider, 1987) suggests that work-unit members tend to become homogeneous over time for three main reasons: a) employees are attracted to others with similar characteristics (e.g., personality, education); b) selection processes in organizations incorporate employees with similar characteristics; and c) employees with characteristics that are different from the typical profile of the organization tend to leave. Although it is reasonable to expect that the homogeneity of work-units would facilitate the exchange of information about justice and shared perceptions (Degoey, 2000), research has provided mixed results (Colquitt, Noe, & Jackson, 2002; Naumann & Bennett, 2000). Therefore, it is possible that the third factor could play a relevant role. Third, the *structuralist approach* argues that mere exposure to similar policies, practices, and procedures is able to create shared perceptions within work-units (Schneider & Reichers, 1983).

Naumann and Bennett (2000) supported this proposal about justice climate. More specifically, the visibility of supervisors increased agreement about the perception of procedural justice.

## Antecedents and Consequences of Organizational Justice

Research has identified both antecedents and consequences of justice. In this section, we summarize the main results (see Figure 3.1 for a general overview).

### *Antecedents*

Research on organizational justice has focused mainly on how fair treatments influence employee reactions. By contrast, the examination of antecedents that could explain justice perceptions is more limited. Beyond the mechanisms underlying the theories described above, here we review specific individual and contextual factors as precursors of justice.

#### *Individual Differences*

It is reasonable to expect that individual differences in stable personality traits would impact justice perceptions in the workplace. After all, personality traits and predispositions describe, among other facets of human behavior, the way persons interpret reality. The same event could be perceived as either fair or unfair, depending on individual personality traits and other stable characteristics.

*Dispositional affectivity, personality traits, and equity sensivity.* Although research on personality-justice perception links is still scarce, some constructs seem relevant in the literature. In their meta-analysis, Ng and Sorensen (2009) included the relationship between *dispositional affectivity* (positive affect—PA and negative affect—NA) and organizational justice (distributive and procedural). Generally speaking, they confirmed the existence of significant relationships between dispositional affectivity and perceptions of organizational justice. In addition, the correlation was especially noteworthy (.47) for the link from PA to procedural justice. Ng and Sorensen (2009) interpreted that high PA— a predisposition to being naturally positive at work—orients employees to perceive the existence of fair procedures in the workplace. Shi et al. (2009) found significant relationships between two of the big five personality constructs (agreeableness and neuroticism) and the four dimensions of organizational justice (distributive, procedural, interpersonal, and informational). Because agreeable employees perceive that others will help them, they perceive fair treatment in their organizations. By contrast, employees with high neuroticism are predisposed to interpreting the environment with negative affect and, therefore, they tend to perceive unfair treatment from others (e.g., the leader). Other research studies have also focused on personality traits. For example, Törnroos et al. (2019)

52

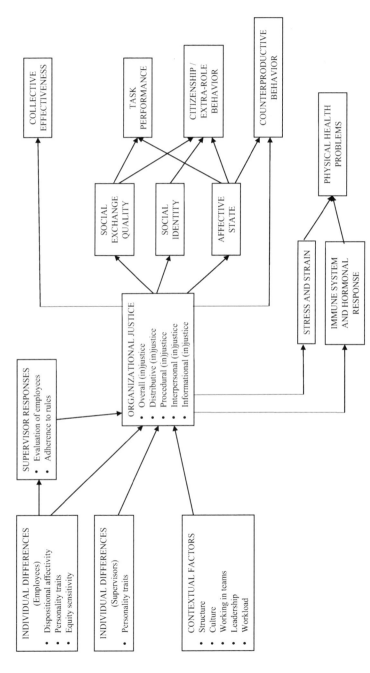

*Figure 3.1* Antecedents and Consequences of Organizational Justice: A General Overview.

found significant positive links from agreeableness to procedural and interactional justice, significant negative links from neuroticism to distributive, procedural, and interactional justice, and a significant positive relationship between openness and distributive justice. Finally, Jeon and Newman (2016) examined *equity sensitivity*, defined as a dispositional tendency to perceive stimuli as fair vs. unfair. They confirmed that equity sensitivity is a strong predictor of organizational justice perceptions.

Recently, Huang and colleagues (2017) concentrated on conscientiousness and agreeableness as personality traits. In general, they meta-analytically corroborated the existence of significant relationships between the two aforementioned employee personality traits and all four dimensions of organizational justice (distributive, procedural, interpersonal, and informational). The researchers proposed and tested, in a set of experiments and a field study, how employee's justice perceptions emerge from their personality traits. They confirmed a mediation model where employees high in conscientiousness and agreeableness receive high effort and likeability ratings from their supervisors, and these positive ratings lead to the supervisor's higher adherence to distributive, procedural, interpersonal, and informational justice rules. The supervisor's adherence to these rules, in turn, leads to employees' justice perceptions. Therefore, employees' conscientiousness and agreeableness stimulate positive reactions from supervisors (in terms of evaluations of employees and adherence to justice rules), facilitating the emergence of justice perceptions.

*Personality traits of the leader.* The consideration of individual differences is not restricted to the employee. These differences are also relevant in understanding the leader as a relevant agent in creating (in)justice in the workplace. Typically, the leader (or supervisor) has been considered the main source of justice because they have an important role in the decision-making processes and in the implementation of policies and practices that affect organizational members and groups. Logically, the leader's personality traits and dispositional tendencies can influence the way justice is created, but empirical studies are limited. As Mayer et al. (2007) pointed out, this omission is surprising because of leaders' strong ability to impact employees' attitudes and perceptions.

Mayer et al. (2007) proposed links from leaders' personality traits—following the big five personality constructs—to three justice climates: procedural, interpersonal, and informational. They found significant relationships between justice climates and three personality constructs. Specifically: a) agreeableness was positively related to all three justice climates considered; b) conscientiousness had a positive relationship with a procedural justice climate; and c) neuroticism was negatively related to procedural, interpersonal, and informational justice climates. Their results confirmed that leaders high in agreeableness, who are more sensitive to the needs of employees, tend to stimulate positive justice climates. By contrast, leaders high in neuroticism, characterized by irritability and emotional instability, are not able to produce shared fairness cognitions among employees. Finally, attributes underlying leaders high in conscientiousness (e.g., dutiful and achievement-oriented) facilitated the creation of a procedural justice climate. Drawing on the HEXACO model of personality, Walker (2015) also confirmed significant relationships between the leader's personality and his/her fairness behaviors: a) agreeableness was positively related to interpersonal justice behavior, b) conscientiousness was positively related to procedural and informational justice behavior, c) openness to experience was positively related to procedural and interpersonal justice behavior, and d) honesty-humility was positively related to interpersonal and informational justice behavior. Unexpectedly, Walker (2015) did not find significant direct links from neuroticism to leader justice behavior.

## Contextual Factors

Three decades ago, Lind and Tyler (1988) argued in favor of considering the context in the investigation of justice. However, research on organizational justice has mainly concentrated on a micro-level approach where individual processes and reactions to justice are emphasized. This approach has produced a limited view because decisions, procedures, and interactions occur within a general organizational context that offers a more complete view of justice antecedents.

*Structure.* One of the relevant contextual factors in understanding justice perceptions is the *structure* of the organization. Schminke, Ambrose, and Cropanzano (2000) analyzed the links from three traditional dimensions of organizational structure—centralization, formalization, and size—to procedural and interactional justice. They found significant relationships between procedural justice and two sub-components of centralization: a) participation in decision-making with regard to policies, and b) an authority hierarchy, describing employees' lack of control over their tasks. Further, they confirmed that centralization (low participation and low control over tasks) works against principles of procedural justice. They also found that the size of the organization is negatively related to interactional justice, supporting the idea that it is difficult to provide respectful treatment to employees in large organizations. By contrast, formalization (the degree to which instructions and procedures are written down) was not related to justice. Other research studies confirmed the significant relationship between structure and organizational justice (Özşahin & Yürür, 2018; Schminke, Cropanzano, & Rupp, 2002). However, results on organizational structures are not totally consistent. For example, research has found both significant (Özşahin & Yürür, 2018; Schminke et al., 2002) and non-significant (Schminke et al., 2000) links from formalization to justice.

*Culture*—which reflects fundamental ideologies, assumptions, and values within the organization—is an important contextual precursor of attitudes and behaviors because it communicates to organizational members the appropriate way to think and feel (Schneider, Ehrhart, & Macey, 2013). For employees, the organizational culture is part of the context where they perform their tasks and interact with co-workers and supervisors. Some assumptions and values of the culture could stimulate or hinder organizational justice perceptions. In fact, theoretical models have suggested relationships between culture and organizational justice (Ambrose & Schminke, 2009; Morris et al., 1999; Steiner & Gilliland, 2001). Schminke, Arnaud, and Taylor (2015) empirically examined the connection between collective culture and justice climate in 108 departments. Drawing on the model by Schwartz (1992), Schminke et al. (2015) considered the opposite higher-order values of self-transcendence vs. self-enhancement. Self-transcendence includes values concerned with the general welfare of others: benevolence (improving the welfare of other people with whom the individual interacts frequently) and universalism (tolerance and concern for the welfare of others). By contrast, self-enhancement refers to values such as achievement (personal success) and power (control over others). Schminke et al. (2015) confirmed positive links from collective self-transcendence to both procedural justice and overall justice climates.

*Working in teams.* Regarding the organization of work, there is a trend toward the use of *teams* in the workplace (e.g., Li, Li, & Lin, 2018). Compared to the individualistic organization of work, working in team contexts could have an impact on justice. Colquitt and Jackson (2006) provided some initial evidence in this regard. They observed that working in teams increases the importance of some rules associated with distributive (equality) and procedural (consistency and decision control) justice rules. They also found that, regarding procedural justice, the accuracy rule was more relevant in small teams, whereas the consistency and bias suppression rules were reinforced in diverse teams. Therefore, working within teams influences the way members define justice.

*Leadership.* Another critical factor for employees in the organizational context is *leadership*. As mentioned above, the leader is probably the main source of justice in the workplace because they represent the organization and have a critical influence on decision-making, policies, and practices. Regarding distributive and procedural justice, leader behaviors inform employees not only about the leader's justice (leader-focused justice) but also about justice from the organization as a whole (organization-focused justice). Very recently, Karam et al. (2019) carried out a meta-analysis of the way the leader's behaviors affect employees' justice perceptions. Based on Yukl's (2012) analysis of 50 years of leadership research, Karam et al. (2019) considered three meta-categories of effective leader behaviors: a) task leader behaviors (efficient use of resources through planning, problem-solving, and monitoring), b) relational leader behaviors (support, recognition, development, and empowerment of employees), and c) change leader behaviors (facilitation and fostering of change and innovation). Karam et al. (2019) found some significant relationships between leader behaviors and justice perceptions. More *task = distribu...* (handwritten)

specifically, task leader behaviors predominated over the other two types of behaviors in the prediction of leader-focused procedural and distributive justice perceptions. Relational leader behaviors were the strongest predictors of organization-focused procedural justice, and change leader behaviors were the most important predictors of organization-focused distributive, interpersonal, and informational justice perceptions. Interestingly, and with regard to distributive and procedural justice, leader behaviors captured more variance in organization-focused justice than in leader-focused justice. This finding supported the idea that the leader is the visible face of the organization and the actor who implements the decisions about organizational outcome allocations (Karam et al., 2019).

*workload* (handwritten)

*Workload.* Despite the argument that the leader is an active agent in decision-making and the implementation of policies and practices, they are subjected to some specific contextual facilitators and constraints in displaying fair behaviors. Workload is especially relevant, given that pressure is usually associated with the leader's activity. Sherf, Venkataramani, and Gajendran (2019) argued that the leader's fair behaviors require efforts (e.g., time) that compete with other tasks, such as completing technical deliverables (e.g., reports). Under workload pressure, performing technical tasks likely takes precedence over displaying fair behaviors, especially if the organization rewards technical achievements. Sherf et al. (2019) supported this idea in three studies: an experience sampling study, a field study, and an experiment.

### *Consequences* of org justice (handwritten annotation)

There are numerous research studies on the consequences of organizational justice. Organizational justice is considered a strong predictor of employee attitudes and behaviors (e.g., Colquitt et al., 2013). To synthesize and articulate this literature, we consider three outcomes: performance, collective outcomes, and health.

*on* (handwritten)

#### *Performance*

Organizational justice is positively associated with relevant constructs that inform about the quality of the relationship between the worker and the organization (or managers), such as trust (Kaltiainen, Lipponen, & Holtz, 2017), commitment (Suifan, Diab, & Abdallah, 2017) and perceived organizational support (Arneguy et al., 2018). Most importantly, these constructs help to understand the processes connecting organizational justice to performance. Colquitt and colleagues, in their meta-analysis and literature reviews (Colquitt et al., 2013; Colquitt & Zipay, 2015), differentiated between cognitive vs. affective routes to understand the impact of organizational justice on attitudes and behaviors related to performance (e.g., task performance, citizenship behavior, cooperation, counterproductive behavior, etc.). Focusing on cognitive-driven behavior,

*trust, commitment, org. support* (handwritten)

social exchange plays a prominent role. Organizational justice facilitates the shift from tangible-based economic exchanges to a social exchange where more unspecified benefits (e.g., advice, appreciation) are considered. In addition, justice leads employees to reciprocate by displaying beneficial behaviors for the organization and its members (e.g., supervisors, co-workers). Colquitt et al. (2013) confirmed this reciprocation phenomenon meta-analytically, considering 493 independent samples. As in social exchange theory, they found a mediation process where indicators of social exchange quality (trust, organizational commitment, perceived organizational support, and leader-member exchange) mediate between organizational justice on the one hand, and task performance and citizenship behavior on the other. However, this mediation did not work for the prediction of counterproductive behaviors. Beyond social exchange theory, Colquitt and Zipay (2015) also suggested that group identification and group engagement could play a significant role in the cognitive aspects of the justice-performance link. Drawing on the group engagement model (Tyler & Blader 2003), it is reasonable to expect that organizational justice would produce employee feelings of being respected and having pride in the group, leading to better performance. Blader and Tyler (2009) confirmed this argument in a study where social identity (identification, pride, and respect) mediates between procedural justice and extra-role behavior.

Regarding affect-driven behavior, Colquitt et al. (2013) incorporated positive and negative state affects in their meta-analysis of the justice-performance link. To do so, they considered appraisal theories—affective events theory (Weiss & Cropanzano, 1996) and cognitive-motivational-relational theory (Lazarus, 1991)—arguing that persons consider whether an event is good or bad for their goals. Persons interpret that unfair events (e.g., violation of a justice rule) hinder the achievement of their goals and produce negative affective states. By contrast, fair events allow persons to achieve their relevant goals (e.g., belonging), stimulating positive affective states. Affective states, in turn, are associated with behaviors. Generally speaking, Colquitt et al. (2013) supported this process. That is, positive and negative affect states mediated the links from organizational justice to task performance, citizenship behavior, and counterproductive behavior.

## Justice-Outcome Links at the Collective Level

As mentioned above, teams and work-units are appropriate contexts for the emergence of shared perceptions of justice. Shared perceptions about how the team or work-unit is treated would likely influence collective efforts to respond to the organization's and leader's requests. Based on this rationale, conducting a meta-analysis, Whitman et al. (2012) confirmed the existence of significant correlations between justice and effectiveness, measuring both constructs at the collective level. Distributive justice climate was the strongest predictor of unit-level performance (e.g., productivity), whereas interactional justice climate was the best predictor of collective processes (e.g., cohesion). Whitman et al. (2012) considered instrumental and relational motives to interpret this differential role of distributive vs. interactional justice climate. Instrumental motives underlie distributive justice because employees try to enhance collective performance in order to maximize their rewards. By contrast, fair interpersonal treatment by leaders stimulates relational motives, improving cooperation and help among employees.

### *Health*

Unfairness has been considered a workplace stressor that can produce health problems (Greenberg, 2004). Scholars have proposed several theories to support this link between injustice and health (e.g., Herr et al., 2018; Robbins, Ford, & Tetrick, 2012). The effort-reward imbalance theory suggests that efforts that are not accompanied by adequate rewards result in distress (Siegrist, 1996). In addition, according to uncertainty management theory (Lind & Van den Bos, 2002), injustice can create a lack of predictability that leads to discomfort and anxiety. In fact, lack of control is traditionally considered a relevant stressor in the workplace (e.g., Karasek, 1979). Injustice situations could also be considered affective events (Weiss & Cropanzano, 1996) that tend to be interpreted as stressful, provoking negative emotions.

Robbins et al. (2012) meta-analytically confirmed the link from organizational injustice to health indicators. Relationships were stronger for stress and psychological strain indicators (mental health, burnout, stress, negative affect) than for indicators of physical health problems (e.g., hypertension, cholesterol) and unhealthy behaviors (e.g., smoking, sedentary lifestyle). Robbins et al. (2012) interpreted these results by suggesting that stress and strain are proximal outcomes of injustice. Therefore, they proposed that stress and strain mediate between injustice and physical health problems. Stress and strain could stimulate negative coping reactions in terms of unhealthy behaviors (e.g., alcohol consumption) that affect physical health negatively. In addition, stress and strain might create physical health problems through the impact on the immune system and cortisol (Robbins et al., 2012).

## Pushing the Field Forward in Research

After several decades of organizational justice research, an impressive amount of evidence has contributed to very relevant advances in our knowledge. We now know much more about the nature of justice and the underlying mechanisms, antecedents, and consequences. Nevertheless, more efforts are necessary in order to continue with additional contributions in research and practice. In the following paragraphs, we focus on three relevant areas for future initiatives: multicultural contexts, justice dynamics, and injustice as a psychosocial stressor. We also discuss practical implications.

59

## *Multicultural Contexts*

Scholars do not usually consider the impact of cultural values on understanding justice. However, cultural differences could have a relevant role with implications for research and practice. Employees around the world are embedded in different cultural values and working conditions. In a globalized context, with increasing interactions among people from different cultures, managing justice perceptions becomes a critical task because their links to well-being and performance could be sensitive to culture. It is important to understand how organizational justice works in different cultures by incorporating cultural diversity in our research and practice in order to have a more complete view of organizational justice and its transfer to professional practice.

Although research has demonstrated the universality of expectations of fair treatment across cultures (Shao et al., 2013), the perception of justice is influenced by the culture. Similar situations may evoke distinct justice perceptions by different cultural groups (Leung & Morris, 2001). In addition, the relative importance of different justice dimensions across cultures may be different (Guo & Giacobbe-Miller, 2015). One situation where cultural differentiation is relevant, impacting the interpretation of justice and its effects, is when local and foreign employees or partners interact or work together. In this context, cultural differences may occur in at least two different ways. First, the use of justice rules may vary depending on the culture. For example, one culture can consider the equality rule to be fair, whereas another culture can use the equity rule to provide fairness treatment. Therefore, different cultures can apply different rules for how to distribute outcomes. Although equity is the preferred rule across cultures (e.g., Kim, Park, & Suzuki, 1990), collectivists tend to follow equality and need rules more than individualists do (Chen, Meindl, & Hui, 1998; Murphy-Berman et al., 1984). Fischer et al. (2007) also showed that the preference for equity is higher in the private sector and in cultures high in mastery values that encourage achievement and domination. However, the preference for equality is higher in organizations that are performing better. Finally, reliance on need is predicted by low unemployment rates and high embeddedness values, which encourage striving toward shared goals and maintaining the status quo (Fischer et al., 2007). Second, cultural differences could impact the criteria used in applying the same justice rule. For instance, although two cultures may adopt the equity rule, collectivistic vertical societies tend to consider aspects such as tenure or social skills (Fischer & Smith 2003; Mueller, Iverson, & Jo, 1999) as adequate contributions, whereas individualistic horizontal societies may emphasize efficiency.

One practical area where cultural differences could be relevant is personnel recruitment and selection. Distributive justice is a major concern for both parties involved (employer and candidate). If they cannot resolve their differences in what can be considered a fair distributive rule for hiring decisions, they may disagree about the results of the process. Procedural justice is also relevant in this context. For example, local employees may not be familiar with the recruitment practices introduced by foreign companies. Consequently, many local candidates could perceive foreign selection procedures as biased and attribute their failure to get a job to procedural injustice in these recruitment practices. This cultural difference may occur in other policies and practices, such as disciplinary actions, training, and development, among others. If the differences are not handled well, they may trigger conflicts (Leung & Stephan, 1998).

### *Justice and Time: A Dynamic Concept of Justice*

The research on organizational justice has mainly focused on between-individual differences in average levels of fair justice treatment—either average levels of justice dimensions (e.g. procedural justice levels) or average levels of overall justice perceptions. Accordingly, this essential premise has been widely acknowledged: "the more justice the better" (Matta et al., 2017). Nevertheless, this perspective has neglected the importance of considering dynamics and within-individual fluctuations in justice treatment. For instance, a supervisor could either treat his/her employees fairly in any event or only now and then, depending on various circumstances, and be inconsistent in the treatment of employees. Justice research has increasingly considered this type of phenomenon, that is, the possible fluctuations in the treatment received by employees over time. Today, researchers acknowledge that trajectories often exist in the variability of a given construct over time. Similarly, scholars have started to investigate the concept of *justice variability*.

Justice variability is broadly defined as "between-person differences in the stability of justice over time" (Matta et al., 2017, p. 2). It is widely based on uncertainty management theory, described above. Uncertainty occurs when the individual is not able to predict her or his future or cannot experience consistency in her/his behaviors, experiences, or cognitions (Van den Bos & Lind, 2002). According to Jones and Skarlicki (2013), new experiences of fairness are compared to prior experiences. In their model, these scholars describe two different types of reactions to justice events. Expected justice events will be automatically processed and reacted to. In this case, the previous perception of justice will be strengthened and remain the same. However, when a justice event is unexpected or takes place in a more risky or threatening environment, the previous (although relatively stable) justice perception can be revised in terms of the recent justice judgment. Similarly, Jones and Skarlicki (2013) stated that the prediction of how the individual will be treated in the future is important. When employees cannot predict the way they will be treated, or they experience inconsistency in their fair treatment, uncertainty emerges as a potential stressor that could negatively impact their overall well-being (Peters, McEwan, & Friston, 2017).

Matta et al. (2017) demonstrated the importance of justice variability in a number of experiments on interpersonal justice. They found that not only was the level of perceived justice relevant but also the extent to which this level was consistent over time. They examined whether inconsistent treatment would influence the overall individual experience of stress. Surprisingly, their results indicated that inconsistent treatment leads to more stress for the individual, regardless of the justice level. In other words, they found that inconsistent fair treatment is more stressful than consistent unfair treatment. These scholars demonstrated that a focus on justice levels that ignores variability over time would lead to an incomplete view of justice within organizations.

The investigation of the evolution of justice over time is a promising avenue for future research. For example, it is possible to examine how changes in objectively measured events (e.g., distribution of tasks throughout the week) impact justice dynamics. In addition, results related to the dynamic of justice are quite relevant for practice in at least two ways. First, monitoring justice is, in itself, an important practical action to diagnose how the treatment by supervisors, organizations, and co-workers evolves. For example, it is possible to check abrupt changes and manage their causes. Second, maintaining stability has positive effects beyond "the more justice, the better." This is relevant for practice because employees, supervisors, and managers could be trained in the importance of justice stability in reducing negative stress.

## Injustice as a Stressor

As mentioned above, injustice can play the role of a stressor with consequences for health. Employees not only perceive that a situation is unfair, they also *feel* that it is unfair. A stressor is generally defined as an unpleasant emotional and physiological state resulting from work experiences that are beyond the control of the person (Hart & Cooper, 2002). In this regard, organizational injustice can be viewed as a psychosocial "stressor"—an aspect of the work environment that causes employees to doubt their ability to cope with work demands (Vermunt & Steensma, 2001). In fact, the number of studies linking organizational justice to work-related stress is increasing (see e.g. Brotheridge, 2003; Fujishiro & Heaney, 2009; Sutinen et al., 2002; Vermunt & Steensma, 2003).

Although more and more evidence exists confirming injustice as a relevant stressor, further research efforts are needed. A challenge for future investigations is to establish more accurate mechanisms. For example, extending the investigation on the mechanisms that integrate justice, psychological health indicators, and physical health is a promising research area that could expand our knowledge significantly. From a practical point of view, programs related to the prevention and management of psychosocial risks could test whether the incorporation of injustice improves the effects of interventions on employee's health.

## Practical Implications

Research on organizational justice has practical implications in at least three different areas. First, *organizational change* is closely connected to justice (e.g., Novelli, Kirkman, & Shapiro, 1995). There are different types of changes, including the redesign of jobs and processes, downsizing, cultural change, and technological innovation, among others. Organizational change is ubiquitous across organizations and over time, and they are associated with justice perceptions. When a change is implemented, workers perceive the degree to which it respects justice criteria related to equity (distributive justice), fair procedures (procedural justice), and adequate or correct treatment (interpersonal and informational justice). Organizations should be aware that justice has an important role, requiring the management of different facets of justice (e.g., implementing procedures without biases and/or sharing adequate information about the change).

*Personnel selection* is another area that is very sensitive to justice (e.g., Bye & Sandal, 2015). Procedural and interactional justice are very relevant here. From a procedural perspective, it is more likely that candidates who apply for a job perceive high justice in the selection process if procedures are consistent, avoid biases, etc. Similarly, justice perception will improve if candidates receive proper information and correct interpersonal treatment. Therefore, professionals involved in personnel selection should consider not only technical issues (e.g., the validity of a test) but also justice facets associated with the procedures implemented and the treatment provided to candidates.

Organizational justice also has relevant implications for *leadership training* (e.g., Skarlicki & Latham, 1997). Leaders are important justice agents in organizations. They make decisions that affect workers significantly (e.g., promotion, distribution of tasks, etc.). Accordingly, it is very recommendable that the design of training for leaders includes competencies related to justice facets such as a fair distribution of rewards (equity) among workers, the implementation of fair procedures, and respectful and decent treatment of team members.

## Final Thoughts

Progress in scientific knowledge is based largely on questioning previous ideas. Research has allowed relevant progress in different aspects of justice, including its definition and nomological network. However, some questions could challenge some assumptions and facilitate additional contributions: Is what we know about justice universal, or is it contextualized knowledge that depends on culture? Can temporal dynamics change a vision of justice based primarily on static approaches? What are the mechanisms underlying the relationship between justice and health, and how are they integrated into other outcomes such as performance?

# References

Adams, J.S. (1965). Inequity in social exchange. In *Advances in experimental social psychology* (Vol. 2, pp. 267–299). Academic Press.

Alkhadher, O. & Gadelrab, H. (2016). Organizational justice dimensions: Validation of an Arabic measure. *International Journal of Selection and Assessment, 24*(4), 337–351.

Ambrose, M.L. & Schminke, M. (2009). Assessing roadblocks to justice: A model of fair behavior in organizations. In Martocchio, J. and Liao, H. (Ed.). *Research in personnel and human resources management* (Vol. 28, pp. 219–263). Emerald Group Publishing Limited.

Arnéguy, E., Ohana, M., & Stinglhamber, F. (2018). Organizational Justice and Readiness for change : A concomitant examination of the mediating role of perceived organizational support and identification. *Frontiers in Psychology, 9*, 1172.

Ambrose, M.L. & Schminke, M. (2009). The role of overall justice judgments in organizational justice research: A test of mediation. *Journal of Applied Psychology, 94*(2), 491–500.

Barclay, L.J. & Kiefer, T. (2014). Approach or avoid? Exploring overall justice and the differential effects of positive and negative emotions. *Journal of Management, 40*(7), 1857–1898.

Bies, R. & Moag, J. (1986). Interactional justice: Communication criteria of fairness. In R. Lewicki, B. Sheppard, & M. Bazerman (Eds.), *Research on negotiation in organizations*, 43–55. JAIPress.

Blader S.L. & Tyler, T.R. (2009). Testing and extending the group engagement model: Linkages between social identity, procedural justice, economic outcomes, and extrarole behavior. *Journal of Applied Psychology, 94*(2), 445–64.

Blau, P.M. (1964). *Exchange and power in social life*. Wiley.

Bosch-Sijtsema, P.M., Fruchter, R., Vartiainen, M., & Ruohomäki, V. (2011). A framework to analyze knowledge work in distributed teams. *Group & Organization Management, 36*(3), 275–307.

Brotheridge, C.M. (2003). The Role of Fairness in Mediating the Effects of Voice and Justification on Stress and Other Outcomes in a Climate of Organizational Change. *International Journal of Stress Management, 10*(3), 253–268.

Bye, H.H. & Sandal, G.M. (2015). Applicant personality and procedural justice perceptions of group selection interviews. *Journal of Business Psychology, 31*(4), 569–582.

Byrne, Z.S. & Cropanzano, R.S. (2000, April). *To which do I attribute this fairness? Differential effects of multi-foci justice on organizational work behaviors.* Presented at the 15th Annual Conference of the Society for Industrial and Organizational Psychology, New Orleans, LA.

Chen, C.C., Meindl, J.R., & Hui, H. (1998). Deciding on equity or parity: A test of situational, cultural, and individual factors. *Journal of Organizational Behavior: The International Journal of Industrial, Occupational and Organizational Psychology and Behavior, 19*(2), 115–129.

Colquitt, J.A. (2001). On the dimensionality of organizational justice: A construct validation of a measure. *Journal of Applied Psychology, 86*(3), 386–400.

Colquitt, J. A., & Jackson, C. L. (2006). Justice in teams: The context sensitivity of justice rules across individual and team contexts. *Journal of Applied Social Psychology, 36*(4), 868–899.

Colquitt, J.A., Noe, R.A., & Jackson, C.L. (2002). Justice in teams: Antecedents and consequences of procedural justice climate. *Personnel Psychology*, *55*(1), 83–109.

Colquitt, J.A., Scott B.A., Rodell J.B., Long D.M., Zapata C.P., Conlon, D.E., & Wesson, M.J. (2013). Justice at the millennium, a decade later: A meta-analytic test of social exchange and affect-based perspectives. *Journal of Applied Psychology*, *98*(2), 199–236.

Colquitt, J.A. & Shaw, J.C. (2005). How should organizational justice be measured? In J. Greenberg & J.A. Colquitt (Eds.), *The handbook of organizational justice* (pp. 113–152). Erlbaum.

Colquitt, J.A., Zapata-Phelan, C.P., & Greenberg, J. (2005). What is organizational justice? A historical overview. *Handbook of Organizational Justice*, *1*, 3–58.

Colquitt, J.A. & Zipay, K.P. (2015). Justice, fairness, and employee reactions. *Annual Review of Organizational Psychology and Organizational Behavior*, *2*(1), 75–99.

Cropanzano, R., Bowen, D.E., & Gilliland, S.W. (2007). The management of organizational justice. *Academy of Management Perspectives*, *21*(4), 34–48.

Cropanzano, R. & Byrne, Z.S. (2000). Workplace justice and the dilemma of organizational citizenship. In M. VanVugt, T. Tyler, & A. Biel (Eds.), *Collective problems in modern society: Dilemmas and solutions* (pp. 142–161). Routledge.

Cropanzano, R., Byrne, Z.S., Bobocel, D.R., & Rupp, D.E. (2001). Moral Virtues, Fairness Heuristics, Social Entities, and Other Denizens of Organizational Justice. *Journal of Vocational Behavior*, *58*(2), 164–209.

Cropanzano, R., Goldman, B., & Folger, R. (2003). Deontic justice: The role of moral principles in workplace fairness. *Journal of Organizational Behavior: The International Journal of Industrial, Occupational and Organizational Psychology and Behavior*, *24*(8), 1019–1024.

Cropanzano, R., Li, A., & Benson, L. (2011). Peer justice and teamwork process. *Group & Organization Management*, *36*(5), 567–596.

Degoey, P. (2000). Contagious justice: Exploring the social construction of justice in organizations. *Research in Organizational Behavior*, *22*(1), 51–102.

Deutsch, M. (1975). Equity, equality, and need: What determines which value will be used as the basis of distributive justice? *Journal of Social Issues*, *31*(3), 137–149.

Fassina, N.E., Jones, D.A., & Uggerslev, K.L. (2008). Meta-analytic tests of relationships between organizational justice and citizenship behavior: Testing agent-system and shared-variance models. *Journal of Organizational Behavior: The International Journal of Industrial, Occupational and Organizational Psychology and Behavior*, *29*(6), 805–828.

Fischer, R. & Smith, P.B. (2003). Reward allocation and culture: A meta-analysis. *Journal of Cross-Cultural Psychology*, *34*(3), 251–268.

Fischer, R., Smith, P.B., Richey, B., Ferreira, M.C., Assmar, E.M.L., Maes, J., & Stumpf, S. (2007). How do organizations allocate rewards? The predictive validity of national values, economic and organizational factors across six nations. *Journal of Cross-Cultural Psychology*, *38*(1), 3–18.

Folger, R. (1998). Fairness as moral virtue. In *Managerial ethics* (pp. 23–44). Psychology Press.

Fujishiro, K. & Heaney, C.A. (2009). Justice at work, job stress, and employee health. *Health Education & Behavior*, *36*(3), 487–504.

Greenberg, J. (1990). Organizational justice: Yesterday, today, and tomorrow. *Journal of management*, *16*(2), 399–432.

Greenberg, J. (1993). The social side of fairness: Interpersonal and informational classes of organizational justice. In R. Cropanzano (Ed.), Series in applied psychology.

*Justice in the workplace: Approaching fairness in human resource management* (pp. 79–103). Lawrence Erlbaum Associates, Inc.

Greenberg, J. (2004). Stress fairness to fare no stress: Managing workplace stress by promoting organizational justice. *Organizational Dynamics*, *33*(4), 352–365.

Guo, C. & Giacobbe-Miller, J.K. (2015). Meanings and dimensions of organizational justice in China: An inductive investigation. *Management and Organization Review*, *11*(1), 45–68.

Hart, P.M. & Cooper, C.L. (2002). Occupational stress: Toward a more integrated framework. In N. Anderson, D.S. Ones, H.K. Sinangil, & C. Viswesvaran (Eds.), *Handbook of industrial, work and organizational psychology, Vol. 2. Organizational psychology* (pp. 93–114). Sage Publications, Inc.

Herr, R.M., Bosch, J.A., Loerbroks, A., Genser, B., Almer, C., van Vianen, A.E., & Fischer, J.E. (2018). Organizational justice, justice climate, and somatic complaints: a multilevel investigation. *Journal of Psychosomatic Research*, *111*(1), 15–21.

Huang, J.L., Cropanzano, R., Li, A., Shao, P., Zhang, X., & Li, Y. (2017). Employee conscientiousness, agreeableness, and supervisor justice rule compliance: A three-study investigation. *Journal of Applied Psychology*, *112*(11), 1564–1589.

Jeon, G. & Newman, D.A. (2016). Equity sensitivity versus egoism: A reconceptualization and new measure of individual differences in justice perceptions. *Journal of Vocational Behavior*, *95*(1), 138–155.

Jones, D.A. & Martens, M.L. (2009). The mediating role of overall fairness and the moderating role of trust certainty in justice–criteria relationships: The formation and use of fairness heuristics in the workplace. *Journal of Organizational Behavior*, *30*(8), 1025–1051.

Jones, D.A. & Skarlicki, D.P. (2013). How perceptions of fairness can change: A dynamic model of organizational justice. *Organizational Psychology Review*, *3*(2), 138–160.

Kaltiainen, J., Lipponen, J., & Holtz, B.C. (2017). Dynamic interplay between merger process justice and cognitive trust in top management: A longitudinal study. *Journal of Applied Psychology*, *102*(4), 636–647.

Karam, E.P., Hu, J., Davison, R.B., Juravich, M., Nahrgang, J.D., Humphrey, S.E., & DeRue, D.S. (2019). Illuminating the "face" of justice: A meta-analytic examination of leadership and organizational justice. *Journal of Management Studies*, *56*(1), 134–171.

Karasek, R. (1979). Job demands, job decision latitude, and mental strain: Implications for job redesign. *Administrative Science Quarterly*, *24*(2), 285–306.

Kim, K.I., Park, H.J., & Suzuki, N. (1990). Reward allocations in the United States, Japan, and Korea: A comparison of individualistic and collectivistic cultures. *Academy of Management Journal*, *33*(1), 188–198.

Koopmann, J., Wang, M., Liu, Y., & Song, Y. (2015). Customer mistreatment: A review of conceptualizations and a multilevel theoretical model. In P.L. Perrewé, J.R.B. Halbesleben, & C.C. Rosen (Eds.), *Research in occupational stress and well-being: Mistreatment in organizations* (Vol. 13, pp. 33–79). Emerald Group Publishing.

Lavelle, J.J., Rupp, D.E., & Brockner, J. (2007). Taking a multifoci approach to the study of justice, social exchange, and citizenship behavior: The target similarity model. *Journal of management*, *33*(6), 841–866.

Lazarus, R.S. (1991). *Emotions and adaptation*. Oxford University Press.

Leung, K. & Morris, M.W. (2001). Justice through the lens of culture and ethnicity. In J. Sanders & V.L. Hamilton (Eds.), *Handbook of justice research in law* (pp. 343–378). Kluwer Academic Publishers.

Leung, K., & Stephan, W. G. (1998). Perceptions of injustice in intercultural relations. *Applied and Preventive Psychology*, 7(3), 195–205.

Leventhal, G.S. (1976). The distribution of rewards and resources in groups and organizations. In *Advances in experimental social psychology* (Vol. 9, pp. 91–131). Academic Press.

Leventhal, G.S. (1980), What should be done with equity theory? New approaches to the study of fairness in social relationships, in Gregen, K., Greenberg, M. and Willis, R. (Eds), *Social exchange: Advances in theory and research*, (pp. 27–55). Plenum.

Li, C.R., Li, C.X., & Lin, C.J. (2018). How and when team regulatory focus influences team innovation and member creativity. *Personnel Review*, 47(1), 95–117.

Lind, E.A. (2001). Fairness heuristic theory: Justice judgments as pivotal cognitions in organizational relations. In J. Greenberg & R. Cropanzano (Eds.), *Advances in organizational justice* (pp. 56–88). Stanford University Press.

Lind, E.A. & Tyler, T.R. (1988). *The social psychology of procedural justice*. Plenum.

Lind, E.A. & Van den Bos, K. (2002). When fairness works: Toward a general theory of uncertainty management. *Research in Organizational Behavior*, 24(1), 181–223.

Martínez-Tur, V. & Moliner, C. (2017). Justice in teams. In A. Brunstein, & O. Braddick (Eds.), *Oxford research encyclopedia of psychology*. Oxford University Press.

Martínez-Tur, V., Peiró, J.M., Ramos, J., & Moliner, C. (2006). Justice perceptions as predictors of customer satisfaction: The impact of distributive, procedural, and interactional justice. *Journal of Applied Social Psychology*, 36(1), 100–119.

Matta, F.K., Scott, B.A., Colquitt, J.A., Koopman, J., & Passantino, L.G. (2017). Is consistently unfair better than sporadically fair? An investigation of justice variability and stress. *Academy of Management Journal*, 60(2), 743–770.

Mayer, D., Nishii, L., Schneider, B., & Goldstein, H. (2007). The precursors and products of justice climates: Group leader antecedents and employee attitudinal consequences. *Personnel Psychology*, 60(4), 929–963.

Molina, A., Moliner, C., Martínez-Tur, V., Cropanzano, R., & Peiró, J.M. (2015). Unit-level fairness and quality within the health care industry: A justice–quality model. *European Journal of Work and Organizational Psychology*, 24(4), 627–644.

Moliner, C., Martínez-Tur, V., Peiró, J.M., Ramos J., & Cropanzano, R. (2005). Relationships between organizational justice and burnout at the work-unit level. *International Journal of Stress Management*, 12(2), 99–116.

Morgeson, F.P. & Hofmann, D.A. (1999). The structure and function of collective constructs: Implications for multilevel research and theory development. *Academy of Management Review*, 24(2), 249–265.

Morris, M., Leung, K., Ames, D., &. Lickel, B. (1999). Views from inside and outside: Integrating emic and etic insights about culture and justice judgment. *Academy of Management Journal*, 24(4), 781–796.

Mueller, C.W., Iverson, R.D., & Jo, D.G. (1999). Distributive justice evaluations in two cultural contexts: A comparison of US and South Korean teachers. *Human Relations*, 52(7), 869–893.

Murphy-Berman, V., Berman, J.J., Singh, P., Pachauri, A., & Kumar, P. (1984). Factors affecting allocation to needy and meritorious recipients: A cross-cultural comparison. *Journal of Personality and Social Psychology*, 46(6), 1267–1272.

Naumann, S.E., & Bennett, N. (2000). A case for procedural justice climate: Development and test of a multilevel model. *Academy of Management journal*, 43(5), 881–889.

Ng, T.W.H. & Sorensen, K.L. (2009). Dispositional affectivity and work-related outcomes: A meta-analysis. *Journal of Applied Social Psychology*, 39(6), 1255–1287.

Novelli, L., Kirkman, B.L., & Shapiro, D.L. (1995). Effective implementation of organizational change: An organizational justice perspective. In C.L. Cooper, & Rousseau, D.M. (Eds.), *Trends in organizational behavior* (Vol. 4, pp. 15–36). John Wiley & Sons Limited.

Özşahin, M. & Yürür, S. (2018). The effect of organizational structure on organizational justice perceptions of employees. *International Journal of Organizational Leadership*, *7*(1), 440–453.

Peters, A., McEwen, B.S., & Friston, K. (2017). Uncertainty and stress: Why it causes diseases and how it is mastered by the brain. *Progress in Neurobiology*, *156*(1), 164–188.

Robbins, J.M., Ford, M.T., & Tetrick, L.E. (2012). Perceived unfairness and employee health: A meta-analytic integration. *Journal of Applied Psychology*, *97*(2), 235–272.

Roberson, Q.M. (2006). Justice in teams: The activation and role of sense-making in the emergence of justice climates. *Organizational Behavior and Human Decision Processes*, *100*(2), 177–192.

Rupp, D.E. & Cropanzano, R. (2002). The mediating effects of social exchange relationships in predicting workplace outcomes from multifoci organizational justice. *Organizational Behavior and Human Decision Processes*, *89*(1), 925–946.

Rupp, D.E., Shapiro, D.L., Folger, R., Skarlicki, D.P., & Shao, R. (2017). A critical analysis of the conceptualization and measurement of organizational justice: Is it time for reassessment?. *Academy of Management Annals*, *11*(2), 919–959.

Schminke, M., Ambrose, M.L., & Cropanzano, R. (2000). The effect of organizational structure on perceptions of procedural fairness. *Journal of Applied Psychology*, *85*(2), 294–304.

Schminke, M., Arnaud, A., & Taylor, R. (2015). Ethics, values, and organizational justice: Individuals, organizations, and beyond. *Journal of Business Ethics*, *130*(3), 727–736.

Schminke, M., Cropanzano, R.S., & Rupp, D.E. (2002). Organization structure and fairness perceptions: The moderating effects of organizational level. *Organizational Behavior and Human Decision Processes*, *89*(1), 881–905.

Schneider, B. (1987). The people make the place. *Personnel Psychology*, *40*(3), 437–453.

Schneider, B. & Reichers, A. (1983). On the etiology of climates. *Personnel Psychology*, *36*(1), 19–40.

Schneider, B., Ehrhart, M.G., & Macey, W.H. (2013). Organizational climate and culture. *Annual Review of Psychology*, *64*(1), 361–388.

Schwartz, S.H. (1992). Universals in the content and structure of values: Theory and empirical tests in 20 countries. In M. Zanna (Ed.), *Advances in experimental social psychology* (Vol. 25, pp. 1–65). Academic Press.

Shao, R., Rupp, D.E., Skarlicki, D.P., & Jones, K.S. (2013). Employee justice across cultures: A meta-analytic review. *Journal of Management*, *39*(1), 263–301.

Shapiro, D.L. (2001). The death of justice theory is likely if theorists neglect the "wheels" already invented and the voices of the injustice victims. *Journal of Vocational Behavior*, *58*(2), 235–242.

Sherf, E., Venkataramani, V., & Gajendran, R. (2019). Too busy to be fair? The effect of workload and rewards on managers' justice rule adherence. *Academy of Management Journal*, *62*(2), 469–502.

Shi, J., Lin, H., Wang, L., & Wang, M. (2009). Linking the big five personality constructs to organizational justice. *Social Behavior and Personality*, *37*(2), 209–222.

Siegrist, J. (1996). Adverse health effects of high-effort/low-reward conditions. *Journal of Occupational Health Psychology*, *1*(1), 27–41.

Skarlicki, D.P. & Latham, G.P. (1997). Leadership training in organizational justice to increase citizenship behavior within a labor union: A replication. *Personnel Psychology*, *50*(3), 617–633.

Steiner, D. & Gilliland, S. (2001). Procedural justice in personnel selection: International and cross-cultural perspectives. *International Journal of Selection and Assessment*, *9*(1–2), 124–131.

Suifan, T.S., Diab, H., & Abdallah, A.B. (2017). Does organizational justice affect turnover-intention in a developing country ? The mediating role of job satisfaction and organizational commitment. *Journal of Management Development*, *36*(9), 1137–1148.

Sutinen, R., Kivimäki, M., Elovainio, M., & Virtanen, M. (2002). Organizational fairness and psychological distress in hospital physicians. *Scandinavian Journal of Public Health*, *30*(3), 209–215.

Thibaut, J. & Walker, L. (1975), *Procedural Justice: A Psychological Analysis*. Lawrence Erlbaum Associates.

Törnroos, M., Elovainio, M., Hintsa, T., Hintsanen, M., Pulkki-Råback, L., Jokela, M., Lehtimäki, T., Raitakari, O.T., & Keltikangas-Järvinen, L. (2019). Personality traits and perceptions of organisational justice. *International Journal of Psychology*, *54*(3), 414–422.

Tyler, T.R. (1987). Procedural justice research. *Social Justice Research*, *1*(1), 41–65.

Tyler, T.R. & Blader, S.L. (2003). The group engagement model: Procedural justice, social identity, and cooperative behavior. *Personality and Social Psychology Review*, *7*(4), 349–361.

Van den Bos, K. (2001). Uncertainty management: the influence of uncertainty salience on reactions to perceived procedural fairness. *Journal of Personality and Social Psychology*, *80*(6), 931–941.

Van den Bos, K. & Lind, E.A. (2002). Uncertainty management by means of fairness judgments. In M.P. Zanna (Ed.), *Advances in experimental social psychology* (Vol. 34, pp. 1–60). Academic Press.

Vermunt, R. & Steensma, H. (2001). Stress and justice in organizations: An exploration into justice processes with the aim to find mechanisms to reduce stress. *Justice in the Workplace: From Theory to Practice*, *2*(1), 27–48.

Vermunt, R. & Steensma, H. (2003). Physiological relaxation: Stress reduction through fair treatment. *Social Justice Research*, *16*(2), 135–149.

Volmer, J. (2015). Followers' daily reactions to social conflicts with supervisors: The moderating role of core self-evaluations and procedural justice perceptions. *Leadership Quarterly*, 26(5), 719–731.

Walker, S.D.S. (2015). Maintaining justice: The effect of managerial personality and trait activation on procedural, interpersonal, and informational fairness. In S.W. Gilliland, D.D. Steiner, & D.P. Skarlicki (Eds.), *Research in social issues in management. The social dynamics of organizational justice* (pp. 143–175). Information Age Publishing.

Weiss, H.M. & Cropanzano, R. (1996). Affective events theory: A theoretical discussion of the structure, causes and consequences of affective experiences at work. In B.M. Staw & L.L. Cummings (Eds.), *Research in organizational behavior* (Vol. 18, pp. 1–74). JAI Press.

Whitman, D.S., Caleo, S., Carpenter, N.C., Horner, M.T., & Bernerth, J.B. (2012). Fairness at the collective level: A meta-analytic examination of the consequences and boundary conditions of organizational justice climate. *Journal of Applied Psychology, 97* (4), 776–791.

Williams, K.D. (1997). Social ostracism. In R.M. Kowalski (Ed.), *Aversive interpersonal behaviors* (pp. 133–170). Plenum Press.

Yukl, G. (2012). Effective leadership behavior: What we know and what questions need more attention. *Academy of Management Perspectives, 26*(4), 66–85.

# 4

# PERCEIVED ORGANIZATIONAL SUPPORT

*Florence Stinglhamber and Gaëtane Caesens*

## Introduction: Definition and Brief History

Paralleling research on organizational commitment, research on perceived organizational support has suggested that just as organizations may be concerned with the engagement of their employees toward them, employees may be interested in their organization's commitment to them. In agreement with this view, the American social psychologist Robert Eisenberger and his colleagues (Eisenberger et al., 1986) have proposed that commitment would be a two-way street, in that employees' inferences concerning the organization's commitment to them would in return influence employees' commitment to the organization. These inferences regarding the organization's commitment to employees make up what is called "perceived organizational support" (POS).

By introducing the POS construct, organizational support theory (OST) was indeed the first theory to consider the employee-organization relationship from the employee's point of view (Kurtessis et al., 2017). Specifically, POS was defined as "employees' *beliefs* about the extent to which the organization values their contributions and cares about their well-being" (Eisenberger et al., 1986, p. 501). In other words, it represents employees' perceptions of the organization's general (positive or negative) orientation toward them or the extent to which the organization favors them or not.

The development of these perceptions of organizational support is fostered by the natural tendency of employees to ascribe anthropomorphic characteristics to organizations (Levinson, 1965). According to Levinson (1965, p. 377),

> people project upon organizations human qualities and then relate to them as if the organizations did in fact have human qualities. They generalize from their feelings about people in the organization who are important to them, to the organization as a whole, as well as extrapolating from those attitudes they bring to the organization.

Thus, employees personify their organization by viewing it as having a personality with benevolent or malevolent intentions toward them (Eisenberger &

Stinglhamber, 2011). This personification process is a kind of pre-requisite to the development of POS.

The objectives pursued throughout this chapter are multiple. After presenting the theoretical framework within which POS is embedded, we will describe its nomological network, both in terms of its antecedents and its consequences. We will then present the few empirical studies that have addressed cultural differences and their impact on research findings related to POS. We will discuss the measurement of the POS construct in the next section. We will continue by discussing the current trends within the POS literature. Then, we will provide HR professionals with practical recommendations derived from the substantial literature on POS. Finally, we will provide a critique of the field, and propose some perspectives for future research.

## Theoretical Frameworks Associated

OST offers various theoretical frameworks for understanding POS and its effects (Eisenberger et al., 1986; Eisenberger & Stinglhamber, 2011). In particular, social exchange and self-enhancement processes were found to be the most successful in accounting for the relationship of POS with its outcomes (Kurtessis et al., 2017).

### Social Exchange Theory

Based on the reciprocity norm (Gouldner, 1960), the social exchange theory (Blau, 1964; Cropanzano & Mitchell, 2005) posits that when an actor does something to benefit a target person, the target person is expected to repay the favorable treatment. Applying this theory to the employee-organization relationship (Baran, Shanock, & Miller, 2012), OST considers employee and employer as partners who exchange valued resources (Blau, 1964). The organization provides employees with material and socio-emotional rewards in exchange for their work effort and dedication to the organization (Baran et al., 2012; Eisenberger et al., 1986). In line with this view, POS initiates a social exchange process wherein employees seek a balance between the organization's orientation toward them and the favorableness of their orientation toward the organization. The norm of reciprocity encourages employees who feel supported by their organization to repay their debt and reciprocate the organization's caring. As a result, supported employees feel obligated to help their supportive organization reach its goals and expect that their increased performance or efforts on behalf of the organization will be rewarded. By contributing to the development and general efficiency of the organization in return for the support received, employees maintain a positive self-image by avoiding the stigmatization related to the violation of the norm of reciprocity and encourage future favorable treatment (Rhoades, Eisenberger, & Armeli, 2001).

Empirical support has been found for these social exchange processes in the realm of POS. Research has indeed shown that employees' felt obligation toward the organization partially mediates the relationship between POS and several positive attitudes and behaviors at work such as affective commitment and citizenship behaviors (e.g., Coyle-Shapiro, Morrow, & Kessler, 2006; Eisenberger et al., 2001). Further supporting this explanation in terms of reciprocity, the relationship between POS and felt obligation was found to be stronger among those who strongly endorse the reciprocity norm as applied to work (Eisenberger et al., 2001).

### Self-Enhancement Processes

While social exchange processes have clearly dominated the literature on POS since the concept first emerged, OST has from the beginning suggested that self-enhancement processes are also at stake. OST indeed holds that POS helps to fulfill employees' socioemotional needs. Just as perceived support from friends and relatives fulfills socioemotional needs in interpersonal relationships, POS was supposed to meet fundamental human needs in the workplace (Armeli et al., 1998; Eisenberger et al., 1986). Following Armeli et al. (1998), POS should satisfy employees' need for recognition or esteem by increasing their inferences that the organization values and is proud of their work accomplishments. POS is also suggested to meet their need for affiliation or need to belong by conveying that the organization accepts them as organizational members and is committed to them. In addition, POS should fulfill employees' need for emotional support by suggesting that help and understanding will be provided to deal with stressful situations at work or at home. Finally, POS may meet employees' need for social approval by promoting the perception that the organization is satisfied that the employee is acting in accordance with established standards and policies. In line with this view, Armeli et al. (1998) reported that patrol police officers with high socioemotional needs showed a stronger positive relationship between POS and performance. Furthermore, Gillet et al. (2012) showed that employees' need satisfaction mediates the relationships between POS and several well-being indicators.

OST further proposes that this fulfillment of socioemotional needs by POS leads employees to "incorporate organizational membership and role status into their social identity" (Rhoades & Eisenberger, 2002, p. 699). Social identity theory (Tajfel & Turner, 1985; Turner, 1985) holds that individuals categorize themselves and others into different social categories in order to define and locate themselves in a given environment. Because individuals are motivated to maintain a positive self-evaluation, they tend to identify with groups who are perceived positively (Tajfel & Turner, 1985; Turner, 1985) and support these groups through their acts (e.g., Ashforth & Mael, 1989; Mael & Ashforth, 1992). In line with this theory, several authors have suggested that, in fulfilling employees' socioemotional needs, POS increases organizational attractiveness which,

→ org Identification

in turn, leads to employees' organizational identification (e.g., Eisenberger & Stinglhamber, 2011; Sluss, Klimchak, & Holmes, 2008). Consistent with this view, empirical evidence has supported the mediating role of organizational identification in the relationship between POS and several outcomes such as affective commitment, turnover intentions, and performance (e.g., Edwards & Peccei, 2010; Marique et al., 2013; Ngo et al., 2013; Stinglhamber et al., 2015a).

In sum, OST holds that both social exchange and self-enhancement processes are at stake and must be mobilized in order to understand POS and its effects. Although presented here separately for the sake of clarity, these two types of processes are not mutually exclusive. Caesens, Marique, and Stinglhamber (2014) found that some of the POS effects should be understood both in terms of exchange and reciprocity and in terms of self-definition and self-categorization. Thereby, they concluded that the two mechanisms do not compete against one another, but instead play a conjoint role. In another vein, other scholars have suggested that these two kinds of processes interplay so that individuals with strong socioemotional needs should find POS very rewarding, thus producing a greater obligation to repay the organization for this favorable treatment (Armeli et al., 1998; see also Kim, Eisenberger, & Baik, 2016).

## Nomological Network

OST has generated considerable interest so that hundreds of empirical studies have been conducted to identify the antecedents and consequences of POS. Several meta-analyses and reviews of the literature were therefore carried out in order to aggregate the multitude of findings concerning the proposed antecedents and consequences of POS (Baran et al., 2012; Eisenberger & Stinglhamber, 2011; Kurtessis et al., 2017; Rhoades & Eisenberger, 2002; Riggle, Edmondson, & Hansen, 2009). Figure 4.1 provides an overview of the nomological network of POS based on this prior work.

### *Antecedents of POS*

As there are many ways to indicate positive regard for employees' contributions and care for their welfare, an impressive list of antecedents is related to POS. In their meta-analytic review, Rhoades and Eisenberger (2002) concluded that POS develops based on the experience of fair treatment from the organization, the receipt of favorable rewards (e.g., salary, promotions) and job conditions (e.g., job autonomy), and the perceived support received from supervisors. More recently, the comprehensive review of the POS literature by Eisenberger and Stinglhamber (2011) and the meta-analysis of 558 studies by Kurtessis et al. (2017) have suggested that POS antecedents can be classified into four main categories: (1) employee-organization relationship quality, (2) HR practices, rewards and job conditions, (3) treatment by organization

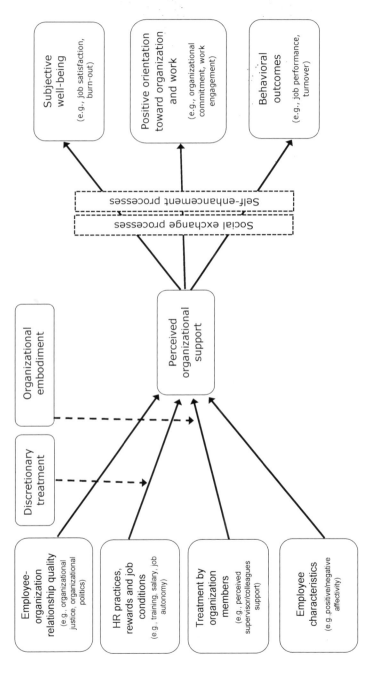

*Figure 4.1* Overview of the Nomological Network of Perceived Organizational Support, Based on Eisenberger and Stinglhamber (2011) and Kurtessis et al. (2017).

members, and (4) employees' characteristics. For each category, we will focus on the most important specific antecedents without seeking to be exhaustive, given the multitude of POS antecedents that have been identified.

### Employee-Organization Relationship Quality

Employee-organization relationship quality refers to contextual factors that convey the organization's (dis)regard for employees (Kurtessis et al., 2017). Among the elements falling into this category, perceptions of fairness are indubitably the most important ones. While all dimensions of organizational justice (i.e., procedural, distributive and interactional justice) were found to be positively related to POS, procedural justice (i.e., the fairness of the ways used to establish the distribution of resources among employees; Colquitt, 2001) is the strongest predictor of POS. Perceptions of fairness and, in particular, fairness regarding how the decisions are made in the organization indicate a concern for employees' welfare and foster POS (Shore & Shore, 1995). On the contrary, organizational politics, defined as "unsanctioned influence attempts that seek to promote self-interest at the expense of organizational goals" (Randall et al., 1999, p. 161), convey the implicit message that the organization cares too little about its personnel to control these harmful behaviors (Kurtessis et al., 2017).

### HR Practices, Rewards, and Job Conditions

OST suggests that HR practices (i.e., developmental opportunities, job security, flexibility in work schedule), rewards (e.g., salary, promotions), and favorable job conditions (i.e., enriching job characteristics such as job autonomy or task variety) enhance POS by making the context and the nature of the work more agreeable (Kurtessis et al., 2017: Rhoades & Eisenberger, 2002). In line with this view, several specific HR practices, rewards, and job conditions have been examined in relationship with POS. In particular, effective training was found to be an HR practice stimulating POS because it indicates an investment in the employee. In the same vein, when employees perceive job security and thus feel that their organization wishes to maintain them as a member of the organization, they are more likely to perceive support and valuation from their organization. Furthermore, job autonomy (i.e., employees' perception of being in control of the way they do their job) is perceived as an indication that the organization trusts its employees to carry out their work and, as such, fosters employee POS. In contrast, role stressors, described as job demands that individuals feel unable to cope with, negatively influence POS. Three main role stressors have been particularly examined as antecedents reducing POS: work overload, role ambiguity, and role conflict.

Importantly, the impact of HR practices, rewards, and job conditions on POS are all the more important, as they are perceived as being given based on a voluntary act on the part of the organization rather than to the result of external constraints. A central tenet of OST is that employees make attributions regarding the origin of the favorable or unfavorable treatment they received from the organization (Eisenberger & Stinglhamber, 2011). Eisenberger et al. (1997), for instance, have shown that favorable HR practices, rewards, and job conditions (e.g., promotion practices, reward systems, fringe benefits, and training opportunities) have a stronger (over six times greater) impact on POS when employees believe that these conditions are the result of their organization's voluntary decisions rather than being impelled by external circumstances, such as governmental policies, safety regulations, or legal compliance (see also Stinglhamber & Vandenberghe, 2004).

## *Treatment by Organization Members*

OST holds that all favorable treatment received from organizational agents or units may contribute to foster a general perception of organizational support (Kurtessis et al., 2017). In particular, because supervisors are representatives or agents of the organization, any (un)favorable treatment from them is perceived as indicative of the (un)favorable treatment from the whole organization. In line with this perspective, numerous studies have shown that leader-member exchange, perceived supervisor support, and transformational leadership are positively related to POS, whereas abusive supervision is negatively related to POS. Further, Eisenberger et al. (2010) suggested that employees might differ in the extent to which they consider their supervisors as being representative of their organization. While some supervisors might strongly embody the organization and be closely aligned with the organization in the eyes of their subordinates, others might be perceived as individuals in their own right possessing characteristics that considerably diverge from those of the organization. This variation in the perceived alignment between the supervisor and the organization was termed "supervisor's organizational embodiment" (SOE) and defined as the extent to which employees identify their supervisor with the organization. Importantly, research has shown that the greater the SOE, the more the treatment received from the supervisor affects the perceived treatment from the organization as a whole and thus POS (Shoss et al., 2013; Stinglhamber et al., 2015b).

Beyond supervisors, OST states that treatment from other entities in the employee's work environment also impacts employee POS. In particular, treatment from colleagues—but also unions, customers, or subordinates—may contribute to the development of high POS (Eisenberger & Stinglhamber, 2011). For instance, employees perceiving their coworkers as supportive are more likely to feel support from the organization as a whole, even though this influence has been found to be more modest than that of the supervisor given his/her power and formal authority over the employee (Ng & Sorensen, 2008).

*Employees' Characteristics*

While OST has focused mainly on the actions of the organization that impact POS, a final category of antecedents refers to the employee's characteristics and, in particular, to his/her personality traits that may influence his/her POS. Significant but weak associations were reported between both positive/negative affectivity and conscientiousness and POS (Rhoades & Eisenberger, 2002). Demographic characteristics (i.e., age, education, gender, and tenure) were found to show very little relationships with POS (Rhoades & Eisenberger, 2002).

*Relative Contribution of Antecedents*

In their meta-analyses, Rhoades and Eisenberger (2002) and Kurtessis et al. (2017) examined the relative contribution of some of these antecedents to POS. First, Rhoades and Eisenberger (2002) concluded that among fairness, supervisor support, and job conditions, fairness is most closely related to POS, followed by supervisor support and job conditions. More recently, Kurtessis et al. (2017) tested the relative contribution of fairness, employees' affectivity, and supervisor support to POS. The results of a multiple regression model predicting POS indicated that fairness is the strongest predictor, followed by employees' negative affectivity, supervisor support, and employees' positive affectivity.

## Consequences of POS

For more than three decades, numerous empirical studies have shown that POS is related to several beneficial outcomes for both organizations and individuals (Baran et al., 2012; Eisenberger & Stinglhamber, 2011; Kurtessis et al., 2017; Rhoades & Eisenberger, 2002; Riggle et al., 2009). Eisenberger and Stinglhamber (2011) proposed to classify these positive consequences into three main categories, namely (1) employees' subjective well-being, (2) a positive orientation (i.e., positive attitudes) toward organization and work, and (3) behavioral outcomes.

*Employees' Subjective Well-Being*

Research has consistently supported the view that the way in which the organization treats and considers employees has a substantial influence on their welfare at work by making the workplace more pleasant. More precisely, because POS fulfills their socio-emotional needs, employees who feel supported are more likely to show greater well-being at work and in general (Baran et al., 2012; Eisenberger & Stinglhamber, 2011; Kurtessis et al., 2017; Rhoades & Eisenberger, 2002). Accordingly, employees who experience high POS have been found to be generally more satisfied with their jobs, to have higher levels of organization-based self-esteem, and to have better general health. They also are less stressed, experience less burn-out, report lower levels of psychological strains and somatic complaints, and experience less work-to-family conflict.

### Positive Orientation toward Organization and Work

By communicating a positive valuation of employees, POS leads employees to develop a more positive orientation toward both their organization and the work it provides them. Regarding the organization, OST (e.g., Eisenberger et al., 1986; Eisenberger & Stinglhamber, 2011) suggests that, based on the social exchange theory and the norm of reciprocity, employees who experience a high level of POS are more likely to develop a stronger emotional attachment to their organization. In accordance with this view, empirical evidence supports a strong relationship between POS and affective organizational commitment so that this outcome is indubitably considered the most important consequence of POS (Stinglhamber et al., 2016). Importantly, Rhoades et al. (2001) went further by providing evidence for the antecedents of POS on affective commitment to the organization using a cross-lagged panel design. Research also reports that employees who perceive a high level of POS more strongly incorporate their organizational membership into their social identity and are thus more likely to show identification with this organization displaying such positive characteristics (e.g., Stinglhamber et al., 2015a). Finally, because POS provides cues to employees regarding the organization's benevolent intentions toward them, it has also been shown to increase their trust in the organization (Kurtessis et al., 2017).

POS also leads employees to experience a better orientation toward the work they perform in this supportive organization. Accordingly, POS has been found to increase employees' job involvement (i.e., the incorporation of the job into their social identity; O'Driscoll & Randall, 1999) and work engagement (i.e., a positive, fulfilling work-related state of mind that is characterized by vigor, dedication, and absorption in one's work; Schaufeli, Salanova, González-Romá, & Bakker, 2002, p. 74) (e.g., Caesens & Stinglhamber, 2014; Kurtessis et al., 2017).

### Behavioral Outcomes

According to OST (Eisenberger & Stinglhamber, 2011; Kurtessis et al., 2017; Rhoades & Eisenberger, 2002), employees who feel supported by their organization are more prone to behave in accordance with the organization's expectations. Again, based on social exchange processes and the reciprocity norm, they are indeed more inclined to return the support received by showing positive work behaviors. Supporting this view, numerous studies (Kurtessis et al., 2017; Rhoades & Eisenberger, 2002) have reported that employees who perceive high POS perform better in their job and work harder. More precisely, POS was found to be positively related to both in-role (i.e., the work activities that employees are expected to carry out as part of their job) and extra-role performance (i.e., the work activities that go beyond what is prescribed by formal job requirements). Furthermore, high-POS employees display more proactive behaviors and propose more creative suggestions in order to help the organization to reach its goals. Finally, POS helps to reduce employees' negative behaviors at work. High levels of POS reduce the propensity to display behaviors that violate organizational norms, i.e., workplace deviance or counter-productive behaviors directed toward the organization or its members. Employees who report feeling supported by their organization also engage less in withdrawal behaviors, such as absenteeism and turnover.

In sum, the literature has so far mainly considered POS as an entirely positive element in the workplace, and empirical research has supported this view by showing its beneficial consequences for both employers and employees (Eisenberger & Stinglhamber, 2011).

## The Relevance of Demographic Diversity and Culture to POS

In recent decades, many organizations in many countries have faced an increase in the demographic diversity of their workforce. On the one hand, major societal changes have led to the emergence of more gender- and age-diversified workforces. On the other hand, the increase of globalization in the world has triggered more interactions between people from different cultures and backgrounds than ever before. While this has created many challenges for organizations to manage this diversity, researchers were not spared and were also challenged to consider whether or not their findings apply to all. POS research was no exception and therefore focused on the fact that the workforce was heterogeneous.

### *Demographic Diversity*

In their meta-analysis, Kurtessis et al. (2017) examined gender and age as possible moderators of POS-outcome relationships. They suggested that women are more inclined to return favorable treatment to their organization and have more pronounced socio-emotional needs for affiliation and support than their male counterparts. Because the norm of reciprocity and the fulfillment of socioemotional needs are the two basic mechanisms explaining the effects of POS (cf. above), they further hypothesized that female employees should show a more positive relationship between POS and outcomes such as performance or organizational citizenship behaviors (or OCB). However, their meta-analytical results did not support their predictions, suggesting that the effects found are equally valid for both men and women.

Similarly, they considered the possibility that age may also influence POS-outcome relationships. Precisely, they expected weaker relationships between

POS and both job satisfaction and organizational commitment among older workers, whose awareness of limited time enhances the appreciation of positive aspects of life (Carstensen, Isaacowitz, & Charles, 1999). Because, by default, they thus tend to have more positive perceptions of their employer, older workers would be less attentive to POS in forming their job attitudes. The findings indicated that while the relationship between POS and job satisfaction was lessened to a small degree among older workers, its relationship with organizational commitment was unaltered by age.

## Culture and POS

### At the National Level

Research on POS also focuses on the impact of national culture. While the vast majority of research on POS has been conducted in the United States, the effects found in the U.S. were replicated around the world, suggesting that the basic principles of OST were somewhat universal (see Baran et al., 2012 for a review). However, this does not exclude the possibility that cultural differences may attenuate or amplify some of the relationships generally reported and composing the nomological network of POS.

In line with this perspective, Chiaburu et al. (2015) examined through a meta-analysis on 78 samples coming from 11 countries to determine whether national cultures (i.e., country-level cultural dimensions from Hofstede) may modify the strength of the POS-OCB relationship. They argued that employees from collectivist countries (i.e., societies characterized by "a tight social framework in which people distinguish between ingroups and outgroups, they expect their ingroup to look after them, and in exchange for they feel they owe absolute loyalty to it"; Hofstede, 1980, p. 45) are more sensitive and appreciative of POS, and that they reciprocate with greater enthusiasm and intensity by displaying more OCB. They further proposed that employees in high power distance cultures (i.e., societies that accept "the fact that power in institutions and organizations is distributed unequally"; Hofstede, 1980, p. 45) do not expect to receive support so that, when it happens, they are particularly grateful and reciprocate through behaviors that go beyond their job roles. In addition, they assumed that, given their feeling of powerlessness toward external forces, employees in high uncertainty avoidance cultures (i.e., societies that feel "threatened by uncertain and ambiguous situations and try to avoid these situations"; Hofstede, 1980, p. 45) might look to organizations for support to a greater extent. When receiving this support, they are more likely to behave in such a way as to return this favorable treatment. Finally, in order to maintain warm personal relationships and solidarity, countries with cultural femininity (i.e., societies "in which gender roles overlap: both men and women are supposed to be modest, tender, and concerned with the quality of life"; Hofstede, 2001, p. 297) are supposed to encourage reciprocity to a greater extent so that employees living in these countries should thus be more sensitive to POS and more willing to reciprocate it. In line with these assumptions, the authors found that the POS-OCB relationship is indeed strengthened in countries with higher levels of collectivism, power distance, uncertainty avoidance, and femininity.

## At the Individual Level

Although these cultural dimensions are usually discussed as part of national culture (e.g., Hofstede, 1980), researchers have also used them as important individual-level self-constructs to distinguish between individuals within the same culture (e.g., Triandis et al., 1988; Wagner, 1995). Several scholars have thus examined whether the degree to which POS resulted in some positive work attitudes and behaviors may depend on these cultural values endorsed at the individual level. In particular, Farh, Hackett, and Liang (2007) found that the relationships between POS and both affective commitment and performance are weaker among employees high in power distance. Eisenberger et al. (2009) found that the relationship between POS and affective commitment might be heightened by employees' collective orientation. In the same vein, Lam, Liu, and Loi (2016) showed that the indirect effect of POS on OCB through organizational identification is stronger among collectivist Chinese nurses.

On the contrary, Van Knippenberg, van Prooijen, and Sleebos (2015) proposed and found that the relationship between POS and OCB is attenuated among collectivist employees from the Netherlands. As we can see, the literature offers mixed results on the role of individual-level collectivism in exchanges between employees and organizations. This discrepancy in results can probably be partly explained by the fact that there are highly varied operationalizations of individualism-collectivism (e.g., Jackson et al., 2006). However, the studies described above do not rely on the same measure, which calls into question the comparability of the findings.

Overall, this line of research certainly deserves to be continued. More research on the role played by these cultural and individual differences would certainly enrich our understanding of employee-employer relationships. In particular, much remains to be done on how the antecedents of POS may differ in their predictive power based upon an organization's demographic composition or within the different cultures. To the best of our knowledge, only one study has so far examined the impact of cultural orientations at the individual level on the relationship between POS and one of its antecedents, i.e. high-performance H.R. practices (see Zhong, Wayne, and Liden's (2016) study conducted in China). Importantly, this research on the cultural and individual differences provides guidance for managers dealing with a diverse and international workforce to manage it successfully. While it shows that OST is useful to organizations within a wide variety of contexts and for everyone, it also shows the nuances that must be taken into account to best match the characteristics of each.

## Measurement of POS

Eisenberger and his colleagues (1986) originally developed a 36-item scale (18 positively and 18 negatively worded items) named the Survey of Perceived Organizational Support (SPOS) in order to assess employees' general beliefs concerning the extent to which the organization values their contributions and cares about their well-being. These 36 statements refer to diverse possible favorable and unfavorable judgments by employees regarding their organization. The results of a factor analysis indicated that the scale was unidimensional (Eisenberger et al., 1986).

For practical reasons (i.e., gain in time and space), scholars then used shorter versions of the SPOS (i.e., using the 17 or 8 highest-loading items of the full SPOS as reported by Eisenberger et al., 1986, see Table 4.1 for the 8-item version). Prior studies provided evidence for the high internal reliability and unidimensionality of these shorter scales (e.g., Eisenberger, Fasolo, & Davis-LaMastro, 1990; Shore & Tetrick, 1991). Importantly, both facets of the definition of the unidimensional construct of POS (valuation of employees' contribution and care about employees' well-being) are represented in these shorter scales, thus preserving the content validity of the concept (Rhoades & Eisenberger, 2002).

## Current Measurement Issues or Approaches

A review of the recent literature on POS led us to identify three current research trends in the study of the concept and its links with the variables belonging to its nomological network: (1) the study of POS as a dynamic

---

*Table 4.1* Eight-Item Version of the Survey of Perceived Organizational Support

---

1. The organization values my contribution to its well-being.
2. The organization fails to appreciate any extra effort from me. (R)
3. The organization would ignore any complaint from me. (R)
4. The organization really cares about my well-being.
5. Even if I did the best job possible, the organization would fail to notice. (R)
6. The organization cares about my general satisfaction at work.
7. The organization shows very little concern for me. (R)
8. The organization takes pride in my accomplishments at work.

---

*Source:* Adapted from Eisenberger & Stinglhamber (2011), p. 3.

*Note:* (R) indicates the item is reverse scored.

phenomenon, (2) the study of POS in combination with support from other constituencies, and (3) the study of POS in relation with a social environment.

## The Study of POS as a Dynamic Phenomenon

The majority of research on POS described above has been cross-sectional and has so far considered POS as a stable variable differing from one individual to another and measuring static perceptions at one time point. Recently, scholars raised the idea that, above and beyond considering POS as an enduring experience (as OST has suggested so far), it is also relevant to consider it as a dynamic phenomenon. According to this view, employees' perceptions of organizational support would be somewhat malleable so that POS can also be considered as a transient or vivid experience. Therefore, current research has started to examine within-person variations of POS and momentary changes of POS over time. Within-person variations of organizational constructs are commonly measured with daily or weekly designs that allow capturing the short-term dynamics of workers' experiences (Schaufeli, 2012). Based on this design, a recent study of Caesens, Stinglhamber, and Ohana (2016) showed that POS fluctuates within employees over short periods of time (i.e., week-to-week). Depending on what happens during the past days, workers showed subsequent higher or lower levels of POS. In addition, their results reported that employees' weekly work engagement was a mediator in the positive relationship between weekly POS and employees' weekly well-being (i.e., weekly positive and negative affect toward the organization and psychological strains). Overall, this study shows the dynamic of work relationships between an employee and his/her organization.

Interestingly, if Caesens et al. (2016) found, for the first time, that employees' organizational support perceptions fluctuated from week to week over a period of three months, these authors did not precisely examine the trajectories of those POS fluctuations, nor to what extent these fluctuations differ from one subgroup of employees to another. A promising avenue for future research might be to examine how POS varies within employees across the course of several days, weeks, months, or years among subgroups of employees (i.e., examining common trajectories of POS over time). This issue should be addressed through the collection of longitudinal data and by applying a growth mixture modeling approach (e.g., Morin, 2016).

## The Study of POS in Combination with Support from Other Constituencies

Recently, several scholars started to raise the idea that POS should not be considered in isolation from other organizational constituencies such as the supervisor (perceived supervisor support) or colleagues (perceived colleagues support) (e.g., Caesens, Stinglhamber, & Luypaert, 2014; Ng & Sorensen, 2008). More precisely, they suggested examining the possible complementary role of these three sources of support as they have been seen as coexisting in various degrees (Caesens et al., 2020). It might indeed be possible that POS is irrelevant or have a less prominent role when employees experience a high level of support from their supervisor or colleagues or, on the contrary, to have a multiplying effect. To address these questions, scholars (e.g., Caesens et al., 2020) adopted a person-centered approach by using a latent profile analysis (e.g., Morin, 2016). This approach led them to identify natural subpopulations of employees differing in their perceptions of sources of support in the workplace, namely POS, perceived supervisor support, and perceived colleagues support.

Interestingly, the results of Caesens et al.'s (2020) study indicated that five profiles of social support at work emerged from two different samples of employees: (1) moderately supported (employees perceiving moderated levels of support from the three sources); (2) isolated (employees perceiving very low levels of social support from both the organization and the supervisor and moderately low levels of social support from colleagues); (3) supervisor supported (employees perceiving high level of social support from the supervisor, low levels of support from the organization and moderate levels of social support from their colleagues); (4) weakly supported (employees perceiving low levels of support from the three sources); and (5) highly supported (employees perceiving high levels of support from the three sources). They further found that the most positive outcomes (i.e., job satisfaction, performance, and affective commitment) were associated with the highly supported profile, while the highest levels of emotional exhaustion were linked to the isolated one. Overall, this study also indicated that for the vast majority of individuals (81.7%), the three sources of support act together, and that employees tend to perceive an overall climate of social support that generalizes across sources. However, research on how POS, PSS, and PCS combine in social support profiles (Caesens et al., 2020) has only just begun. More research on this important issue is certainly warranted and will provide valuable information for practice.

### The Study of POS in Relation to a Social Environment

Rooted in the social exchange theory (Blau, 1964), POS was essentially considered so far as a construct capturing the quality of a dyadic exchange relationship between an employee and his/her personified organization (Levinson, 1965). In agreement with this view and as we have seen in the section devoted to its antecedents, most POS studies have examined "how people *personally* perceive to be more or less supported by their organization based on their *own* work experiences" (Stinglhamber et al., 2020). This literature has thus mainly focused on individual-level psychological explanations in order to explain the development of POS. Recently, a handful of studies have begun to consider that OST would benefit from adopting a broader vision of the POS develop-ment and influence, i.e., a vision that exceeds the two-way relationship between an employee and his/her organization. Precisely, this research expands and deepens the comprehension of POS by considering that the social context is useful in understanding how POS is shaped and impacts employees' attitudes and behaviors. Two different perspectives emerged in this recent stream of research.

On the one hand, some scholars examined the social contagions or rip-ple effects that may occur in the formation of POS. Zagenczyk et al. (2010) suggested that a focal employee's POS is influenced by information that this employee acquires from the social context. Through his/her interactions with coworkers within the organization, he/she collects a great deal of information. He/she then interprets it in order to understand, analyze, and form an opinion about the organizational environment in which he/she finds himself/herself. Sharing perceptions of organizational support among colleagues would thus provide clues that the focal employee uses to form his/her own views regarding the organization's valuation of him/herself. Relying on a social network analy-sis, Zagenczyk et al. (2010) indeed found that employees sharing advice ties in the organization (i.e., "instrumental relationships through which employees share job- and organization-related information," p.129) have similar levels of POS. They further showed that it is also the case for employees having ties with similar others in the organization, i.e., colleagues who occupy struc-turally equivalent positions in organizational friendship and advice networks (Zagenczyk et al., 2010).

In the same vein, Stinglhamber et al. (2020) recently tested this contagion effect by examining whether a focal employee's POS is associated with the POS of his/her direct coworkers, i.e., the people pertaining to the same workgroup and with whom the focal employee has no choice but to interact. They found that the POS of his/her direct coworkers is related to the focal employee's POS, with positive consequences in terms of increasing job satisfaction and then OCB. However, the influence of coworkers' POS on the focal employee's POS and its subsequent outcomes was significant only when the focal employee experiences low voice in the workplace. This finding suggests that employees would rely on others' judgments to a greater extent to build their own POS when they feel uncertain and feel like non-valued organizational members. Overall, these two studies suggest that if employees pay attention to the treat-ment they receive from the organization to shape their POS, they also con-sider how this treatment is perceived by both coworkers with whom they share advice or who reside in structurally equivalent network positions (Zagenczyk et al., 2010) and coworkers who are by default part of their work environment (Stinglhamber et al., 2020).

On the other hand, some authors considered the possible social compari-son processes that may be at play in the formation of POS or its impact on employees' work attitudes and behaviors. Vardaman et al. (2016) recently proposed that, beyond making inferences about their own POS in absolute value, employees are also motivated to determine whether they are more or less supported than others. They suggested that the most salient reference group for a focal employee to determine this *relative* POS is that of direct coworkers, i.e., coworkers pertaining to the same workgroup and with whom they frequently interact at work. Accordingly, they objectively compare the individual POS of a focal employee to the group average to construct a measure of relative POS that best reflects reality. They found that a favorable relative POS (i.e., favorable within-group comparisons) is positively associated with affective commitment and retention. In contrast, an unfavorable relative POS (i.e., unfavorable within-group comparisons) is negatively related to these outcomes, especially in less-supported workgroups.

In a similar vein, Tsachouridi and Nikandrou (2019) recently introduced the relative POS (RPOS) construct, defined as a focal employee's global perceptions that the organization supports him/her more than his/her coworkers. Contrary to what Vardaman et al. (2016) did, they considered that perceptions of reality are more influential than reality in their effects on attitudes and behaviors, and therefore directly asked participants in their study to assess their POS in comparison with that of their coworkers. Their main findings indicate that this subjective comparison between their POS and that of their coworkers contribute to their own POS. The more the comparison is favorable (i.e., a high RPOS), the more the individual POS increases. This RPOS-POS relationship is further mediated by organizational identification and has consequences in terms of intention to quit the organization and willingness to help and support it. Overall, by demonstrating how social comparisons operate in the realm of POS, these studies help to highlight the significant role of the self-enhancement processes in OST (Vardaman et al., 2016). While unfavorable comparisons of one's POS with that of a reference group could harm self-enhancement and have negative consequences, favorable comparisons could instead increase self-enhancement and foster positive perceptions, attitudes, and behaviors at work.

In sum, the few studies described in this section show that POS does not develop or operate in isolation of social context. If they all argue for an effect of the social environment, the processes at stake are, however, different. A key challenge for upcoming studies will thus be to determine what would lead employees to engage in contagion versus comparison processes.

## Practical Implications

Given the favorable consequences of POS, identifying levers on which organizations can act on to foster, among employees, this feeling of being supported by their organization is of utmost importance for practitioners. As a plethora of antecedents were already identified and, to some extent, prioritized by research, practitioners have many courses of action that they can follow and rely on (e.g., organizational justice; see section 3.1). Rather than reiterating each of these identified determinants of POS, we propose to list some basic principles that should be followed in allocating resources to foster POS.

First, organizations must ensure that they communicate the voluntary nature of any favorable action taken or, on the contrary, that they communicate the unintended nature of any unfavorable action (Eisenberger & Stinglhamber, 2011). Proper treatment of employees indeed generates more POS when it is seen as discretionary rather than the consequence of external constraints such as the law (Eisenberger et al., 1997; Stinglhamber & Vandenberghe, 2004).

Second, organizations should consider that having an impact on the employee's POS does not only mean that the employee must be the direct target of any favorable organizational treatment. Practitioners must pay attention to the indirect dissemination of POS. Actions and words of representatives of the organization (e.g., recruiters), managers, and opinion leaders may indeed have a greater impact on employees' views of the organization than might be expected (Shanock et al., 2019).

Finally, organizations should tailor supportive treatment to cultural norms but also individual needs or expectations. What employees find supportive or not depends on national culture (Shanock et al., 2019) and individual differences so that a greater personalization of the supportive treatment is undoubtedly necessary. In sum, by using these three principles as a basis for developing their human resource policies and practices, practitioners should achieve good results in terms of increasing employees' POS.

## Critique of the Field Up Until Now

As we have seen above, much research has examined the consequences of POS for both organizations and employees (e.g., Kurtessis et al., 2017). So far, this literature has mainly considered POS as a positive element within the workplace: The greater the POS, the more positive the outcomes for organizations and employees will be. A positive view of POS and its effects has thus dominated the literature so far. Nevertheless, some scholars started to suggest that POS might have some negative consequences or, at least, more limited positive consequences (e.g., Burnett et al., 2015). For instance, Eisenberger and Stinglhamber (2011) suggested that "the employee's organizational identification and affective commitment resulting from POS can also cause employees to become complicit with poorly planned, risky, or unethical activities" (p. 208). A more systematic examination of the potential dark side of POS would undoubtedly open the possibility of new insights and refinements for OST.

Although seldom discussed, there is some empirical evidence that indicates that POS has negative consequences or, at the very least, less positive consequences for both organizations and employees under certain circumstances. First, Armeli et al. (1998) unexpectedly found in their study that, for patrol officers having low socioemotional needs, the relationship between POS and performance was actually negative. The authors explained this unexpected finding by "the possibility that employees with low socioemotional needs may view high POS as a bank of goodwill that provides an opportunity to rest on one's laurels" (p. 295). In other words, employees having low socioemotional needs might assume that their organization will forgive them for poor performance (Armeli et al., 1998). More importantly, recently, Kurtessis et al. (2017) also reported in their recent meta-analysis that many relationships between POS and outcomes showed substantial variability across samples. This suggests that sample-level moderators might account for these relationships and that contextual variables also play a role. Overall, future research that considers individual or contextual moderators that weaken the relationships between POS and several outcomes would, therefore, be beneficial (see also the section above on diversity issues).

Second, based on the "too much of a good thing effect" proposed in the management literature (Pierce & Aguinis, 2013) and the vitamin model (Warr, 1987), some scholars started to examine potential nonlinear relationships between POS and several outcomes. In line with this view, Burnett et al. (2015) demonstrated that the relationship between POS and employees taking charge (i.e., a kind of proactive behavior characterized by change- or improvement-making actions) is characterized by a curvilinear inverted U-shaped curve. They suggested that when good things are present in excess (e.g., supportiveness), it can backfire. More particularly, too much support from the organization might be perceived as overwhelming, overly controlling, or excessive for employees, so that the employee may feel threatened and incompetent and finally reduce his/her felt obligation to help the organization reach its goals through proactive behaviors (Burnett et al., 2015). Interestingly, this curvilinear relationship was also found to be stronger for employees having serious concerns or perceiving high anticipated costs related to a potential non-receptivity to their proactive behavior.

Finally, even more recently, Harris and Kacmar (2018) also proposed that employees perceiving high levels of support might at some point consider that they have made enough efforts to reciprocate the favorable treatments received from the organization leading to a plateau in the POS-outcomes relationships. In line with this view, they found that the relationships between POS and in-role performance, extra-role performance, affective commitment and deviance (all rated by supervisors) were curvilinear (characterized by an inverted U-shaped curve for in-role, extra-role performance, and affective commitment, and a U-shaped curve for deviance).

Based on this prior research, it seems of particular relevance to consider and explore in the future years the conditions under which POS might lead to negative consequences, or at least to cease to have positive consequences. Overall, this future research perspective will help managers to optimize their allocation of resources and certainly warrants future investigations.

# What is Next: Pushing the Field Forward in Research and Practice

In the previous sections of this chapter, we have already identified several new lines of research on POS that we believe should be pursued to help develop OST in general. In addition, several authors have proposed in their prior works perspectives for future research that are still relevant today.

With a few exceptions (e.g., Caesens et al., 2016; Chen et al., 2009; Rhoades et al., 2001), most of the research conducted on the antecedents and consequences of POS was based on cross-sectional designs. Experimental studies and field studies using longitudinal designs with repeated measures (i.e., panel designs) are certainly needed to establish the direction of the relationship between POS and any other variable. Research on causal relationships between POS and related constructs would be critical in order to both build a solid foundation for theory development and draw informed and practice-oriented conclusions for managers in organizations.

Because organizations tend to try and preserve a competitive advantage, the workforce is becoming increasingly dependent upon non-traditional work relationships such as temporary workers (Kalleberg, 2000). It would certainly be interesting for future research to examine in detail whether the development of POS is different for contingent employees. These are only two examples among others of research perspectives that have already been highlighted by other researchers before us and to which we refer the interested reader for further details (e.g., Baran et al., 2012; Eisenberger & Stinglhamber, 2011; Kurtessis et al., 2017; Stinglhamber et al., 2016). We prefer to focus here on three avenues of research which, to our knowledge, have been less regularly proposed or developed in previous work.

## Dynamic of POS Over Time

As noted above, it might be relevant to examine in the future the dynamic of POS over time. A promising avenue for future research is indeed to examine whether POS evolves over the course of several days, weeks, months, or years among subgroups of employees (e.g., Beal et al., 2005). Do the majority of employees perceive stable POS perceptions, high or low, over time? Do certain employees experience a linear decreasing or increasing trajectories of POS over time or, on the contrary, nonlinear trajectories? More importantly, it would be interesting to examine both the predictors and outcomes of these trajectories. For instance, it may be relevant to analyze whether employees who typically perceive high levels of organizational support may react more negatively to a slight decrease in their POS over time, as compared to employees who are characterized by stable perceptions of moderate support from their organization over time.

Interestingly, examining these within-person POS fluctuations may be particularly relevant at certain times in employees' working lives. More precisely, analyzing how POS varies among a population of newcomers may be of particular interest since organizational socialization is inherently dynamic (Ashforth, 2012) and implies adjustments among employees' perceptions over time. Based on the organization's reputation, the information provided by acquaintances currently working in that organization, interactions with recruiters and information provided by the organization itself (Zheng et al., 2016), future employees of an organization develop perceptions of the extent to which that organization will value their contributions and care about their well-being when they join it (anticipated organizational support; Casper & Buffardi, 2004). Employees might, however, perceive discrepancies between this anticipated organizational support and the actual support they finally receive from the organization a few months after organizational entry, which might lead to negative consequences. Therefore, exploring how anticipated organizational support translates to actual POS through an examination of employees' perceptions trajectories certainly warrants future investigations.

### Mechanisms Underlying the Relationship between POS and its Antecedents

While much is known about the mechanisms that explain the relationships between POS and its consequences, comparatively little is known about the mechanisms that underlie the relationships between POS and its antecedents. Beyond the employees' attributions regarding the origin of the favorable or unfavorable treatment they received from the organization, much indeed remains to be done on the other factors that may be at play in the development of POS. In particular, Eisenberger and Stinglhamber (2011) stated that expressions of positive regard should contribute more to POS when they are given with sincerity and authenticity. Many employees indeed question the sincerity of the intentions behind some of their organization's actions. Is the organization trustworthy and is it sincerely putting the human being at the core of its management, or is it a cynical attempt of manipulation? Although this principle of sincerity is at the heart of OST (Eisenberger & Stinglhamber, 2011), it has never been empirically tested.

Future research might also examine other moderators of the relationships between favorable treatments offered by the organization and POS. For instance, if the organization uses expressions of gratitude in a discriminating, contingent, and proportionate fashion, the employee will certainly think that he/she really deserves this favorable treatment with more implications in terms of POS. In addition, the coherence of the recognition practices with the organizational culture and policies, in general, should be another factor to consider. Specifically, verbal praise and approval must be followed by concrete actions and tangible indications of positive regard and must be part of an organizational logic consistent with these signs of consideration. Advancing OST on these principles would contribute to a better understanding of the conditions under which favorable treatment by the organization will effectively translate into a greater sense of support among the employee. For practitioners, these research results would be all the more important because they would allow them to assess better the probability that the actions taken will have an impact on their employees' POS with all the (essentially positive) consequences associated with it so far (see also Kurtessis et al., 2017).

### Multilevel POS

As we have seen, POS has been initially conceptualized as an individual-level variable capturing an employee's beliefs regarding the organizational support received. OST holds that these beliefs may vary highly from one individual to another based on the personal treatment that is provided by the organization. Since this initial development there are, however, a few signs suggesting that beyond the individual perceptions, there may also be a more or less supportive climate in organizations. Studies on the trickle-down effect (e.g., Shanock & Eisenberger, 2006) suggest that the support received at one hierarchical level of an organization can percolate to lower levels, creating an interesting snowball or multiplying effect. As explained above, in their latent profile analysis, Caesens et al. (2020) reported that for most employees a greater or lesser degree of support from the organization is generally accompanied by a greater or lesser degree of support from other sources (such as the supervisor or colleagues), suggesting that supports from different sources go hand in hand and thus create a more or less important supportive climate in organizations.

Finally, studies on the social contagion effect of POS (Stinglhamber et al., 2020; Zagenczyk et al., 2010) also suggest that these perceptions have a more collective dimension that should not be overlooked. This idea of climate has, to some extent, been implicitly suggested in a few prior studies (Frear et al., 2018; Tremblay, Gaudet, & Vandenberghe, 2019; Vandenberghe et al., 2007) but, undoubtedly, needs further development. More precisely, POS research would benefit from multilevel studies that disentangle POS as an individual perception and POS as a climate variable (i.e., conceived of at the group and organization level; see also Baran et al., 2012). Since these two perspectives are conceptually distinct, they can lead to conflicting findings across levels of analysis. Support for the homology of relationships across levels will contribute to the parsimony of OST. Conversely, differences in relationships across levels will lead to its refinement (Caesens et al., 2016). At a time when many organizations have evolved or are increasingly evolving toward the adoption of recognition practices that are no longer only individual but also collective, such a line of research seems to make particular sense.

## Conclusion

In conclusion, OST has generated substantial research literature and offers a robust theoretical framework for scholars to build on. Many aspects still require further investigation to improve the theory and assist practitioners. The topic certainly deserves the full attention of researchers given the implications of a high POS or, on the contrary, of a lack of POS, which is unfortunately still a reality for many employees. Overall, the results accumulated so far suggest that POS plays a central role in the employee-organization relationship. Supporting employees is a win-win situation for employers and employees.

## References

Armeli, S., Eisenberger, R., Fasolo, P., & Lynch, P. (1998). Perceived organizational support and police performance: The moderating influence of socioemotional needs. *Journal of Applied Psychology, 83*, 288–297.

Ashforth, B.E. (2012). The role of time in socialization dynamics. In C.R. Wanberg (Ed.), *Oxford library of psychology. The Oxford handbook of organizational socialization* (pp. 161–186). New York, NY, U.S.: Oxford University Press.

Ashforth, B.E. & Mael, F. (1989). Social identity theory and the organization. *Academy of Management Review, 14*, 20–39.

Baran, B.E., Shanock, L.R., & Miller, L.R. (2012). Advancing organizational support theory into the twenty-first century world of work. *Journal of Business and Psychology, 27*, 123–147.

Beal, D.J., Weiss, H.M., Barros, E., & MacDermid, S.M. (2005). An episodic process model of affective influences on performance. *Journal of Applied psychology, 90*, 1054–1068.

Blau, P.M. (1964). *Exchange and power in social life*. New York, NY: Wiley.

Burnett, M.F., Chiaburu, D.S., Shapiro, D.L., & Li, N. (2015). Revisiting how and when perceived organizational support enhances taking charge: An inverted U-shaped perspective. *Journal of Management, 41*, 1805–1826.

Caesens, G., Gillet, N., Morin, A., Houle, S.A., & Stinglhamber, F. (2020). A person-centered perspective on social support in the workplace. *Applied Psychology: An International Review, 69*, 686–714.

Caesens, G., Marique, G., Hanin, D., & Stinglhamber, F. (2016). The relationship between perceived organizational support and proactive behavior directed toward the organization. *European Journal of Work and Organizational Psychology, 25*, 398–411.

Caesens, G., Marique, G., & Stinglhamber, F. (2014). The relationship between perceived organizational support and affective commitment: More than reciprocity, it is also a question of organizational identification. *Journal of Personnel Psychology, 13*, 167–173.

Caesens, G., & Stinglhamber, F. (2014). The relationship between perceived organizational support and work engagement: The role of self-efficacy and its outcomes. *European Review of Applied Psychology, 64*, 259–267.

Caesens, G., Stinglhamber, F., & Luypaert, G. (2014). The impact of work engagement and workaholism on well-being: The role of work-related social support. *Career Development International, 19*, 813–835.

Caesens, G., Stinglhamber, F., & Ohana, M. (2016). Perceived organizational support and well-being: A weekly study. *Journal of Managerial Psychology, 31*, 1214–1230.

Carstensen, L., Isaacowitz, D., & Charles, S. 1999. Taking time seriously: A theory of socioemotional selectivity. *American Psychologist, 54*, 165–181.

Casper, W.J., & Buffardi, L.C. (2004). Work-life benefits and job pursuit intentions: The role of anticipated organizational support. *Journal of Vocational Behavior, 65*, 391–410.

Chen, Z., Eisenberger, R., Johnson, K.M., Sucharski, I.L., & Aselage, J. (2009). Perceived organizational support and extra-role performance: Which leads to which? *Journal of Social Psychology, 149*, 119–124.

Chiaburu, D.S., Chakrabarty, S., Wang, J., & Li, N. (2015). Organizational support and citizenship behaviors: A comparative cross-cultural meta-analysis. *Management International Review, 55*, 707–736.

Colquitt, J.A. (2001). On the dimensionality of organizational justice: A construct validation of a measure. *Journal of Applied Psychology, 86*, 386–400.

Coyle-Shapiro, J. A-M., Morrow, P.C., & Kessler, I. (2006). Serving two organizations: Exploring the employment relationship of contracted employees. *Human Resource Management, 45*, 561–583.

Cropanzano, R. & Mitchell, M.S. (2005). Social exchange theory: An interdisciplinary review. *Journal of Management, 31*, 874–900.

Edwards, M.R. & Peccei, R. (2010). Perceived organizational support, organizational identification, and employee outcomes testing a simultaneous multifoci model. *Journal of Personnel Psychology, 9*, 17–26.

Eisenberger, R., Armeli, S., Rexwinkel, B., Lynch, P.D., & Rhoades, L. (2001). Reciprocation of perceived organizational support. *Journal of Applied Psychology, 86*, 42–51.

Eisenberger, R., Cummings, J., Armeli, S., & Lynch, P. (1997). Perceived organizational support, discretionary treatment, and job satisfaction. *Journal of Applied Psychology, 82*, 812–820.

Eisenberger, R., Fasolo, P., & Davis-LaMastro, V. (1990). Perceived organizational support and employee diligence, commitment, and innovation. *Journal of Applied Psychology, 75*, 51–59.

Eisenberger, R., Huntington, R., Hutchinson, S., & Sowa, D. (1986). Perceived organizational support. *Journal of Applied Psychology, 71*, 500–507.

Eisenberger, R., Karagonlar, G., Stinglhamber, F., Neves, P., Becker, T.E., & Steiger-Mueller, M. (2010). Leader-member exchange and affective organizational commitment: The contribution of supervisor's organizational embodiment. *Journal of Applied Psychology, 95*, 1085–1103.

Eisenberger, R. & Stinglhamber, F. (2011). *Perceived organizational support: Fostering enthusiastic and productive employees.* Washington, DC: APA Books.

Eisenberger, R., Stinglhamber, F., Shanock, L.R., Jones, J.R., & Aselage, J. (2009). *Extending the social exchange perspective of perceived organizational support: Influences of collectivism and competitiveness.* Unpublished manuscript, University of Delaware.

Farh, J.L., Hackett, R.D., & Liang, J. (2007). Individual-level cultural values as moderators of perceived organizational support–employee outcome relationships in China: Comparing the effects of power distance and traditionality. *Academy of Management Journal, 50,* 715–729.

Frear, K.A., Donsbach, J., Theilgard, N., & Shanock, L.R. (2018). Supported supervisors are more supportive, but why? A multilevel study of mechanisms and outcomes. *Journal of Business and Psychology, 33,* 55–69.

Gillet, N., Fouquereau, E., Forest, J., Brunault, P., & Colombat, P. (2012). The impact of organizational factors on psychological needs and their relations with well-being. *Journal of Business and Psychology, 27,* 437–450.

Gouldner, A.W. (1960). The norm of reciprocity: A preliminary statement. *American Sociological Review, 25,* 161–178.

Harris, K.J. & Kacmar, K.M. (2018). Is more always better? An examination of the nonlinear effects of perceived organizational support on individual outcomes. *The Journal of Social Psychology, 158,* 187–200.

Hofstede, G. (1980). Culture and organizations. *International Studies of Management & Organization, 10,* 15–41.

Hofstede, G. (2001). *Culture's consequences: Comparing values, behaviors, institutions and organizations across nations.* Thousand Oaks, CA: Sage publications.

Jackson, C.L., Colquitt, J.A., Wesson, M.J., & Zapata-Phelan, C.P. (2006). Psychological collectivism: A measurement validation and linkage to group member performance. *Journal of Applied Psychology, 91,* 884–899.

Kalleberg, A.L. (2000). Nonstandard employment relations: Part-time, temporary, and contract work. *Annual Review of Sociology, 16,* 341–365.

Kim, K.Y., Eisenberger, R., & Baik, K. (2016). Perceived organizational support and affective organizational commitment: Moderating influence of perceived organizational competence. *Journal of Organizational Behavior, 37,* 558–583.

Kurtessis, J.N., Eisenberger, R., Ford, M.T., Buffardi, L.C., Stewart, K.A., & Adis, C.S. (2017). Perceived organizational support: A meta-analytic evaluation of organizational support theory. *Journal of Management, 43,* 1854–1884.

Lam, L.W., Liu, Y., & Loi, R. (2016). Looking intra-organizationally for identity cues: Whether perceived organizational support shapes employees' organizational identification. *Human Relations, 69,* 345–367.

Levinson, H. (1965). Reciprocation: The relationship between man and organization. *Administrative Science Quarterly, 9,* 370–390.

Mael, F. & Ashforth, B.E. (1992). Alumni and their alma mater: A partial test of the reformulated model of organizational identification. *Journal of Organizational Behavior, 13,* 103–123.

Marique, G., Stinglhamber, F., Desmette, D., Caesens, G., & De Zanet, F. (2013). The relationship between perceived organizational support and affective commitment: A social identity perspective. *Group & Organization Management, 38,* 68–100.

Morin, A.J.S. (2016). Person-centered research strategies in commitment research. In J.P. Meyer (Ed.), *Handbook of employee commitment* (pp. 490–508). Northampton, MA: Edward Elgar.

Ng, T.W. & Sorensen, K.L. (2008). Towards a further understanding of the relationships between perceptions of support and work attitudes: A meta-analysis. *Group & Organization Management, 33*, 243–268.

Ngo, H.Y., Loi, R., Foley, S., Zheng, X., & Zhang, L. (2013). Perceptions of organizational context and job attitudes: The mediating effect of organizational identification. *Asia Pacific Journal of Management, 30*, 149–168.

O'Driscoll, M.P. & Randall, D.M. (1999). Perceived organisational support, satisfaction with rewards, and employee job involvement and organisational commitment. *Applied Psychology: An International Review, 48*, 197–209.

Pierce, J.R. & Aguinis, H. (2013). The too-much-of-a-good-thing effect in management. *Journal of Management, 39*, 313–338.

Randall, M.L., Cropanzano, R., Bormann, C.A., & Birjulin, A. (1999). Organizational politics and organizational support as predictors of work attitudes, job performance, and organizational citizenship behavior. *Journal of Organizational Behavior, 20*, 159–174.

Rhoades, L. & Eisenberger, R. (2002). Perceived organizational support: A review of the literature. *Journal of Applied Psychology, 87*, 698–714.

Rhoades, L., Eisenberger, R., & Armeli, S. (2001). Affective commitment to the organization: The contribution of perceived organizational support. *Journal of Applied Psychology, 86*, 825–836.

Shanock, L., Eisenberger, R., Heggestad, E.D., Malone, G., Clark, L., Dunn, A.M., … & Woznyj, H. (2019). Treating employees well: The value of organizational support theory in human resource management. *The Psychologist-Manager Journal, 22*, 168–191.

Riggle, R.J., Edmondson, D.R., & Hansen, J.D. (2009). A meta-analysis of the relationship between perceived organizational support and job outcomes: 20 years of research. *Journal of Business Research, 62*, 1027–1030.

Schaufeli, W.B. (2012). Work engagement: What do we know and where do we go? *Romanian Journal of Applied Psychology, 14*, 3–10.

Schaufeli, W.B., Salanova, M., González-Romá, V., & Bakker, A.B. (2002). The measurement of engagement and burnout: A two sample confirmatory factor analytic approach. *Journal of Happiness Studies, 3*, 71–92.

Shanock, L.R. & Eisenberger, R. (2006). When supervisors feel supported: Relationships with subordinates' perceived supervisor support, perceived organizational support, and performance. *Journal of Applied Psychology, 91*, 689–695.

Shore, L.M. & Shore, T.H. (1995). Perceived organizational support and organizational justice. In R.S. Cropanzano & K.M. Kacmar (Eds.), *Organizational politics, justice, and support: Managing the social climate of the workplace* (pp. 149–164). Westport, CT: Quorum.

Shore, L.M. & Tetrick, L.E. (1991). A construct-validity study of the Survey of Perceived Organizational Support. *Journal of Applied Psychology, 76*, 637–643.

Shoss, M.K., Eisenberger, R., Restubog, S.L.D., & Zagenczyk, T.J. (2013). Blaming the organization for abusive supervision: The roles of perceived organizational support and supervisor's organizational embodiment. *Journal of Applied Psychology, 98*, 158–168.

Sluss, D.M., Klimchak, M., & Holmes, J.J. (2008). Perceived organizational support as a mediator between relational exchange and organizational identification. *Journal of Vocational Behavior, 73*, 457–464.

Stinglhamber, F., Caesens, G., Clark, L., & Eisenberger, R. (2016). Perceived organizational support and organizational commitment. In J. Meyer (Ed.), *Handbook of Employee Commitment* (pp. 333–345). Northampton, MA: Edward Elgar Publishers.

Stinglhamber, F., Marique, G., Caesens, G., Desmette, D., Hansez, I., Hanin, D., & Bertrand, F. (2015a). Employees' organizational identification and affective organizational commitment: An integrative approach. *PLoS ONE, 10*, e0123955.

Stinglhamber, F., Marique, G., Caesens, G., Hanin, D., & De Zanet, F. (2015b). The influence of transformational leadership on followers' affective commitment: The role of perceived organizational support and supervisor's organizational embodiment. *Career Development International, 20*, 583–603.

Stinglhamber, F., Ohana, M., Caesens, G., & Meyer, M. (2020). Perceived organizational support: An examination of the role of coworkers' perceptions and employees' voice. *Employee Relations, 42*, 107–124.

Stinglhamber, F. & Vandenberghe, C. (2004). Favorable job conditions and perceived support: The role of organizations and supervisors. *Journal of Applied Social Psychology, 34*, 1470–1493.

Tajfel, H. & Turner, J.C. (1985). The social identity theory of intergroup behavior. In S. Worchel & W.G. Austin (Eds.), *Psychology of intergroup relations* (2nd ed., pp. 7–24). Chicago: Nelson-Hall.

Tremblay, M., Gaudet, M.-C., & Vandenberghe, C. (2019). The role of group-level perceived organizational support and collective affective commitment in the relationship between leaders' directive and supportive behaviors and group-level helping behaviors. *Personnel Review, 48*, 417–437.

Triandis, H.C., Bontempo, R., Villareal, M.J., Asai, M., & Lucca, N. (1988). Individualism and collectivism: Cross-cultural perspectives on self-ingroup relationships. *Journal of Personality and Social Psychology, 54*, 323–338.

Tsachouridi, I. & Nikandrou, I. (2019). Integrating social comparisons into Perceived Organisational Support (POS): The construct of Relative Perceived Organisational Support (RPOS) and its relationship with POS, identification and employee outcomes. *Applied Psychology: An International Review, 68*, 276–310.

Turner, J.C. (1985). Social categorization and the self-concept: A social cognitive theory of group behavior. In E.J. Lawler (Ed.), *Advances in group processes* (Vol. 2, pp. 77–122). Greenwich, CT: JAI Press.

Vandenberghe, C., Bentein, K., Michon, R., Chebat, J.-C., Tremblay, M., & Fils, J.-F. (2007). An examination of the role of perceived support and employee commitment in employee-customer encounters. *Journal of Applied Psychology, 92*, 1177–1187.

Van Knippenberg, D., van Prooijen, J.W., & Sleebos, E. (2015). Beyond social exchange: Collectivism's moderating role in the relationship between perceived organizational support and organizational citizenship behaviour. *European Journal of Work and Organizational Psychology, 24*, 152–160.

Vardaman, J.M., Allen, D.G., Otondo, R.F., Hancock, J.I., Shore, L.M., & Rogers, B.L. (2016). Social comparisons and organizational support: Implications for commitment and retention. *Human Relations, 69*, 1483–1505.

Wagner III, J.A. (1995). Studies of individualism-collectivism: Effects on cooperation in groups. *Academy of Management Journal, 38*, 152–173.

Warr, P. (1987). *Work, Unemployment, and Mental Health*. Clarendon Press, Oxford.

Zagenczyk, T.J. Scott, K.D., Gibney, R., Murrell, A.J., & Thatcher, J.B. (2010). Social influence and perceived organizational support: A social networks analysis. *Organizational Behavior and Human Decision Processes, 111*, 127–138.

Zheng, D., Wu, H., Eisenberger, R., Shore, L.M., Tetrick, L.E., & Buffardi, L.C. (2016). Newcomer leader–member exchange: the contribution of anticipated organizational support. *Journal of Occupational and Organizational Psychology, 89*, 834–855.

Zhong, L., Wayne, S.J., & Liden, R.C. (2016). Job engagement, perceived organizational support, high-performance human resource practices, and cultural value orientations: A cross-level investigation. *Journal of Organizational Behavior, 37*, 823–844.

# 5

♥

# ORGANIZATIONAL IDENTIFICATION

*Chia-Huei Wu, Hannah Weisman,*
*Katsuhiko Yoshikawa, and Hyun-Jung Lee*

## Organizational Identification

When will employees be willing to devote themselves to their organizations? This question has many answers, such as when employees are satisfied with their jobs (Judge, Zhang, Glerum, Chapter 9), when they are treated fairly in their organizations (Martínez-Tur, Moliner, Alice Maniezki, Chapter 3), or when they receive support from their organizations (Stinglhamber & Caesens, Chapter 4). Beyond these answers concerning employees' views and treatment, there is another answer that reflects an intrinsic reason: when employees see their organizations as an integral part of themselves. When employees possess a strong social identity based on their organizations (i.e., defining themselves based on their organizational memberships), they tend to define their self-concepts as interchangeable with the organization. As people strive to maintain a positive view of themselves, having a self-conception based on one's group or organizational membership can therefore:

> *Energize* people to exert themselves on behalf of the group, facilitate the *direction* of efforts toward collective (instead of individual) outcomes, and help workers *sustain* their loyalty to the team or organization through times in which this is not individually rewarding.
>
> (Ellemers, De Gilder, & Haslam, 2004, p. 461)

Accordingly, organizational identification, a construct capturing the extent to which employees define themselves in terms of organizational membership and attributes (Ashforth, Harrison, & Corley, 2008), has been found as a factor that can motivate employees to devote themselves to their organizations and shape employees' work attitudes and behavior.

In this chapter, we first introduce the concept of organizational identification. Next, we summarize research findings regarding the antecedents and consequences of organizational identification and review existing measurement tools for assessing organizational identification (see Table 5.1 for a summary).

Finally, we discuss key gaps in the literature on organizational identification and offer directions for future research that would address those gaps, before concluding with a discussion of the concept's practical implications.

## The Concept of Organizational Identification

The interest in ideas similar to organizational identification can be traced back to early management studies that suggested that the coalescence (Barnard, 1938/1968) between the worker and the organization motivates employees to devote their effort to their organizations. However, the study of organizational

*Table 5.1* Summary of a Nomological Net of Organizational Identification

| Antecedents of Organizational Identification | Concept of Organizational Identification | Consequences of Organizational Identification |
| --- | --- | --- |
| **Individual Factors**<br><br>• Demographic variables<br>  - Tenure, Age, Employment status<br>• Work perception and feelings<br>  - Sense of fit (Person-organization fit, Person-job fit)<br>  - Feelings about work (e.g., passion, relative deprivation, ostracism)<br><br>**Job Factors**<br><br>• Enriched job characteristics<br>  - Job challenge, Job autonomy<br>• Relational job characteristics<br>  - Social outreach via one's job, Communication for virtual work, Formal mentoring<br>• Physical distance<br>  - Physical isolation, Physical distance from the company's corporate headquarters | **Definition of Organizational Identification**<br><br>"perception of oneness with or belongingness to an organization, where the individual defines him or herself in terms of the organization(s) in which he or she is a member" (Mael & Ashforth, 1992, p. 104).<br><br>**Key Measurement Tools**<br><br>• The Mael Scale<br>• Organizational Identification Questionnaire<br>• Edwards and Peccei's Scale<br>• Multidimensional Identity Scale<br>• Cognitive Organizational Identification Scale | **Bright Side of Organizational Identification**<br><br>• Employee attitudes<br>  - Job involvement, Job satisfaction, Organizational commitment, Engagement, Lower turnover intentions<br>• Employee behavior<br>  - Job performance, Work effort, In-role performance<br>  - Organizational citizenship behaviors, Actions to improve work processes, Readiness for change, Extra-role performance,<br>  - Lower organizational deviance<br>• Employee well-being<br>  - Psychological well-being<br>  - Organization-based self-esteem<br>  - Lower emotional exhaustion |

*Table 5.1* (Cont.)

| Antecedents of Organizational Identification | Concept of Organizational Identification | Consequences of Organizational Identification |
|---|---|---|
| **Leadership Factors**<br><br>• Leaders' style and characteristics<br>  - Charismatic leadership, Transformational leadership, Ethical leadership, Servant leadership, Self-sacrificial leadership, Leader humility, Leaders' organizational identification<br>• Quality of leader-member exchange (LMX) relationship<br><br>**Organizational Factors**<br><br>• External views of the organization<br>  - Perceptions of organizational prestige, distinctiveness, reputation, and stereotypes<br><br>• Internal practices<br>  - Corporate social responsibility, Socialization practices, Fair practices, Psychological contract management | | **Dark Side of Organizational Identification**<br><br>• Vulnerability<br>  - Negative feelings during the presence of identity threats<br>  - Resource depletion in the face of psychological contract violation<br>• Compulsive and unhealthy work ethic<br>  - Lower creativity<br>  - Workaholism<br>  - Unethical pro-organizational behavior |

identification first emerged as a research topic in the 1980s when Ashforth and Mael (1989) used social identity theory to understand organizational identification.

Social identity theory (Tajfel, 1978, p.63) suggests individuals can define themselves based on the groups to which they belong, or their social identity, that is, "that part of an individual's self-concept which derives from his knowledge of his membership of a social group (or groups) together with the value and emotional significance attached to that membership." Social identity not only helps individuals construct a self-concept but also serves to distinguish individuals and members of their social groups from out-groups. Social identification with a group is not all or nothing, but rather a matter of degree, as individuals in the same social group may vary in the strength of their identification with the social group.

Because an organization can be viewed as a structured social unit consisting of people who work together to pursue specific goals (Etzioni, 1964), it can be an entity with which employees can identify and build a social identity. From this perspective, organizational identification, therefore, is defined as the "perception of oneness with or belongingness to an organization, where the individual defines him or herself in terms of the organization(s) in which he or she is a member" (Mael & Ashforth, 1992, p. 104). Organizational identification involves cognitive (i.e., I am A; self-definition), evaluative (i.e., I value A; importance), and affective (i.e., I feel about A; affect) components (Ashforth et al., 2008) that jointly denote the perception of oneness with or belongingness to an organization. Organizational identification is organization-specific and functions to distinguish employees in a specific organization (i.e., in-group) relative to employees in other organizations (out-groups). Finally, employees in the same organization can have different levels of organizational identification, depending on how strongly they define themselves based on their organizational membership.

Employees can identify with their organizations with different motives (see Ashforth & Schinoff, 2016, for a review). For example, employees can be motivated to identify with their organizations due to a desire to belong. Employees can also be motivated to identify in order to boost their positive conceptions of the self (i.e., self-enhancement), for example, by linking themselves to organizations with higher prestige. Other self-related motives include

> self-knowledge (locating the self within a context to define the self), self-expression (enacting valued identities), self-coherence (maintaining a sense of wholeness across a set of identities), self-continuity (maintaining a sense of wholeness across time), and self-distinctiveness (valuing a sense of uniqueness).
>
> (Ashforth et al., 2008, p.335)

Finally, identifying with the organization can help employees reduce feelings of uncertainty in changing business environments as it can help them associate with and be part of collective actions.

Since the inception of research on organizational identification, researchers have questioned and investigated the extent to which organizational identification is distinguishable from a variety of related constructs. One of the most challenging tasks has been distinguishing organizational identification from organizational commitment (Ashforth et al., 2008; Mael & Ashforth, 1992), particularly the affective form of organizational commitment that reflects the individual's emotional attachment (Bergami & Bagozzi, 2000) and desire to remain with the organization (Allen & Meyer, 1990). Nevertheless, organizational identification and commitment are distinguishable (see also Klein, 2020 in Chapter 7). Specifically, the cognitive overlap—the overlap between the employee's sense of self and the employee's organizational membership—is central to organizational identification, but not to organizational commitment. Organizational commitment mainly concerns the employee's emotional reaction or positive attitude toward the organization, as a separate entity from themselves, and does not involve the cognitive element. Empirically, numerous scholars have demonstrated that organizational identification and organizational commitment are indeed empirically discriminant constructs (e.g., Cole & Bruch, 2006; Herrbach, 2006; Lee, Park, & Koo, 2015; Ng, 2015).

Organizational identification is also distinct from other psychological constructs discussed in this book, such as job involvement (i.e., "the extent to which one is mentally focused on, cognitively preoccupied with, and concerned with one's present job") (Diefendorff et al., Chapter 6, [page 133]), job satisfaction (i.e., an overall, evaluative judgment of one's job ranging from positive to negative) (Judge et al., Chapter 9, [page 210]), and employee engagement (i.e., a multidimensional motivational state that involves the simultaneous investment of an individual's complete self and personal resources in the performance of a role and one's work) (Saks & Gruman, Chapter 10, [page 244]). Whereas organizational identification concerns the perceived oneness between an employee and his/her organization, these constructs focus on an employee's job experience or state while performing a job. Nevertheless, organizational identification could be a precursor for developing those positive attitudes in organizations because employees are likely to build stronger emotional bonds with their organizations when they have a sense of oneness with them. In support of this view, Lee et al. (2015) examined the association between organizational identification and attitudinal constructs (i.e., job involvement, job satisfaction, and affective organizational commitment) by comparing two models. The first model assumed organizational identification, along with job involvement, job satisfaction, and affective organizational commitment, was a component of one's general attitude toward the organization. The second model assumed that organizational identification was an antecedent that helps employees develop a positive general attitude toward an organization, indicated by job involvement, job satisfaction, and affective organizational commitment. The authors ultimately found that the second model had a better model fit to the meta-analytic data than the first model, indicating organizational identification can be regarded as the basis for developing positive attitudes toward the organization.

Finally, organizational identification is positively related to, but distinguishable from, different forms of identification in the workplace, such as supervisor identification (e.g., Zhang & Chen, 2013), team identification (e.g., Bartels et al., 2007; Christ et al., 2003; van Dick et al., 2008), and professional identification (e.g., Bamber & Iyer, 2002; Bartels et al., 2010). Studies have not only shown that different forms of identification have differential associations with the same or different outcomes (e.g., Deng, Coyle-Shapiro, & Yang, 2018; Hekman et al., 2009b; Olkkonen & Lipponen, 2006; Zhang & Chen, 2013), but also that organizational identification has an interactional effect with other forms of identification in predicting employee outcomes (e.g., Hekman et al., 2009a; Hekman, et al., 2009b; van Dick et al., 2008).

# Nomological Network of Organizational Identification

## Antecedents of Organizational Identification

Scholars have examined a wide range of theoretical antecedents of organizational identification. Below, we place antecedents into four categories: (1) individual factors (e.g., demographics and individuals' work perceptions and feelings), (2) job factors (e.g., task and social characteristics of the job), (3) leadership factors (e.g., leadership styles and leader-member exchange), and (4) organizational factors (e.g., external views of the organization and internal practices).

### Individual Factors

The individual antecedents of organizational identification include demographic variables (e.g., age and tenure), as well as individuals' perceptions and feelings about their jobs (e.g., person-job fit). In terms of demographic variables, research has examined tenure, age, employment status, and minority status. Tenure may be positively related to organizational identification due to the increased organizational contact that comes with greater tenure (Dutton, Dukerich, & Harquail, 1994). As contact with the organization increases, individuals come to understand the "collective organizational identity" better, and they are better able to define themselves in terms of the organization (Dutton et al., 1994, p. 247). In a meta-analysis (Riketta, 2005), tenure had a positive but weak correlation with organizational identification. Because the meaning of long tenure might be different for those who climb the hierarchical ladder and move into the core of the organization versus those who stay in the periphery, tenure may not be a good predictor of who is more likely to have a stronger organizational identification. Age has also been found to have a positive but weak association with organizational identification in two meta-analytic studies (Ng & Feldman, 2010; Riketta, 2005). One explanation for the link between age and organizational identification concerns socioemotional selectivity theory; as individuals get older, they select themselves into organizations that maximize social and emotional gains and minimize social and emotional losses (Carstensen, 1992). Through that selection process, older individuals may be more likely to end up in organizations that make them feel comfortable and naturally inclined to identify. Employment status (i.e., limited-term vs. permanent) can also shape one's organizational identification. For instance, a study of workers from a large international service organization found that having a limited-term work contract as opposed to a more open-ended, permanent contract was negatively associated with organizational identification (Johnson & Ashforth, 2008).

Moving on to individuals' work perceptions and feelings about their jobs, several factors may serve as antecedents of organizational identification. For instance, research has shown a sense of fit, such as person-organization fit (Anaza, 2015; Cable & Derue, 2002; Demir, Demir, & Nield, 2015) and person-job fit (Anaza, 2015; Saks & Ashforth, 1997), is positively related to organizational identification because employees with a higher sense of fit can more easily form a perception of oneness with the organization. Positive feelings, such as satisfaction with the organization (Mael & Ashforth, 1992; Pratt, 1998) and passion for the work (Astakhova & Porter, 2015), can also promote organizational identification because they signal a promising fit with the organization that motivates individuals to internalize their organizational memberships. By contrast, negative feelings, such as relative deprivation (Cho, Lee, & Kim, 2014), cynicism (Bedeian, 2007), and workplace ostracism (Wu et al., 2016), can undermine employees' organizational identification because employees tend to distance themselves from entities where they have been or could be mistreated.

### Job Factors

Beginning with job design, research demonstrates that job challenge (Carmeli, Cohen-Meitar, & Elizur, 2007) and job autonomy (Bamber & Iyer, 2002) are positively related to organizational identification. These findings suggest that individuals who have enriched tasks and freedom to take the initiative on the job are more likely to identify with their organizations. Additionally, the extent to which the job is designed to be physically isolated or distant from the organization may also affect organizational identification. In a study of virtual employees, for example, researchers found that physical isolation was negatively associated with employees' perceptions of respect in the organization, and thus with their organizational identification (Bartel, Wrzesniewski, & Wiesenfeld, 2012). Similarly, a study by Wieseke et al., (2012) revealed that physical distance from the company's corporate headquarters was associated with reduced organizational identification in a sample of salespeople. The social characteristics of jobs also play a role. For example, involvement in social outreach efforts through one's job and employing organization may enhance one's identification with the organization (Bartel, 2001). Other social characteristics of the job that may promote organizational identification include frequent electronic communication in the context of virtual work (Wiesenfeld, Raghuram, & Garud, 1999), as well as the provision of formal mentoring (Chen & Wen, 2016).

### Leadership Factors

Several leadership styles tend to foster organizational identification among followers, including charismatic leadership (Lindblom, Kajalo, & Mitronen, 2016), ethical leadership (DeConinck, 2015; Demirtas et al., 2017; Walumbwa et al., 2011), servant leadership (de Sousa & van Dierendonck, 2014; Zhang et al., 2012), and self-sacrificial leadership (Li, Zhang, & Tian, 2016). Research findings suggest followers may be more inclined to define themselves in terms of the organization when they perceive the leader as charismatic (Lindblom et al., 2016) and when they are able to see that ethics are central to the organization's values, as embodied by the ethical nature of the organization's leader. Transformational and transactional leadership are also positively associated with followers' organizational identification (Effelsberg, Solga, & Gurt, 2014; Epitropaki & Martin, 2005), with transformational leadership being the more beneficial of the two (Epitropaki & Martin, 2005). Research findings suggest organizational members more readily identify with the organization when the leader goes beyond simply clarifying performance expectations and role responsibilities, and instead acts as a role model who inspires, stimulates, and considers members' individual needs (Epitropaki & Martin, 2005). Leaders who are high in humility also tend to encourage followers' organizational identification (Li et al., 2018), perhaps because organizational members are more likely to develop a sense of belongingness when leaders highlight their strengths and demonstrate concern for their well-being. Research has also found leaders' own organizational identification predicts employees' organizational identification (Van Dick et al., 2007), likely because leaders with can emphasize the value of being an organizational member and cultivate followers' sense of oneness.

The quality of social exchange between the leader and organizational member (LMX) is a final leadership-related antecedent of organizational identification (e.g., Jungbauer et al., 2018; Katrinli et al., 2008; Loi, Chan, & Lam, 2014; Lu & Sun, 2017). Because employees often perceive supervisors as agents representing the organization, employees who have high-quality LMX relationships with their supervisors tend to see themselves as in-group, valued members of the organization. In turn, they tend to identify more strongly with the organization than those employees who have lower quality LMX relationships.

*Organizational Factors*

Research has also investigated a range of organizational factors as antecedents of organizational identification. These antecedents can be classified into two broader categories: external views of organizations and internal practices.

Antecedents pertaining to external views of organizations include perceptions of the organization's prestige, distinctiveness, reputation, and stereotypes. Organizational prestige is positively associated with employees' levels of organizational identification (e.g., Bartels, Pruyn, & de Jong, 2009; Bartels et al., 2007; Fuller et al., 2006) because employees may identify more strongly with respected, admired, and well-regarded organizations as a way to enhance their self-esteem. Members' beliefs about the organization's central, distinct, and enduring attributes (Dutton et al., 1994), such as organizational distinctiveness (Mael & Ashforth, 1992), reputation (Baer et al., 2018), and stereotypes (Bergami & Bagozzi, 2000), can also be antecedents of organizational identification because such organizational characteristics help individuals differentiate themselves from others outside of the organization.

An organization's internal practices, such as corporate social responsibility (De Roeck & Delobbe, 2012; Goswami et al., 2018), socialization practices (Ashforth & Saks, 1996), and fair practices (e.g., Cho & Treadway, 2011; Dunford, Jackson, Boss, Tay, & Boss, 2015; Frenkel, Restubog, & Bednall, 2012; He, Zhu, & Zheng, 2014), also play a role. These internal practices, in brief, help construct a sense of positivity and belongingness, which motivates employees to identify with their organizations. Organizations can also directly shape employees' organizational identification via managing their psychological contract (i.e., employees' beliefs regarding the terms and conditions of a reciprocal exchange agreement with their employers) (Rousseau, 1989). Because the breach or fulfillment of a psychological contract shapes the quality of the employee-organization relationship, it can reduce (Epitropaki, 2013; Kreiner & Ashforth, 2004) or enhance (Ali Arain et al,, 2018) the extent to which employees define themselves in terms of the organizational membership.

## Consequences of Organizational Identification

Researchers have conducted numerous studies to examine the positive and negative consequences of organizational identification for individual employees. We review each aspect in order.

### Bright Side of Organizational Identification

Because employees tend to devote themselves to their work and the organization when being an organizational member is important to defining who they are, the literature has found that organizational identification shapes positive employee attitudes in organizations, such as job involvement, job satisfaction, organizational commitment (see Lee et al., 2015, for a meta-analysis study), higher work engagement (He et al., 2014; Karanika-Murray et al., 2015), and lower turnover intentions (Bilinska, Wegge, & Kliegel, 2016; Das, Dharwadkar, & Brandes, 2008).

Organizational identification is also linked to positive performance and behavior such as greater work effort (Bartel, 2001; Lu & Sun, 2017), higher job performance (Chughtai & Buckley, 2010; Finch et al., 2018), and organizational citizenship behavior (Bell & Menguc, 2002; Cho & Treadway, 2011; Dukerich, Golden, & Shortell, 2002; Wu et al., 2016), as well as more continuous actions to improve work processes (Lee, 2004), higher readiness for change (Hameed, Roques, & Ali Arain, 2013), and lower organizational deviance (Al-Atwi & Bakir, 2014). A recent meta-analysis revealed organizational identification is positively related to both extra-role and in-role behaviors; the mean correlation between identification and in-role behaviors (e.g., job performance, productivity, and customer-oriented service behavior) was .27, whereas the mean correlation between identification and extra-role behavioral outcomes (e.g., organizational citizenship behavior, helping behavior, and voice behavior) was .42 (Lee et al., 2015). These findings provide evidence that organizational identification is linked to beneficial behavioral consequences, especially extra-role behavioral consequences.

In general, the effects of organizational identification on attitudinal and behavioral outcomes are observed in samples with different cultural backgrounds, showing that organizational identification is a significant predictor of important work-related outcomes across cultural contexts. For example, higher organizational identification is associated with lower turnover intentions in studies directly comparing samples of Japanese and British employees (Abrams, Ando, & Hinkle, 1998). Nevertheless, in a meta-analytic study, Lee et al. (2015) found the effects of organizational identification on attitudinal and behavioral outcomes were stronger in studies that were conducted in collectivist cultures than in studies that were conducted in individualist cultures, perhaps because employees from collectivist cultures are more prone to define who they are based on their group membership.

Finally, because humans have a fundamental need to belong (Baumeister & Leary, 1995; Ryan & Deci, 2000), a stronger organizational identification, which reflects a stronger sense of belongingness to an organization, can fulfill employees' need to belong and contribute to employee well-being. In line with this view, organizational identification has been linked to better psychological well-being after job loss owing to a personal reason (Tosti-Kharas, 2012), higher organization-based self-esteem (Bergami & Bagozzi, 2000), and lower emotional exhaustion (Baer et al., 2018).

*Dark Side of Organizational Identification*

Organizational identification is not always associated with positive feelings or outcomes. It can be associated with negative experiences and outcomes, depending on the organizational context and the presence of any identity threats. For instance, in a qualitative study of Penn State alumni identification in the wake of the Jerry Sandusky scandal, Eury et al. (2018) found the identified alumni experienced positive emotions toward the organization before the scandal (e.g., pride, love, and favorable feelings), but negative emotions toward the organization during the scandal (e.g., shame, embarrassment, and anger), and contradictory emotions toward the organization looking ahead to the future (e.g., love and embarrassment). In addition, across two studies of Chinese medical employees, Deng, Coyle-Shapiro, and Yang (2018) found that employees with a stronger organizational identification are more vulnerable to psychological contract violation, an emotional manifestation of a broken promise by one's organization (Morrison & Robinson, 1997), by experiencing a significant loss of mental energy and regulatory resources.

In addition, evidence suggests a strong organizational identification may endanger a compulsive and unhealthy work ethic among employees. For example, Avanzi et al. (2012) report a curvilinear link between organizational identification and workaholism—the felt obligation and compulsion to work incessantly beyond one's formal role requirements. The researchers found that the association between organizational identification and workaholism was negative at first but became positive when identification was strong. This negative implication is perhaps unsurprising considering the positive link between organizational identification and extra-role performance, and the notion that workaholism involves transcending one's formal role requirements. This finding shows a too-much-of-a-good-thing effect (Pierce & Aguinis, 2013) of organizational identification. Strong organizational identification may also reduce creativity (Rotondi, 1974, 1975) and hinder initiatives that diverge from accepted norms in the organization (Bouchikhi & Kimberly, 2003), because it may lead employees to reinforce, rather than challenge, their existing views of the organization and themselves. Additionally, strong organizational identification may induce a propensity to engage in unethical behaviors that serve the organization's interests (Chen, Chen, & Sheldon, 2016) because employees with strong organizational identification may be more concerned with benefitting the organization than with any ethical consequences.

## Measurements of Organizational Identification

Researchers have used a variety of measurement tools to assess individuals' levels of organizational identification. Below, we review four measurement tools that assess identification by asking employees to indicate their agreement with various statements. Two of these tools are commonly used, unidimensional measurements (Cheney, 1983; Mael & Ashforth, 1992), and the other two are measurements based on a multidimensional structure (Edwards & Peccei, 2007; Stoner, Perrewé, & Hofacker, 2011). We then review a measurement tool that assesses identification in a visual, graphic format (Bergami & Bagozzi, 2000).

### *The Mael Scale*

The Mael scale (Mael & Ashforth, 1992) is the most commonly used instrument, whether in its original form or an adapted form (Lee et al., 2015; Riketta, 2005). The six items (see Table 5.2) that constitute the Mael scale derive from a previously developed, 10-item scale measuring "Identification with a Psychological Group" (Mael, 1988). The six-item version of the Mael scale was initially used in a 1992 study to measure alumni's identification with their alma mater (Mael & Ashforth, 1992). This scale showed good internal consistency reliability ($\alpha = .87$) in the study. The scale has been adapted, as follows, to measure individuals' identification with the organization on a 5-point scale (1 = *Strongly agree*, 5= *Strongly disagree*). A total score is used to indicate the level of organizational identification.

*Table 5.2* The Mael Scale

| |
|---|
| 1. When someone criticizes [name of organization], it feels like a personal insult. |
| 2. I am very interested in what others think about [name of organization]. |
| 3. When I talk about this organization, I usually say "we" rather than "they." |
| 4. This organization's successes are my successes. |
| 5. When someone praises this organization, it feels like a personal compliment. |
| 6. If a story in the media criticized the organization, I would feel embarrassed. |

*Source:* Items retrieved from Mael & Ashforth (1992).

## Organizational Identification Questionnaire (OIQ)

This scale by Cheney (1982) was the second most common scale, following the Mael scale, and was actually more common than the Mael scale in research from the communications discipline (Riketta, 2005). The OIQ has 25 items capturing three components of identification suggested by Patchen (1970): (a) similarity of values, (b) membership, and (c) loyalty toward the organization. Although items in this scale were developed based on the three components, Cheney (1982) did not examine the factor structure of the items but only used a total or average score to indicate the level of organizational identification. Table 5.3 presents items in the OIQ. They were assessed with a 7-point scale in Cheney's (1983) study and had higher internal-consistency reliability ($\alpha = .95$).

## Edwards and Peccei's Scale

Edwards and Peccei (2007) measured organizational identification with six items that were intended to capture three dimensions of organizational identification (i.e., self-categorization and labeling; sharing organizational goals and values; sense of attachment, belonging, and membership of the organization). The three dimensions are key features of organizational identification highlighted in the literature and capture affective and cognitive components of organizational identification. Edwards and Peccei (2007) used them to develop items that individually have specific meanings but collectively capture a comprehensive conceptualization of organizational identification. They examined the factor structure of the six items and found that a three-factor model based on the three dimensions fit better than a one-factor model. However, they found the three factors were highly correlated and did not have differential associations with other variables such as justice and work involvement. They thus suggest using a total score but not three subscale scores to indicate the level of organizational identification. The internal consistency reliability of this scale was .89 in Study 1 and .93 in Study 2 (Edwards & Peccei, 2007). The items are shown in Table 5.4, adapted to a general organizational context. Likert-type scales were used with 5-point responses ranging from "strongly disagree" to "strongly agree" (Edwards, 2009).

*Table 5.3* The Organizational Identification Questionnaire

Think of your role as an employee of [organization]. For each item below, select the answer that best represents your belief about or attitude toward [organization]. Please respond to all the items. The possible responses are:

YES! I agree very strongly with the statement.

YES I agree strongly with the statement.

yes I agree with the statement.

? I neither agree nor disagree with the statement.

No I disagree with the statement.

NO I disagree strongly with the statement.

NO! I disagree very strongly with the statement.

1. *I would probably continue working for [Organization X] even if I didn't need the salary.*
2. *In general, the people employed by [Organization X] are working towards the same goals.*
3. *I am very proud to be an employee of [Organization X].*
4. *[Organization X]'s image in the community represents me well.*
5. *I often describe myself to others by saying, "I work for [Organization X]" or "I am from [Organization X]."*
6. *I try to make on-the-job decisions by considering the consequences of my actions for [Organization X].*
7. *We at [Organization X] are different from others in our field.*
8. *I am glad I chose to work for [Organization X] rather than another company.*
9. *I talk up [Organization X] to my friends as a great company to work for.*
10. *In general, I view [Organization X]'s problems as my problems.*
11. *I am willing to put in a great deal of effort beyond that normally expected to help [Organization X] be successful.*
12. *I become irritated when I hear others outside [Organization X] criticize the company.*
13. *I have warm feelings toward [Organization X] as a place to work.*
14. *I would be quite willing to spend the rest of my career with [Organization X].*
15. *I feel that [Organization X] cares about me.*
16. *The record of [Organization X] is an example of what dedicated people can achieve.*
17. *I have a lot in common with others employed by [Organization X].*
18. *I find it difficult to agree with [Organization X]'s policies on important matters relating to me. (reverse scored)*
19. *My association with [Organization X] is only a small part of who I am. (reverse scored)*
20. *I like to tell others about projects that [Organization X] is working on.*
21. *I find that my values and the values of [Organization X] are very similar.*
22. *I feel very little loyalty to [Organization X]. (reverse scored)*
23. *I would describe [Organization X] as a large "family" in which most members feel a sense of belonging.*
24. *I find it easy to identify with [Organization X].*
25. *I really care about the fate of [Organization X].*

*Source:* Reprinted with permission from Cheney (1982).

*Table 5.4* The Edwards and Peccei (2007) Scale

---

1. *My employment in [Organization X] is a big part of who I am.* [self-categorization and labeling]
2. *I consider myself an [Organization X] person.* [self-categorization and labeling]
3. *What [Organization X] stands for is important to me.* [sharing organizational goals and values]
4. *I share the goals and values of [Organization X].* [sharing organizational goals and values]
5. *My membership of [Organization X] is important to me.* [belongingness and membership]
6. *I feel strong ties with [Organization X].* [belongingness and membership]

---

*Source:* Items retrieved from Edwards & Peccei (2007).

## Multidimensional Identity Scale

This scale, developed by Stoner et al. (2011), contains 15 items that reflect four components of organizational identification: (a) self-categorization, (b) goodness of fit, (c) affective attachment, and (d) behavioral involvement. These four dimensions altogether capture cognitive, affective, and behavioral features of organizational identification. Stoner et al. (2011) have conducted an exploratory and confirmatory factor analysis to validate a four-factor structure based on the four dimensions. Correlations among the four factors were modest. Nevertheless, they also used a total score but not subscale scores to indicate the level of organizational identification. In their study, respondents indicated their agreement with these items on a 5-point scale (1 = *Strongly disagree*, 5 = *Strongly agree*). The internal-consistency reliability of the four subscales ranged from .69 to .87 in Stoner et al.'s (2011) Study 1. These items are shown in Table 5.5, adapted toward a general organizational context.

## Cognitive Organizational Identification Scale

Unlike the previous four measurements we reviewed, the two-item "Cognitive Organizational Identification" scale (Bergami & Bagozzi, 2000) (see Table 5.6) includes a visual, graphic item in addition to an item that is purely verbal. The visual item asks respondents to indicate the degree to which their identity overlaps with the organization's identity by selecting the Venn diagram that best reflects this overlap. See Table 5.6 for this visual item, which was used to measure respondents' identification with an organization called "CAMST" in the original study (Bergami & Bagozzi, 2000). Then, the verbal item asks respondents to indicate the degree to which their self-image overlaps with the organization's image using a 7-point scale (1 = *Not at all*, 7 = *Very much*), and may be adapted toward any organization in the following format: "Please indicate to what degree your self-image overlaps with [Organization X]'s image." The reliability of the two-item scale was .71 in the original study (Bergami &

*Table 5.5* Multidimensional Identity Scale

1. *I am a member of this [organization].* [Self-Categorization]
2. *I consider myself a member of this [organization].* [Self-Categorization]
3. *If asked if I belong to this [organization], I would say "Yes."* [Self-Categorization]
4. *I do not consider myself a member of this [organization]. (reverse scored)* [Self-Categorization]
5. *I perceive myself to be similar to other members of this [organization].* [Goodness of Fit]
6. *I have attributes traits, features, and behaviors that are normal for a member of this [organization].* [Goodness of Fit]
7. *I represent a typical member of this [organization].* [Goodness of Fit]
8. *I am like other members of this [organization].* [Goodness of Fit]
9. *When something bad happens to this [organization], I personally feel hurt.* [Affective-Attachment]
10. *When this [organization] is in pain, I empathize.* [Affective-Attachment]
11. *I have a feeling of connection with this [organization].* [Affective-Attachment]
12. *I am personally concerned about what happens to other members of this [organization].* [Affective-Attachment]
13. *At work, I decorate my "office space" with pictures pertaining to this [organization].* [Behavioral Involvement]
14. *At home, I have lots of [organization] paraphernalia.* [Behavioral Involvement]
15. *I display objects (i.e., bumper stickers, pins, T-shirts) that illustrate that I am member of this [organization].* [Behavioral Involvement]

*Source:* Items retrieved from Stoner, Perrewé, & Hofacker (2011).

Bagozzi, 2000). The development of the COI also ultimately paved the way for the development of an alternative, visual measure of organizational identification known as the "Graphic Scale of Organizational Identification" (Shamir & Kark, 2004).

As reviewed above, different measurements of organizational identification contain different elements in their assessments. A significant debate centers on the inclusion of items that assess individuals' emotional response to organizational membership, because these items may reflect organizational commitment. For instance, several items included in OIQ assess the individual's emotional response to membership in the organization (e.g., "I have warm feelings toward [Organization X] as a place to work"), which is very similar to items for assessing organizational commitment. For this reason, a recent meta-analysis of the organizational identification literature (Lee et al., 2015) excluded studies that had used the OIQ to measure organizational identification. This issue with the OIQ reflects a broader tension in the organizational identification literature between scholars who view organizational identification as strictly cognitive (e.g., Bergami & Bagozzi, 2000; Dutton et al., 1994; Lee et al., 2015) and those who view identification as also having an affective component (e.g., Ashforth et al., 2008; Cheney, 1983; Johnson, Morgeson, & Hekman, 2012; Stoner et al., 2011).

*Table 5.6* Cognitive Organizational Identification Scale

---

**The visual item**

Imagine that one of the circles at the left in each row represents your own self-definition or identity and the role circle at the tight represents CAMST's identity. Please indicate which case (A, B, C, D, E, F, G or H) best describes the level of overlap between your own and CAMST's identities.

Me      CAMST

A — Far Apart

B — Close Together but Separate

C — Very Small Overlap

D — Small Overlap

E — Moderate Overlap

F — Large Overlap

G — Very Large Overlap

H — Complete Overlap

**The verbal item**

Please indicate to what degree your self-image overlaps with Camst's image on a 7-point scale (1 = Not at all, 4 = moderately, 7 = very much).

---

*Source*: Reprinted with permission from Bergami & Bagozzi (2000).

## Directions For Future Research

Although organizational identification has been studied extensively, we identify issues that should be further addressed, including multilevel examinations, identification with multiple organizations, and organizational identification in a global business context.

### *Multilevel Examinations*

We advocate for a multilevel examination of organizational identification to understand how factors at different levels from the individual to the organization can shape one's organizational identification, and in turn, how organizational identification can bring consequences at different levels. Research so far has identified antecedents of organizational identification at different levels (e.g., individual characteristics, job-design factors, leadership, and organizational characteristics and practices). However, the literature has not used a multilevel design to examine how these multilevel factors would jointly affect one's organizational identification. For example, how will inconsistent experiences between different levels shape employees' organizational identification? As we reviewed above, employees tend to identify more strongly with prestigious organizations. However, what happens to employees in prestigious organizations who are not treated fairly or are ostracized by their colleagues? Do feelings of ambivalence arising from this inconsistency push employees away from identifying the organization? How do employees reconcile these inconsistent experiences? The answers to these questions are practically relevant yet poorly understood due to a lack of multilevel perspective and examination in the literature. Ashforth and Schinoff (2016) drew on interpretive research to describe the process of identity construction in organizations through sense-breaking and sense-giving, which could provide a lens to help us understand how employees identify with their organizations when different experiences are taken into account.

We also advocate for a multilevel examination in terms of consequences of organizational identification. So far, researchers mainly focus on the effects of organizational identification on employees' work attitudes and behaviors or outcomes at the individual levels. Nevertheless, would having stronger organizational identification affect operation and thus outcomes at the dyadic, team, and organizational level? For example, in the leadership context at the dyadic level, will strong organizational identification motivate followers to accept and react to leaders' expectations? Would leaders be more likely to provide resources and support for followers who have higher organizational identification in turn, and thus build better leader-member exchange relationships? Although the quality of leader-member exchange relationships has been viewed as an antecedent of organizational identification, we argue it can be the outcome of organizational identification, and both shape each other in the leadership dynamics at the dyadic level.

At the team level, how can the collective levels of organizational identification among team members shape the team process, such as cohesion, communication, and coordination, and thus team outcomes? What happens if members of the same team vary in their levels of organizational identification? How will such variation influence the team process, and thus team performance? Kraus et al., (2015) reported that agreement between sales managers' and salespersons' organizational identification is beneficial to the salesperson's performance and customer satisfaction. In contrast, differences between sales managers' and salespersons' organizational identification can undermine the salesperson's performance and customer satisfaction. We speculate that such effects could also occur in a team context because agreement or differences in organizational identification across team members can determine working relationships between team members and influence the team processes and outcomes. In addition to processes and outcomes within a team, organizational identification can play a role in shaping inter-team or group dynamics. For example, in a sample consisting of 92 teams from an organization, Porck and colleagues (in press) found that a group's organizational identification helps enhance intergroup strategic consensus, but such an effect will be undermined when groups possess stronger group identification. The authors replicated the same effects in a sample consisting of 37 teams from another organization. We encourage future studies to unpack the role of organizational identification in shaping team or inter-team dynamics and outcomes.

At the organizational level, how do the collective levels of organizational identification across all employees shape organizational-level activities and outcomes? Although strong organizational identification might have a detrimental effect on the organization's capacity to engage in radical changes that considerably reshape the identity of the organization, strong organizational identification may facilitate the flexible exchange of resources (e.g., knowledge) among organization members through generalized social exchange. Generalized exchange is a collective form of social exchange that takes place in a social group with three or more members, and in this form, participants do not receive reciprocation directly from the one who receives resources from them, but indirectly from someone in the group (Levine & Prietula, 2012; Molm, 2003; Yamagishi & Cook, 1993; Yoshikawa, Wu, & Lee, 2019). Generalized exchange is particularly valuable for large organizations because unlike dyadic forms of social exchange, it can facilitate a more flexible flow of resources among a large number of employees beyond established social ties (Levine & Prietula, 2012). Because organizational identification blurs the distinction between self-interests and other-interests, knowledge and resource exchange across employees will likely be more prominent in organizations with a higher collective level of organizational identification, which then contributes to organizational operation and performance. So far, only Millward and Postmes (2010) have empirically examined the association between organizational identification and organizational outcomes by reporting a positive association between customer business managers' organizational identification and sales turnover of the business unit across 51 units. More studies are needed to understand how organizational identification can shape organizational outcomes.

### Identification with Multiple Organizations

Studies that we reviewed largely assume one person has only a single target of organizational identification, whereas in contemporary organizations, there are opportunities that individuals can identify with different organizations. First, in multinational corporations (MNCs), one typically belongs simultaneously to a subsidiary (or the headquarters) and its parent MNC. Both are typically considered organizations in day-to-day conversation, and evidence suggests individuals develop distinct identification with the subsidiary they work for and the parent MNC (Reade, 2001a, 2001b; Smale et al., 2015; Vora & Kostova, 2007). Such dual identification might be distinct, compound, or nested, and the interplay might have complex consequences for individual attitudes and behaviors toward the subsidiary and the MNC (Vora & Kostova, 2007). Second, the increase of agency workers who work for one organization while being employed by another (Buch, Kuvaas, & Dysvik, 2010) and freelancers, who may simultaneously join multiple projects in different organizations, also create opportunities for those workers to develop identification with multiple organizations. Third, individuals might also maintain identification with organizations that they previously worked for, along with identification with the current organization. Many organizations invest in the development and maintenance of alumni networks, and interactions with other alumni in such networks stimulate individuals' identity as an "ex-" member of the organization (Bardon, Josserand, & Villesèche, 2015). How does identification with different organizations shape their behaviors and attitudes, interplaying with their identification with the current organization? Overall, the literature has paid little attention to these emerging issues, and we posit that investigations into such multiple targets of identification will expand the literature of organizational identification and further promote its relevance to contemporary organizations.

### Organizational Identification in a Global Business Context

Future studies can also explore the function of organizational identification in a global business context. The growth of global business and multinational corporations (MNCs) may pose a unique challenge of dual identification (Lee, 2014; Reade, 2001b; Vora, Kostova, & Roth, 2007). Individuals working for foreign MNCs may be encouraged to identify with the local subsidiary organization as well as the global MNC, and the interests of the global MNC and local organization may not always be perfectly aligned, thus leading to dilemmas of dual identification for local employees. Furthermore, organizational identification in a global business context may be even more complex when national identity comes into play (Vaara, Tienari, & Koveshnikov, in press) because working with MNCs can create tension between one's organizational and national identity if the values, norms, and practices of the firm do not align with what local employees are accustomed to in the national cultural context. Supporting this view, Das, Dharwadkar, and Brandes (2008), in their study of Indian call center workers, found the centrality of national identity (i.e., "the extent to which individuals define themselves by their citizenship or the subjective importance of one's national identity in the hierarchy of different social identities," p. 1507) moderates the effect of organizational identification on employee performance. In such a context, national (Indian) identity has different values, norms, and practices than those embedded in the organizational identity of being a worker in a global call center. Specifically, they found that organizational identification is positively related to employee performance among workers with lower national identity centrality but is negatively related to employee performance among those with higher national identity centrality. The extant literature suggests local employees who have cosmopolitan orientation (Lee, 2015) can transcend the conventionally defined values, norms, and ways of doing things, and are less conflicted in these dilemmas and are more likely to identify and commit to the MNC (Lee & Reade, 2018). Furthermore, local employees of minority status tend to be more attracted to foreign MNCs and are likely to identify with them more strongly, compared to non-minority individuals, because foreign firms are less embedded in the national context and thus are relatively free from the local-specific social prejudices and biases (Reade & Lee, 2012).

Another possible circumstance under which an employee's culture may significantly affect his or her organizational identification concerns the employee's possession of multiple cultural identities (i.e., individuals who identify themselves as members of multiple cultures). For such employees, the relationship between multicultural identification and personal, social, and task outcomes will be stronger if the organization adopts a multiculturalism ideology and weaker if the organization adopts a color-blindness ideology that downplays cultural differences and emphasizes shared characteristics (Fitzsimmons, 2013). All in all, our review suggests that managing employees' organizational identification thus becomes a more significant issue than performance management in a global setting.

## Practical Implications of Organizational Identification

Based on what we know so far from studies on organizational identification, we offer several implications for practice. Firstly, although organizational identification reflects employees' self-conception, organizations and managers have multiple ways (as we reviewed earlier on the antecedents of organizational identification) to cultivate employees' organizational identification. In addition to considering using specific or different approaches to shape employees' organizational identification, organizations and managers may want to pay attention to whether those adopted approaches provide experiences that can consistently cultivate employees' organizational identification.

Second, whereas organizational identification is associated with various positive employee attitudinal and behavioral outcomes, it also can lead to negative consequences, especially when organizational identification becomes too strong. The dilemma for organizations and managers is how to maintain employees' organizational identification at the level at which employees will be neither too rigid to explore new activities and reshape the conception of the organization, nor too preoccupied with the organization's interests that their work-life balance and ethical responsibilities to other stakeholders are compromised.

Third, organizations and managers should not neglect the fact that employees have different degrees of organizational identification and that different employees may value social identities other than the one they have with the organization. For instance, as we mentioned earlier, employees' national identities can play a role in shaping employees' work attitudes and behavior in a global business context. Organizations and managers thus must pay attention to more than the development and the function of organizational identification, because organizational identification is one of an employee's social identities, but not the only one.

Finally, organizational identification not only functions at the individual level. As indicated earlier, several studies have shown that organizational identification can shape dyadic dynamics between leaders and followers and inter-group dynamics within an organization. Although more studies are needed to discover the function of organizational identification beyond the individual level, organizations and managers could consider how to leverage the function of organizational identification to facilitate organizational operations at different levels.

## Conclusion

In this chapter, we reviewed studies on organizational identification, identified gaps in the literature, and offered directions for future research. Whereas the existing studies mainly concern organizational identification at the individual level, we encourage future research to extend studies to different contexts with a multilevel lens within and beyond the organization level. Ultimately, organizational identification not only matters for individual employees, but also has implications for leadership dynamics, team functioning, and organizational operations on a global scale.

# References

Abrams, D., Ando, K., & Hinkle, S. (1998). Psychological attachment to the group: Cross-cultural differences in organizational identification and subjective norms as predictors of workers' turnover intentions. *Personality and Social Psychology Bulletin, 24,* 1027–1039. doi: dx.doi.org/10.1177/01461672982410001

Al-Atwi, A.A. & Bakir, A. (2014). Relationships between status judgments, identification, and counterproductive behavior. *Journal of Managerial Psychology, 29,* 472–489. doi: 10.1108/JMP-02-2012-0040

Ali Arain, G., Bukhari, S., Hameed, I., Lacaze, D.M., & Bukhari, Z. (2018). Am I treated better than my co-worker? A moderated mediation analysis of psychological contract fulfillment, organizational identification, and voice. *Personnel Review, 47,* 1138–1156. doi: 10.1108/PR-04-2016-0090

Allen, N.J. & Meyer, J.P. (1990). The measurement and antecedents of affective, continuance and normative commitment to the organization. *Journal of Occupational Psychology, 63,* 1–18. doi: 10.1111/j.2044-8325.1990.tb00506.x

Anaza, N.A. (2015). Relations of fit and organizational identification to employee-customer identification. *Journal of Managerial Psychology, 30,* 925–939. doi: 10.1108/JMP-12-2012-0389

Ashforth, B.E., Harrison, S.H., & Corley, K.G. (2008). Identification in organizations: An examination of four fundamental questions. *Journal of Management, 34,* 325–374. doi: doi.org/10.1177/0149206308316059

Ashforth, B.E. & Mael, F. (1989). Social identity theory and the organization. *Academy of Management Review, 14,* 20–39. doi: doi.org/10.2307/258189

Ashforth, B.E. & Saks, A.M. (1996). Socialization tactics: Longitudinal effects on newcomer adjustment. *Academy of Management Journal, 39,* 149–178. doi: dx.doi.org/10.2307/256634

Ashforth, B.E. & Schinoff, B.S. (2016). Identity under construction: How individuals come to define themselves in organizations. *Annual Review of Organizational Psychology and Organizational Behavior, 3,* 111–137. doi: 10.1146/annurev-orgpsych-041015-062322

Astakhova, M.N. & Porter, G. (2015). Understanding the work passion–performance relationship: The mediating role of organizational identification and moderating role of fit at work. *Human Relations, 68,* 1315–1346. doi: 10.1177/0018726714555204

Avanzi, L., van Dick, R., Fraccaroli, F., & Sarchielli, G. (2012). The downside of organizational identification: Relations between identification, workaholism and well-being. *Work & Stress, 26,* 289–307. doi: 10.1080/02678373.2012.712291

Baer, M.D., Bundy, J., Garud, N., & Kim, J.K. (2018). The benefits and burdens of organizational reputation for employee well-being: A conservation of resources approach. *Personnel Psychology, 71,* 571–595. doi: 10.1111/peps.12276

Bamber, E.M. & Iyer, V.M. (2002). Big 5 Auditors' Professional and Organizational Identification: Consistency or Conflict? *Auditing: A Journal of Practice & Theory, 21,* 21–38. doi: doi.org/10.2308/aud.2002.21.2.21

Bardon, T., Josserand, E., & Villesèche, F. (2015). Beyond nostalgia: Identity work in corporate alumni networks. *Human Relations, 68*, 583–606. doi: 10.1177/0018726714532967

Barnard, C.I. (1938/1968). *The functions of the executive* (30th anniversary ed.). Cambridge, MA: Harvard University Press.

Bartel, C.A. (2001). Social comparisons in boundary-spanning work: Effects of community outreach on members' organizational identity and identification. *Administrative Science Quarterly, 46*, 379–414. doi: doi.org/10.2307/3094869

Bartel, C.A., Wrzesniewski, A., & Wiesenfeld, B.M. (2012). Knowing where you stand: Physical isolation, perceived respect, and organizational identification among virtual employees. *Organization Science, 23*, 743–757. doi: dx.doi.org/10.1287/orsc.1110.0661

Bartels, J., Peters, O., de Jong, M., Pruyn, A., & van der Molen, M. (2010). Horizontal and vertical communication as determinants of professional and organisational identification. *Personnel Review, 39*, 210–226. doi: dx.doi.org/10.1108/00483481011017426

Bartels, J., Pruyn, A., & de Jong, M. (2009). Employee identification before and after an internal merger: A longitudinal analysis. *Journal of Occupational & Organizational Psychology, 82*, 113–128. doi: doi.org/10.1348/096317908X283770

Bartels, J., Pruyn, A., de Jong, M., & Joustra, I. (2007). Multiple organizational identification levels and the impact of perceived external prestige and communication climate. *Journal of Organizational Behavior, 28*, 173–190. doi: doi.org/10.1002/job.420

Baumeister, R.F. & Leary, M.R. (1995). The need to belong: Desire for interpersonal attachments as a fundamental human motivation. *Psychological Bulletin, 117*, 497–529. doi: dx.doi.org/10.1037/0033-2909.117.3.497

Bedeian, A.G. (2007). Even if the tower is "Ivory," It isn't "White:" Understanding the consequences of faculty cynicism. *Academy of Management Learning & Education, 6*, 9–32. doi: 10.5465/AMLE.2007.24401700

Bell, S.J. & Menguc, B. (2002). The employee-organization relationship, organizational citizenship behaviors, and superior service quality. *Journal of Retailing, 78*, 131–146. doi: dx.doi.org/10.1016/S0022-4359%2802%2900069-6

Bergami, M. & Bagozzi, R.P. (2000). Self-categorization, affective commitment and group self-esteem as distinct aspects of social identity in the organization. *British Journal of Social Psychology, 39*, 555–577. doi: dx.doi.org/10.1348/014466600164633

Bilinska, P., Wegge, J., & Kliegel, M. (2016). Caring for the elderly but not for one's own old employees? Organizational age climate, age stereotypes, and turnover intentions in young and old nurses. *Journal of Personnel Psychology, 15*, 95–105. doi: dx.doi.org/10.1027/1866-5888/a000144

Bouchikhi, H. & Kimberly, J. (2003). Escaping the identity trap. *MIT Sloan Management Review, 44*, 20–26.

Buch, R., Kuvaas, B., & Dysvik, A. (2010). Dual support in contract workers' triangular employment relationships. *Journal of Vocational Behavior, 77*, 93–103. doi: 10.1016/j.jvb.2010.02.009

Cable, D.M. & Derue, D.S. (2002). The convergent and discriminant validity of subjective fit perceptions. *Journal of Applied Psychology, 87*, 875–884. doi: doi.org/10.1037/0021-9010.87.5.875

Carmeli, A., Cohen-Meitar, R., & Elizur, D. (2007). The role of job challenge and organizational identification in enhancing creative behavior among employees in the workplace. *Journal of Creative Behavior, 41*, 75–90. doi: dx.doi.org/10.1002/j.2162-6057.2007.tb01282.x

Carstensen, L.L. (1992). Social and emotional patterns in adulthood: Support for socioemotional selectivity theory. *Psychology and Aging, 7*, 331–338. doi: 10.1037/0882-7974.7.3.331

Chen, C. & Wen, P. (2016). The effect of mentoring on proteges' organizational deviance. *Psychological Reports, 119*, 200–220. doi: dx.doi.org/10.1177/0033294116659456

Chen, M., Chen, C.C., & Sheldon, O.J. (2016). Relaxing moral reasoning to win: How organizational identification relates to unethical pro-organizational behavior. *Journal of Applied Psychology, 101*, 1082–1096. doi: dx.doi.org/10.1037/apl0000111

Cheney, G. (1982). *Organization identification as a process and product: A field study.* Unpublished master's thesis, Purdue University, West Lafayette, IN.

Cheney, G. (1983). On the various and changing meanings of organizational membership: A field study of organizational identification. *Communication Monographs, 50*, 342–362. doi: 10.1080/03637758309390174

Cho, B., Lee, D., & Kim, K. (2014). How does relative deprivation influence employee intention to leave a merged company? The role of organizational identification. *Human Resource Management, 53*, 421–443. doi: 10.1002/hrm.21580

Cho, J. & Treadway, D.C. (2011). Organizational identification and perceived organizational support as mediators of the procedural justice–citizenship behaviour relationship: A cross-cultural constructive replication. *European Journal of Work & Organizational Psychology, 20*, 631–653. doi: 10.1080/1359432X.2010.487363

Christ, O., Dick, R., Wagner, U., & Stellmacher, J. (2003). When teachers go the extra mile: Foci of organisational identification as determinants of different forms of organisational citizenship behaviour among schoolteachers. *British Journal of Educational Psychology, 73*, 329–341. doi: 10.1348/000709903322275867

Chughtai, A.A. & Buckley, F. (2010). Assessing the effects of organizational identification on in-role job performance and learning behaviour. *Personnel Review, 39*, 242–258. doi: 10.1108/00483481011017444

Cole, M.S. & Bruch, H. (2006). Organizational identity strength, identification, and commitment and their relationships to turnover intention: does organizational hierarchy matter? *Journal of Organizational Behavior, 27*, 585–605. doi: doi.org/10.1002/job.378

Das, D., Dharwadkar, R., & Brandes, P. (2008). The importance of being "Indian": Identity centrality and work outcomes in an off-shored call center in India. *Human Relations, 61*, 1499–1530. doi: doi.org/10.1177/0018726708096636

De Roeck, K. & Delobbe, N. (2012). Do environmental CSR initiatives serve organizations' legitimacy in the oil industry? Exploring employees' reactions through organizational identification theory. *Journal of Business Ethics, 110*, 397–412. doi: dx.doi.org/10.1007/s10551-012-1489-x

de Sousa, M.J.C. & van Dierendonck, D. (2014). Servant leadership and engagement in a merge process under high uncertainty. *Journal of Organizational Change Management, 27*, 877–899. doi: 10.1108/JOCM-07-2013-0133

DeConinck, J.B. (2015). Outcomes of ethical leadership among salespeople. *Journal of Business Research, 68*, 1086–1093. doi: 10.1016/j.jbusres.2014.10.011

Demir, M., Demir, S.S., & Nield, K. (2015). The relationship between person-organization fit, organizational identification and work outcomes. *Journal of Business Economics & Management, 16*, 369–386. doi: 10.3846/16111699.2013.785975

Demirtas, O., Hannah, S., Gok, K., Arslan, A., & Capar, N. (2017). The moderated influence of ethical leadership, via meaningful work, on followers' engagement, organizational identification, and envy. *Journal of Business Ethics, 145*, 183–199. doi: 10.1007/s10551-015-2907-7

Deng, H., Coyle-Shapiro, J., & Yang, Q. (2018). Beyond reciprocity: A conservation of resources view on the effects of psychological contract violation on third parties. *Journal of Applied Psychology, 103*, 561–577. doi: 10.1037/apl0000272

Dukerich, J.M., Golden, B.R., & Shortell, S.M. (2002). Beauty is in the eye of the beholder: The impact of organizational identification, identity, and image on the cooperative behaviors of physicians. *Administrative Science Quarterly, 47*, 507–533. doi: dx.doi.org/10.2307/3094849

Dunford, B.B., Jackson, C.L., Boss, A.D., Tay, L., & Boss, R.W. (2015). Be fair, your employees are watching: a relational response model of external third-party justice. *Personnel Psychology, 68*, 319–352. doi: 10.1111/peps.12081

Dutton, J.E., Dukerich, J.M., & Harquail, C.V. (1994). Organizational images and member identification. *Administrative Science Quarterly, 39*, 239–263. doi: 10.2307/2393235

Edwards, M.R. (2009). HR, perceived organisational support and organisational identification: An analysis after organisational formation. *Human Resource Management Journal, 19*, 91–115. doi: 10.1111/j.1748-8583.2008.00083.x

Edwards, M.R. & Peccei, R. (2007). Organizational identification: Development and testing of a conceptually grounded measure. *European Journal of Work & Organizational Psychology, 16*, 25–57. doi: 10.1080/13594320601088195

Effelsberg, D., Solga, M., & Gurt, J. (2014). Getting followers to transcend their self-interest for the benefit of their company: Testing a core assumption of transformational leadership theory. *Journal of Business & Psychology, 29*, 131–143. doi: 10.1007/s10869-013-9305-x

Ellemers, N., De Gilder, D., & Haslam, S.A. (2004). Motivating individuals and groups at work: A social identity perspective on leadership and group performance. *Academy of Management Review, 29*, 459–478. doi: 10.2307/20159054

Epitropaki, O. (2013). A multilevel investigation of psychological contract breach and organizational identification through the lens of perceived organizational membership: Testing a moderated-mediated model. *Journal of Organizational Behavior, 34*, 65–86. doi: 10.1002/job.1793

Epitropaki, O. & Martin, R. (2005). The moderating role of individual differences in the relation between transformational/transactional leadership perceptions and organizational identification. *Leadership Quarterly, 16*, 569–589. doi: 10.1016/j.leaqua.2005.06.005

Etzioni, A. (1964). *Modern organizations*. Englewood Cliffs, NJ: Prentice-Hall.

Eury, J.L., Kreiner, G.E., Trevino, L.K., & Gioia, D.A. (2018). The past is not dead: Legacy identification and alumni ambivalence in the wake of the Sandusky scandal at Penn state. *Academy of Management Journal, 61*, 826–856. doi: dx.doi.org/10.5465/amj.2015.0534

Finch, D.J., Abeza, G., O'Reilly, N., & Hillenbrand, C. (2018). Organizational identification and independent sales contractor performance in professional services. *Journal of Services Marketing, 32*, 373–386. doi: 10.1108/JSM-07-2016-0278

Fitzsimmons, S.R. (2013). Multicultural employees: A framework for understanding how they contribute to organizations. *Academy of Management Review, 38*, 525–549. doi: 10.5465/amr.2011.0234

Frenkel, S.J., Restubog, S.L.D., & Bednall, T. (2012). How employee perceptions of HR policy and practice influence discretionary work effort and co-worker assistance: evidence from two organizations. *International Journal of Human Resource Management, 23*, 4193–4210. doi: 10.1080/09585192.2012.667433

Fuller, J.B., Hester, K., Barnett, T., Frey, L., Relyea, C., & Beu, D. (2006). Perceived external prestige and internal respect: New insights into the organizational identification process. *Human Relations, 59*, 815–846. doi: doi.org/10.1177/0018726706067148

Goswami, A., O'Brien, K.E., Dawson, K.M., & Hardiman, M.E. (2018). Mechanisms of corporate social responsibility: The moderating role of transformational leadership. *Ethics & Behavior, 28*, 644–661. doi: dx.doi.org/10.1080/10508422.2018.1467764

Hameed, I., Roques, O., & Ali Arain, G. (2013). Nonlinear moderating effect of tenure on organizational identification (OID) and the subsequent role of oid in fostering readiness for change. *Group & Organization Management, 38*, 101–127. doi: 10.1177/1059601112472727

He, H., Zhu, W., & Zheng, X. (2014). Procedural justice and employee engagement: roles of organizational identification and moral identity centrality. *Journal of Business Ethics, 122*, 681–695. doi: 10.1007/s10551-013-1774-3

Hekman, D.R., Bigley, G.A., Steensma, H.K., & Hereford, J.F. (2009a). Combined effects of organizational and professional identification on the reciprocity dynamic for professional employees. *Academy of Management Journal, 52*, 506–526. doi: 10.5465/amj.2009.41330897

Hekman, D.R., Steensma, H.K., Bigley, G.A., & Hereford, J.F. (2009b). Effects of organizational and professional identification on the relationship between administrators' social influence and professional employees' adoption of new work behavior. *Journal of Applied Psychology, 94*, 1325–1335. doi: 10.1037/a0015315

Herrbach, O. (2006). A matter of feeling? The affective tone of organizational commitment and identification. *Journal of Organizational Behavior, 27*, 629–643. doi: doi.org/10.1002/job.362

Johnson, M.D., Morgeson, F.P., & Hekman, D.R. (2012). Cognitive and affective identification: Exploring the links between different forms of social identification and personality with work attitudes and behavior. *Journal of Organizational Behavior, 33*, 1142–1167. doi: 10.1002/job.1787

Johnson, S.A. & Ashforth, B.E. (2008). Externalization of employment in a service environment: the role of organizational and customer identification. *Journal of Organizational Behavior, 29*, 287–309. doi: 10.1002/job.477

Jungbauer, K.-L., Loewenbrück, K., Reichmann, H., Wendsche, J., & Wegge, J. (2018). How does leadership influence incident reporting intention in healthcare? A dual process model of leader–member exchange. *German Journal of Human Resource Management / Zeitschrift für Personalforschung, 32*, 27–51. doi: 10.1177/2397002217745315

Karanika-Murray, M., Duncan, N., Pontes, H.M., & Griffiths, M.D. (2015). Organizational identification, work engagement, and job satisfaction. *Journal of Managerial Psychology, 30*, 1019–1033. doi: 10.1108/JMP-11-2013-0359

Katrinli, A., Atabay, G., Gunay, G., & Guneri, B. (2008). Leader-member exchange, organizational identification and the mediating role of job involvement for nurses. *Journal of Advanced Nursing, 64*, 354–362. doi: dx.doi.org/10.1111/j.1365-2648.2008.04809.x

Kraus, F., Haumann, T., Ahearne, M., & Wieseke, J. (2015). When sales managers and salespeople disagree in the appreciation for their firm: The phenomenon of organizational identification tension. *Journal of Retailing, 91*, 486–515. doi: doi.org/10.1016/j.jretai.2015.03.001

Kreiner, G.E. & Ashforth, B.E. (2004). Evidence toward an expanded model of organizational identification. *Journal of Organizational Behavior, 25*, 1–27. doi: 10.1002/job.234

Lee, E.-S., Park, T.-Y., & Koo, B. (2015). Identifying organizational identification as a basis for attitudes and behaviors: A meta-analytic review. *Psychological Bulletin, 141*, 1049–1080. doi: 10.1037/bul0000012

Lee, H.-J. (2004). The role of competence-based trust and organizational identification in continuous improvement. *Journal of Managerial Psychology, 19*, 623–639. doi: dx. doi.org/10.1108/02683940410551525

Lee, H.-J. (2014). Identities in the global world of work. In B. Gehrke & M.-T. Claes (Eds.), *Global leadership practices: A cross-cultural management perspective* (pp. 85–101). London: Palgrave Macmillan.

Lee, H.-J. (2015). Cosmopolitanism. In C.L. Cooper, M. Vodosek, D.N. Hartog & J.M. McNett (Eds.), *Wiley Encyclopedia of Management* (3rd edition ed., Vol. 6, pp. 1–2). Chichester: John Wiley and Sons.

Lee, H.-J. & Reade, C. (2018). The role of Yin-Yang leadership and cosmopolitan followership in fostering employee commitment in China: A paradox perspective. *Cross Cultural and Strategic Management, 25*, 276–298. doi: 10.1108/CCSM-12-2016-0216

Levine, S.S. & Prietula, M. (2012). How knowledge transfer impacts performance: A multilevel model of benefits and liabilities. *Organization Science, 23*, 1748–1766. doi: 10.1287/orsc.1110.0697

Li, J., Liang, Q., Zhang, Z., & Wang, X. (2018). Leader humility and constructive voice behavior in China: a dual process model. *International Journal of Manpower, 39*, 840–854. doi: 10.1108/IJM-06-2017-0137

Li, R., Zhang, Z.-Y., & Tian, X.-M. (2016). Can self-sacrificial leadership promote subordinate taking charge? The mediating role of organizational identification and the moderating role of risk aversion. *Journal of Organizational Behavior, 37*, 758–781. doi: dx.doi.org/10.1002/job.2068

Lindblom, A., Kajalo, S., & Mitronen, L. (2016). Does a retailer's charisma matter? A study of frontline employee perceptions of charisma in the retail setting. *Journal of Services Marketing, 30*, 266–276. doi: 10.1108/JSM-05-2015-0160

Loi, R., Chan, K.W., & Lam, L.W. (2014). Leader-member exchange, organizational identification, and job satisfaction: A social identity perspective. *Journal of Occupational & Organizational Psychology, 87*, 42–61. doi: 10.1111/joop.12028

Lu, X. & Sun, J.-M. (2017). Multiple pathways linking leader-member exchange to work effort. *Journal of Managerial Psychology, 32*, 270–283. doi: 10.1108/JMP-01-2016-0011

Mael, F.A. (1988). *Organizational identification: Construct redefinition and a field application with organizational alumni:* Unpublished doctoral dissertation, Wayne State University, Detroit, MI.

Mael, F.A. & Ashforth, B.E. (1992). Alumni and their alma mater: A partial test of the reformulated model of organizational identification. *Journal of Organizational Behavior, 13*, 103–123. doi: doi.org/10.1002/job.4030130202

Millward, L.J. & Postmes, T. (2010). Who we are affects how we do: The financial benefits of organizational identification. *British Journal of Management, 21*, 327–339. doi: 10.1111/j.1467-8551.2009.00667.x

Molm, L.D. (2003). Theoretical comparisons of forms of exchange. *Sociological Theory, 21*, 1–17. doi: 10.1111/1467-9558.00171

Morrison, E.W. & Robinson, S.L. (1997). When employees feel betrayed: A model of how psychological contract violation develops. *Academy of Management Review*, *22*, 226–256. doi: 10.2307/259230

Ng, T.W.H. (2015). The incremental validity of organizational commitment, organizational trust, and organizational identification. *Journal of Vocational Behavior*, *88*, 154–163. doi: dx.doi.org/10.1016/j.jvb.2015.03.003

Ng, T.W.H. & Feldman, D.C. (2010). The relationships of age with job attitudes: A meta analysis. *Personnel Psychology*, *63*, 677–718. doi: doi.org/10.1111/j.1744-6570.2010.01184.x

Olkkonen, M.-E. & Lipponen, J. (2006). Relationships between organizational justice, identification with organization and work unit, and group-related outcomes. *Organizational Behavior and Human Decision Processes*, *100*, 202–215. doi: doi.org/10.1016/j.obhdp.2005.08.007

Patchen, M. (1970). *Participation, achievement, and involvement on the job*. New Jersey: Prentice- Hall.

Pierce, J.R. & Aguinis, H. (2013). The too-much-of-a-good-thing effect in management. *Journal of Management*, *39*, 313–338. doi: 10.1177/0149206311410060

Porck, J.P., van Knippenberg, D., Tarakci, M., Ateş, N.Y., Groenen, P.J.F., & de Haas, M. (in press). Do group and organizational identification help or hurt intergroup strategic consensus? *Journal of Management*. doi: 10.1177/0149206318788434

Pratt, M.G. (1998). To be or not to be: Central questions in organizational identification. In D. A. Whetten & P. C. Godfrey (Eds.), *Foundations for organizational science. Identity in organizations: Building theory through conversations*, (pp. 171–207). Thousand Oaks, CA: Sage Publications. doi: dx.doi.org/10.4135/9781452231495.n6

Reade, C. (2001a). Antecedents of organizational identification in multinational corporations: fostering psychological attachment to the local subsidiary and the global organization. *International Journal of Human Resource Management*, *12*, 1269–1291. doi: 10.1080/09585190110083794

Reade, C. (2001b). Dual identification in multinational corporations: local managers and their psychological attachment to the subsidiary versus the global organization. *The International Journal of Human Resource Management*, *12*, 405–424. doi: 10.1080/713769627

Reade, C. & Lee, H.-J. (2012). Organizational commitment in time of war: Assessing the impact and attenuation of employee sensitivity to ethnopolitical conflict. *Journal of International Management*, *18*, 85–101. doi: 10.1016/j.intman.2011.09.002

Riketta, M. (2005). Organizational identification: A meta-analysis. *Journal of Vocational Behavior*, *66*, 358–384. doi: dx.doi.org/10.1016/j.jvb.2004.05.005

Rotondi, T. (1974). Creativity and organizational identification in research and development environments. *Public Personnel Management*, *3*, 53–58. doi: dx.doi.org/10.1177/009102607400300111

Rotondi, T. (1975). Organizational identification: Issues and implications. *Organizational Behavior and Human Performance*, *13*, 95–109. doi: doi.org/10.1016/0030-5073(75)90007-0

Rousseau, D.M. (1989). Psychological and implied contracts in organizations. *Employee Responsibilities and Rights Journal*, *2*, 121–139. doi: 10.1007/bf01384942

Ryan, R.M. & Deci, E.L. (2000). Self-determination theory and the facilitation of intrinsic motivation, social development, and well-being. *American Psychologist*, *55*, 68–78. doi: doi.org/10.1037/0003-066X.55.1.68

Saks, A.M. & Ashforth, B.E. (1997). A longitudinal investigation of the relationships between job information sources, applicant perceptions of fit, and work outcomes. *Personnel Psychology, 50*, 395–426. doi: doi.org/10.1111/j.1744–6570.1997.tb00913.x

Shamir, B. & Kark, R. (2004). A single-item graphic scale for the measurement of organizational identification. *Journal of Occupational and Organizational Psychology, 77*, 115–123. doi: 10.1348/096317904322915946

Smale, A., Björkman, I., Ehrnrooth, M., John, S., Mäkelä, K., & Sumelius, J. (2015). Dual values-based organizational identification in MNC subsidiaries: A multilevel study. *Journal of International Business Studies, 46*, 761–783. doi: 10.1057/jibs.2015.18

Stoner, J., Perrewé, P.L., & Hofacker, C. (2011). The development and validation of the multidimensional identification scale (MDIS). *Journal of Applied Social Psychology, 41*, 1632–1658. doi: 10.1111/j.1559-1816.2011.00770.x

Tajfel, H. (1978). Social categorization, social identity and social comparison. In H. Tajfel (Ed.), *Differentiation between social groups: Studies in the social psychology of intergroup relations* (pp. 61–76). London: Academic Press.

Tosti-Kharas, J. (2012). Continued organizational identification following involuntary job loss. *Journal of Managerial Psychology, 27*, 829–847. doi: 10.1108/02683941211280184

Vaara, E., Tienari, J., & Koveshnikov, A. (in press). From cultural differences to identity politics: A critical discursive approach to national identity in MNCs. *Journal of Management Studies,* doi: 10.1111/joms.12517

Van Dick, R., Hirst, G., Grojean, M.W., & Wieseke, J. (2007). Relationships between leader and follower organizational identification and implications for follower attitudes and behaviour. *Journal of Occupational and Organizational Psychology, 80*, 133–150. doi: 10.1348/096317905x71831

Van Dick, R., van Knippenberg, D., Kerschreiter, R., Hertel, G., & Wieseke, J. (2008). Interactive effects of work group and organizational identification on job satisfaction and extra-role behavior. *Journal of Vocational Behavior, 72*, 388–399. doi: dx.doi.org/10.1016/j.jvb.2007.11.009

Vora, D. & Kostova, T. (2007). A model of dual organizational identification in the context of the multinational enterprise. *Journal of Organizational Behavior, 28*, 327–350. doi: doi.org/10.1002/job.422

Vora, D., Kostova, T., & Roth, K. (2007). Roles of subsidiary managers in multinational corporations: The effect of dual organizational identification. *Management International Review (MIR), 47*, 595–620. doi: doi.org/10.1007/s11575-007-0031-3

Walumbwa, F.O., Mayer, D.M., Wang, P., Wang, H., Workman, K., & Christensen, A.L. (2011). Linking ethical leadership to employee performance: The roles of leader–member exchange, self-efficacy, and organizational identification. *Organizational Behavior & Human Decision Processes, 115*, 204–213. doi: 10.1016/j.obhdp.2010.11.002

Wieseke, J., Kraus, F., Ahearne, M., & Mikolon, S. (2012). Multiple identification foci and their countervailing effects on salespeople's negative headquarters stereotypes. *Journal of Marketing, 76*, 1–20. doi: 10.1509/jm.10.0444

Wiesenfeld, B.M., Raghuram, S., & Garud, R. (1999). Communication patterns as determinants of organizational identification in a virtual organization. *Organization Science, 10*, 777–790. doi: doi.org/10.1287/orsc.10.6.777

Wu, C.-H., Liu, J., Kwan, H.K., & Lee, C. (2016). Why and when workplace ostracism inhibits organizational citizenship behaviors: An organizational identification perspective. *Journal of Applied Psychology, 101*, 362–378. doi: dx.doi.org/10.1037/apl0000063

Yamagishi, T. & Cook, K.S. (1993). Generalized exchange and social dilemmas. *Social Psychology Quarterly, 56*, 235–248. doi: 10.2307/2786661

Yoshikawa, K., Wu, C.-H., & Lee, H.-J. (2020). Generalized exchange orientation: Conceptualization and scale development. *Journal of Applied Psychology, 105*, 294–311. doi: doi.org/10.1037/apl0000438

Zhang, H., Kwong Kwan, H., Everett, A.M., & Jian, Z. (2012). Servant leadership, organizational identification, and work-to-family enrichment: The moderating role of work climate for sharing family concerns. *Human Resource Management, 51*, 747–767. doi: 10.1002/hrm.21498

Zhang, Y. & Chen, C.C. (2013). Developmental leadership and organizational citizenship behavior: Mediating effects of self-determination, supervisor identification, and organizational identification. *The Leadership Quarterly, 24*, 534–543. doi: doi.org/10.1016/j.leaqua.2013.03.007

# 6

# JOB INVOLVEMENT

*James M. Diefendorff, Megan T. Nolan, Steven T. Tseng,*
*Megan E. Kenworthy, and Nicole L. Fiorentino*

## Introduction

The relationship an individual has with their work has been of interest to researchers for many years. A central idea in this area is that individuals differ in terms of how important they view their jobs, with high importance being associated with a variety of beneficial outcomes. One construct lens through which to view this idea is that of job involvement. The concept of job involvement was coined 55 years ago by Lodahl and Kejner (1965), who defined it as "the degree to which a person is identified psychologically with his work, or the importance of work in his total self-image" (p. 24) and as "the degree to which a person's work performance affects his [or her] self-esteem" (p. 25). Building on these ideas, Kanungo (1982a) conceptualized job involvement as the degree to which one identifies psychologically with one's job. This idea was further elaborated by Paullay, Alliger, and Stone-Romero (1994), who defined job involvement as "the degree to which one is cognitively preoccupied with, engaged in, and concerned with one's present job" (p. 225). Job involvement has been referenced in more than 1,817 peer-reviewed articles in the PsycINFO database since its introduction. Work on this construct has focused on understanding its antecedents, including personality and job characteristics (e.g., Brown, 1996; Hackman & Lawler, 1971; Hackman & Oldham, 1975), and outcomes, such as motivation (Hackman & Lawler, 1971) and performance (Diefendorff et al., 2002). Interestingly, although research on job attitudes and related constructs has seen tremendous growth over the past 30 years, research on job involvement has been relatively stagnant. For instance, the number of peer-reviewed papers referring to the job attitude of job satisfaction in PsycINFO over 10-year spans has nearly tripled during the past 30 years (5,039 papers from 1990 to 1999, 9,422 from 2000 to 2009, and 14,564 from 2010 to 2019), whereas the papers referencing job involvement during the same period has been steady (394 papers from 1990 to 1999, 469 from 2000 to 2009, and 409 from 2010 to 2019).

Although it is hard to pinpoint the reason for this lack of growth in research on job involvement, we suspect it may be attributable, in part, to (a) conceptual ambiguities and different construct definitions of job involvement (Highhouse, Nye, & Matthews, 2017; Schleicher, Hansen, & Fox, 2011), (b) meta-analytic findings showing that job involvement has only weak relations with important outcomes, like job performance (Brown, 1996), and (c) the emergence of similar variables with richer theoretical foundations, including organizational identification (Dutton, Dukerich, & Harquail, 1994) and engagement (Kahn, 1990). We discuss each of these issues in more detail throughout the chapter.

The goals of this chapter are to provide (a) a review of significant theoretical and empirical contributions to the job involvement literature and (b) an overview of contemporary issues, future directions, and practical considerations. Specifically, in the first half of the chapter, we take a historical perspective on the job involvement construct, focusing on prominent conceptualizations and associated measures. In the second half of the chapter, the focus shifts to a discussion of contemporary research findings, challenges facing research on job involvement, directions for future research, and managerial implications.

## Emergence of Job Involvement: Construct Definitions and Measures

### Precursors of the Job Involvement Construct

In tracing job involvement to its early roots, Blau (1985) discussed three classic ideas reflecting the importance *of the job to a person*, which serve as the theoretical underpinnings of job involvement: active participation in one's job (Allport, 1943), the job as a central life interest (Dubin, 1956), and ego involvement in one's job (Allport, 1943; French & Kahn, 1962; Gurin, Veroff, & Feld, 1960). Allport (1943) discussed the personal importance of one's job as being reflected by whether the person is actively participating in the job and whether the job helps to satisfy the person's needs for prestige or autonomy. Dubin (1956) focused on the idea of one's job being a central versus peripheral life interest and investigated the extent to which industrial workers valued *work-related compared to nonwork-related social experiences*. Other researchers considered job importance as being reflected by ego involvement, which was indicated by whether a person's self-esteem was dependent on how well they performed their job (French & Kahn, 1962; Gurin et al., 1960). Vroom (1962) empirically examined the concept of ego involvement (operationalized as one item focused on whether a person will focus on a work-related problem when not at work) and found that more ego-involved individuals received higher performance ratings. The definitions and measures of job involvement reviewed in the following section are derived from and build on one or more of these early theoretical ideas.

## *Lodahl and Kejner's (1965) Foundational Work*

The term "job involvement" was introduced in 1965 by Lodahl and Kejner, who defined it as reflecting both the strength of one's identification with one's work and the extent to which one's self-esteem is contingent on one's job performance. This latter notion stemmed, in part, from earlier research on "ego involvement" and pursuit of the "status seeking motive" in one's work (Allport, 1943, p. 459; Vroom, 1962). The central idea was that when "ego involvement" in one's job is high, job performance will affect individuals' self-esteem to a greater extent (French & Kahn, 1962; p. 19). High ego involvement essentially means that accomplishment, praise, and positive evaluations from performing the *work is more important* and meaningful to the individual (Rabinowitz & Hall, 1977).

Based on this conceptual definition, Lodahl and Kejner (1965) developed the first widely used measure of job involvement. The 20-item measure included items such as "I'll stay overtime to finish a job, even if I'm not paid for it" and "I feel depressed when I fail at something connected with my job." Although Lodahl and Kejner's definition of job involvement continues to be cited today (e.g., Welbourne & Sariol, 2017), their original 20-item measure has been criticized for (a) conflating job involvement with work centrality (Elloy, Everett, & Flynn, 1991; Kanungo, 1982a; Paullay et al., 1994) and (b) including items tapping into two related but distinct concepts: identification with one's job and job-based contingent self-esteem (Kanungo, 1982b). Interestingly, Lodahl and Kejner concluded that their measure was comprised of at least three dimensions, but the dimensions were never clearly labeled or defined (Rabinowitz & Hall, 1977). Further, subsequent researchers failed to find stability in the factor structure across samples (e.g., Blau, 1985; Schwyhart & Smith, 1972; Wood, 1974). Lodahl and Kejner (1965) offered a 6-item version of their scale, choosing items that loaded highest on the first principal component and shared 76% of the variance with the full scale. This measure is still used in research today (e.g., Lin, Koopman, & Wang, 2018).

Reeve and Smith (2001) attempted to revise the Lodahl and Kejner (1965) measure by removing the contingent self-esteem items. This effort produced a 9-item scale that tapped into a single latent construct (i.e., job involvement as a key source of personal identity) and had better psychometric properties and other conceptual advantages compared to Lodahl and Kejner's 20-item and 6-item measures. This revised scale has been adopted by researchers interested in job involvement (e.g., Welbourne & Sariol, 2017; Wittmer & Martin, 2011).

## *Kanungo's (1982a) Conceptualization*

The next most significant work in defining and measuring job involvement was that of Kanungo (1982a). A key impetus for this work was the belief that Lodahl and Kejner (1965) had conflated two definitions of job involvement with items representing (a) psychological identification (e.g., "I live, eat, and breathe my job") and (b) performance self-esteem (e.g., "sometimes I'd like to kick myself for the mistakes I made"; see also Gorn & Kanungo, 1980; Kanungo, 1981). In addition, Kanungo (1982b) quibbled with Lodahl and Kejner's description of job involvement as a cognitive state and an emotional state, arguing that emotional states better aligned with job satisfaction. To more clearly differentiate job involvement from job satisfaction, Kanungo (1982b) argued that involvement was a belief (i.e., cognition) about one's job, whereas satisfaction was an affective reaction to one's job.

Kanungo (1982a) also noted that involvement in a specific job is different from involvement with work in general, a distinction that Lodahl and Kejner (1965) had not clearly made. Kanungo labeled this construct work involvement, though it has more often been referred to as work centrality, defined as the extent to which one psychologically identifies with work in general and views the act of working as a key component of one's identity. Unlike job involvement, which is thought to vary as a function of the particular job one holds, work centrality (Dubin, 1956; Dubin, Champoux, & Porter, 1975) should be a more stable set of beliefs shaped by one's socialization history and experiences (Dubin, 1956).

Kanungo (1982a) developed the second prominent measure of job involvement, the 10-item Job Involvement Questionnaire (JIQ), which captured cognitive states only. See Table 6.1 for items. Unlike Lodahl and Kejner's (1965) measure, which includes a mixture of identification and performance self-esteem items, the items in the JIQ focus on psychological identification with the job only. Empirical evidence supports the usefulness of the JIQ, as the reliability and criterion-related validity of the scale are high (Paterson & O'Driscoll, 1990). With that said, Blau (1985) recommended the removal of one item from the JIQ—"Usually I feel detached from my job"—after an empirical analysis of the items (see also Paterson & O'Driscoll, 1990). With the removal of the aforementioned item, Blau (1985) concluded that Kanungo's (1982a) measure is a slightly

*Table 6.1* Job Involvement Scale

---

1. The most important things that happen to me involve my present job.
2. To me, my job is only a small part of who I am (R).
3. I am very much involved personally in my job.
4. I live, eat, and breathe my job.
5. Most of my interests are centered around my job.
6. I have very strong ties with my present job that would be very difficult to break.
7. Usually I feel detached from my job (R).
8. Most of my personal life goals are job-oriented.
9. I consider my job to be very central to my existence.
10. I like to be absorbed in my job most of the time.

---

*Source:* Revised with permission from Kanungo (1982a).

*Note:* All items use a 7-point scale with anchors of 1 "disagree very much" to 7 "agree very much".

"purer" operationalization of job involvement compared to the short-form (six-items) by Lodahl and Kejner (1965). Variations of Kanungo's 10-item scale have been used in several studies since its introduction. For example, Blau and Boal (1989) used a six-item version, though they did not specify which 6 items were retained and why. Boswell and Olson-Buchanan, (2007) also used six of the original ten items (e.g., "The most important things that happen to me involve my job" and "I like to be absorbed in my job most of the time").

### *Paullay et al.'s (1994) Conceptualization*

In perhaps the second most significant conceptual and measurement revision of Lodahl and Kejner's (1965) work (after Kanungo, 1982), Paullay, Alliger, and Stone-Romero (1994) defined job involvement as the degree to which one is cognitively preoccupied with, engaged in, and concerned with one's present job, which reflects the idea of job involvement as active participation in one's job (Allport, 1943). Further, they argued that job involvement consists of two dimensions: *job involvement-role* and *job involvement-setting*. Job involvement-role is the degree to which one is engaged in the specific tasks that make up one's job, whereas job involvement-setting is the "degree to which one finds carrying out the tasks of one's job in the present job environment to be engaging" (p. 225). They posited that job involvement is highest when an individual is involved in both components, but viewed these components as distinct since, for example, someone may be involved in carrying out daily tasks of his or her job yet may not be involved in the current office setting in which he or she works. To capture this distinction and also further distinguish job involvement from job satisfaction, Paullay et al. developed a 27-item measure of job involvement, with 13 items assessing job involvement-role and 14 items assessing job involvement-setting. In subsequent research, researchers used the full 27-item measure to assess job involvement as a global construct (Diefendorff et al., 2002). See Table 6.2 for items.

### *Our Definition of Job Involvement*

Building on and integrating the definitions outlined above, we define job involvement as *the importance of one's current job to one's self-concept, as indicated by the extent to which one is mentally focused on, cognitively preoccupied with, and concerned with one's present job.* We believe this overarching definition best characterizes this construct and also helps to distinguish job involvement from other job-related attitudes and evaluations. This definition suggests that job involvement is a set of job-related cognitions (i.e., the degree to which one views the job as an important part of one's identity) and can be indicated by one's focus on, preoccupation with, and concern with one's job. Highly involved workers are more likely to become immersed in their work and have "flow experiences" than less involved workers. They are also more likely to think about their jobs when not working, which can result in "constructive" rumination about work, better

*Table 6.2* Job Involvement and Work Centrality Scales

---

*STATEMENTS 1–27 PERTAIN TO YOUR*
*ATTITUDES TOWARD YOUR <u>PRESENT JOB</u>*

---

1  I don't mind spending a half hour past quitting time if I can finish something I've been working on.
2  Often when I am not at work, I find myself thinking about things that I have done or things that need to be done at work.
3  I feel myself to be a part of the workgroup on which I work.
4  Generally, I feel detached from the type of work that I do in my present job (R).
5  This work environment really inspires the very best in me in the way of job performance.
6  There is something about the workgroup on which I work that makes me want to do my best.
7  I'll stay overtime to finish something I'm working on.
8  I just do my own job and forget about such things as parties at work and work activities (R).
9  I enjoy doing things with my coworkers.
10 I really feel as if the workgroup's problems are my problems.
11 I am willing to put in a great deal of effort beyond that normally expected in order to help the company be successful.
12 Sometimes I lie awake at night thinking about the things I have to do the next day at work.
13 In my current job I often do extra work that isn't required.
14 I am absorbed in the type of work that I do in my present job.
15 I'm really a perfectionist about the work that I do.
16 In general I am involved in my "work environment" (for example, my workgroup or in the company in general).
17 If once a week, after the work day is over, the administration had the employees get together in groups for the purpose of discussing possible job changes or problems, I would remain after quitting time to participate in these discussions.
18 If I had the choice between going to the company picnic or staying home, I would probably stay home (R).
19 I am very much involved personally in the type of work that I do in my present job.
20 I would prefer to work in a different setting or organization (R).
21 At work, I am very involved in what goes on with others (for example, my coworkers or supervisor).
22 I usually show up for work a little early to get things ready.
23 I am extremely glad that I chose this company to work for over the other places I was considering at the time I joined.
24 I often try to think of ways of doing my job more effectively.
25 I am really interested in my own work.
26 I do only what my job requires, no more, no less (R).
27 I am willing to put in a great deal of effort beyond that normally expected in order to help my workgroup be successful.

*Table 6.2* (Cont.)

---

### STATEMENTS 28–39 REFER TO YOUR
### ATTITUDES TOWARD WORK IN GENERAL

---

28 Work should only be a small part of one's life (R).
29 In my view, an individual's personal life goals should be work-oriented.
30 Life is worth living only when people get absorbed in work.
31 The major satisfaction in my life comes from my work.
32 The most important things that happen to me involve my work.
33 I have other activities more important than my work (R).
34 Work should be considered central to life.
35 I would probably keep working even if I didn't need the money.
36 To me, my work is only a small part of who I am (R).
37 Most things in life are more important than work.
38 If unemployment benefit was really high, I would still prefer to work.
39 Overall, I consider work to be very central to my existence.

---

*Source*: Items retrieved from Paullay, Alliger, & Stone-Romero (1994).

*Notes*: All items use a 7-point scale with anchors of 1 "Disagree very much" to 7 "agree very much." Scoring: Job Involvement Total Items: 1 – 27 [alpha = .91], Job Involvement – Setting Items: 3, 5, 6, 8, 9, 10, 11, 16, 17, 18, 20, 21, 23, 27 [alpha = .87], Job Involvement – Role Items: 1, 4, 2, 7, 12, 13, 14, 15, 19, 22, 24, 25, 26 [alpha = .84], Work Centrality Items: 28 – 39 [alpha = .80].

connection with activities in one's workday, and smoother re-entry into work. However, highly involved workers may find it more difficult to detach after work psychologically, may experience greater work-to-family spillover, and may find it difficult to relax and/or fully engage with non-work activities (e.g., hobbies, family time). Thus, having very high job involvement may have a dark side, something we consider more fully later in the chapter.

## Distinguishing Job Involvement from Other Job Constructs

Part of clearly defining and measuring a construct is ensuring that it is conceptually and empirically distinct from other constructs. A variety of constructs reflect evaluations of or reactions to work that stem in part from the importance of work to the worker, including work centrality (Paullay et al., 1994), job engagement (see Kuhnel, Sonnentag, & Westman, 2009; Hallberg & Schaufeli, 2006), job satisfaction (Locke, 1976), organizational commitment (Hallberg & Schaufeli, 2006), and organizational identification (Riketta, 2005). Table 6.3 presents the definition of job involvement and each of these other constructs, as well as ways these constructs differ from job involvement. We also present meta-analytic correlations of job involvement with these other constructs, as reported in previously published papers.

*Table 6.3* Job Involvement and Related Constructs

**Definition of Job Involvement**: *The importance of one's current job for one's self-concept, reflected by the extent to which one is mentally focused on, cognitively preoccupied with, and concerned with one's present job* (Kanungo, 1982a; Paullay et al. 1994).

| *Related Constructs* | *Definition and Distinction from Job Involvement (JI)* | *r with Job Involvement* |
|---|---|---|
| Work Centrality | **Definition**: Degree of importance that work, in general, plays in one's life (Paullay et al., 1994). | .53<br><br>(Brown, 1996) |
| | **Distinction from JI:** The focus is on work in general and not on one's particular job. Work centrality is thought to be more stable and enduring than job involvement (i.e., it will not vary across jobs) as it reflects one's values and beliefs, which come from one's unique familial and socialization history. | |
| Organizational Identification | **Definition:** One's "perception of oneness with or belongingness to an organization, where the individual defines him or herself in terms of the organization(s) in which he or she is a member" (Mael & Ashforth, 1992, p. 104; see also Wu et al., Chapter 5). | .61<br><br>(Riketta, 2005) |
| | **Distinction from JI:** Organizational identification develops based on one's perceived relationship with the organization and involves negotiating one's personal identity with one's social identity. Job involvement develops based on the job itself. | |
| Organizational Commitment | **Definition:** A volitional psychological bond reflecting dedication to and responsibility for the organization (Klein et al., Chapter 7); the strength of attachment to an organization. | .50<br><br>(Brown, 1996) |
| | **Distinction from JI:** Organizational commitment is focused on the organization as a whole versus job involvement's focus on the specific job. Further, commitment is about one's attachment to likely future actions, versus involvement focusing on the immersion of the self into the job. | |

*Table 6.3* (Cont.)

| Related Constructs | Definition and Distinction from Job Involvement (JI) | r with Job Involvement |
|---|---|---|
| Job Satisfaction | **Definition:** Overall, an evaluative judgment of one's job ranging from positive to negative (Judge et al., Chapter 9). | .45<br><br>(Brown, 1996) |
| | **Distinction from JI:** Job satisfaction reflects an evaluation of one's job (i.e., often a "have-want" comparison) and is tightly intertwined with affect. Job involvement does not reflect an evaluation of one's job, but rather the extent to which one is immersed in and preoccupied with one's job. | |
| Job Engagement | **Definition:** Investment of an individual's complete self and personal resources into a role and one's work (Saks et al., Chapter 10); expression of a person's "preferred self" (physical, cognitive, and emotional) in task behaviors. | .47<br><br>(Rich et al., 2010) |
| | **Distinction from JI:** Investment of the self (physical, cognitive, emotional) into work versus the importance of one's job to the self-concept. Engagement may be more dynamic (momentary) than job involvement. | |

## Work Centrality

As previously noted, work centrality is the degree of importance that work plays in one's life (Paullay et al., 1994), which is different from how vital a particular job is in a person's life. Certainly, work centrality may overlap with job involvement to a large extent, especially for individuals who have worked for a long time in one job. However, we argue that they are distinct in that work centrality reflects more of a value that develops from how a person is raised and what they are taught about the value of hard work, providing for one's family, and contributing to the greater good by being gainfully employed and paying one's taxes. Thus, a person may exhibit high work centrality because they view work as an essential component of one's life (e.g., working hard for five days a week in return for a wage and providing for one's family), but not be immersed in their job while working or preoccupied with their job when not working (low job involvement).

## Organizational Identification

Organizational identification has been defined as one's "perception of oneness with or belongingness to an organization, where the individual defines himself or herself in terms of the organization(s) in which he or she is a member" (Mael

& Ashforth, 1992, p. 104; see also Wu et al., Chapter 5). According to social identity theory, "identity" at the individual level has two parts (Brewer, 1991; 2003): personal identity (i.e., characteristics that differentiate one individual from others) and social identity (i.e., categorizations of the self into social units including race, gender, occupational roles, etc.; Ashforth & Fugate, 2001). As a result, individuals engage in an ongoing identification process whereby they negotiate personal identity (the "Who am I?" question) and social identity ("This is who we are" messages; Kreiner, Hollensbe, & Sheep, 2006; p. 1032). Thus, organizational identification can describe both a state (i.e., feeling that one's identity is derived in part from the organization) and a process (i.e., aligning one's identity with that of the organization; Ashforth & Fugate, 2001). Perhaps the most obvious way that job involvement differs from organizational identification is the focus on job versus organization, respectively. To the extent that identity is implicated, job involvement may also have state (i.e., seeing the job as being a large part of one's self-definition) and process (i.e., integrating and reconciling this job-based identity with other identities) components. Further, these two constructs may reciprocally influence each other, such as when strong identification with one's organization leads to high job involvement, or when being very immersed in one's job leads to a strong identification with one's organization.

## Organizational Commitment

Organizational commitment has been defined as a force that binds an individual to a course of action of relevance to the organization (Meyer & Herscovitch, 2001). It reflects the level of dedication and responsibility to the organization (Klein et al., Chapter 7). One's commitment is characterized by a belief in and acceptance of organizational goals and values, a willingness to exert effort on behalf of the organization, and a desire to maintain membership in the organization (Mowday, Porter, & Steers, 1982, p. 27). Organizational commitment is typically focused on the attachment an individual has with the organization as a whole rather than with the job, as would be reflected by job involvement. Further, commitment is thought to reflect more of a "want to" bond, as compared to a "self-definition" bond seen with job involvement and organizational identification (Klein, Malloy, & Brinsfield, 2012). It is also worth mentioning that organizational commitment is often aimed at understanding a person's likely future course of action with a particular focus on leaving versus staying with a company (Klein et al., 2012; Meyer, Becker, & Vandenberghe, 2004).

## Job Satisfaction

Job satisfaction has been defined as a positive emotional state, reflecting an affective response to the job situation (Locke, 1976). Judge et al. (Chapter 9) focus the construct more specifically on the evaluation of the job as being positive or negative. Job satisfaction differs from job involvement in that job satisfaction involves evaluating the job as good or bad (i.e., as meeting one's expectations/needs or not), whereas job involvement is more of a cognitive assessment of how important and tightly integrated the job is with one's identity. In addition, because of its close links to affect, job satisfaction may vary more within-person over time than job involvement.

### Engagement

Engagement is one of the more recently developed job-related constructs that has conceptual overlap with job involvement. Work engagement has been conceptualized in two primary ways (Byrne et al., 2016): (a) the Maslach and Leiter (1997) view where engagement is essentially the opposite of burnout and (b) the Kahn (1990) view where engagement reflects the investment of cognitive, physical, and emotional energy in one's work (see also Saks et al., Chapter 10). The "opposite of burnout" conceptualization (Schaufeli, Salanova, Gonzalez-Roma, & Bakker, 2002) views engagement as a composed of vigor, absorption, and dedication, with low levels of these variables corresponding to high burnout (emotional exhaustion, low personal accomplishment, and cynicism). Because burnout is a syndrome that develops over time in response to chronic workplace stress (Maslach & Jackson, 1981), engagement from this perspective should be relatively stable over days or weeks. The "investment of self" perspective (Kahn, 1990) is based on the idea that engagement occurs when one is fully invested in one's work, cognitively, emotionally, and behaviorally, and is viewed as an optimal state.

We view engagement from the "lack of burnout" conceptualization to be fairly distinct from job involvement given that engagement would result from low levels of chronic stressors at work (i.e., engagement is the psychological state when burnout is not present). The engagement as "investment of the self" view is more similar to job involvement, though we suspect that it is more dynamic than job involvement as engagement from this perspective reflects the investment of cognitive, emotional, and physical energies which are known to vary by tasks and across situations in one's work. In contrast, job involvement is thought to pertain to the job as a whole with little evidence that it varies within-person and across work tasks.

## Antecedents and Consequences of Job Involvement

In this section, we review past work linking job involvement to antecedents and consequences. Figure 6.1 presents a schematic overview of these connections. Antecedents of job involvement can be categorized as including individual characteristics, such as personality and behavior, or environmental variables, such as job characteristics (Brown, 1996) and organizational characteristics.

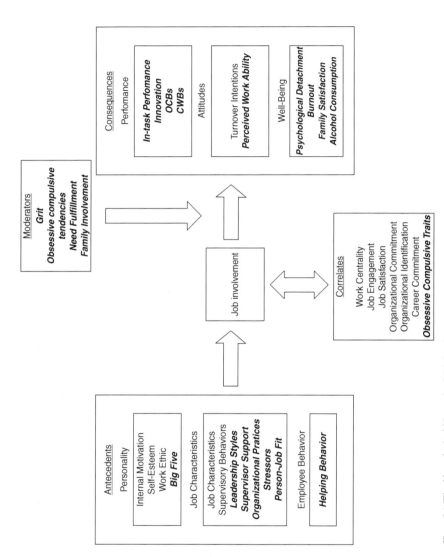

*Figure 6.1* The Nomological Network of Job Involvement.

*Note.* Non-italic/non-bold variables were included in Brown's (1996) meta-analysis.

Furthermore, the outcomes of job involvement include work motivation and job performance.

## *Antecedents: Employee Characteristics and Behaviors*

According to the individual difference perspective, job involvement results, in part, from stable traits grounded in inherited characteristics (e.g., Big Five) or early socialization experiences that speak to the importance of work as a virtuous and necessary activity (Brown, 1996). Regarding personality variables, Brown's (1996) meta-analytic findings suggest that those high in internal motivation (i.e., similar to intrinsic or autonomous motivation; Gagné & Deci, 2005), self-esteem, and work ethic tend to be highly involved in their jobs. In contrast, the traits of growth need strength and locus of control were unrelated to job involvement (Brown, 1996). More recently, a study of Taiwanese employees showed that the Big Five personality dimensions of extraversion, openness to experience, agreeableness, and conscientiousness positively related to job involvement, whereas neuroticism was negatively related to job involvement (Liao & Lee, 2009). Brown (1996) found that demographic characteristics, such as age, gender, education, length of service, and salary, were unrelated to job involvement.

## *Antecedents: Job Characteristics and Work Context*

Research on contextual antecedents assumes that job involvement depends, in part, on features of the job and work environment (Hackman & Oldham, 1980; Kanungo, 1979). These variables include job characteristics, work environment features, and managerial practices. In support of this notion, Brown's (1996) meta-analysis found that numerous job characteristics (skill variety, task identity, feedback, task significance, job challenge, and motivating potential) were positively related to job involvement. Interestingly, role perceptions (role ambiguity and role conflict) were not significantly related to job involvement (Brown, 1996). More recently, research has replicated significant links of skill variety, feedback, and task significance with job involvement but also found a relationship with autonomy (Akinbobola & Bamigbola, 2017; Van den Broeck et al., 2010; Hassan, 2014; Lambert & Paoline, 2012). Finally, person-job fit was positively associated with job involvement (Huang, Yuan, & Li, 2019), suggesting that employees who fit well with their job requirements are more likely to identify with the job and feel cognitively immersed in their work (Zhao & Han, 2016).

Regarding organizational characteristics, Brown and Leigh (1996) found that employee perceptions of the organizational environment (i.e., the extent to which management is perceived as flexible and supportive, role clarity, job challenge, freedom of self-expression, the employees' perceived contribution toward organizational goals, and adequacy of recognition received from the organization) related to job involvement across two samples. High-performance work systems (i.e., coherent sets of human resource practices aimed at improving firm performance by improving employee work experiences; e.g., Farndale, Hope-Hailey, & Kelliher, 2011; Guthrie, 2001) were found to result in greater job involvement (Huang et al., 2016).

Managerial factors, including supervisory behaviors (participatory decision making and consideration), were found to be positively related to job involvement (Brown, 1996). Recent work on leadership styles found that transformational and transactional leadership styles were both positively associated with job involvement (Cheng, Yen, & Chen, 2012; Rana, Malik, & Hussain, 2016). Furthermore, leader-member exchange was positively associated with job involvement (Lawrence & Kacmar, 2012), and supervisor support accounted for incremental variance in job involvement above and beyond the support provided by co-workers, friends, and family (Lambert et al., 2016).

### *Outcomes: Motivation and Performance*

Theoretically, the outcomes of job involvement include motivation (Hackman & Lawler, 1971; Lawler, 1986) and performance (Park et al., 2019). These conceptual links originate from the notion that being involved in your job increases motivation (i.e., goal choice, effort, persistence), which in turn influences job performance, as well as other work behaviors such as turnover and absenteeism. Brown (1996) found in his meta-analysis that job involvement was related to motivation but, counter to expectations, was unrelated to work behaviors such as effort, performance, absenteeism, and turnover. He concluded that "job involvement, in and of itself, does not directly stimulate significantly higher levels of job performance" (p. 244), but can influence the more proximal internal state of motivation.

In an attempt to understand this nonsignificant link with performance, Diefendorff et al., (2002) argued the measurement of job involvement, as well as the performance construct, may have contributed to this finding. Diefendorff et al. found that when using the relatively new Paullay et al. (1994) measure of job involvement (which captured both involvement in the role and setting and did not capture work centrality) and focusing on both in-role performance and organizational citizenship behaviors (OCBs), job involvement was a significant and positive predictor. Subsequent work supports the association of job involvement with OCBs (Chen & Chiu, 2009; Chiu & Tsai, 2006), as well as with helping behaviors (Lin, Koopman, & Wang, 2018) and innovation (Huang, Yuan, & Li, 2019). Thus, job involvement may do a better job of predicting more discretionary, volitional behaviors at work.

Interestingly, Lin, Koopman, and Wang (2018) suggest the causal direction may go from helping to job involvement with multiple competing pathways at work. These authors found that, on the one hand, helping behaviors were associated with increased psychological meaningfulness and safety, which, in turn, were associated with higher job involvement. On the other hand, helping behaviors were also associated with increased emotional exhaustion, which in turn was associated with lower job involvement. Importantly, these authors explored and ruled out job involvement as an antecedent of helping. Lin and colleagues argued that helping behavior has both enrichment- and depletion-based mechanisms that promote job meaningfulness and psychological satisfaction as well as exhaustion.

Finally, another behavioral outcome recently linked to job involvement is absenteeism. Although Brown's (1996) meta-analysis concluded that job involvement was not significantly related to absenteeism, Wegge et al., (2007) demonstrated that job involvement was negatively related to absenteeism when job satisfaction was low but was not related when satisfaction was high. Perhaps these two attitudes are substitutable for discouraging absenteeism, such that being high on one or the other is sufficient, but there is no added value in being high on both.

### *Outcome: Well-Being and Work-Family*

Another class of outcome variables of interest pertains to employee well-being and work-family connections. Early work by Meissner (1971) linked job involvement with positive mental health, arguing that positive feelings towards one's work role (i.e., high job involvement as a result of praise and positive feedback) would spillover and produce benefits in other areas of life, including general levels of well-being (Gechman & Wiener, 1975). In Brown's (1996) meta-analysis, job involvement was found to be more strongly related to intrinsic satisfaction (i.e., satisfaction with the work) than extrinsic satisfaction (i.e., satisfaction with supervisor, promotion, coworker, and pay), and that it was not significantly related to somatic health complaints, life satisfaction, and work-family conflict (WFC). However, more recent work found significant negative associations of job involvement with work stress and burnout (López-Araújo, Osca Segovia, & Rodríguez Muñoz, 2008; Lambert & Paoline, 2012), suggesting implications for emotion-related processes.

Recent research by Prottas and Hyland (2011) has re-examined the relationship of job involvement with WFC. These authors found that job involvement and home involvement (i.e., non-work responsibilities and social involvement) were positively related to positive affective spillover (e.g., being in a positive mood at work spills over to home and vice versa) and positive instrumental spillover (e.g., successfully performing tasks at work helped the individual accomplish tasks at home and vice versa). Importantly, job involvement and home involvement were not associated with home-to-family conflict or family-to-home conflict. More recently, Konradt and Garbers (2016) re-examined the collective impact of job and family involvement, focusing on job and family satisfaction trajectories as the outcome variable. They found that, although people who were highly involved across domains had higher initial job and family satisfaction scores, these individuals also had more negative (declining) family satisfaction trajectories. These results suggest that job involvement may contribute to positive work-family spillover, but high involvement may produce a negative trend in family satisfaction.

Although a common assumption in the literature is that high job involvement is desirable and associated with beneficial outcomes, high job involvement may be harmful to well-being in some situations. Consistent with this line of thought, Frone, Russell, and Cooper (1995) found that employees with high job involvement were more likely to consume heavy amounts of alcohol when they experienced role ambiguity (stressor) compared to employees low in job involvement (Frone et al., 1995). In essence, experiencing ambiguity with regard to something central to one's self-definition—in this case, one's job—is especially stressful, so individuals are more likely to use alcohol to cope. Other studies have also found that employees with high levels of job involvement experience stronger adverse effects of work stress on their health compared to employees with low job involvement. For instance, job involvement exacerbated the relationship between work stress and the desire to drink (Liu et al., 2009) as well as the relationship between role conflict and quality of work-life (Igbaria, Parasuraman, & Badawy, 1994). Furthermore, individuals who are highly involved in their jobs find it more difficult to detach from work, a factor which is shown to strengthen the stressor-strain relation and prevent recovery from stressors (Sonnentag & Fritz, 2015).

Recently, Welbourne and Sariol (2017) examined the role of job involvement in the relationship between incivility and counterproductive work behaviors (CWBs). These authors suggest that experiencing incivility in a domain that is important to the self may prompt employees to engage in more CWBs as a retaliatory coping response. In support of these predictions, high levels of job involvement were found to strengthen the positive relationship between experienced incivility and enacted CWBs, including withdrawal and production deviance (e.g., taking long breaks, coming to work late, purposely doing work slowly).

Consistent with the notion that high job involvement may have a "dark side," Mudrack (2004) examined how job involvement interacts with obsessive-compulsive traits to predict workaholism. Specifically, they found that job involvement interacted with obstinacy (i.e., trait tendency to be stubborn, opinionated, and defiant) and superego (i.e., believing that one is more ethical than others) to predict a facet of workaholism focused on performing non-required work behaviors (i.e., spending free time thinking of ways to improve job performance; Mudrack & Naughton, 2001). Building on the idea that job involvement may combine with situational and trait factors to predict outcomes, Kabat-Farr, Walsh, and McGonagle (2017) found that supervisor incivility posed particularly high risks for employees high in job involvement and low in grit (individual differences in "perseverance and passion for long-term goals"; Duckworth et al., 2007, p. 1087), which the authors conceptualized as a personal resource that protects employees from stress. Specifically, they found that the negative relationship between incivility and perceived work ability (employees' appraisals of their ability to continue working in their job) was stronger for employees high in job involvement and low in grit, illustrating that high involvement was harmful in the context of low grit and high incivility (Kabat-Farr et al., 2017).

# Unresolved Issues and Opportunities in Research on Job Involvement

As noted at the beginning of this chapter, research on job involvement has not advanced at the same rate as research on other related constructs. Further, relatively few papers have appeared in "top tier" industrial-organizational (I-O) and organizational behavior (OB) outlets. It may be that this lack of growth in job involvement is due to other job-related constructs (e.g., engagement) drawing attention away from job involvement, but this begs the question of why. In this section, we discuss some unresolved issues surrounding job involvement that may have led to its relative stagnation, as well as opportunities for research that they present.

## *Conceptualization and Measurement*

As previously noted, several conceptualizations of the job involvement construct have been proposed and continue to persist. For instance, Chiu and Tsai (2006) relied on Lodahl and Kejner's (1965) definition and measure, Lambert and Paoline (2012) relied on Kanungo's (1982a) definition and measure, and Diefendorff et al. (2002) used the Paullay et al. (1994) definition and measure. This lack of consistency across studies creates ambiguity about how to define the construct and its nature, as well as how it should be operationalized. Further, when studies use different operationalizations that rely on different definitions and find conflicting results, it can be hard to pinpoint the source of the difference (e.g., measures, samples). This leads to difficulty in understanding the cumulative state of the literature.

Clearly defining the construct of interest is an essential first step in developing theory and hypotheses in any empirical study. The last systematic review of job involvement (of which we are aware) was Brown's (1996) meta-analysis, which was conducted nearly 25 years ago. We suspect it may be time to update the state of literature with regard to job involvement, including re-examining the nature of the construct, its nomological network (antecedents, correlates, consequences), and potential differences in measures, as well as considering potential moderators grounded in cultural, country, or regional differences.

We argue that job involvement is best viewed as a unidimensional construct (i.e., the importance of one's current job for one's self-concept) though our definition suggests it can be observed in multiple ways (i.e., being mentally focused on, cognitively preoccupied with, and concerned with one's present job). As such, future work using this definition should revisit the dimensionality of job involvement. Interestingly, the status of job involvement as being either a job attitude, evaluation, perception, or reaction to one's job is unclear. It has been referred to as a job attitude (Schleicher et al., 2011), yet common definitions of job involvement (including our own) do not seem to align with that of an attitude (i.e., an evaluation of an entity along a dimension of favorability; Eagly & Chaiken, 1993).

## Job Involvement as a Stable or Dynamic Construct

An unexplored area for future research on job involvement is whether it is indeed relatively stable or if there is a dynamic component. In Rabinowitz and Hall's (1977) review, they cited research suggesting that job involvement is a relatively stable internal characteristic, relying primarily on test-retest reliability data over relatively long periods (e.g., 20 months in Hall & Mansfield, 1971; six months in Lawler, Hackman, & Kaufman, 1973). Steel and Rentsch (1997) measured job involvement again after 10 years, and Mauno and Kinnunen (2000) measured job involvement three times after one-year periods. However, the idea that job involvement can reflect a developmental process (similar to organizational identity) suggests it might change as individuals become socialized and seek to incorporate the job they perform into their identity.

To the extent that individuals can become more or less immersed in different work activities on the job, there may be the potential for job involvement to fluctuate in even shorter timeframes. A method that can be employed to examine fluctuations in job involvement and its relationships with other variables is experience sampling methodology (ESM; Beal, 2015). Research has documented that a variety of job attitudes and/or job perceptions exhibit substantial within-person variability over short periods (e.g., over hours, across days; e.g., Judge & Ilies, 2002; Gabriel et al., 2014). For instance, Judge and Ilies (2002) found that 36% of the variance in job satisfaction can be attributed to within-individual states, and 29% of that within-person variance was explained by mood (Judge & Ilies, 2002). No published research appears to have used ESM to examine job involvement stability and relations with other dynamic constructs (e.g., mood, task perceptions). Interestingly, if job involvement is shown to exhibit substantial within-person variation, this could call into question its distinctiveness from the "investment of self" conceptualization of job engagement (Kahn, 1990).

## Interaction Effects in Examining Job Involvement

Given the lack of main effects of job involvement on key outcomes in the Brown (1996) meta-analysis and the emergence of studies finding interactive effects of job involvement (see the consequences section above), one potential avenue for future research is to theorize about and further examine the ways job involvement might combine with other constructs to predict outcomes of interest. As previously noted, highly job involved employees were more likely to engage in CWBs as a retaliatory response to incivility compared to employees with low job involvement (Welbourne & Sariol, 2017), shedding light on instances when job involvement is associated with detrimental outcomes. In another study, the relationship between incivility and perceived work ability was stronger for employees high in job involvement and low in grit (Kabat-Farr et al., 2017), demonstrating that many individual differences may interact with situational variables to predict outcomes. Diefendorff and colleagues (2002) found that sex moderated the effect of job involvement on the OCB dimensions of courtesy and sportsmanship, with women demonstrating positive relations and men showing negative relationship for courtesy and null relationship for sportsmanship. It seems that highly involved men may be less likely to focus on the socio-emotional parts of the job, perhaps because men define their jobs more narrowly than women (i.e., involved women are more likely to be courteous, whereas involved men are less likely to be courteous).

Future research should continue to examine how job involvement combines with other traits and contextual variables to predict critical well-being and performance outcomes. Although previous research has found that highly involved employees find it difficult to detach from work (Sonnentag & Fritz, 2015), it is possible that this effect can be mitigated by other traits (e.g., resilience) or boundary-management strategies. Having strategies that facilitate detachment may maximize the beneficial outcomes for high involvement employees while minimizing adverse effects.

It may also be worthwhile for researchers to examine how job involvement interacts with (a) involvement in other life domains (e.g., family involvement, leisure), (b) typically "positive" or typically "negative" individual difference traits (e.g., conscientiousness and neuroticism respectively), and (c) a host of job-based (e.g., job characteristics) or work context variables (e.g., high involvement HR practices, mean group or leader job involvement) to name a few. Additionally, although Rabinowitz and Hall (1977) discussed an interactionist perspective with regard to the antecedents of involvement, little research has examined how personality and situational variables jointly influence one's level of job involvement. As such, it may be worthwhile for researchers to explore further job involvement as an outcome variable from a more complex perspective.

### Dark Side of Job Involvement

Relatively little research has explored the potential dark side of job involvement. For instance, given the importance of the job to self-concept, high levels of job involvement may appear similar to what has been labeled as workaholism. Indeed, research has demonstrated that job involvement can impede detachment from work and further exhibit a distal negative impact on work engagement (Kuhnel et al., 2009). Furthermore, high job involvement is thought to reflect a state in which an individual's identity is closely associated with his or her job (Lodahl & Kejner, 1965). Thus, for individuals with high job involvement, job-related experiences may exhibit a significant impact on how individuals view themselves. In essence, job involvement may amplify the attitudinal and behavioral consequences of job-related experiences, making positive experiences more positive and negative experiences more negative. In support of this idea, research has shown that job involvement strengthened the positive relationship between job stressors and strain (Frone et al., 1995).

Interestingly, it might be worth examining whether job involvement has a curvilinear relationship with positive outcomes, such that from low to moderate job involvement, there are benefits, but from moderate to high job involvement, there are costs. In essence, there may be "too much of a good thing" with job involvement. Finally, to the extent that high job involvement is a desirable outcome, it may be worth investigating whether organizational interventions can produce improvements in job involvement. Indeed, there is a class of HR practices considered to be high involvement, suggesting that they are aimed at increasing the involvement of workers (Paré & Tremblay, 2007).

## *Job Involvement in a Global Context*

There is a considerable dearth in empirical research examining job involvement globally and cross-culturally. Although there is some research that studies job involvement outside of the United States and Canada (e.g., Bolelli & Durmuş, 2017), most studies do not compare samples across countries or cultures. Results from a handful of exceptions suggest that the impact of predictors on job involvement may vary as a function of national or cultural differences. For instance, facets of job characteristics were differentially related to job involvement between a sample of US employees and a sample of Indian employees (Sekaran & Mowday, 1981). Specifically, skill variety appeared to be a stronger predictor of job involvement for Indian employees, while feedback was a stronger predictor of job involvement for US employees. In another study, Gomez-Mejia (1984) determined that occupational membership (i.e., job title) was a stronger predictor of job involvement than cultural variables (i.e., geographical area, political system, shared historical background of society, and level of economic development). Indeed, across ten countries that provided the largest sample size for this study (e.g., Brazil, Israel, Korea, South Africa, United States), results indicated that average job involvement was similar among employees in the same occupational level across countries, suggesting that cultural differences may not be as important of a determinant of job involvement. Finally, in a more recent study, Cohen (2007) examined the relationship between culture variables and job involvement. Results indicated that job involvement was positively related to individualism-collectivism and uncertainty avoidance, but not significantly related to power distance.

Although the research summarized above gives a hint of interesting implications for job involvement in a global context, more research is needed to replicate and extend such findings. Beyond the articles reviewed above, we were unable to find further empirical work comparing job involvement across nations and cultures. In contrast, a quick Google Scholar search reveals that the implications of national and cultural differences on other job attitudes, such as job satisfaction and organizational commitment, appear to have received relatively more attention.

## Implications for Practice

Job involvement reflects, to some extent, a personal stake in the job, and this can be beneficial or detrimental under different situations. Highly job-involved employees see their job as very important on a personal level, so they may be more motivated and perform at a high level. On the one hand, it almost seems obvious that organizations would prefer highly involved employees compared to low job-involved employees, who do not see their job as personally important. On the other hand, because the job holds high importance, highly job-involved employees may also be more prone to deleterious outcomes when job situations are unfavorable.

Managers should also have an eye out for creating work tasks that help to satisfy a person's needs for autonomy, competence, and relatedness (Gagné & Deci, 2005). Part of doing this is also creating a work environment that is autonomy-supportive and allows individuals to have a choice by actively engaging and otherwise having input in what they do and how they do it. These factors are more likely to produce autonomous motivation, which is comprised of both intrinsic motivation (i.e., performing tasks because they are fun or interesting) and identified motivation (i.e., performing tasks because they are aligned with important values). Identified motivation is definitionally similar to job involvement as both reflect alignment between internal and external values as well as activation and investment of the self in what one is doing.

## Conclusion

The purpose of this chapter was to provide a conceptual review of job involvement theory and research, as well as to consider potential future directions on this topic. The first conceptualizations of job-involvement date back about seven decades and has since made considerable progress in terms of defining, measuring, and differentiating between separate constructs. Future research opportunities are plentiful, and researchers are encouraged to examine the stability, interactive effects, and the dark side of job involvement.

# References

Akinbobola, O. & Bamigbola, O. (2017). Organizational role stress and job involvement of employees in post consolidation nationalized bank: Job involvement of employees in post consolidation nationalized bank. *International Journal of Interdisciplinary Organizational Studies*, *12*(1), 1–11.

Allport, G.W. (1943). The ego in contemporary psychology. *Psychological Review*, *50*, 451–478.

Ashforth, B.E. & Fugate, M. (2001). Role transitions and the life span. In B.E. Ashforth (Ed.), *Role transitions in organizational life: An identity-based perspective*. Mahwah, NJ: Lawrence Erlbaum, pp. 225–257.

Beal, D. J. (2015). ESM 2.0: State of the art and future potential of experience sampling methods in organizational research. *Annual Review of Organizational Psychology and Organizational Behavior*, *2*(1), 383–407.

Blau, G.J. (1985). A multiple study investigation of the dimensionality of job involvement. *Journal of Vocational Behavior*, *27*, 19–36.

Blau, G. & Boal, K. (1989). Using job involvement and organizational commitment interactively to predict turnover. *Journal of Management*, *15*(1), 115–127.

Bolelli, M. & Durmuş, B. (2017). Work attitudes influencing job involvement among "Y" generation. *International Journal of Commerce and Finance*, *3*(1), 1–11.

Boswell, W.R. & Olson-Buchanan, J.B. (2007). The use of communication technologies after hours: the role of work attitudes and work-life conflict. *Journal of Management*, *33*(4), 592–610.

Brewer, M.B. (1991). The social self: On being the same and different at the same time. *Personality and social psychology bulletin*, *17*(5), 475–482.

Brewer, M.B. (2003). Optimal distinctiveness, social identity, and the self. In M.R. Leary & J.P. Tangney (Eds.), *Handbook of self and identity*: 480–491. New York: Guilford Press.

Brown, S.P. (1996). A meta-analysis and review of organizational research on job involvement. *Psychological Bulletin*, *120*(2), 235–255.

Brown, S.P. & Leigh, T.W. (1996). A new look at psychological climate and its relationship to job involvement, effort, and performance. *Journal of Applied Psychology*, *81*(4), 358–368.

Byrne, Z. S., Peters, J. M., & Weston, J. W. (2016). The struggle with employee engagement: Measures and construct clarification using five samples. *Journal of Applied Psychology*, *101*(9), 1201–1227.

Cheng, Y.N., Yen, C.L., & Chen, L.H. (2012). Transformational leadership and job involvement: The moderation of emotional contagion. *Military Psychology*, *24*(4), 382–396.

Chen, C.C. & Chiu, S. (2009). The mediating role of job involvement in the relationship between job characteristics and organizational citizenship behavior. *The Journal of Social Psychology*, *149*(4), 474–494.

Chiu, S. & Tsai, M. (2006). Relationships among burnout, job involvement, and organizational citizenship behavior. *The Journal of Psychology*, *140*(6), 517–530.

Cohen, A. (2007). One nation, many cultures: A cross-cultural study of the relationship between personal cultural values and commitment in the workplace to in-role performance and organizational citizenship behavior. *Cross-cultural research*, *41*(3), 273–300.

Diefendorff, J.M., Brown, D.J., Kamin, A.M., & Lord, R.G. (2002). Examining the roles of job involvement and work centrality in predicting organizational citizenship behaviors and job performance. *Journal of Organizational Behavior, 23*, 93–108.

Dubin, R. (1956). Industrial workers' worlds: A study of the "central life interests" of industrial workers. *Social Problems, 3*, 131–142.

Dubin, R., Champoux, J.E., & Porter, L.W. (1975). Central life interest and organizational commitment of blue-collar and clerical workers. *Administrative Science Quarterly*, 1975, *20*, 411–421.

Duckworth, A.L., Peterson, C., Matthews, M.D., & Kelly, D.R. (2007). Grit: Perseverance and passion for long-term goals. *Journal of Personality and Social Psychology, 92*, 1087–1101.

Dutton, J.E., Dukerich, J.M., & Harquail, C.V. (1994). Organizational images and member identification. *Administrative Science Quarterly, 39*(2), 239–263.

Eagly, A. H., & Chaiken, S. (1993). *The psychology of attitudes*. Fort Worth, TX: Harcourt Brace Jovanovich.

Elloy, D.E., Everett, J.E., & Flynn, W.R. (1991). An examination of the correlates of job involvement. *Group & Organization Studies, 16*, 160–177.

Farndale, E., Hope-Hailey, V., & Kelliher, C. (2011). High commitment performance management: The roles of justice and trust. *Personnel Review, 40*(1), 5–23.

French, J.R.P. & Kahn, R.L. (1962). A programmatic approach to studying the industrial environment and mental health. *Journal of Social Issues, 18*, 1–47.

Frone, M.R., Russell, M., & Cooper, M.L. (1995). Job stressors, job involvement and employee health: A test of identity theory. *Journal of Occupational and Organizational Psychology, 68*(1), 1–11.

Gabriel, A.S., Diefendorff, J.M., Chandler, M.M., Moran, C.M., & Greguras, & G.J. (2014). The dynamic relationships of work affect and job satisfaction with perceptions of fit. *Personnel Psychology, 67*, 389–420.

Gagné, M. & Deci, E.L. (2005). Self-determination theory and work motivation. *Journal of Organizational Behavior, 26*(4), 331–362.

Gechman, A. S., & Wiener, Y. (1975). Job involvement and satisfaction as related to mental health and personal time devoted to work. *Journal of Applied Psychology, 60*(4), 521–523.

Gomez-Mejia, L.R. (1984). Effect of occupation on task related, contextual and job involvement orientation: a cross-cultural perspective. *Academy of Management Journal, 27*(4), 706–720.

Gorn, G.J. & Kanungo, R.N. (1980). Job involvement and motivation: Are intrinsically motivated managers more job involved? *Organizational Behavior and Human Performance, 26*, 265–277.

Gurin, G., Veroff, J., & Feld, S. (1960). *Americans view their mental health: A nationwide interview survey*. New York, NY: Basic Books.

Guthrie, J.P. (2001). High-involvement work practices, turnover, and productivity: Evidence from New Zealand. *Academy of Management Journal, 44*(1), 180–190.

Hackman, J.R. & Lawler, E.E. (1971). Employee reactions to job characteristics. *Journal of Applied Psychology Monograph, 55*(3), 259–286.

Hackman, J.R. and Oldham, G.R. (1975). Development of the job diagnostic survey. *Journal of Applied Psychology, 60*(2), 159–170.

Hackman, J. R., & Oldham, G. R. (1980). *Work redesign*. Reading, MA: Addison-Wesley.

Hall, D.T. & Mansfield, R. (1971). Organizational and individual response to external stress. *Administrative Science Quarterly, 16*, 533–547.

Hallberg, U.E. & Schaufeli, W.B. (2006). "Same" but different? Can work engagement be discriminated from job involvement and organizational commitment? *European Psychologist, 11*(2), 119–127.

Hassan, S. (2014). Sources of professional employees job involvement: An empirical assessment in a government agency. *Review of Public Personnel Administration, 34*, 356–378.

Highhouse, S., Nye, C., & Matthews, R.A. (2017). Finding meaning in the struggle of work: Construct redundancy in work importance measurement. *Journal of Personnel Psychology, 16*(3), 1–13.

Huang, L.C., Ahlstrom, D., Lee, A.Y.P., Chen, S.Y., & Hsieh, M.J. (2016). High performance work systems, employee well-being, and job involvement: An empirical study. *Personnel Review, 45*, 296–314.

Huang, W., Yuan, C., & Li, M. (2019). Person–job fit and innovation behavior: Roles of job involvement and career commitment. *Frontiers in Psychology, 10*, 1134.

Igbaria, M., Parasuraman, S., & Badawy, M.K. (1994). Work experiences, job involvement, and quality of work life among systems personnel. *MIS Quarterly, 18*, 175–201.

Ilies, R., & Judge, T. A. (2002). Understanding the dynamic relationships among personality, mood, and job satisfaction: A field experience sampling study. *Organizational Behavior and Human Decision Processes, 89*(2), 1119–1139.

Judge, T.A. & Ilies, R. (2002). Relationship of personality to performance motivation: a meta- analytic review. *Journal of Applied Psychology, 87*(4), 797–807.

Kabat-Farr, D., Walsh, B.M., & McGonagle, A.K. (2017). Uncivil supervisors and perceived work ability: The joint moderating roles of job involvement and grit. *Journal of Business Ethics, 26*, 1–15.

Kahn, W.A. (1990). Psychological conditions of personal engagement and disengagement at work. *Academy of Management Journal, 33*, 692–724.

Kanungo, R.N. (1979). The concepts of alienation and involvement revisited. *Psychological Bulletin, 86*, 119–138.

Kanungo, R.N. (1981). Work alienation and involvement: Problems and prospects. *International Review of Applied Psychology, 30*, 1–15.

Kanungo, R.N. (1982a). Measurement of job and work involvement. *Journal of Applied Psychology, 67*(3), 341–349.

Kanungo, R.N. (1982b). *Work alienation: An integrative approach*. ABC-CLIO.

Klein, H.J., Molloy, J.C., & Brinsfield, C.T. (2012). Reconceptualizing workplace commitment to redress a stretched construct: Revisiting assumptions and removing confounds. *Academy of Management Review, 37*(1), 130–151.

Konradt, U. & Garbers, Y. (2016). The role of job and family involvement for satisfaction in job and family. *Zeitschrift für Psychologie, 224*, 15–24.

Kreiner, G.E., Hollensbe, E.C., & Sheep, M.L. (2006). Where is the "me" among the "we"? Identity work and the search for optimal balance. *Academy of Management Journal, 49*(5), 1031–1057.

Kuhnel, J., Sonnentag S., & Westman, M. (2009). Does work engagement increase after a short respite? The role of job involvement as a double-edged sword. *Journal of Occupational and Organizational Psychology, 82*, 575–594.

Lambert, E.G., Minor, K.I., Wells, J.B., & Hogan, N.L. (2016). Social support's relationship to correctional staff job stress, job involvement, job satisfaction, and organizational commitment. *The Social Science Journal*, *53*(1), 22–32.

Lambert, E. & Paoline, E. (2012). Exploring the possible antecedents of job involvement: An exploratory study among jail staff. *Criminal Justice and Behavior*, *39*, 264–286.

Lawler, E.E., III. (1986). *High-involvement management: Participative strategies for improving organizational performance*. San Francisco: Jossey-Bass.

Lawler, E.E. III, Hackman J.R., & Kaufman, S. (1973). Effects of job redesign: A field experiment. *Journal of Applied Social Psychology*, *3*, 49–62.

Lawrence, E.R. & Kacmar, M.K. (2012). Leader-member exchange and stress: The mediating role of job involvement and role conflict. *Institute of Behavioral & Applied Management*, 39–52.

Liao, C. & Lee, C. (2009). An empirical study of employee job involvement and personality traits: The case of Taiwan. *International Journal of Economics and Management*, *3*(1), 22–36.

Lin, W., Koopmann, J., & Wang, M. (2018). How does workplace helping behavior step up or slack off? Integrating enrichment-based and depletion-based perspectives. *Journal of Management*, 1–29.

Liu, S., Wang, M., Zhan, Y., & Shi, J. (2009). Daily work stress and alcohol use: Testing the cross-level moderations effects of neuroticism and job involvement. *Personnel Psychology*, *62*, 575–597.

Locke, E.A. (1976). The nature and causes of job satisfaction. In M.D. Dunnette (Ed.), *Handbook of Industrial and Organizational Psychology*. Chicago, IL: Rand McNally, pp. 1297–1347.

Lodahl, T.M. & Kejner, M. (1965). The definition and measurement of job involvement. *Journal of Applied Psychology*, *49*(1), 24–33.

López-Araújo, B., Osca Segovia, A., & Rodríguez Muñoz, M. (2008). Role stress, implication with work and burnout in professional soldiers. *Revista Latinoamericana de Psicologia*, *40*(2), 293–304.

Maslach, C. & Jackson, S.E. (1981). The measurement of experienced burnout. *Journal of Organizational Behavior*, *2*(2), 99–113.

Maslach, C., & Leiter, M. P. (2008). *The truth about burnout: How organizations cause personal stress and what to do about it*. John Wiley & Sons.

Mael, F. & Ashforth, B.E. (1992). Alumni and their alma mater: A partial test of the reformulated model of organizational identification. *Journal of Organizational Behavior*, *13*, 103–123.

Mauno, S. & Kinnunen, U. (2000). The stability of job and family involvement: applying the multi-wave, multi-variable technique to longitudinal data. *Work and Stress*, *14*, 51–64.

Meissner, W. W. (1971). Notes on identification: II. Clarification of related concepts. *The Psychoanalytic Quarterly*, *40*(2), 277–302.

Meyer, J.P., Becker, T.E., & Vandenberghe, C. (2004). Employee commitment and motivation: a conceptual analysis and integrative model. *Journal of Applied Psychology*, *89*(6), 991–1007.

Meyer, J.P. & Herscovitch, L. (2001). Commitment in the workplace: Toward a general model. *Human Resource Management Review*, *11*, 299–326.

Mowday, R.T., Porter, L.W., & Steers, R. (1982). Organizational linkages: The psychology of commitment, absenteeism, and turnover.

Mudrack, P.E. (2004). Job involvement, obsessive-compulsive personality traits, and workaholic behavioral tendencies. *Journal of Organizational Change Management, 17*(5), 490–508.

Mudrack, P.E. & Naughton, T.J. (2001). The assessment of workaholism as behavioral tendencies: Scale development and preliminary empirical testing. *International Journal of Stress Management, 8*(2), 93–111.

Paré, G., & Tremblay, M. (2007). The influence of high-involvement human resources practices, procedural justice, organizational commitment, and citizenship behaviors on information technology professionals' turnover intentions. *Group & Organization Management, 32*(3), 326–357.

Park, J., Kim, S., Lim, M., & Sohn, Y. W. (2019). Having a calling on board: Effects of calling on job satisfaction and job performance among South Korean newcomers. *Frontiers in Psychology, 10*, 1–12.

Paterson, J.M. & O'Driscoll, M.P. (1990). An empirical assessment of Kanungo's (1982) concept and measure of job involvement. *Applied Psychology: An International Review, 39*, 293–306.

Paullay, I.M., Alliger, G.M., & Stone-Romero, E.F. (1994). Construct validation of two instruments designed to measure job involvement and work centrality. *Journal of Applied* Psychology, 79, 224–228.

Prottas, D.J. & Hyland, M.M. (2011). Is high involvement at work and home so bad? Contrasting scarcity and expansionist perspectives. *The Psychologist-Manager Journal, 14*(1), 29–51.

Rabinowitz, S. & Hall, D.T. (1977). Organizational research on job involvement. *Psychological bulletin, 84*(2), 265.

Rana, S., Malik, N., & Hussain, R. (2016). Leadership styles as predictors of job involvement in teachers. *Pakistan Journal of Psychological Research, 31*(1), 161–182.

Reeve, C.L. & Smith, C.S. (2001). Refining Lodahl and Kejner's job involvement scale with a convergent evidence approach: Applying multiple methods to multiple samples. *Organizational Research Methods, 4*(2), 91–111.

Rich, B. L., Lepine, J. A., & Crawford, E. R. (2010). Job engagement: Antecedents and effects on job performance. *Academy of Management Journal, 53*(3), 617–635.

Riketta, M. (2005). Organizational identification: A meta-analysis. *Journal of Vocational Behavior, 66*(2), 358–384.

Schaufeli, W. B., Salanova, M., González-Romá, V., & Bakker, A. B. (2002). The measurement of engagement and burnout: A two sample confirmatory factor analytic approach. *Journal of Happiness Studies, 3*(1), 71–92.

Schleicher, D.J., Hansen, D., & Fox, K.E. (2011). Job attitudes and work values. In S. Zedeck (Ed.), *APA Handbooks in Psychology. APA handbook of industrial and organizational psychology, Maintaining, expanding, and contracting the organization*, 3, 137–189.

Schwyhart, W.R. & Smith, P.C. (1972). Factors in the job involvement of middle managers. *Journal of Applied Psychology, 56*, 227–233.

Sekaran, U. & Mowday, R.T. (1981). A cross-cultural analysis of the influence of individual and job characteristics on job involvement. *International Review of Applied Psychology, 30*, 51–64.

Sonnentag, S. & Fritz, C. (2015). Recovery from job-stress: The stressor-detachment model as an integrative framework. *Journal of Organizational Behavior, 36*, 72–103.

Steel, R.P. & Rentsch, J.R. (1997). The dispositional model of job attitudes revisited: Findings of a 10-year study. *Journal of Applied Psychology, 82*, 873–879.

Vroom, V. H. (1962). Ego-involvement, job satisfaction, and job performance. *Personnel Psychology, 15*, 159–177.

Wegge, J., Schmidt, K.H., Parkes, C., & Van Dick, R. (2007). Taking a sickie: Job satisfaction and job involvement as interactive predictors of absenteeism in a public organization. *Journal of Occupational and Organizational Psychology, 80*(1), 77–89.

Welbourne, J.L. & Sariol, A.M. (2017). When does incivility lead to counterproductive work behavior? Roles of job involvement, task interdependence, and gender. *Journal of Occupational Health Psychology, 22*, 194–206.

Wittmer, J.L.S. & Martin, J.E. (2011). Work and personal role involvement of part-time employees: Implications for attitudes and turnover intentions. *Journal of Organizational Behavior, 32*, 767–787.

Wood, D. (1974). Effect of worker orientation differences on job attitude correlates. *Journal of Applied Psychology, 59*, 54–60.

Zhao B. & Han P. (2016). The impact of people-work matching and abusive management on innovation behaviors: the mediating role of basic psychological needs. *Soft Sci., 30*, 74–79.

# 7

# WORKPLACE COMMITMENTS

*Howard J. Klein and Hee Man Park*

## Workplace Commitments

Commitment has been demonstrated to impact outcomes important to workers and organizations alike, such as absenteeism, turnover, motivation, prosocial behaviors, performance, and wellbeing (Cooper-Hakim & Viswesvaran, 2005; Meyer, 2016). As such, it is a frequently examined construct in Management and Industrial/Organizational Psychology. We use the term workplace commitments to refer to the full array of commitments that people have at work and the term target to refer to the specific things or foci to which they can be committed (e.g., an organization, team, person, idea). Workplace commitments have been studied for over 70 years and have been defined in a wide variety of ways and from multiple perspectives. There are primarily models of commitment, rather than commitment theories, with theoretical support for relationships imported from various areas, most frequently theories of social exchange (Cropanzano & Mitchell, 2005), to support the formation and consequences of commitment.

Klein, Molloy, and Brinsfield, (2012) drew from several theories, including field theory (Lewin, 1943), action identification theory (Vallacher & Wegner, 1985), theory of planned behavior (Ajzen, 1991), affective events theory (Weiss & Cropanzano, 1996), social cognitive theory (Bandura, 1997) and self-determination theory (Gagné & Deci, 2005) to support their target neutral model of commitment. More recently, systems theory has been used to explain the interrelationships among multiple commitments (Klein, Solinger, & Duflot, in press). In this chapter, we briefly summarize the history of commitment research and discuss the various ways it has been conceptualized. We also overview the different workplace commitment targets that have been studied, review the different approaches to the measurement of commitment, summarize what is known about the antecedents and outcomes of commitment, and outline current issues and future research needs as well as practical implications.

## Evolution of the Construct

The study of workplace commitments originated in separate literatures and thus is multidisciplinary. The earliest commitment work was done by sociologists and economists, and the target of most of this early research was commitment to the employing organization, although there were exceptions that acknowledge multiple workplace targets of commitment (e.g., Merton, 1957; Simon, Smithburg, & Thompson, 1950). Examples of this earliest research include Barnard (1938), which introduced the inducement-contribution model, and Whyte (1956), which explored how work provides a sense of social belongingness and why employees conform to the demand of the organization. The focus of this early work was often on (a) how group attachments generate and sustain social order, and (b) how commitment to social institutions facilitates collective actions to cope with power differentials between workers and management and enhances social welfare. Although commitment research can be traced to this early work, the term "commitment" was not always used and rarely explicitly defined.

The study of workplace commitments largely moved to organizational behavior and industrial-organizational psychology, but within these disciplines, the study of commitment is highly fragmented with commitments to different targets studied by different researchers in different literatures. In some cases, the study of commitment emerged relatively independently of the work on organizational commitment (e.g., goal commitment by motivation researchers, union commitment in labor relations, escalation of commitment in decision-making literature). In other cases (e.g., career commitment, commitment to teams, supervisors, projects, change efforts), scholars initially borrowed from organizational or goal commitment and then further explored the concept, again in distinct literatures (i.e., careers, teams, leadership, etc.).

Scholars in psychology and management began to pay more attention to commitment and to use the term "commitment" more regularly in the 1960s. The research in this era took two different perspectives, reflecting either a behavioral or psychological view. The behavioral view, exemplified by Becker (1960), considered commitment to be the result of past choices with behavior committing people to future actions due to a desire for consistency, sense of obligation, "side-bets" and "sunk costs" leading one to maintain a course of action. In contrast, the psychological view, exemplified by Keisler and Sakamura (1966), was based on the attitude literature and held that commitment, based on one's relationship or identification with the target, drove behavior.

There was tremendous growth in the study of workplace commitment during the mid 1970s–mid 1980s. The attitudinal perspective began to gain prominence, aided by the introduction of the first widely used commitment measure, the Organizational Commitment Questionnaire (OCQ; Mowday,

Steers, & Porter, 1979). During this time, commitment was widely accepted as an important outcome construct that managers could measure and attempt to influence. Steers (1977), taking the psychological view, grouped commitment antecedents into personal characteristics, job characteristics, and work experiences, the last one explaining the most variance in organizational commitment. There were also important extensions during this time from the behavioral view. Hrebiniak and Alutto (1972), for example, found that despite the demographic correlates of commitment, worker perception of the inducement to contributions and the accumulation of side-bets or investments determined organizational commitment and Salancik (1977) showed that commitments take many forms and are primarily beneficial in sustaining actions in the face of difficulties, even though they carry both benefits and costs. A final development during this time was the re-emergence of research on commitment targets other than the employing organization, including union commitment (Gordon et al., 1980), career commitment (Blau, 1985), and escalation of commitment (Staw, 1981).

Research on workplace commitment from the mid-1980s put even greater emphasis on multiple targets of commitment and began to integrate those different commitments as exemplified by Morrow (1983), Reichers (1985), and Becker (1992). Greater attention was also paid to the multiple bases of commitment during this time, with attempts made to integrate the variety of conceptualizations that existed in the literature. For example, O'Reilly and Chatman (1986) suggested three independent dimensions—compliance, identification, and internalization—as bases for one's psychological attachment. Similarly, Meyer and Allen (1991) presented their three-component model (TCM), which became the predominant perspective in the study of commitment for the next 25 years, aided by a corresponding measure that largely replaced the OCQ. The TCM model holds that commitment is experienced as one or more of three mindsets: affective (want to), continuance (need to), normative (ought to).

More recent work has challenged the inclusive approach of this era (e.g., Klein et al., 2012; Solinger, Van Olffen, & Roe, 2008), examined new targets of commitment (e.g., Swart et al., 2014), and repositioned the construct to better reflect the current workplace (e.g., van Rossenberg et al., 2018)—a work context that differs in significant ways from the time workplace commitments were first examined in terms of the nature of work, organizations, and the employment relationship. These recent developments are discussed in more detail in the following sections.

## Conceptualizations of Commitment

As noted above, commitment has been conceptualized from several different theoretical perspectives and defined in a wide variety of ways—some more popular than others, some more defensible than others. Some definitions have been criticized as confounding commitment with its antecedents, namely viewing commitment as an investment, exchange, identification, or congru-ence. Other definitions have been similarly criticized as being confounded, but with the outcomes of commitment, namely those viewing commitment as not leaving (i.e., continuation) or motivation. Other common conceptualiza-tions view commitment as an attitude, a binding force, an attachment or bond, or a specific type of bond. In addition, some conceptualizations incorporate more than one of these different perspectives. Examples of these views are summarized below.

### Investment/Exchange

From this perspective, commitment is viewed as an economic, behavioral, or social investment or exchange, or a combination thereof. In the case of invest-ments (e.g., Brockner, 1992), a person expects some future valued outcome that will be lost or diminished if the person does not continue the behavior or relationship with the target. For exchange (e.g., Angle & Perry, 1981), there is a felt obligation to reciprocate because something valuable is expected or has already been received from the commitment target. It has been argued that these conceptualizations are problematic because investments and exchanges can lead to commitment but are not commitment itself (e.g., Klein, Molloy, & Cooper, 2009b).

### Identification/Congruence

Others define commitment as identification with the target and/or congruence between the person and the target in terms of goals and/or values. These defi-nitions originated earlier but became more popular based on the Porter et al. (1974) definition of organizational commitment, which included identification with the organization and a belief in and acceptance of the organization's goals and values. These perspectives have also been criticized. For identifica-tion, there is conceptual and empirical evidence for viewing commitment and identification as distinct concepts (Klein et al., 2014), and identification has become viewed as its own construct (Van Dick, Becker, & Meyer, 2006). Klein et al. (2012) argued that identification and commitment are different types of psychological bonds, with identification involving the merging of the self with the target (Chapter 5). In contrast, commitment involves a volitional dedication to and caring for the target, without requiring the merging of the self with the target. In the case of congruence, it has been argued that this leads to commit-ment rather than itself being commitment (e.g., Klein et al., 2009b).

### Motivation

The difference between commitment and motivation is sometimes unclear because motivation is frequently defined as a set of forces (internal and external; Pinder, 1998), and commitment is sometimes similarly defined as a force (e.g., Meyer & Herscovitch 2001). Although some authors equate commitment with the willingness to expend effort (i.e., motivation) on behalf of the commitment target, this perspective has been criticized as the two constructs are distinct in other respects, and because motivation is often viewed as a primary outcome of commitment and not commitment itself (e.g., Klein et al., 2009b).

## Continuation

Continuance refers to the desire or intention to continue, or an unwillingness to withdraw from the target. This perspective can be traced back to the focus of many earlier researchers (e.g., Kanter, 1968) on explaining why people stay with an organization. This view was further popularized by Porter et al. (1974), who characterized organizational commitment as including a strong desire to maintain membership in the organization. This perspective has received criticism because commitment and the desire to continue with a target are distinct phenomena, with the latter being a primary outcome of commitment (Klein et al., 2009b). The notion of job embeddedness (Chapter 8), from turnover literature, is similar to these views on continuation as it reflects different ways one's life would be disrupted because of fit, links, and sacrifice if one left the organization (and/or community). Like notions of continuance commitment, job embeddedness reflects the perceived costs of leaving (Mitchell et al., 2001). The distinction between embeddedness and commitment is more apparent for commitment conceptualizations that do not view being stuck or having too much to lose as part of the definition or even antecedents of commitment.

## Attitude

Commitment is commonly presented as a work attitude, and some authors explicitly define commitment as an attitude or an overall evaluation of a target (e.g., Chusmir, 1982; Solinger et al., 2008). Conceptualizing commitment as an attitude has been criticized because the word "attitude" was vaguely used as a part of commitment definitions without defining exactly what was meant. Whether or not commitment can be considered an attitude thus depends on the definitions of both commitment and attitude being used. If attitudes are defined as a summary evaluation, such as good-bad or harmful-beneficial (Ajzen & Fishbein, 2000), that does not sufficiently capture or explain the commitment construct (Klein et al., 2009b). If one used the older view that attitudes have affective, behavioral, and cognitive dimensions (e.g., Olson & Zanna, 1993), then some definitions of commitment fit with that depiction (e.g., Solinger et al., 2008) while many other definitions are still incongruent. Most, but not all, recent commitment conceptualizations (e.g., Klein et al,

2012; Meyer & Herscovitch, 2001) consider commitment to be a psychological state rather than an attitude, with that psychological state reflecting how an object is represented in the mind (on a multitude of dimensions, not just the summary evaluation) at a particular point in time.

### Force vs. Bond

Even among authors defining commitment as a psychological state, there is disagreement about the specific nature of that state. For example, Meyer and Herscovitch (2001) view commitment as a force that binds an individual to a target, similar to a motivational force. From this perspective, committed antecedents create a force that is commitment, and which serves to bind a person to the target of commitment. Others define commitment as the attachment that results from that force (e.g., O'Reilly & Chatman, 1986; Neubert & Cady, 2001; Rusbult & Farrell, 1983). That is, the strength of a commitment is the strength of the adhesion or bond a person has to the commitment target. Others define commitment still more narrowly, as a specific type of attachment or bond (Klein et al., 2012), with other bond types constituting distinct constructs rather than different bases, forms, or types of commitment. Specifically, Klein et al. (2012) assert that commitment is a psychological state defined as "a volitional psychological bond reflecting dedication to and responsibility for a particular target" (p. 137) and distinguish commitment from other bond types including acquiescence, instrumental, and identification bonds. From this view, commitment is a particular type of attachment one feels to a target that is characterized by choice, dedication, and felt responsibility.

### Unidimensional vs. Multidimensional

The dimensionality of the construct is a final difference across the above conceptualizations (see Allen, 2016; Klein & Park, 2016). Prior conceptualizations of organization commitment reflect both uni- and multidimensional perspectives, with the unidimensional perspective being more prevalent for other workplace targets, though there are exceptions (e.g., union commitment). Multidimensional definitions largely reflect multiple bases for, rather than targets of, commitment. Indeed, even for some multidimensional models (i.e., Kanter; 1968; Meyer & Allen, 1991), commitment is defined singularly despite there being different types of commitment or commitment mindsets. Examples of authors presenting multidimensional frameworks include Buchanan (1974)— organizational commitment consisting of identification, involvement, and loyalty; Gordon et al. (1980)—union commitment having four factors: union loyalty, a responsibility to the union, willingness to work for the union, and belief in unionism; Kanter (1968)—commitments to social systems reflecting continuance, cohesion, or control; Meyer and Allen (1991)—organizational commitment reflecting a combination of three mindsets: affective, normative, and continuance; and O'Reilly and Chatman (1986)—organizational commitment consisting of three dimensions of psychological attachment: compliance, identification, and internalization.

Examples of authors defining commitment as unidimensional include Becker (1960; organizational commitment), Bishop and Scott (2000; team commitment), Blau (1985; career commitment), Klein et al. (2012, target neutral), Locke, Latham, and Erez (1988; goal commitment), and Porter et al. (1974; organizational commitment). Despite the widespread acceptance of some multidimensional frameworks, those frameworks have been challenged conceptually and empirically in terms of both structure and confounded content (e.g., Bayazit, Hammer, & Wazeter, 2004; Jaros, 2009; Klein et al., 2014). Klein and Park (2016) argue that a unidimensional view is more defensible conceptually in terms of parsimony, consistency across commitment targets (i.e., not all dimensions of other frameworks are applicable for all targets), and eliminating confounding elements (i.e., aspects of most multidimensional models conflate commitment with its antecedents, outcomes, or distinct constructs such as identification). Empirically, there are valid measures, discussed below, reflecting both approaches.

### Conceptualizations Summary

From the above discussion, it should be evident that commitment has been conceptualized in a wide variety of ways, which has hindered progress in understanding this phenomenon and created confusion regarding the nature of the construct and its relationship to other constructs such as job satisfaction, identification, involvement, engagement, and embeddedness. When there are alternative conceptualizations of a construct, the relative validity of the measures used to operationalize those conceptualizations can be compared, but doing so does not reveal which is the "correct" conceptualization. That determination is made by the consensus of the field, based on the perceived theoretical and empirical utility of each approach. Over the history of the study of commitment, there has never been a complete consensus regarding the definition of the construct. However, there have been shifts in the predominant operationalization—from the behavioral view rooted in sunk costs, side-bets, and continuing a course of action (e.g., Becker, 1960) to the attitudinal view focusing on identification and involvement (e.g., Mowday et al., 1979) to TCM provided by Meyer and Allen (1991). In our opinion, another shift is occurring, with the TCM model increasingly challenged. Unsurprisingly, we believe that the unidimensional, target neutral definition provided by Klein et al. (2012; i.e., as a volitional psychological bond reflecting dedication to and responsibility for a target), and the corresponding measure (Klein et al., 2014), to be the most defensible and best option for advancing commitment scholarship and informing practice. This conclusion is based on that conceptualization proving (a) a concise, parsimonious definition with clear boundaries to better differentiate commitment from other constructs and (b) applicability across the full range of targets within and outside of the workplace.

## Workplace Commitment Targets

As noted previously, workers have a wide array of workplace commitments, something that has been recognized for decades. Simon et al (1950), for example, noted that commitment to the organization is distinct from commitment to the organization's values, policies, and goals. The majority of research attention, however, has been given to commitment to the employing organization even though it has been suggested that this may not be as relevant as other workplace targets due to changes in the nature of work and the employment relationship (e.g., Cappelli, 2006; van Rossenberg et al., 2018). Those changes include but are not limited to shorter employment tenures, the increased prominence of short-term, project-based and contract workers, and advancements in technology that facilitate the spatial separation of work (e.g., flex offices, geographically dispersed teams). Because of these and other changes, commitment is as important as ever, as organizations still need committed workers. The issue is committed to what (e.g., goals, values, teams, projects), and for how long?

In addition, although it has long been recognized that people simultaneously hold multiple commitments to different work-related targets, those commitments have primarily been studied independently, with similarities obscured by the above noted definitional ambiguity and inconsistency. More studies are now examining multiple commitments, and recent target neutral definitions (Klein et al. 2012; Meyer & Herscovitch, 2001) and measures (Klein et al. 2014) facilitate the examination of multiple commitments. Below, we categorized potential workplace commitment targets into three groups (organizations/organizational units, people, and ideals and actions) and noted key articles summarizing what is known about commitment to these targets.

### Organizations and Organizational Units

These targets include not only the employing organization but also other organizations (e.g., unions, professional associations, client organizations) and organizational units (e.g., top management team, divisions, departments, work teams). Indeed, while it was previously evident that organizational commitment referred to the commitment to the employing organization, that is no longer necessarily the case with many workers performing tasks for organizations that are not their employer. There are several comprehensive summaries of what we know about organizational commitment (e.g., Klein, Becker, & Meyer, 2009a; Meyer, 2016; Meyer et al., 2002). Research on union commitment has generally sought to understand the makeup of union commitment, factors that influence workers to join, stay, and actively participate in unions as well as other outcomes of union commitment (e.g., Fullagar et al., 2004;

Tetrick et al., 2007). Research on team commitment, exemplified by Bishop and Scott (2000) and Wombacher and Felfe (2017), has focused on how predictors differentially influence team and organizational commitment as well as on how team commitment interacts with organizational commitment in affecting team processes and outcomes.

One change in the nature of work since early commitment research is that organizational boundaries have blurred, with more people working in boundary-spanning roles or working with stretched, porous, or no organizational boundaries (e.g., joint ventures, virtual structures, positions in client organizations, contract employment, telework, etc.), sometimes interacting with other organizations more closely than the one that employs them. Researchers have begun to examine commitments to these other organizations and the implications of being committed to multiple organizations. McElroy, Morrow, and Laczniak (2001) articulate a conceptualization of external organizational commitment, and Lapalme, Simard, and Tremblay (2011) and Swart et al. (2014) are examples of studies investigating this phenomenon.

## People

This category pertains to specific individuals (rather than groups) within or outside the organization (e.g., coworkers, supervisors, suppliers, customers). Of these specific individuals, most research has focused on commitment to supervisors. Much of this work examines the relationships between supervisor commitment and other commitments, most often team and organization (e.g., Cheng, Jiang, & Riley, 2003; Vandenberghe & Bentein, 2009). Interestingly, this research suggests that, depending on the context, supervisor commitment may align closely with either organizational commitment or with team commitment (e.g., Redman & Snape, 2005). Another theme in the supervisor commitment literature is identifying how this target uniquely predicts commitment outcomes such as turnover (e.g., Landry, Panaccio, & Vandenberghe, 2010).

## Ideals and Actions

The final set of workplace targets covers representations within the individual, including commitments to values, goals, decisions, strategies, policies, and change efforts as well as commitments to one's profession, occupation, and career. Because goals will not operate as intended without commitment, goal commitment plays a critical role in self-regulation (Klein, Cooper, & Monahan, 2013). Despite this important role, commitment was most often ignored or assumed in goal setting research prior to the late 1980s. Two reviews (Hollenbeck & Klein, 1987; Locke et al., 1988) highlighted the need for research on this key construct, and it has since received increased attention. Klein et al., (1999) presented a meta-analytic summary of that research, which was updated by Klein et al. (2013). Action commitments include commitments to specific planned activities, including strategies or strategic initiatives (e.g., Ford, Weissbein & Plamondon, 2003), change efforts (Herscovitch & Meyer, 2002), or other organizational programs (e.g., Ehrhardt et al., 2014; Neubert & Cady, 2001). These actions could be organization-wide efforts, focused on a unit within the organization, or an individual effort.

With decisions as to the commitment target, the literature has largely focused on the negative effects of escalating commitment to a course of action despite failures or worsening conditions that might rationally suggest ending that course of action. Foundational articles (e.g., Staw, 1981; Staw & Ross, 1978) documented this phenomenon and posited reasons for this illogical strengthening of commitment. Subsequent research has identified alternative mechanisms and moderators (e.g., ego threat, public evaluation of decision, resistance to decision from others) to better understand the phenomena, with a recent summary provided by Sleesman et al. (2012). Finally, commitment to one's profession (e.g., Jauch, Glueck, & Osborn, 1978; Wallace, 1995) occupation (e.g., Lee, Carswell, & Allen, 2000) and career (e.g., Blau, 1985) have each been studied as related but distinct targets. Research on these commitments has focused on how they relate to organizational commitment and the distinctiveness of these commitments in terms of unique antecedents and outcomes or by accounting for variance above and beyond organizational commitment in outcomes like turnover.

## Measurement of Commitment

With the exception of commitment to decisions, which is typically assessed behaviorally, commitments to most other workplace targets are assessed with self-report measures. A variety of different instruments have been used within and across the study of different commitment targets. There has also been considerable research addressing the dimensionality and validity of those different measures.

### *Organizational Commitment*

The dominant measure of organizational commitment has shifted over time, along with changes in the dominant conceptualization. Specifically, the OCQ (Mowday et al., 1979) was widely used up until the mid-1990s when it was supplanted by the TCM measures first provided by Allen and Meyer (1990), in part because of criticisms that the OCQ was confounded with withdrawal intentions. Despite its popularity, concerns have also been raised regarding the TCM measures (e.g., Jaros, 2007). In some cases, measures of commitment to other targets are adaptations of organizational commitment measures (e.g., Meyer, Allen, & Smith, 1993) whereas unique, target-specific measures were developed in other cases (e.g., Carson and Bedeian, 1994). Because organizational commitment measures were explicitly designed with the employing organization as the target, adapting these measures to other targets required extensive rewording of some items, raising questions of equivalence (Klein et al., 2014). Measures used for other targets are summarized below.

### Career/Professional/Occupational Commitment

Commitment to these targets has been measured in a variety of ways, some unique to the career literature, such as Blau (1985) and Carson and Bedeian (1994), while others have been adapted from measures of organizational commitment (e.g., Blau & Holladay, 2006; Meyer et al. 1993).

### Goal Commitment

Early goal setting research mainly assumed commitment rather than measuring it, and when it was measured, there was considerable variability in how it was assessed. A nine-item measure was presented by Hollenbeck, Williams, and Klein (1989), and variations of that measure have been widely used since, but not all studies used all of the items, and the dimensionality of the scale was criticized. A measurement model meta-analysis by Klein et al., (2001) recommended the use of a five-item version.

### Union Commitment

Gordon et al. (1980) presented a forty-eight item measure assessing four distinct dimensions. This measure was widely adapted, but like the Hollenbeck et al. (1989) goal commitment measure, different studies used different variations of the measure with several authors suggesting that a shorter version assessing fewer dimensions is sufficient (e.g., Friedman & Harvey, 1986; Kelloway, Catano, & Southwell, 1992).

### Target Neutral Measure

As evidenced above, a variety of measures of commitments has been used both within and across targets. This inconsistency makes it difficult to compare commitments to multiple targets directly. To facilitate the examination of multiple targets, Klein et al. (2012) purposefully defined commitment in a manner applicable to any target (i.e., a volitional psychological bond reflecting dedication to and responsibility for a target), and Klein et al. (2014) developed and validated a target neutral measure corresponding to that definition that is easily adaptable to any target. This measure, referred to as the K.U.T. (Klein et al., Unidimensional, Target neutral) commitment scale, consistently proves to be unidimensional as designed, with reliabilities above .80 even though it is just four, non-redundant items, presented in Table 7.1.

*Table 7.1* Target Neutral K.U.T. Commitment Items and Response Format[a]

| How committed are you to [your/the/this] [target]? | | | | |
| --- | --- | --- | --- | --- |
| To what extent do you care about [your/the/this] [target]? | | | | |
| How dedicated are you to [your/the/this] [target]? | | | | |
| To what extent have you chosen to be committed to [your/the/this] [target]? | | | | |
| 1 | 2 | 3 | 4 | 5 |
| Not at all | Slightly | Moderately | Quite a bit | Extremely |

*Source*: Klein et al. (2014) based on the conceptual definition provided in Klein et al. (2012). Translations into other languages can be found at u.osu.edu/commitmentmeasure/.

*Note*: a A 7-point response scale can also be used (Not at all, Slightly, Somewhat, Moderately, Mostly, Very, Completely) if restricted variance is a concern.

Having summarized the nature of commitment and its measurement, we next turn to what we know about the antecedents and outcomes of commitment.

## Antecedents of Commitment

Several factors have been identified as antecedents of commitment. It should be noted, however, that these have largely been identified through correlational rather than experimental research. To organize these numerous antecedents, we use the process model presented by Klein et al. (2012) and shown in Figure 7.1. Based on field theory (Lewin, 1943), promotion-prevention focus (Higgins, 1997), prospect theory (Kahneman & Tversky, 1979), and social cognitive theory (Bandura, 1997), this model posits that four proximal states are the immediate determinants of commitment to any target—salience, positive affect, trust, and perceived control—with an inclusive set of more distal antecedents, organized by level of analysis, that can influence the development of commitment through those four proximal states.

In terms of the more distal factors, individual level factors are attributes of the worker, such as values and personality traits. Personal values such as work ethic and work centrality have been shown to lead to commitment, as has value congruence with the target (Dubin, Champoux, & Porter, 1975; Mirels & Garrett, 1971). Several personality traits have been found to relate to commitment, including locus of control, conscientiousness, extraversion, and regulatory focus (Johnson, Chang, & Yang, 2010; Klein et al., 1999). Other individual differences shown to influence perceptual evaluations, such as trait affect, also influence commitment via the above proximal states. Target characteristics constitute the second category of antecedents and include factors such as the psychological proximity of the target, which impacts salience (Becker et al., 1996; Mueller & Lawler, 1999). Similarly, characteristics such as the legitimacy and reputation of the target can influence commitment through evaluations of trust and positive affect.

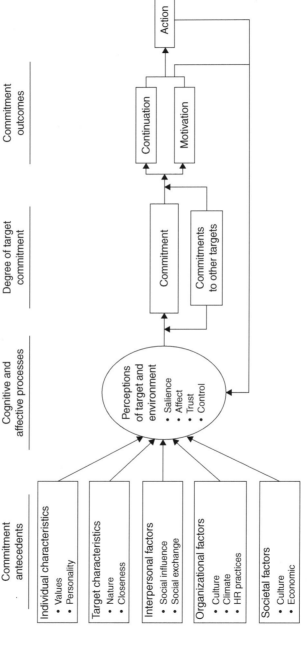

*Figure 7.1* Process Model of Commitment. Klein et al. (2012).

A third set of antecedents centers on work and nonwork social relationships. For example, research has shown that commitment is positively related to having a dense friendship network (Morrison, 2002). In addition, both social influences and exchanges resulting from social relationships can impact the identified perceptual evaluations and, subsequently, commitment. For example, Lawler, Thye, & Yoon (2000) found that frequent interactions among actors increases commitment via positive emotion and group salience. Other examples of these social influences include what others think and say about the target and the commitment of others. Social exchanges can similarly impact commitments, through such processes as supervisor supportiveness, leader-member exchange, and perceived organizational support.

Organizational and societal factors represent the final two categories of antecedents. Organizational-level antecedents that impact the more proximal states include culture (and subcultures) and climate as well as the organization's human resource practices. For example, both employee support programs (Grant, Dutton, & Rosso, 2008) and family supportive human resource practices (Wayne et al., 2013) have been found to be positively related to organizational commitment. Societal-level factors reflect the broader socioeconomic environment in which the individual and organization are embedded. Included here are national culture, as cultural factors such as power distance and collectivism can impact perceptions of control and trust, and have been shown to influence commitment (e.g., Cheng, Jiang, & Riley, 2003). Macroeconomic factors, including a country or region's economic conditions, business system characteristics, and labor market features (e.g., segmentation, strength, and role of unions), can similarly impact perceptions and, in turn, commitment (e.g., Hult, 2005).

## Commitment Outcomes

As noted previously, commitment is associated with a number of desirable consequences. The Klein et al. (2012) model, shown in Figure 7.1, proposes two immediate outcomes (i.e., continuation and motivation) with action and the results of those actions (e.g., performance) being more distal outcomes. Continuation includes both the intention to continue with the target and continuation behaviors. In short, committed individuals are less likely to withdraw from the target. Commitments to goals and decisions, for example, have been shown to be associated with an unwillingness to abandon goals (Hollenbeck & Klein, 1987) and decisions (e.g., Staw, 1981), and meta-analyses (e.g., Mathieu & Zajac, 1990; Meyer et al., 2002) have consistently demonstrated negative relationships between organizational commitment and turnover intentions, actual turnover, and other withdrawal behaviors (e.g., tardiness, absenteeism).

In terms of motivation, high commitment results in individuals' allocating more effort and resources in support of the target and being more willing to make trade-offs in favor of the target when allocating constrained resources such as time and attention (Klein et al., 2012). The relationship between commitment and motivation has been supported in prior research, summarized in the above referenced meta-analyses. Higher performance, both in-role and extra-role (e.g., organizational citizenship and prosocial behaviors) and at the individual, team, and organizational levels, is another frequently examined outcome of commitment. The Klein et al. (2012) model in Figure 7.1 holds that the effects of commitment on performance are indirect, through the effects of continuation and motivation. Of the various dimensions of performance examined, results have been the strongest in predicting extra-role or discretionary behavior.

Worker wellbeing is another commitment outcome being examined with increasing frequency. As summarized by Meyer and Maltin (2010), commitment has shown positive associations with various types of wellbeing (including physical wellbeing, general physical health, and mental health) and negative associations with strain such as physical and mental health complaints (including anxiety and depression), burnout and stress. Although wellbeing has generally been examined as an outcome of commitment, some studies (e.g., Vandenberghe, Mignonac, & Manville, 2015) have examined the role of commitment in either buffering or exacerbating the adverse effects of perceived stressors on tension, anxiety, burnout, and depression. Empirical evidence of the moderating role of commitment has supported both the buffering and exacerbating effects. Other studies (e.g., Jain, Giga, & Cooper, 2009) also have examined wellbeing as an antecedent of commitment, and Klein et al. (2017) identified negative effects on wellbeing as one of the reasons workers cease being committed to workplace targets.

## Current Issues and Future Research Needs

We conclude by identifying several current issues that need to be addressed in order to advance our understanding of workplace commitments and provide a better prescription for managing the multiple commitments workers hold in the contemporary workplace.

### *Meaning and Measurement*

As covered in this chapter, numerous conceptualizations of commitment can be found in the literature. A diversity of perspectives can be useful, but a lack of consensus regarding the meaning, structure, and measurement of commitment creates confusion about the nature, operation, and usefulness of the construct. As such, it would help if a greater consensus was reached about some fundamental issues relating to (a) whether commitment is a bond or the force that creates that bond, (b) whether commitment is uni- or multidimensional, and (c) the location of the construct boundary (e.g., does commitment include behavioral intentions or are those intentions an outcome of commitment?). Relatedly, further theoretical work is needed articulating the mechanisms by which commitment operates. There are numerous models in the commitment literature, but most theoretical explanations are imported from other topics. For example, a predominant theoretical explanation is social exchange theory, but this theory is not relevant for all conceptualizations or targets of commitment (e.g., Weng & McElroy, 2012).

These issues are critical because the conceptual definition of a construct is the basis for determining the construct validity of measures meant to assess that construct, issues of construct redundancy, and whether or not observed empirical relationships may be inflated due to the measure including elements of the other examined constructs (Klein et al., 2014). Given these conceptual disagreements, it is not surprising that there are also questions regarding the proper measurement of commitment (e.g., whether to use a uni-or multidimensional scale, whether to use the same measure across targets or target specific measures). These issues cannot be addressed through critical studies comparing alternative views. The relative validity of the different measures used to operationalize distinct conceptualizations can be compared, but doing so does not reveal which is the more accurate or useful conceptualization.

### *Target Differences*

Klein and colleagues (2012, 2014) have presented a target neutral model and measure of commitment, but that does not mean that the target does not matter or that targets are interchangeable, only that distinct constructs are not needed to reflect commitments to different targets. Indeed, Klein et al. (2012) acknowledge that there are likely variations in key antecedents or other aspects of commitment that vary by target. Systematic research is needed to identify those differences, which is more easily accomplished with a common definition and measure. Relatedly, Klein et al. (2012) noted the need to develop a parsimonious typology for organizing the numerous potential workplace commitment targets, as the current set of targets is rather unwieldy and there is insufficient evidence to support the groupings that have been used (including the three categories used above in this chapter).

Without understanding how commitments to different targets are similar or different from each other, it is difficult to explain or predict what commitments are most desirable in what contexts, an increasingly important issue for organizations and managers in a changing workplace. Despite the recognized need for a target typology, van Rossenberg et al. (2018) concluded that new theory or considerable additional research evidence is needed to be able to have more confidence in what target commitments operate similarly. Examples of needed research across commitment targets include identifying how the relative importance of the antecedents and outcomes might vary across targets and whether there are systematic differences in the development, maintenance, or dissipation of commitment over time and across targets.

## Commitment Dynamics

Commitment has historically been viewed as largely stable once established. However, it is now more commonly thought of as a fluid psychological state. Commitment theory is just beginning to catch up with the recognition that commitments are dynamic. Understanding the temporality of commitment is increasingly vital because organizations now need employees who can readily develop and relinquish commitments. A contract worker, for example, needs to commit quickly to their tasks, then move past those commitments, and commit to their next assignment. If this relinquishment does not occur, their success and well-being may suffer. There is a large body of cross-sectional research examining correlates of commitment, but relatively little longitudinal research examining exactly how commitment develops, variation in commitment within individuals over time, or the dissipation of commitment. Exceptions here include Bentein et al., (2005) and Solinger, Hofmans, and Olffen (2015). In addition, evidence suggests that the key factors that alter commitment often differ from those that initially facilitate the development of commitment (e.g., Klein et al., 2017). Thus, despite the increased attention being given to the temporality of commitment, additional theory is needed to explain better that dynamism and the dynamic aspects of commitment need to be more systematically examined. In doing so, it is recommended that more studies take a within-person approach.

The recognition of the dynamic nature of commitment and the fact that commitment is distinct from attachment has led to the identification of two new related constructs—residual and quondam commitments. Residual commitments (Breitsohl & Ruhle, 2013, 2016) involve the continuation of a commitment over time even after separating from the commitment target (e.g., remaining committed to a former team member even if no longer on the same team). The determinants and consequences of these residual commitments require further study as these remaining commitments may have implications for the formation of new commitments and/or create conflicting demands (Breitsohl & Ruhle, 2013). In contrast, quondam commitments (Klein et al., 2017) are commitments that no longer exist, but once were consequential for an individual and, as such, may still influence the way they think, feel, and act. We know little about the consequences of such quondam commitments on work attitudes, behavior, or well-being; or how those effects differ depending on the reasons the commitment ends. The Klein et al. (2017) study suggests that quondam commitments can occur gradually or abruptly, for a variety of reasons, most of which are distinct from established commitment antecedents, and may result from intra-individual factors (e.g., shifts in personal values), or factors in the external environment (e.g., a new supervisor).

## *Multiple Commitments*

As noted previously, it has long been recognized that workers have multiple commitments, but those commitments have largely been studied independently. Several workplace trends make understanding multiple commitments more important, and studies are increasingly looking at more than one commitment. From that research, we know that commitments to multiple targets predict workplace outcomes over and above each other, and in distinct ways. Yet, this has typically been in dual combinations or occasionally in larger, one-off groupings. Such efforts are difficult to integrate, and ignore the broader interconnectedness among other unexamined targets. Indeed, it has been suggested that in most cases, examining any one, or even a pair of, commitments in isolation from the full interrelated set of commitments associated with a given role will result in incomplete understanding and prediction (Klein et al., in press).

In addition, although theorists have regularly recognized the existence of multiple commitments (e.g., Gouldner, 1960; Klein et al., 2012; Reichers, 1986), current commitment theory does not provide much guidance or a sufficient explanation for some key questions. Specifically, commitment theory needs to be extended to better understand and predict the multiple commitments individuals simultaneously hold, the inter-relationships among those commitments, how those inter-relationships change over time, and how sets of target commitments collectively impact behavior. A more systemic approach is needed to account for different target commitments being synergistic, unrelated, or conflicting, to provide an explanation as to when each type of relationship can be expected, and to provide guidance for helping individuals manage their multiple commitments, particularly when they do conflict.

Some recent multiple commitment studies have taken a person-centered approach (e.g., Morin et al., 2011). These studies show that commitments to different targets may or may not cluster together, with the same targets being compatible or conflicting, depending on the person and context. Although the person-centered approach can identify multiple sub-groups with different commitment target profiles, this research has not examined the mechanisms or contingent factors that might explain profile emergence or membership (Meyer & Morin, 2016). As an alternative, Klein et al. (in press) propose taking a systems perspective to provide a theoretical basis for understanding the dynamic interrelationships among multiple commitments. Klein et al. (in press) define a commitment system as a network of inter-relating commitments to a bounded set of targets, define several system attributes that can be studied, discuss the formation and operation of commitment systems, and note that tools exist in other fields that can be applied to model commitment systems, and more importantly, track changes in commitment systems over time. One important implication of this perspective is that in most cases, because of the inter-relationships among target commitments, examining a single commitment in isolation from other related commitments will result in an incomplete understanding or prediction.

## *Dark Sides of Commitment*

Another critical future research need is to understand better the potential negative effects of commitment (e.g., Randall, 1988). Except for the work on the escalation of commitment in decision-making, the literature has largely assumed that more or stronger commitment is always better without sufficiently recognizing that the consequences of high commitment can be either positive or negative for the individual, the organization, or both. That is, the "too much of a good thing" effect (Pierce & Aguinis, 2013) is clearly applicable to the study of commitment. There are several different ways in which commitments can be problematic. First, an extremely strong commitment can become overzealousness, negatively impacting judgment and decision-making, blinding workers to the need for change, and possibly resulting in detrimental, perhaps even illegal or unethical actions. This suggests that researchers should examine the potential non-linear effects of commitment on various workplace outcomes. Second, even if not extreme, strong commitments can be detrimental when the target of that commitment is problematic (e.g., a flawed decision or strategy, rogue supervisor, misguided goal). Third, workers remaining committed to targets that are no longer relevant or needed by the organization can create rigidity and hinder the organization's ability to adapt.

A fourth potential issue is that workers can have too many commitments, leading to conflicting commitments or being unable to act upon them all, hindering performance and creating stress. Fifth, even if an individual does not have too many commitments, negative outcomes can still result if the demands of a single commitment lead to the individual expending levels of effort that are not sustainable without sacrificing other commitments or well-being. Research suggests that individuals can simultaneously commit to multiple targets and that such commitments need not conflict (Randall 1988). There are, however, limits to an individual's resources (e.g., time, attention), and conflict is likely to result when multiple commitments create incompatible demands. Additional research is needed to better understand both over-commitment and competing commitments, as well as whether there are individual (e.g., self-regulation, trait self-control) or situational (e.g., supportiveness, complexity) factors that moderate a person's ability to manage multiple, competing commitments. Finally, there are costs of developing and maintaining commitments. In some situations, those costs may outweigh the benefits, particularly if another type of bond would suffice.

### *Cultural Differences*

Commitment research has been conducted in numerous countries, and it appears that commitment is relevant across cultures and that national culture influences workplace commitments (e.g., Meyer et al., 2012). As an example, Fisher (2014) found that power distance influences the moderating effects of empowerment and cooperative climate on the relationship between role overload and organizational commitment. However, we do not yet fully understand cultural differences in how commitment develops, is experienced, and influences behavior. There is some evidence that commitment conceptualizations, models, and measures developed in North America can be applied reasonably well to other cultures. That view has, however, been challenged (e.g., Wasti & Önder, 2009), and those results, largely using an imposed etic approach, questioned. More in-depth, qualitative research is warranted, taking an emic approach, to understand better what commitment means to individuals with different cultural backgrounds and values rather than simply evaluating the transportability of existing models. After doing so, and after revising our models if needed, other issues, including the appropriate translation of items and equivalence of commitment measures and the effects of culture, values, and norms on the development and experience of commitment, can be examined.

## Implications for Practice

Managers and human resource (HR) professionals are concerned with facilitating desired workplace commitments because of the positive effects of those commitments on outcomes important to organizations and employees, namely motivation, extra role behaviors, retention, and wellbeing (Meyer, 2016). Managers are in a position to influence the objective features of the work environment and, perhaps more importantly, how that environment is perceived by workers (e.g., Berg, Janoff-Bulman, & Cotter, 2001). As such, managers can use the four immediate antecedents of commitment identified by Klein et al. (2012) to facilitate the formation and maintenance of commitments. The first of these is salience. Managers can increase the salience of a target in several ways, including communicating why that target is important and making that target meaningful for the employee. Another way to facilitate that salience is to have employees make their commitments public (e.g., Klein et al., 2019). Two other immediate antecedents are trust and affect. Employees are more likely to commit to something they view positively and feel good about, and without trust, employees are unlikely to have the dedication that is at the core of commitment. Managers can thus influence commitments by helping ensure that desired commitment targets are trusted and positively evaluated. Research has shown, for example, that developing positive team climates enhances team commitment (e.g., Liao & Rupp, 2005; Simons & Roberson, 2003). Finally, employees must believe that they have some control or influence relating to the target. Hence, managers can also help build and maintain desired commitments through empowerment (e.g., Avolio et al., 2004) and facilitating efficacy (e.g., Mills & Fullagar, 2017).

An organization's human resource (HR) management practices can similarly be designed to help facilitate commitments. Most HR practices are aimed at enhancing motivation, performance, and/or retention—outcomes that result from commitment. That is, commitment is often an assumed mediator between HR practices and the intended outcomes of those practices. Commitments can begin to form during the talent acquisition process through the treatment of applicants and fit-based selection (e.g., Truxillo, Bauer, & Garcia, 2017). Commitments can continue to be built through talent development, starting with onboarding (e.g., Klein & Weaver, 2000) and using training and development to signal opportunity and provide recognition (e.g., Breitsohl & Ruhle, 2013). Talent management, rewards, and employee/labor relations can similarly foster commitment by facilitating positive affect and perceptions of trust, fairness, and being appreciated. The macro HR literature often invokes commitment as a key "black box" construct connecting HR policies and practices to organizational outcomes, as evidenced by the notion of high commitment work systems (e.g., Arthur, 1994). Specifically, practices associated with such HR systems, including but not limited to involvement in decision making, training for skill development and group problem solving, and corporate volunteering, should also facilitate worker commitments (e.g., Gellatly et al., 2009; Grant et al. 2008). Given changes to the employment relationship, however, it is important that the full range of desired workplace commitments, as well as the dynamic nature and interdependencies among those multiple commitments, are considered when designing those policies and practices, and not just organizational commitment (van Rossenberg et al., 2018).

## Conclusion

This chapter has summarized the history of commitment research, discussed the various ways it has been conceptualized, highlighted the different workplace commitment targets that have been studied, overviewed the different commitment measures, summarized what we know about the antecedents and outcomes of commitment, and outlined a set of current issues and future research needs. Commitment has been one of the most frequently examined constructs within the study of organizational phenomena. From that attention, there is much we know about the correlates and consequences of commitment, but much remains unknown. A better understanding of commitment is important from both academic and practice perspectives, requiring further investigation and clarification. Despite substantial changes in the nature of organizations, work, and employment relationship since the origins of commitment scholarship, organizations still need committed workers and individuals predisposed to form commitments.

# References

Ajzen, I. (1991). The theory of planned behavior. *Organizational Behavior and Human Decision Processes, 50(2)*, 179–211.

Ajzen, I. & Fishbein, M. (2000). Attitudes and the attitude-behavior relation: Reasoned and automatic processes. *European Review of Social Psychology, 11(1)*, 1–33.

Allen, N.J. (2016). Commitment as a multidimensional construct. In J.P. Meyer (Ed.) *The Handbook of Employee Commitment*. Northampton, MA: Edward Elgar Publishing. 28–42.

Allen, N.J. & Meyer, J.P. (1990). The measurement and antecedents of affective, continuance and normative commitment to the organization. *Journal of Occupational Psychology, 63*(1), 1–18.

Angle, H.L. & Perry, J.L. (1981). An empirical assessment of organizational commitment and organizational effectiveness. *Administrative Science Quarterly, 26*(1), 1–14.

Arthur, J.B. (1994). Effects of human resource systems on manufacturing performance and turnover. *Academy of Management Journal, 37*(3), 670–687.

Avolio, B.J., Zhu, W., Koh, W., & Bhatia, P. (2004). Transformational leadership and organizational commitment: Mediating role of psychological empowerment and moderating role of structural distance. *Journal of Organizational Behavior, 25(8)*, 951–968.

Bandura, A. (1997). *Self-efficacy: The exercise of control*. New York, NY: W.H. Freeman and Company.

Barnard, J. (1938). *The Functions of the Executive*. New York, NY: McGraw Hill.

Bayazit, M., Hammer, T.H., & Wazeter, D.L. (2004). Methodological challenges in union commitment studies. *Journal of Applied Psychology, 89(4)*, 738.

Bentein, K., Vandenberghe, C., Vandenberg, R.J., & Stinglhamber, F. (2005) The role of change in the relationship between commitment and turnover: A latent growth modeling approach. *Journal of Applied Psychology, 90(3)*, 468–482.

Becker, H.S., (1960). Notes on the concept of commitment. *American Journal of Sociology, 66(1)*, 32–40.

Becker, T.E., (1992). Foci and bases of commitment: are they distinctions worth making? *Academy of Management Journal, 35(1)*, 232–244.

Becker, T.E., Billings, R.S., Eveleth, D.M., & Gilbert, N.L. (1996). Foci and bases of employee commitment: Implications for job performance. *Academy of Management Journal, 39(2)*, 464–482.

Berg, M.B., Janoff-Bulman, R., & Cotter, J. (2001). Perceiving value in obligations and goals: Wanting to do what should be done. *Personality and Social Psychology Bulletin, 27(8)*, 982–995.

Bishop, J.W. & Scott, K.D. (2000). An examination of organizational and team commitment in a self-directed team environment. *Journal of Applied Psychology, 85(3)*, 439–450.

Blau, G.J. (1985). The measurement and prediction of career commitment. *Journal of Occupational Psychology, 58(4)*, 277–288.

Blau, G. & Holladay, E.B. (2006). Testing the discriminant validity of a four dimensional occupational commitment measure. *Journal of Occupational and Organizational Psychology, 79(4)*, 691–704.

Breitsohl, H. & Ruhle, S.A. (2013), Residual affective commitment to organizations: concept, causes and consequences. *Human Resource Management Review, 23(2)*, 161–173.

Breitsohl, H. & Ruhle, S.A. (2016). The end is the beginning–The role of residual affective commitment in former interns' intention to return and word-of-mouth. *European Journal of Work and Organizational Psychology, 25(6)*, 833–848.

Brockner, J. (1992) The escalation of commitment to a failing course of action: Toward theoretical progress. *Academy of Management Review, 17(1)*, 39–61.

Buchanan, B., (1974). Building organizational commitment: the socialization of managers in work organizations. *Administrative Science Quarterly, 19*, 533–546.

Carson, K.D. & Bedeian, A.G. (1994): Career commitment: Construction of a measure and examination of its psychometric properties. *Journal of Vocational Behavior, 44(3)*, 237–262.

Cappelli, P. (2006). Changing career paths and their implications. In *America at Work* (pp. 211–224). New York: Palgrave Macmillan.

Cheng, B.S., Jiang, D.Y., & Riley, J.H. (2003). Organizational commitment, supervisory commitment, and employee outcomes in the Chinese context: proximal hypothesis or global hypothesis? *Journal of Organizational Behavior, 24(3)*, 313–334.

Chusmir, L.H. (1982). Job commitment and the organizational woman. *Academy of Management Review, 7(4)*, 595–602.

Cooper-Hakim, A. & Viswesvaran, C. (2005). The construct of work commitment: Testing an integrative framework. *Psychological Bulletin, 131(2)*, 241–259.

Cropanzano, R. & Mitchell, M.S. (2005). Social exchange theory: An interdisciplinary review. *Journal of Management, 31(6)*, 874–900.

Dubin, R., Champoux, J.E., & Porter, L.W. (1975). Central life interests and organizational commitment of blue-collar and clerical workers. *Administrative Science Quarterly, 20*, 411–421.

Ehrhardt, K., Miller, J.S., Freeman, S.J., & Hom, P.W. (2014). Examining project commitment in cross functional teams: Antecedents and relationship with team performance. *Journal of Business and Psychology, 29(3)*, 443–461.

Fisher, D.M. (2014). A multilevel cross-cultural examination of role overload and organizational commitment: Investigating the interactive effects of context. *Journal of Applied Psychology, 99(4)*, 723–736.

Ford, J.K., Weissbein, D.A., & Plamondon, K.E. (2003). Distinguishing organizational from strategy commitment: Linking officers' commitment to community policing to job behaviors and satisfaction. *Justice Quarterly, 20(1)*, 159–185.

Friedman, L. & Harvey, R.J. (1986). Factors of union commitment: The case for a lower dimensionality. *Journal of Applied Psychology, 71(3)*, 371–376.

Fullagar, C.J., Gallagher, D.G., Clark, P.F., & Carroll, A.E. (2004). Union commitment and participation: A 10 year longitudinal study. *Journal of Applied Psychology, 89(4)*, 730–737.

Gagné, M. & Deci, E.L. (2005). Self-determination theory and work motivation. *Journal of Organizational behavior, 26(4)*, 331–362.

Grant, A.M., Dutton, J.E., & Rosso, B.D. (2008). Giving commitment: Employee support programs and the prosocial sensemaking process. *Academy of Management Journal, 51(5)*, 898–918.

Gellatly, I.R., Hunter, K.H., Currie, L.G., & Irving, P.G. (2009). HRM practices and organizational commitment profiles. *The International Journal of Human Resource Management, 20(4)*, 869–884.

Gordon, M.E., Philpot, J.W., Burt, R.E., Thompson, C.A., & Spiller, W.E. (1980). Commitment to the union: Development of a measure and an examination of its correlates. *Journal of Applied Psychology, 65(4)*, 479–499.

Gouldner, H.P. (1960). Dimensions of organizational commitment. *Administrative Science Quarterly, 4*(4), 468–490.

Herscovitch, L. & J.P. Meyer. (2002). Commitment to organizational change: Extension of a three component model. *Journal of Applied Psychology, 87(3)*, 474–487.

Higgins, E.T. (1997). Beyond pleasure and pain. *American Psychologist, 52(12)*, 1280–1300.

Hollenbeck, J.R. & Klein, H.J. (1987). Goal commitment and the goal setting process: Problems, prospects and proposals for future research. *Journal of Applied Psychology, 72(2)*, 212–220.

Hollenbeck, J.R., Williams, C.R., & Klein, H.J. (1989). An empirical examination of the antecedents of commitment to difficult goals. *Journal of Applied Psychology, 74(1)*, 18–23.

Hrebiniak, L.G. & J.A. Alutto. (1972). Personal and role related factors in the development of organizational commitment. *Administrative Science Quarterly, 17(4)*, 555–573.

Hult, C. (2005). Organizational commitment and person- environment fit in six western countries. *Organization Studies, 26(2)*, 249–270.

Jain, A.K., Giga, S.I., & Cooper, C.L. (2009). Employee wellbeing, control and organizational commitment. *Leadership & Organization Development Journal, 30(3)*, 256–273.

Jaros, S.J. (2007). Meyer and Allen model of organizational commitment: Measurement issues. *The Icfai Journal of Organizational Behavior, 6(4)*, 7–25.

Jaros, S. (2009). Measurement of commitment. In: Klein, H.J., Becker, T.E., Meyer, J.P. (Eds.), *Commitment in Organizations: Accumulated Wisdom and New Directions* (pp. 347–381). New York, NY: Routledge/Taylor and Francis..

Jauch, L.R., Glueck, W.F., & Osborn, R.N. (1978). Organizational loyalty, professional commitment, and academic research productivity. *Academy of Management Journal, 21(1)*, 84–92.

Johnson, R.E., Chang, C., & Yang, L. (2010). Commitment and motivation at work: The relevance of employee identity and regulatory focus. *Academy of Management Review, 35(2)*, 226–245.

Kahneman, D. & Tversky, A. (1979). Prospect theory: An analysis of decision under risk. *Econometrica, 47(2)*, 263–291.

Kanter, R.M. (1968). Commitment and social organization: A study of commitment mechanisms in utopian communities. *American Sociological Review, 33(4)*, 499–517.

Keisler, C. & Sakamura, J. (1966). A test of a model for commitment. *Journal of Personality and Social Psychology, 3(3)*, 349–353.

Kelloway, E.K., Catano, V.M., & Southwell, R.R. (1992). Construct validity of union commitment: Development and dimensionality of a shorter scale. *Journal of Occupational and Organizational Psychology, 65(3)*, 197–211.

Klein, H.J., Becker, T.E., & Meyer, J.P. (2009a). *Commitment in Organizations: Accumulated Wisdom and New Directions*. New York, NY: Routledge/Taylor and Francis.

Klein, H.J., Molloy, J.C., & Cooper, J.T. (2009b). Conceptual foundations: Construct definitions and theoretical representations of workplace commitments. In H.J. Klein, T.E. Becker, & J.P. Meyer (Eds.) *Commitment in Organizations: Accumulated Wisdom and New Directions* (pp. 3–36). New York, NY: Routledge/Taylor and Francis Group.

Klein, H.J., Brinsfield, C.T., Cooper, J.T., & Molloy, J.C. (2017). Quondam commitments: An examination of commitments employees no longer have. *Academy of Management Discoveries, 3*(4), 331–357.

Klein, H.J., Cooper, J.T., Molloy, J.C., & Swanson, J.A. (2014). The assessment of commitment: Advantages of a unidimensional, target-free approach. *Journal of Applied Psychology, 99(2)*, 222–238.

Klein, H.J., Cooper, J.T., & Monahan C.A. (2013). Goal commitment. In E.A. Locke & G.P. Latham (Eds.) *Developments in Goal Setting and Task Performance* (pp. 65–89). New York, NY: Routledge/Taylor and Francis.

Klein, H.J., Lount, R.B., Park, H.M., & Linford, B.J. (2019). When goals are known: The effects of audience relative status on goal commitment and performance. *Journal of Applied Psychology, 105(4)*, 372–389.

Klein, H.J., Molloy, J.C., & Brinsfield, C.T. (2012). Reconceptualizing workplace commitment to redress a stretched construct: revisiting assumptions and removing confounds. *Academy of Management Review, 37(1)*, 130–151.

Klein, H.J., Molloy, J.C., & Cooper, J.T. (2009). Conceptual foundations: Construct definitions and theoretical representations of workplace commitments. In H. J. Klein, T. E. Becker, & J. P. Meyer (Eds.) *Commitment in Organizations: Accumulated Wisdom and New Directions* (p.3–36). Routledge/Taylor and Francis Group.

Klein, H.J. & Park, H.M. (2016). Commitment as a unidimensional construct. In J.P. Meyer (Ed.) *The Handbook of Employee Commitment* (pp. 15–27). Northampton, MA: Edward Elgar Publishing.

Klein, H.J., Solinger, O., & Duflot, V. (in press). Commitment system theory: The evolving structure of commitments to multiple targets. *Academy of Management Review*.

Klein, H.J & Weaver, N. (2000). The effectiveness of an organizational-level orientation training program in the socialization of new hires. *Personnel Psychology, 53(1)*, 47–66.

Klein, H.J., Wesson, M.J., Hollenbeck, J.R., & Alge, B.J. (1999). Goal commitment and the goal setting process: Conceptual clarification and empirical synthesis. *Journal of Applied Psychology, 84(6)*, 885–896.

Klein, H.J., Wesson, M.J., Hollenbeck, J.R., Wright, P.M., & DeShon, R.D. (2001). The assessment of goal commitment: A measurement model metaanalysis. *Organizational Behavior and Human Decision Processes, 85(1)*, 32–55.

Landry, G., Panaccio, A., & Vandenberghe, C. (2010). Dimensionality and consequences of employee commitment to supervisors: A two study examination. *The Journal of Psychology, 144(3)*, 285–312.

Lapalme, M.È., Simard, G., & Tremblay, M. (2011). The influence of psychological contract breach on temporary workers' commitment and behaviors: A multiple agency perspective. *Journal of Business and Psychology, 26(3)*, 311–324.

Lawler, E.J., Thye, S.R., & Yoon, J. (2000). Emotion and group cohesion in productive exchange. *American Journal of Sociology, 106*(3), 616–657.

Liao, H. & Rupp, D.E. (2005). The impact of justice climate and justice orientation on work outcomes: A cross-level multifoci framework. *Journal of Applied Psychology, 90*(2), 242–256.

Lee, K., Carswell, J.J., & Allen, N.J. (2000). A meta analytic review of occupational commitment: Relations with person and work related variables. *Journal of Applied Psychology*, 85(5), 799–811.

Lewin, K. (1943). Defining the "field at a given time." *Psychological Review, 50(3)*, 292–310.

Locke, E.A., Latham, G.P., & Erez, M. (1988). The determinants of goal commitment. *Academy of Management Review, 13(1)*, 23–39.

Mathieu, J.E. & Zajac, D.M. (1990). A review and meta-analysis of the antecedents, correlates, and consequences of organizational commitment. *Psychological Bulletin, 108(2)*, 171–194.

McElroy, J.C., Morrow, P.C., & Laczniak, R.N. (2001). External organizational commitment. *Human Resource Management Review, 11(3)*, 237–256.

Merton, R.K. (1957). *Social Theory and Social Structure*. Glencoe, IL: Free Press.

Meyer, J.P. (2016). *The Handbook of Employee Commitment*. Northampton, MA: Edward Elgar.

Meyer, J.P. & Allen, N.J. (1991). A three-component conceptualization of organizational commitment. *Human Resource Management Review, 1(1)*, 61–89.

Meyer, J.P., Allen, N.J., & Smith, C.A. (1993). Commitment to organizations and occupations: Extension and test of a three component conceptualization. *Journal of Applied Psychology, 78(4)*, 538–551.

Meyer, J.P. & Herscovitch, L. (2001). Commitment in the workplace: toward a general model. *Human Resource Management Review, 11(3)*, 299–326.

Meyer, J.P. & Maltin, E.R. (2010). Employee commitment and wellbeing: a critical review, theoretical framework and research agenda. *Journal of Vocational Behavior, 77(2)*, 323–337.

Meyer, J.P. & Morin, A.J.S. (2016). A person centered approach to commitment research: Theory, research, and methodology. *Journal of Organizational Behavior, 37(4)*, 584–612.

Meyer, J.P., Stanley, D.J., Herscovitch, L., & Topolnytsky, L. (2002). Affective, continuance, and normative commitment to the organization: a meta-analysis of antecedents, correlates, and consequences. *Journal of Vocational Behavior, 61(1)*, 20–52.

Meyer, J.P., Stanley, D.J., Jackson, T.A., McInnis, K.J., Maltin, E.R., & Sheppard, L. (2012). Affective, normative, and continuance commitment levels across cultures: A meta analysis. *Journal of Vocational Behavior, 80 (2)*, 225–245.

Mills, M.J. & Fullagar, C.J. (2017). Engagement within occupational trainees: Individual difference predictors and commitment outcome. *Journal of Vocational Behavior, 98*, 35–45.

Mirels, H.L. & Garrett, J.B. (1971). The Protestant ethic as a personality variable. *Journal of Consulting and Clinical Psychology, 36(1)*, 40–44.

Mitchell, T.R., Holtom, B.C., Lee, T.W., Sablynski, C.J., & Erez, M. (2001). Why people stay: Using job embeddedness to predict voluntary turnover. *Academy of Management Journal, 44(6)*, 1102–1121.

Morin, A.J.S., Morizot, J., Boudrias, J.S., & Madore, I. (2011). A Multifoci Person Centered Perspective on Workplace Affective Commitment: A Latent Profile/Factor Mixture Analysis. *Organizational Research Methods, 14(1)*, 58–90.

Morrison, E.W. (2002). Newcomers' relationships: The role of social network ties during socialization. *Academy of Management Journal, 45(6)*, 1149–1160.

Morrow, P.C. (1983). Concept redundancy in organizational research: The case of work commitment. *Academy of Management Review, 8(3)*, 486–500.

Mowday, R.T., Steers, R.M., & Porter, L.W. (1979). The Measurement of Organizational Commitment. *Journal of Vocational Behavior, 14(2)*, 224–247.

Mueller, C.W. & Lawler, E.J. (1999). Commitment to nested organizational units: Some basic principles and preliminary findings. *Social Psychology Quarterly, 62(4)*, 325–346.

Neubert, M.J. & S.H. Cady. (2001). Program commitment: A multi study longitudinal field investigation of its impact and antecedents. *Personnel Psychology, 54(2)*, 421–448.

O'Reilly, C. & Chatman, J. (1986). Organizational commitment and psychological attachment: The effects of compliance, identification, and internalization on prosocial behavior. *Journal of Applied Psychology, 71(3)*, 492–499.

Olson, J.M. & Zanna, M.P. (1993). Attitudes and attitude change. *Annual Review of Psychology, 44*(1), 117–154.

Pierce, J.R. & Aguinis, H. (2013). The too-much-of-a-good-thing effect in management. *Journal of Management, 39(2)*, 313–338.

Pinder, C.C. (1998). *Motivation in Work Organizations*. Upper Saddle River, NJ: Prentice Hall.

Porter, L.W., Steers, R.M., Mowday, R.T., & Boulian, P.V. (1974). Organizational commitment, job satisfaction, and turnover among psychiatric technicians. *Journal of Applied Psychology, 59(5)*, 603–609.

Randall, D.M. (1988). Multiple roles and organizational commitment. *Journal of Organizational Behavior, 9(4)*, 309–317.

Redman, T. & Snape, E. (2005). Unpacking commitment: multiple loyalties and employee behaviour. *Journal of Management Studies, 42(2)*, 301–328.

Reichers, A.E. (1985). A review and reconceptualization of organizational commitment. *Academy of Management Review, 10(3)*, 465–476.

Reichers, A.E. (1986). Conflict and organizational commitments. *Journal of Applied Psychology, 71(3)*, 508.

Rusbult, C.E. & Farrell, D. (1983). A longitudinal test of the investment model: The impact on job satisfaction, job commitment, and investments. *Journal of Applied Psychology, 68(3)*, 429–438.

Salancik, G.R. (1977). Commitment and the control of organizational behavior. In: Staw, B.M., Salancik, G.R. (Eds.), *New Directions in Organizational Behaviour* (pp. 1–54). Chicago, IL: St. Clair Press.

Simon, H.A., Smithburg, D.W., & Thompson, V.A. (1950). *Public Administration*. New York, NY: Knopf.

Simons, T. & Roberson, Q. (2003). Why managers should care about fairness: The effects of aggregate justice perceptions on organizational outcomes. *Journal of Applied Psychology, 88(3)*, 432–443.

Sleesman, D., Conlon, D., McNamara, G., & Miles, J. (2012). Cleaning up the big muddy: A meta analytic review of the determinants of escalation of commitment. *Academy of Management Journal, 55(3)*, 541–562.

Solinger, O.N., Hofmans, V., & Olffen, W. (2015). The dynamic microstructure of organizational commitment. *Journal of Occupational and Organizational Psychology*, 88(4), 773–796.

Solinger, O.N., Van Olffen, W., & Roe, R.A. (2008). Beyond the three component model of organizational commitment. *Journal of Applied Psychology, 93(1)*, 70–83.

Staw, B.M. (1981). The escalation of commitment to a course of action. *Academy of Management Review, 6(4)*, 577–587.

Staw, B.M., & Ross, J. (1978). Commitment to a policy decision: A multi theoretical perspective. *Administrative Science Quarterly, 23(1)*, 40–64.

Steers, R.M. (1977). Antecedents and Outcomes of Organizational Commitment. *Administrative Science Quarterly, 22(1)*, 46–56.

Swart, J., Kinnie, N., van Rossenberg, Y., & Yalabik, Z. (2014). Why should I share my knowledge? A multiple foci of commitment perspective. *Human Resource Management Journal, 24(3)*, 241–254.

Tetrick, L.E., Shore, L.M., McClurg, L.N., & Vandenberg, R.J. (2007). A model of union participation: The impact of perceived union support, union instrumentality, and union loyalty. *Journal of Applied Psychology, 92(3)*, 820–828.

Truxillo, D.M., Bauer, T.N., & Garcia, A.M. (2017). Applicant reactions to hiring procedures. In H. W. Goldstein, E. D. Pulakos, J. Passmore, & C. Semedo (Eds.), *The Wiley Blackwell Handbook of the Psychology of Recruitment, Selection and Employee Retention* (pp. 53–70). Hoboken, NJ: Wiley-Blackwell.

Vallacher, R.R. & Wegner, D.M. (1985). *A Theory of Action Identification*. Hillsdale, NJ: Lawrence Erlbaum Associates.

Vandenberghe, C., Mignonac, K., & Manville, C. (2015). When normative commitment leads to lower well being and reduced performance. *Human Relations, 68(5)*, 843–870.

Vandenberghe, C. & Bentein, K. (2009). A closer look at the relationship between affective commitment to supervisors and organizations and turnover. *Journal of Occupational and Organizational Psychology, 82(2)*, 331–348.

Van Dick, R., Becker, T.E., & Meyer, J.P. (2006). Commitment and identification: forms, foci, and future. *Journal of Organizational Behavior, 27(5)*, 545–548.

Van Rossenberg, Y.G.T., Klein, H.J., Asplund, K., Bentein, K., Breitsohl, H., Cohen, A., ... & Ali, N. (2018). The future of workplace commitment: Key questions and directions. *European Journal of Work and Organizational Psychology, 27(2)*, 153–167.

Wallace, J.E. (1995). Organizational and professional commitment in professional and non professional organizations. *Administrative Science Quarterly, 40(2)*, 228–255.

Wasti, S.A. & Önder, C. (2009). Commitment across cultures: Progress, pitfalls and propositions. In: Klein, H.J., Becker, T.E., Meyer, J.P. (Eds.), *Commitment in Organizations: Accumulated Wisdom and New Directions* (pp. 309–343). New York, NY: Routledge/Taylor and Francis.

Wayne, J.H., Casper, W.J., Matthews, R.A., & Allen, T.D. (2013). Family-supportive organization perceptions and organizational commitment: the mediating role of work–family conflict and enrichment and partner attitudes. *Journal of Applied Psychology, 98(4)*, 606–622.

Weiss, H.M. & Cropanzano, R. (1996). Affective events theory: A theoretical discussion of the structure, causes and consequences of affective experiences at work. *Research in Organizational Behavior, 18*, 1–74.

Weng, Q. & McElroy, J.C. (2012). Organizational career growth, affective occupational commitment and turnover intentions. *Journal of Vocational Behavior, 80(2)*, 256–265.

Whyte, W.H. (1956). *The Organization Man*. New York, NY: Doubleday.

Wombacher, J.C. & Felfe, J. (2017). The interplay of team and organizational commitment in motivating employees' interteam conflict handling. *Academy of Management Journal, 60(4)*, 1554–1581.

# 8

# JOB EMBEDDEDNESS

*Beni Halvorsen, Katrina Radford, Geoffrey Chapman,
and Brad Nikolic*

The material that follows is organized into seven sections. In the first section, we define job embeddedness. In the second section, we outline a brief history of the emergence of job embeddedness theory in turnover and retention literature through the unfolding model of voluntary employee turnover (Lee & Mitchell, 1994), and we compare it to similar constructs used in turnover and retention research. The third section focuses on the nomological network of job embeddedness. Section four examines job embeddedness in different cultural contexts, and section five focuses on the issues in measuring job embeddedness. In the sixth section of the chapter, we present a critique of the field up until now, and in the final section, we propose practical implications for organizations.

## Job Embeddedness: A Definition

Job embeddedness is *both* a theory and a model of retention (Halvorsen, Treuren, & Kulik, 2015). Job embeddedness theory is defined as a broad constellation of psychological, social, and financial influences on employee retention (Yao et al., 2004; Zhang, Fried, & Griffith, 2012). These influences are present as either on-the-job ("on-the-job embeddedness" or "organizational embeddedness") or outside the job environment, such as in the community where employees live ("off-the-job embeddedness" or "community embeddedness"). Both on-the-job and off-the-job influences are intertwined and create an overall "web" of attachments where a person can become "stuck" (Mitchell et al., 2001). The greater these attachments are to a person, the harder it then becomes to leave a job. Additionally, the more an employee will lose by leaving, the more likely they will stay (Reitz, Anderson, & Hill, 2010). The strength of connectedness between employees' organization and community is proposed to be a function of three components, which are called *fit*, *links*, and *sacrifice*.

### Fit

Fit is defined as an employee's perceived compatibility with the organization (Lee et al., 2004). It is here an employee makes a judgment as to how they perceive themselves as similar to, or to "fit" with, their organization and community. Good person-organization fit occurs when an employee's values, career aspirations, knowledge, skills, and ability are compatible with the organization's culture, and with the requirements of his or her job (Zhang et al., 2012). On-the-job fit also encompasses person-job fit (a person's skillset matching the requirements of the job) and supervisor-subordinate fit (how well a person navigates his or her relationship with their immediate supervisor). This also includes their perceived compatibility with future career development opportunities, job demands, knowledge, skills and abilities, as well as their personal and organizational values alignment, and any alignment or fit with any community service activities sponsored by the organization (Holtom et al., 2006a; Reitz & Anderson, 2011).

Off-the-job fit refers to how well an individual feels connected to and suits the broader community where they live (Clinton, Knight, & Guest, 2012). Factors influencing this perception include the weather conditions, schools, location, community amenities, political and religious climate, and entertainment activities available to them in their local community that align with their personal and family commitments (Holtom et al., 2006a; Reitz & Anderson, 2011). Off-the-job fit might result when a person's community offers opportunities to pursue his or her interests (Halvorsen et al., 2015). Off-the-job fit also occurs when a person considers how well he or she fits with aspects of the community and surrounding environments, such as climate, weather conditions, religious beliefs, and entertainment (Mitchell et al., 2001; Zhang et al., 2012).

For both organizational and community fit, job embeddedness posits that the stronger the fit, the more likely employees will remain at their organization.

### *Links*

According to job embeddedness, the "links" an individual has to other people and activities within their organization and broader community play a strong role in determining how long they will stay within that organization (Mitchell et al., 2001; Reitz & Anderson, 2011).

On-the-job links are defined as the formal and informal connections between a person, institution(s), or other people (Lee et al., 2004; Zhang et al., 2012). According to job embeddedness theory, the sheer volume of links an individual creates and has at work—such as working within a team or holding membership with professional associations through their employer (e.g., SIOP or AOM)—makes it increasingly difficult for an employee to quit his or her job (Mitchell et al., 2001). Off-the-job links are defined as the informal and formal relationships an individual has with people outside of the workplace as well as institutions and community groups. This could be in the format of volunteering at local schools or community organizations, and it can include extended family (Halvorsen et al., 2015; Holtom et al., 2006a).

The premise that job embeddedness argues is that the more links or threads an employee has within their organization and the broader community, the harder it will be for an employee to disentangle these links in order to leave their job. Therefore, they will have higher intentions to stay at their job. Additionally, research investigating these links has found that employees who have a longer tenure at an organization will have stronger links with their organization and community and, therefore, will be less likely to leave (Holtom et al., 2006a).

### *Sacrifice*

The final component that is argued to explain why employees stay is how easy those links and that fit can be broken. This is often referred to as "sacrifice," or in the form of a question: what sacrifices would employees have to make, both at work and in the community, if they chose to stay or leave? (Anderson & Hill, 2010; Mitchell et al., 2001; Reitz & Anderson, 2011).

On-the-job sacrifice is defined as the real or perceived psychological, social, or material cost of leaving one's organization (Lee et al., 2004; Mitchell et al., 2001). When an individual leaves an organization, job-related losses occur, such as giving up favorite colleagues, interesting projects, and financial and non-financial benefits. Off-the-job sacrifice is defined in a similar manner to its respective on-the-job counterpart: the real or perceived psychological, social, or material cost of leaving the community (Mitchell et al., 2001) to facilitate a move to a new job. Furthermore, sacrifice more generally refers to the ease with which both on-and off-the-job fit, and links can be broken (Holtom et al., 2006a).

This element of the job embeddedness framework was heavily influenced by the earlier turnover theory proposed by March and Simon (1958), which argued that an employee's intentions to leave an organization are a function of their perceived desirability and ease of movement from one organization to another. In job embeddedness terms, sacrifice is represented as the cost versus benefits of the lost links they have made within their organization and the broader community in comparison with the gains they will make or benefits they will receive if they left. Such losses include the loss of key networks, relationships, friends, projects, and the benefits they receive from their organization (Holtom et al., 2006a; Reitz & Anderson, 2011). In other words, the more an employee will lose by leaving, the more likely they will stay at their job. Mitchell et al. (2001) did acknowledge that community sacrifices, as well as community links and fit, are more likely to play a significant role in an employee's intentions to leave if they have to relocate as a consequence of their new job (Radford, 2013).

## A History of Job Embeddedness and Theoretical Underpinnings

Prior to the notion of job embeddedness, researchers investigating turnover primarily focused on the broad question of why people leave their job and why people stay (Hom & Griffeth, 1995). By asking these questions, the concepts of job attachment (Koch & Steers, 1978), job satisfaction (Carsten & Spector, 1987), organizational commitment (Allen & Meyer, 1990), and continuance commitment (Shore & Wayne, 1993) became prominent terms and avenues of research in the field, with the simple answers being that when other opportunities arose, employees who were satisfied with their jobs and committed to their organization would be more likely to stay, and those who were dissatisfied and not committed would be more likely to leave (Mitchell et al., 2001). However, these concepts only provided partial explanations for employee turnover, as a satisfied and committed employee may still leave their job. Studies have shown that as an individual construct, job embeddedness is more useful in measuring intent to leave than job attachment, job satisfaction, organizational commitment, continuance commitment, and affective commitment (Crossley et al. 2007; Richards & Schat, 2011).

Job embeddedness emerged as a concept capable of providing a more complete explanation of employee turnover. Originally, the concept was established from two questions that arose from an analysis of Lee and Mitchell's (1994) Unfolding Model of Voluntary Turnover. The first of which involved determining what constituted a "shock," eventually being defined as a "particular, jarring event that initiates the psychological analyses involved in quitting a job" (Lee et al., 1999). The more pressing question was why some shocks led to certain employees quitting their job, whereas those same shocks did not prompt other employees to quit. The answer to this question came through the suggestion that there were forces—such as off-the-job factors and non-attitudinal variables, as well as attachments at work more generally—that would keep an employee in his or her job. This ultimately led to Mitchell et al. (2001) articulating their new construct and calling it job embeddedness.

In their initial conceptualization, Mitchell and Lee (2001) presented field theory (Lewin, 1951), and the research on the embedded figures test (Witkin et al., 1962) as influences on the idea of job embeddedness. Field theory argues that behavior is derived from the totality of coexisting and interdependent psychological forces in a person's living space and that behavioral change arises from changes to these forces (Burnes & Cooke, 2013; Lewin, 1951). These attachments may be few or many, close or distant, and strong or weak. In a similar fashion, research on the embedded figures test shows that embedded figures are completely immersed in their background and are attached and linked in various ways. A person who is deeply embedded will have many strong and close attachments, whereas a person who is not will experience the opposite.

Building on this, Mitchell et al. (2001) argued that a broad set of influences would impact employees' intentions to stay, ranging from factors within their organization as well as factors outside the organization in which they work, that all have a range of psychological, social, and financial implications to the employee (Reitz & Anderson, 2011; Zhang et al., 2012). While these influences can vary in strength and size for each employee, they have a combined influence on employees' intentions to stay (Clinton et al., 2012). Consequently, job embeddedness incorporates each of these components.

Theoretically, support for the dimensions of job embeddedness emerges from turnover and attachment literatures. Job attachment is most relevant to job embeddedness when discussing the connections and links formed by employees (Richards & Schat, 2011). Both on- and off-the-job links have support from published research; however, the majority of research has focused on the links an employee develops at work. For example, employees can become committed to "constituencies" within an organization (e.g., coworkers, supervisors, mentors, work teams, and unions), in contrast to the more general measure of their commitment to an organization (Maertz & Campion, 1998; Reichers, 1985). If an employee does not wish to lose those valued relationships with other individuals at work by quitting, he or she therefore becomes more psychologically attached to the organization.

An employee's relationships outside of the workplace also carry influence in the turnover decision and lend further support to the job embeddedness concept of links. Family relationships immediately spring to mind as a spouse, children, or parents exert a lot of influence on the turnover decision. Kinship responsibilities such as marriage and having children have been shown to be a stronger predictor of employee retention than organizational commitment (Abelson, 1987; Blegen, Mueller, & Price, 1988; Lee & Maurer, 1999). In addition, activities that are likely to help an employee develop external links with the community, such as social hobbies and church activities, have also been shown to increase retention (Cohen, 1995; Halvorsen et al., 2015).

The underpinnings of on-and off-the-job embeddedness have a rich research history. Much like the research on links, the focus of studies in this field has tended to be on fit at work. For example, person-job fit, person-organization fit, person-occupation fit, perceived fit, and actual fit (Kristof, 1996) all provide solid theoretical foundations for job embeddedness' fit dimensions. Specifically, the chance of voluntary employee turnover increases substantially with a perception of miss-fit (Kristof, 1996). Moreover, organizations prefer homogeneity, and people who do not fit with the majority will ultimately leave (Schneider, 1987).

There are many other dimensions of fit that have been studied over the years—for example, the fit between organizational climate and personal values (Hom & Griffeth, 1995). O'Reilly, Chatman, and Caldwell (1991) found that employees whose values did not match the organization's would subsequently leave. Furthermore, when newcomers' perception of organizational culture fit with their supervisors, intention to stay was higher than where there was a lack of fit (Van Vianen, 1999).

Research on factors relating to off-the-job fit is scarce. However, an examination of community-based research that focuses on a community's demography and its impact on turnover intentions proves fruitful. Extending the ideas from this field of research suggest that if an individual is similar to the people he or she is around in the community, then he or she will experience a better fit. For example, people with a Caucasian ethnicity who were racially dissimilar to their communities expressed stronger intentions to leave their community *and* their jobs (Ragins et al., 2012). Other studies in this area highlight the idea that when community demographics become more diverse, the majority group exhibits resistance to the integration of dissimilar others, making it harder to form off-the-job fit, which in turn may lead to higher instances of employee turnover (Halvorsen et al., 2015).

While there has been less widely reported findings with respect to the sacrifice component of job embeddedness, some studies do focus on capturing this idea in other constructs. An example of this is the concept of on-the-job perks. Meyer and Allen (1997) reported on a scale that included items about sacrificing financial benefits, and prior research tends to support the idea that having to give up financial perks reduces both the intention to leave and actual turnover (e.g., Gupta & Jenkins, 1980; Shaw et al., 1998).

It is important to note that while job embeddedness does have similarities with the concepts of organizational continuance and affective commitment (Shore & Wayne, 1993), it is a distinctly different concept to each of these (Crossley et al., 2007). Although there are many different definitions and measures of organizational commitment (e.g., Allen & Meyer, 1990; Mowday, Steers, & Porter, 1979; Steers, 1977), the concept of job embeddedness provides a much broader picture of the factors involved with turnover decisions made by employees. The same can be said for the concepts of job satisfaction (Carsten & Spector, 1987) and job attachment (Koch & Steers, 1978), with each of these concepts only providing partial explanations for turnover. As this section has shown, many of these existing concepts are related to various aspects of job embeddedness, and the next section of this chapter will explore these connections further.

## Nomological Network of Job Embeddedness: Antecedents and Consequences

While the nature of job embeddedness itself has been discussed above, this section will provide an overview of the nomological network of job embeddedness, or in other words, describe the various factors that influence job embeddedness (antecedents), and the various factors that job embeddedness influences (consequences). Figure 8.1 presents a diagram that displays these relationships in pictorial format

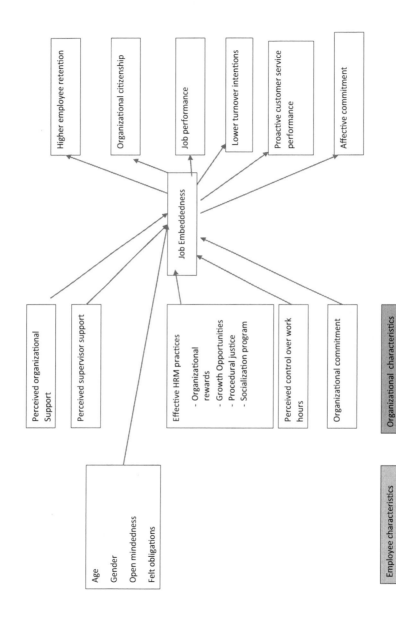

*Figure 8.1* The Nomological Network of Job Embeddedness.

## *Antecedents*

### *Employee Characteristics*

Age, gender, personality, and employees' felt obligations to the organization have all been identified as antecedents to job embeddedness. Specifically, the influence that an employee's *age* has on job embeddedness is raised with literature suggesting that older employees are more likely to have developed links and made sacrifices on and off the job, and thus demonstrate higher levels of job embeddedness. Moreover, organizations can use job embeddedness as a way of retaining older workers in the workplace (McEvoy & Henderson, 2012). In addition, an employees' gender has been found to have both a direct and indirect moderating effect on job embeddedness (Jiang et al., 2012; Lee, Burch, & Mitchell, 2014). Specifically, the meta-analysis by Jiang et al. (2012) found that gender significantly moderated the on-the-job embeddedness-turnover intentions linkage, but did not moderate the off-the-job embeddedness-turnover relationship. In particular, this study found that female employees had a stronger relationship between their on-the-job embeddedness and turnover intentions than male employees in that study (Jiang et al., 2012). After reviewing the influence that personality plays on job embeddedness, Chen, Chou, and Wang (2010) demonstrated that *open-mindedness* was significantly correlated with job embeddedness, suggesting that the individual traits of employees have an important role to play in determining levels of job embeddedness.

Furthermore, Chan et al. (2019) found that the level of *felt obligation* that an employee had towards an organization significantly influenced their level of job embeddedness, with employees that felt more obligated to their company reporting higher levels of job embeddedness. While this chapter is unable to provide a complete review of the characteristics that influence job embeddedness, these papers clearly highlight the role that recruitment plays in ensuring the right fit for the job exists in the first place. The next section will highlight the evidence that surrounds the organizational characteristics that are needed to influence job embeddedness.

### *Organizational Characteristics*

There is extensive literature available that examines the consequences and outcomes of job embeddedness in organizational environments. Job embeddedness was initially developed as a construct to help explain why employees stay at an organization. Allen (2006) verified this with a study that demonstrated that significantly *higher rates of retention* were found among employees that had higher levels of job embeddedness. Halbesleben and Wheeler (2008) further supported the idea that job embeddedness could explain why employees stay in an organization by demonstrating that higher levels of job embeddedness also resulted in significantly *lower turnover intentions*.

Shortly after Mitchell et al. (2001) proposed the concept, many researchers began to examine what factors in the workplace influenced the development of job embeddedness. One of the first of these studies was presented by Giosan, Holtom, and Watson (2005), who demonstrated that both *organizational support* and *supervisor support* influenced the development of job embeddedness. This early finding highlighted the role of the organization in developing job embeddedness among its employees.

Building on these findings, Wheeler, Harris, and Harvey (2010) showed that *effective HRM practices* significantly increased the level of job embeddedness for employees. However, not all studies focused solely on the role that the organization plays in building job embeddedness among employees.

More recently, Nguyen, Taylor, and Bergiel (2017) returned to the focus on organizational factors that influence job embeddedness and their results support the earlier views of Wheeler et al. (2010) by finding that *organizational rewards* was significantly correlated with higher levels of job embeddedness. In addition to this, Nguyen et al. (2017) also found that providing employees with *growth opportunities* resulted in higher levels of job embeddedness, as did the presence of *procedural justice* in the workplace.

Chan et al. (2019) presented a study that built further on the individual focus that Chen et al. (2010) began, examining specific individual characteristics of hospitality workers and the influence they had on levels of job embeddedness. The findings of this study suggested that the *level of control over work hours* positively correlated with job embeddedness, which contrasted earlier findings in the literature that suggested that there was no connection between autonomy and job embeddedness.

While this brief overview cannot report on every factor that has been reported as a potential antecedent of job embeddedness, several studies present much more comprehensive accounts of the nomological network of job embeddedness. One such study is presented by Ghosh and Gurunathan (2015), who identify a range of antecedents for job embeddedness that has been reported in the literature. In addition to the factors discussed above, they also highlight the role that *organizational commitment* plays as a separate construct from job embeddedness. Ghosh and Gurunathan (2015) also indicate that specific actions that can be taken by the organization, such as *socialization programs*, often have a significant positive influence on the development of job embeddedness among employees.

### *Job Embeddedness as an Antecedent and Moderator to Other Outcomes*

One of the first studies to specifically focus on the consequences of job embeddedness was presented by Lee et al. (2004), who indicated that higher levels of job embeddedness among employees had a significant positive influence on *organizational citizenship behaviors*, effectively increasing the inclination of employees to go above and beyond the requirements of their position. Further to this, the findings demonstrated by Lee et al. (2004) indicated that job embeddedness had a significant positive correlation with *job performance*. Both of these findings have been replicated many times in studies over the last 15 years.

Beyond the direct consequences, several studies have explored the role that job embeddedness plays as a moderator for other relationships. For example, Mallol, Holtom, and Lee (2007) found that job embeddedness moderates the effect of *absences, citizenship, and performance on turnover.* The suggestion here being that employees who demonstrate high absenteeism, low citizenship, and low performance are usually more likely to leave an organization, but this relationship is not as strong if employees have high levels of job embeddedness.

Chan et al. (2019) explored some of the consequences of job embeddedness among hospitality workers, finding a significant positive impact of job embeddedness on *proactive customer service performance.* This finding was of interest as most previous studies examined performance in terms of purely task-based behaviors and outcomes, but Chan et al. (2019) demonstrated that job embeddedness could also be linked to employees proactively engaging in relationship-based elements of their job roles.

Ghosh and Gurunathan's (2015) review also highlighted many of the reported consequences of job embeddedness among employees in organizational contexts. Among several other outcomes, including those already discussed above, these authors indicate that higher levels of job embeddedness can also lead to higher levels of *affective commitment* among employees. In other words, if an employee is embedded in their role, they will have higher levels of emotional and attitudinal commitment to their tasks.

When discussing the consequences of job embeddedness, it is important to note that not all studies report beneficial outcomes. From early on, Lee et al. (2004) recognized the potential "dark side" of job embeddedness or the possibility of employees and organizations experiencing detrimental outcomes as a result of higher levels of job embeddedness. Early reports of negative consequences focused primarily on off-the-job embeddedness, with findings suggesting that higher levels of off-the-job embeddedness result in *higher levels of absenteeism and turnover.* This effect can be explained by the fact that employees who are more committed to their family and community will be more likely to prioritize these domains over their work roles.

Ng and Feldman (2010) also examined the potential for negative consequences, suggesting that increasing organizational embeddedness leads to a decline in *social and human capital development* over time. This finding was extended by the same authors two years later, with a study indicating that higher organizational embeddedness was also associated with higher levels of *work-to-family and family-to-work conflict* (Ng and Feldman, 2012).

## Job Embeddedness in Different Cultural Contexts

Since its emergence in the turnover literature in 2001, job embeddedness studies have primarily emanated from the United States. Researchers since then have called for research that explores job embeddedness' predictive powers of turnover in other cultural contexts. In an effort to heed those calls, some researchers have used Hofstede's (1996) cultural dimensions of individualism and collectivism to compare job embeddedness' predictive powers of turnover. In one study, employees from a Hispanic (i.e., collectivist) culture were shown not only to be more embedded within the community than non-Hispanics (mirroring a theory consistent effect that collectivist cultures are more entrenched in the "we" rather than the "I" both at work and away from work), but also that job embeddedness predicted Hispanic employee turnover at two kinds of organizations over and above the traditional models of turnover in job satisfaction and organizational commitment (Mallol et al., 2007).

In a similar vein, several studies have emerged that use a collectivist sample from a collectivist society in China. These studies had mixed results. The first study to use China as the country from which employees' job embeddedness was examined found that social exchange and job embeddedness mediated mutual investment and over-investment affected quit propensity (Hom et al., 2009). Another study examined the factors (i.e., fit, links, and sacrifice) of job embeddedness and how they predicted the intention to leave, and found that on-the-job sacrifice was associated with *increased* turnover intention with the Chinese sample. This relationship is *not* consistent with job embeddedness theory. Rather, job embeddedness theory suggests that high levels of sacrifice should be associated with lower turnover intentions (Mitchell & Lee, 2001). Interestingly, on-the-job fit was associated with decreased turnover intentions— a relationship that is consistent with job embeddedness theory (Bambacas & Kulik, 2013).

Another collectivist approach took place using India as the setting for a job embeddedness study. Much like some studies emanating from China, the initial studies using India brought mixed results. The first study compared the job embeddedness of an Indian sample against a sample of US employees, and found that on-the-job fit was associated with lower turnover for US employees, but not for Indian employees. The finding for US employees mirrors what job embeddedness theory suggests should happen, whereas the finding for Indian employees does *not* mirror job embeddedness theory. US employees who reported high off-the-job links also reported higher turnover, whereas Indian employees with high off-the-job links reported lower turnover. The finding for US employees is *not* consistent with job embeddedness theory, whereas the finding for Indian employees is (Ramesh & Gelfand, 2010).

Utilizing large government datasets, other authors used proxies for items related to job embeddedness' six factors to examine turnover in European countries. These countries—Spain, Italy, Denmark, and Finland—are all individualistic countries, and shared similar findings in that job embeddedness significantly predicted employee turnover (Tanova & Holtom, 2008).

Continuing in the European expansion of job embeddedness, another study examined employee turnover in Albania (a collectivist country). This study used a sample of bank employees and found that job embeddedness did not predict intention to leave above organizational commitment and job satisfaction (Harman et al., 2009).

These studies indicate that there is more work to be done to explore and refine the measure of job embeddedness across different cultural contexts. Given that the measure was developed and mostly tested in the US, this is something researchers can contribute to the field. There is also a need to explore the impact that job embeddedness has in countries that have large spaces between cities, such as Australia and some countries in Africa, where it is likely people travel further for work. These findings combined suggest that further work on the global reach of this variable is needed.

## Issues in Measuring Job Embeddedness

As the literature evolved in the early 2000s, scale development and refinement became a trend in the job embeddedness literature. This came about as researchers became warier of survey fatigue in respondents (Cunningham, Fink, & Sagas, 2005), but also because researchers began to debate whether it was more useful to measure the specific embeddedness factors (fit, links and sacrifice) or to measure embeddedness as a global construct. Researchers introducing global measures (Crossley et al., 2007; Cunningham et al., 2005) argued that a global assessment of job embeddedness allowed the entire construct (job embeddedness) to be assessed with relatively few questions (Crossley et al., 2007). Advocates of the earlier embeddedness scales argued that measuring the fit, links, and sacrifice factors permitted a more fine-grained analysis; researchers could identify which factor(s) carried the most weight in a given sample (Mitchell et al., 2001). Further, the global measures focused on on-the-job attachments more than off-the-job attachments. The off-the-job aspects are important in job embeddedness theory, and by neglecting this facet of embeddedness, the global scales are not addressing all of the forces that bind an employee to an organization.

The first global measure of job embeddedness came out in 2005 and used only six items (one item to measure each of the factors of job embeddedness), and significantly predicted intention to leave in two samples (Cunningham et al., 2005). This was promptly followed up with a seven-item measure of job embeddedness, which also proved to be highly predictive of employee turnover (Crossley et al., 2007). It should be noted, however, the Crossley measure only focused on on-the-job embeddedness.

While the development of global measures emerged, researchers attempted to shorten the original job embeddedness scale. The original job embeddedness scale had 42 items (Lee et al., 2004; Mitchell et al., 2001) that assessed each of the six factors (on- and off-the-job fit, links, and sacrifice) of embeddedness separately. The items in the original 2001 job embeddedness scale were a mix of dichotomous (yes/no) questions and questions rated on a Likert scale. Some researchers standardized each item, then averaged across the items to calculate an overall job embeddedness score, whereas others would simply standardize the dichotomous items and then add them to the other items to create an over-all score. In 2006, a shortened version of the original job embeddedness scale (18 items) was created and had a strong relationship with the original long-form 2001 scale ($r = .92$). This short version predicted voluntary turnover in one study, and involuntary turnover in a second (Holtom, Mitchell, Lee, & Tidd, 2006b).

Similarly, in 2009, another version of the long-form scale appeared, which used 21 items and used Holtom et al. (2006b) as the basis for their measure (Felps et al., 2009). The 21-item short form of job embeddedness was a signifi-cant predictor of turnover. A final 12-item scale emerged in 2012, where six items were used to measure off-the-job embeddedness, and six items were used to measure on-the-job embeddedness. This scale was found to be a reliable predictor of the intention to leave (Clinton et al., 2012).

Running parallel to the development of short-form scales and global meas-ures of job embeddedness was debate as to the actual nature of job embedded-ness. A reflective construct differs from a formative construct in the direction of causality between the indicators and the construct. In a reflective construct, the direction of causality flows from the construct (in this case, job embeddedness) to the indicators (the items) (Jarvis et al., 2003; Zhang et al., 2012). The global measures (Crossley et al., 2007; Cunningham et al., 2005) of job embedded-ness are reflective scales (Rossiter, 2002).

In a formative—sometimes called composite—construct, the direction of causality flows from the indicators (the items) to the construct (job embedded-ness) (Clinton et al., 2012; Lee et al., 2014; Yao et al., 2004). The original job embeddedness measure (Mitchell & Lee, 2001; Mitchell et al., 2001) is a forma-tive/composite measure (Clinton et al., 2012; Zhang et al., 2012). For example, owning a home (an off-the-job fit item) causes an individual to become embed-ded; being embedded does not cause an individual to own a home. Table 8.1 presents a sample of global and formative measures of job embeddedness that are used frequently in the literature.

The global (reflective) and formative (composite) measures of job embed-dedness each have their own strengths and weaknesses. As Zhang et al. (2012, p. 223) conclude,

> if a study aims to explore the associations between components of job embeddedness and outcomes, the study should probably use the com-posite measure…if a study aims to test models using latent constructs, the reflective measure would be a better choice…

*Table 8.1* Sample Job Embeddedness Measures

| Measure Type | Measure Name | Scaling | Item |
|---|---|---|---|
| Global, multiple item measure | Global measure of job embedded-ness (Crossley et al, 2007) | 5-point Likert-type scale (1 = *Strongly Disagree* to 5 = *Strongly Agree*) | 1. I feel attached to this organization. 2. It would be difficult for me to leave this organization. 3. I'm too caught up in this organization to leave. 4. I feel tied to this organization. 5. I simply could not leave the organization that I work for. 6. It would be easy for me to leave this organization. (reverse scored) 7. I am tightly connected to this organization. |
| Global, multiple item measure | Global measure of job embedded-ness (Cunningham et al., 2005) | 5-point Likert-type scale (1 = *Strongly Disagree* to 5 = *Strongly Agree*) | 1. I feel compatible with my organization. 2. I feel a strong link to my organization. 3. I would sacrifice a lot if I left this job. 4. I feel compatible with where I live. 5. I feel a strong link to my community. 6. I would sacrifice a lot if I left this community. |
| Formative, multiple item measure | "Short form" job embedded-ness scale (Felps et al, 2009) | 5-point Likert-type scale (1 = *Strongly Disagree* to 5 = *Strongly Agree*) Three items (items 19, 20, and 21) are yes/no. These are standardized before being added to the relevant factor of job embedded-ness. | 1. My job utilizes my skills and talents well. 2. I feel like I am a good match for my organization. 3. If I stay with my organization, I will be able to achieve most of my goals. 4. I really love the place where I live. 5. The place where I live is a good match for me. 6. The area where I live offers the leisure activities that I like (sports, outdoor activities, cultural events & arts). 7. I have a lot of freedom on this job to pursue my goals. 8. I would sacrifice a lot if I left this job. |

*(continued)*

*Table 8.1* (Cont.)

| Measure Type | Measure Name | Scaling | Item |
|---|---|---|---|
| | | | 9. I believe the prospects for continuing employment with my organization are excellent. |
| | | | 10. Leaving the community where I live would be very hard. |
| | | | 11. If I were to leave the community, I would miss my non-work friends. |
| | | | 12. If I were to leave the area where I live, I would miss my neighborhood. |
| | | | 13. I am a member of an effective work group. |
| | | | 14. I work closely with my coworkers. |
| | | | 15. On the job, I interact frequently with my work group members. |
| | | | 16. My family roots are in this community. |
| | | | 17. I am active in one or more community organizations (e.g., churches, sports teams, schools, etc.). |
| | | | 18. I participate in cultural and recreational activities in my local area. |
| | | | 19. Are you currently married? |
| | | | 20. If you are currently married, does your spouse work outside the home? |
| | | | 21. Do you own a home (with or without a mortgage)? |

## A Critique of the Field

While research establishing this construct has been predominately contextualized within white-collar occupations, the fact that a significant proportion of the research conducted has been limited to a US context has attracted criticism from some authors. This was of particular concern to Zhang et al. (2012), who expressed concern that the construct of job embeddedness could not be applied reliably outside of the US context without extensive revalidation studies. These authors raised questions about how well the specific nature of the questions could be translated into different languages, and whether the perceptions of what constituted the various components of job embeddedness would translate across cultures.

These concerns have been reflected in some of the research that has been conducted outside the US. For example, Peltokorpi (2013) questions the applicability of the validated scale used to measure the construct to a Japanese context. However, through a qualitative inquiry, they found that the construct does broadly apply to a Japanese context. Further supporting this, Mallol et al. (2007) found the scale to be a robust predictor of employee retention across diverse populations, albeit populations that all resided within the US. Additionally, a meta-analysis by Jiang et al. (2012) found support for the construct across cultures and even more so within female-dominant sectors.

Some authors have questioned the value of measuring the construct with a 40-item tool, suggesting that the number and specificity of the items further exaggerate the context-specific issues raised above. This led to Cunningham et al. (2005) and Crossley et al. (2007) developing their 7-item global scale for job embeddedness, as previously discussed. However, it should be noted that the original authors who proposed the construct of job embeddedness caution that this simplified scale measures only a perception of job embeddedness, rather than providing an accurate measure of the construct itself (Lee et al. 2014).

Further to this, a study by Radford and Chapman (2015) found that the applicability of the off-the-job links to an Australian aged care setting may be limited, and as such, a more thorough investigation of where off-the-job links are more important, considering context and culture, are needed. To achieve this, more consideration of how job embeddedness may be explored qualitatively may be required, as some authors in the field have expressed doubts about how readily this construct could benefit qualitative and mixed-method studies.

## Future Research Directions

This chapter has highlighted the background and overview of job embeddedness in the literature to date. While the majority of studies of this construct have been conducted in the US, the relatively few studies that examine the construct outside the US have failed to validate the use of community-level variables to support this theory.

This is not to say the community level variables are insignificant, just that further refinement of what exactly influences community links, fits, and sacrifices are needed. This is particularly important for examining situations where contexts have changed. For example, employees happily travel up to 1.5 hours each way to get to work in some areas of Australia, but this kind of commute in the US is unheard of. Therefore, further refinement to what constitutes community links, fit, and sacrifice in different cultural contexts is needed as part of future research on this construct.

Another avenue for future research lies within the links and sacrifice dimensions of job embeddedness. Links, as initially conceptualized, measure the sheer volume of links an individual has at work and in the community. What is currently not understood is the strength of the links an individual has, and how to measure these links. Finally, the component of sacrifice is the least well-researched of all three, and would benefit from additional exploration both in terms of on- and off-the-job forms of sacrifice.

As the job embeddedness literature has unfolded, studies have used the components of job embeddedness as mediators and moderators of relationships between important organizational outcomes. One notable study examined on-the-job embeddedness as a mediator between off-the-job embeddedness, its relationship with job motivation, networking behavior, and organizational identification, and found that there was a significant mediation effect (Ng & Feldman, 2013). Other studies have examined job embeddedness's role in employee organizational citizenship behavior and found that job embeddedness's sacrifice factor significantly mediated the relationship between psychological contract fulfillment and employee extra-role behavior (Kiazad, Kraimer, & Seibert, 2019). Further, this study found that fit and links moderated this mediated relationship. Another study examined job embeddedness as a mediator between workplace ostracism and employee attitudes and found that job embeddedness mediated the relationships between workplace ostracism and intention to leave, as well as affective commitment (Lyu & Zhu, 2019). Future research could continue to focus on job embeddedness as mediators or moderators of important organizational relationships and outcomes.

Further research would also benefit from taking into account the role of organizational leadership as a moderating variable in the relationship of job embeddedness and various positive or negative outcomes. Extensive research on organizational leadership has shown that leaders are a critical factor that determines organizational outcomes and influences workplace behaviors through their interaction with subordinates (e.g., Babalola, Stouten, & Euwema, 2015, Bass, 2008, DeChurch et al., 2010, Yukl, 2012). Specifically, depending on the quality of the relationship between leaders and their subordinates, this could have various degrees of impact on job embeddedness. Therefore, it is suggested to investigate the moderating effect of various leadership constructs and the degree of influence on job embeddedness.

In line with Zhang et al. (2012), the role of cultural differences and their impact on job embeddedness deserves further attention. Culture provides individuals as well as groups with clear guidelines of desired and applicable conduct within an organized context (Schein, 2010). The question, therefore, remains: To what extent can the composite scale of job embeddedness be generalized to other cultural settings, and what are some differences that can be observed, for example, between individualist cultures and collectivist cultures?

Can we generalize, or can future studies identify if differences exist and how that influences employees' job embeddedness?

Tracking job embeddedness trajectories or changes across time in longitudinal studies is also a fruitful avenue for future research. Little is known about how embeddedness changes within individuals across time. Also unknown is what the long-term effects of embeddedness are on important organizational outcomes. For example, if the level of job embeddedness of an employee goes down by one point, is that difference in embeddedness going to carry more of an impact in a turnover/retention decision than an employee whose embeddedness goes up by two points?

## Implications for Practice

With the well-documented costs of employee turnover continuing to impact the productivity and profitability of organizations around the globe, obtaining a better understanding of why employees leave is vital. Even more importantly, the concept of job embeddedness helps managers to understand why employees choose to stay within an organization, completing the partial explanations provided by the concepts of job attachment, organizational commitment, and job satisfaction. Understandably then, there are several implications of job embeddedness for managers and practitioners in the global business environment.

First, managers can focus on improving the various forms of fit that their employees will experience. Knowing that both on-the-job and off-the-job fit plays a significant role in an employee's decision to stay at an organization means that a manager will be able to take specific actions to minimize the risk of key personnel leaving the company. This could be through traditional means, such as improving job design and work environment, but also through a more focused effort to understand and improve off-the-job fit for employees.

Second, the concept of job embeddedness has added to the knowledge gained through the application of job/organizational commitment and job attachment in terms of the relationships an employee establishes within and outside of the organization. Equipped with the knowledge of how these links influence an employee's decision to stay in their job, a manager can ensure that there is sufficient opportunity for employees to develop these links. On-the-job links can be fostered through team-based activities and social events, while off-the-job links can be fostered through the provision of community-service leave, and a strong focus on engagement with the local community.

Finally, managers can utilize job embeddedness through a better understanding of the influence that both on-the-job and off-the-job sacrifices have on employee turnover. Demonstrating an awareness of these sacrifices will not only reinforce their importance to employees but also has the potential to improve relationships between managers and employees.

# Conclusion

Over the past 20 years, job embeddedness has proven to be a paradigm shifting move in the turnover and retention literature, focusing on why people *stay* in their jobs. It has further been shown to be a useful predictor of other outcomes and has consistently been used as a mediator or moderator in several studies. We firmly believe that there is still plenty of life left with the construct, and have outlined several potential future directions for the literature, which may keep researchers occupied for many more years to come.

# References

Abelson, M.A. (1987). Examination of avoidable and unavoidable turnover. *Journal of Applied Psychology*, *72*, 382–386.

Allen, D.G. (2006). Do organizational socialization tactics influence newcomer embeddedness and turnover? *Journal of Management*, *32*(2), 237–256.

Allen, N.J. & Meyer, J.P. (1990). The measurement and antecedents of affective, continuance and normative commitment to the organization. *Journal of Occupational Psychology*, *63*(1), 1–18.

Anderson, M. & Hill, P.D. (2010). Job embeddedness and nurse retention. *Nurse Administration Quarterly*, *34*(3), 190–200.

Babalola, M.T., Stouten, J., & Euwema, M. (2015). Frequent change and turnover intention: The moderating role of ethical leadership. *Journal of Business Ethics*, *134*(2), 1–12.

Bambacas, M. & Kulik, C.T. (2013). Job embeddedness in China: How HR practices impact turnover intentions. *The International Journal of Human Resource Management*, *24*, 1933–1952.

Bass, B.M. (2008). *The Bass Handbook of Leadership: Theory, research and managerial application* (4th ed.). New York: Free Press.

Blegen, M.A., Mueller, C.W., & Price, J.L. (1988). Measurement of kinship responsibility for organizational research. *Journal of Applied Psychology*, *73*, 402–409.

Burnes, B. & Cooke, B. (2013). Kurt Lewin's field theory: A review and re-evaluation. *International Journal of Management Reviews*, *15*, 408–425.

Carsten, J.M. & Spector, P.E. (1987). Unemployment, job satisfaction, and employee turnover: A meta-analytic test of the Muchinsky model. *Journal of Applied Psychology*, *72*, 374.

Chan, W.L., Ho, J.A., Sambasivan, M., & Ng, S.I. (2019). Antecedents and outcome of job embeddedness: Evidence from four and five-star hotels. *International Journal of Hospitality Management*, *83*, 37–45.

Chen, J.-R., Chou, T.-C., & Wang, T.-W. (2010). The organizational context, job embeddedness, and effectiveness of managing knowledge work teams. *Journal of Applied Business Research (JABR)*, *26*(5), 19–28.

Clinton, M., Knight, T., & Guest, D.E. (2012). Job embeddedness: A new attitudinal measure. *International Journal of Selection and Assessment*, *20*, 111–117.

Cohen, A. (1995). An examination of the relationships between work commitment and nonwork domains. *Human Relations*, *48*, 239–263.

Crossley, C.D., Bennett, R.J., Jex, S.M., & Burnfield, J.L. (2007). Development of a global measure of job embeddedness and integration into a traditional model of voluntary turnover. *Journal of Applied Psychology*, *92*, 1031–1042.

Cunningham, G.B., Fink, J.S., & Sagas, M. (2005). Extensions and further examination of the job embeddedness construct. *Journal of Sport Management*, *19*, 319–335.

DeChurch, L.A., Hiller, N.J., Murase, T., Doty, D., & Salas, E. (2010). Leadership across levels: Levels of leaders and their levels of impact. *The Leadership Quarterly*, *21*(6), 1069–1085.

Felps, W., Mitchell, T.R., Hekman, D.R., Lee, T.W., Holtom, B.C. & Harman, W.S., 2009. Turnover contagion: How coworkers' job embeddedness and job search behaviors influence quitting. *Academy of Management Journal*, *52*(3), 545–561.

Ghosh, D. & Gurunathan, L. (2015). Job embeddedness: A ten-year literature review and proposed guidelines. *Global Business Review*, *16*(5), 856–866.

Giosan, C., Holtom, B., & Watson, M. (2005). Antecedents to job embeddedness: The role of individual, organizational and market factors. *Journal of Organizational Psychology*, *5*(1), 31–44.

Gupta, N. & Jenkins, G.D. (1980). *The structure of withdrawal: Relationships among estrangement, tardiness, absenteeism, and turnover.* Springfield, VA: National Technical Information Service.

Halbesleben, J.R.B. & Wheeler, A.R. (2008). The relative roles of engagement and embeddedness in predicting job performance and intention to leave. *Work & Stress*, *22*(3), 242–256.

Halvorsen, B., Treuren, G., & Kulik, C.T. (2015). Job embeddedness among migrants: Fit and links without sacrifice. *International Journal of Human Resource Management*, *26*, 1298–1317.

Harman, W.S., Blum, M., Stefani, J., & Taho, A. (2009). Albanian turnover: Is the job embeddedness construct predictive in an albanian context? *Journal of Behavioral and Applied Management*, *10*(2), 192.

Holtom, B.C., Mitchell, T.R., & Lee, T.W. (2006a). Increasing human and social capital by applying job embeddedness theory. *Organizational Dynamics*, 35, 316–331.

Holtom, B.C., Mitchell, T.R., Lee, T.W., & Tidd, S. (2006b). Less is more: Validation of a short form of the job embeddedness measure and theoretical extensions. Paper presented at the meeting of the Academy of Management, Atlanta, Georgia.

Hom, P.W. & Griffeth, R.W. (1995). *Employee turnover*. Cincinnati, OH: South-Western College Publishing.

Hom, P.W., Tsui, A.S., Wu, J.B., Lee, T.W., Zhang, A.Y., Fu, P.P., & Li, L. (2009). Explaining employment relationships with social exchange and job embeddedness. *Journal of Applied Psychology*, *94*, 277–297.

Jarvis, C.B., Mackenzie, S.B., Podsakoff, P.M., Mick, D.G., & Bearden, W.O. (2003). A critical review of construct indicators and measurement model misspecification in marketing and consumer research. *Journal of Consumer Research*, *30*, 199–218.

Jiang, K., Liu, D., McKay, P.F., Lee, T.W., & Mitchell, T.R. (2012). When and how is job embeddedness predictive of turnover? A meta-analytic investigation. *Journal of Applied Psychology*, *97*, 1077–1096.

Kiazad, K., Kraimer, M.L., & Seibert, S.E. (2019). More than grateful: How employee embeddedness explains the link between psychological contract fulfillment and employee extra-role behavior. *Human Relations*, *72*, 1315–1340.

Koch, J.L. & Steers, R.M. (1978). Job attachment, satisfaction, and turnover among public sector employees. *Journal of Vocational Behavior, 12,* 119–128.

Kristof, A.L. (1996). Person-organization fit: An integrative review of its conceptualizations, measurement and implications. *Personnel Psychology, 48,* 1–49.

Lee, T.W., Burch, T.C., & Mitchell, T.R. (2014). The story of why we stay: A review of job embeddedness. *Annual Review of Organizational Psychology and Organizational Behavior, 1*(1), 199–216. doi:10.1146/annurev-orgpsych-031413-091244

Lee, T.W. & Maurer, S. (1999). The effects of family structure on organizational commitment, intention to leave and voluntary turnover. *Journal of Managerial Issues, 11,* 493–513.

Lee, T.W. & Mitchell, T.R. (1994). An alternative approach: The unfolding model of voluntary employee turnover. *Academy of Management Review, 19,* 51–89.

Lee, T.W., Mitchell, T.R., Holtom, B.C., McDaniel, L.S., & Hill, J.W. (1999). The unfolding model of voluntary turnover: A replication and extension. *Academy of Management Journal, 42,* 450–462.

Lee, T.W., Mitchell, T.R., Sablynski, C.J., Burton, J.P., & Holtom, B.C. (2004). The effects of job embeddedness on organizational citizenship, job performance, volitional absences, and voluntary turnover. *Academy of Management Journal, 47,* 711–722.

Lewin, K. (1951). *Field theory in social science: Selected theoretical papers.* Edited by D. Cartwright. New York: Harper.

Lyu, Y. & Zhu, H. (2019). The predictive effects of workplace ostracism on employee attitudes: A job embeddedness perspective. *Journal of Business Ethics, 158,* 1083–1095.

Maertz, C. & Campion, M.A. (1998). 25 years of voluntary turnover research: A review and critique. In C.L. Cooper and I.T. Robertson (Eds). *International Review of Industrial and Organizational Psychology,* vol. 13, pp. 49–81. Chichester, England: Wiley.

Mallol, C.M., Holtom, B.C., & Lee, T.W. (2007). Job embeddedness in a culturally diverse environment. *Journal of Business and Psychology, 22*(1), 35–44.

March, J.G. & Simon, H.A. (1958). *Organizations.* New York: Wiley.

McEvoy, G.M. & Henderson, S. (2012). The retention of workers nearing retirement: A job embeddedness approach. *Journal of Workplace Behavioral Health, 27*(4), 250–271. doi:10.1080/15555240.2012.725595

Meyer, J.P. & Allen, N.J. (1997). *Commitment in the workplace.* Thousand Oaks, CA: Sage Publications.

Mitchell, T.R. & Lee, T.W. (2001). The unfolding model of voluntary turnover and job embeddedness: Foundations for a comprehensive theory of attachment. *Research in Organizational Behavior, 23,* 189–246.

Mitchell, T.R., Holtom, B.C., Lee, T.W., Sablynski, C., & Erez, M. (2001). Why people stay: Using job embeddedness to predict voluntary turnover. *Academy of Management Journal, 44,* 1102–1121.

Mowday, R.T., Steers, R.M., & Porter, L.W. (1979). The measurement of organizational commitment. *Journal of Vocational Behavior, 14*(2), 224–247.

Ng, T.W. & Feldman, D.C. (2010). The effects of organizational embeddedness on development of social capital and human capital. *Journal of Applied Psychology, 95*(4), 696.

Ng, T.W. & Feldman, D.C. (2012). The effects of organizational and community embeddedness on work-to-family and family-to-work conflict. *Journal of Applied Psychology, 97:* 1233–1251.

Ng, T.W. & Feldman, D.C. (2013). Community embeddedness and work outcomes: The mediating role of organizational embeddedness. *Human Relations, 67,* 71–103.

Nguyen, V.Q., Taylor, G.S., & Bergiel, E. (2017). Organizational antecedents of job embeddedness. *Management Research Review*, *40*(11), 1216–1235.

O'Reilly, C.W., Chatman, J., & Caldwell, D.F. (1991). People and organizational culture: A profile comparison approach to person-organization fit. *Academy of Management Journal*, *34*, 487–516.

Peltokorpi, V. (2013). Job embeddedness in Japanese organizations. *The International Journal of Human Resource Management*, *24*, 1551–1569.

Radford, K. (2013). Two sides of the same coin? An investigation into factors influencing employees' intentions to stay and leave. Unpublished Doctoral Dissertation, Griffith University, Gold Coast, Queensland, Australia.

Radford, K. & Chapman, G. (2015). Are all workers influenced to stay by similar factors, or should different retention strategies be implemented? Comparing younger and older aged-care workers in Australia. *Australian Bulletin of Labour*, *41*(1), 58–81.

Ragins, B.R., Gonzalez, J.A., Ehrhardt, K., & Singh, R. (2012). Crossing the threshold: The spillover of community racial diversity and diversity climate to the workplace. *Personnel Psychology*, *65*, 755–787.

Ramesh, A. & Gelfand, M.J. (2010). Will they stay or will they go? The role of job embeddedness in predicting turnover in individualistic and collectivistic cultures. *Journal of Applied Psychology*, *95*, 807–823.

Reichers, A. (1985). A review and reconceptualization of organizational commitment. *Academy of Management Review*, *10*, 465–476.

Reitz, O.E. & Anderson, M.A. (2011). An overview of job embeddedness. *Journal* of Professional Nursing, *27*(5), 320–327.

Reitz, O.E., Anderson, M.A., & Hill, K.S. (2010). Job embeddedness and nurse retention. *Nursing Administration* Quarterly, *34*(3), 190–200.

Richards, D.A. & Schat, A.C. (2011). Attachment at (not to) work: Applying attachment theory to explain individual behavior in organizations. *Journal of Applied Psychology*, *96*, 169.

Rossiter, J.R. (2002). The c-oar-se procedure for scale development in marketing. *International Journal of Research in Marketing*, *19*, 1–31.

Schein, E.H. (2010). *Organizational culture and leadership* (4th ed.). Hoboken, NJ: Jossey-Bass.

Schneider, B. (1987). People make the place. *Personnel Psychology*, *40*, 437–453.

Shaw, J.D., Delery, J.E., Jenkins, G.D., & Gupta, N. (1998). An organization-level analysis of voluntary and involuntary turnover. *Academy of Management Journal*, *41*, 511–525.

Shore, L.M. & Wayne, S.J. (1993). Commitment and employee behavior: Comparison of affective commitment and continuance commitment with perceived organizational support. *Journal of Applied Psychology*, *78*(5), 774.

Steers, R.M. (1977). Antecedents and outcomes of organizational commitment. *Administrative Science Quarterly*, *22*(1), 46–56.

Van Vianen, A.E.M. (1999). Person-organization fit: The match between newcomers' and recruiters' preferences for organizational cultures. Paper presented at the Annual Meeting of the Academy of Management, Chicago.

Wheeler, A.R., Harris, K.J., & Harvey, P. (2010). Moderating and mediating the HRM effectiveness-intent to turnover relationship: The roles of supervisors and job embeddedness. *Journal of Managerial Issues*, *22*, 182–196.

Witkin, H.A., Dyk, R.B., Faterson, H.F., Goodenough, D.R., & Karp, S.A. (1962). *Psychological differentiation*. New York: Wiley.

Yao, X., Lee, T.W., Mitchell, T.R., Burton, J.P., & Sablynski, C. (2004). Job embeddedness: Current research and future directions. In R. Griffeth & P. Hom (Eds.), *Understanding employee retention and turnover*. Greenwich, CT: Information Age.

Yukl, G.A. (2012). *Leadership in organizations* (8th ed.). New York: Pearson Education.

Zhang, M., Fried, D.D., & Griffeth, R.W. (2012). A review of job embeddedness: Conceptual, measurement issues, and directions for future research. *Human Resource Management Review*, *22*, 220–231.

# 9

# JOB SATISFACTION

*Timothy A. Judge, Shuxia (Carrie) Zhang, and David R. Glerum*

## Job Satisfaction

Researchers have been attempting to capture the way people experience and relate to their work since the inception of Organizational Psychology and Behavior as a field. Within the universe of job attitudes, job satisfaction has been the single most studied of these constructs (Judge et al., 2017). The importance of job satisfaction has been demonstrated in numerous studies, which have found that job satisfaction is related to a variety of individually and organizationally relevant behaviors including task performance, absenteeism, turnover, organizational citizenship behavior (OCB), counterproductive work behavior (CWB), and organizational profitability (Judge & Kammeyer-Mueller, 2012). Given the various implications of job satisfaction in the workplace, we intend to provide a thorough review of job satisfaction that describes the etiology of the construct, how it is operationalized, and its nomological network. In this review, we first provide a brief review of the historical trends in job satisfaction research. Second, we discuss the definitions and facets of job satisfaction. Third, we summarize various approaches to measuring job satisfaction. Fourth and fifth, we review the antecedents and outcomes of job satisfaction. Finally, we provide a critique of the job satisfaction literature, practical implications, and directions for future research.

## Historical Trends in Job Satisfaction Research

### The Dawn of Job Satisfaction Research

The study of job satisfaction began in the late 1920s and 1930s, which was greatly influenced by the industrial and employment crises of the Great Depression. Given widespread job dissatisfaction in the workplace during this period, researchers sought to uncover the causes of such dissatisfaction, with early work identifying emotions as an important factor. For example, in Fisher and Hanna's (1931) *The Dissatisfied Worker*, they concluded that chronic emotional maladjustments were the primary causes of job dissatisfaction.

## *Mid-Century Advancements in the Study of Job Satisfaction*

During the mid-century, several conceptual and methodological advancements revolutionized the study of job satisfaction. Looking back on early century work on job satisfaction, researchers critiqued the approaches in prior job satisfaction research (e.g., Brayfield & Crockett, 1955), while additional work during this period enhanced the study of job satisfaction. For example, job satisfaction measurement was improved during this period with initial work on the study of the components of job satisfaction (Brayfield & Rothe, 1951; Kunin, 1955). In the 1950s, influenced by the pragmatically oriented culture developed during the war, researchers began studying the effects of job satisfaction, including those on job performance (e.g., Brayfield & Crockett, 1955) and turnover (e.g., Weitz & Nuckols, 1955). Theoretical developments were also significant during this period. One of the most influential contributions to job satisfaction theory during this period was Herzberg's two-factor theory (Herzberg, Mausner, & Snyderman, 1959), which states that factors that cause job satisfaction are different from factors that cause job dissatisfaction. However, subsequent research casts doubts concerning the veracity of this theory (Ewen, 1964; House & Wigdor, 1967; Hulin & Smith, 1964).

## *Humanist Perspectives on Job Satisfaction*

This mid-century period also inspired a series of epochs comprised of unique perspectives on job satisfaction. The first epoch (1950s) was primarily influenced by humanistic psychology and included a focus on need fulfillment and humanistic models of job satisfaction, such as those developed by Morse (1953), Schaffer (1953), and McGregor (1960). This humanistic approach to job satisfaction emphasized employee personal transformation and development, as well as the role of work in fulfilling inherent human needs. As an example application, McGregor (1960) suggested that job design should provide employees opportunities to participate in decision-making, autonomy, and self-direction, as well as a chance to enrich their jobs. By doing so, employees' universal needs for self-actualization would be fulfilled, and job satisfaction could be improved.

## *Cognitive Perspectives on Job Satisfaction*

Job satisfaction research in the 1960s to 1980s was influenced by developments in cognitive psychology, particularly on the attitude formation process. For example, the Cornell model of job satisfaction (Smith, Kendall, & Hulin, 1969) proposed that frames of reference influence the evaluation of job outcomes. Frames of reference refer to the relative standards individuals use in evaluating their job outcomes, and these standards are influenced by individuals' past experiences, the economy, and living standards. Specifically, the model posits that frames of reference moderate the effect of job outcomes on job satisfaction: in other words, the influence of job outcomes on job satisfaction judgments depends on each individual's frame of reference. Another influential theory developed during the cognitive epoch was the value-percept model by Locke (1969), which posits that discrepancies between wants (i.e., what is desired by the person) and haves (i.e., what is received from the job) will lead to dissatisfaction—but only if the job facet is important to the individual.

## Dispositional Perspectives on Job Satisfaction

In the 1980s, researchers began to focus on the dispositional sources of job satisfaction (Adler & Weiss, 1988; Arvey et al., 1989; Staw, Bell, & Clausen, 1986; Staw & Ross, 1985). This work suggested that satisfaction evaluations were heavily influenced by individuals' dispositions, such as their personality traits. As a catalyst to the continued development of this perspective in the following decade, the predictive power of personality on job satisfaction was invigorated by Digman's (1990) review on the emergence of the five-factor model in psychology research. During the following decade, researchers continued to examine dispositional influences on job satisfaction. For example, core self-evaluations (CSE) had been found to be a predictor of job satisfaction (Judge et al., 1998).

## Affective Perspectives on Job Satisfaction (1990s–Present)

Compared with the growing volume of research on cognitive perspectives of job satisfaction after the turn of the mid-century, the affective component of job satisfaction was relatively ignored throughout much of the construct's history—despite seminal work that suggested emotions play a large role in job satisfaction (Fisher & Hanna, 1931; Hersey, 1932). Over time, researchers began to note that many job satisfaction surveys lacked affective content and that emotions were not measured as either antecedents or consequences of job satisfaction (e.g., Organ & Near, 1985). Cranny, Smith, and Stone (1992) even proposed that job satisfaction *is* an affective reaction. Noticing the field's neglect for the affective aspects of job satisfaction, Weiss and Cropanzano (1996) proposed Affective Events Theory (AET). AET proposes that affective reactions have a direct influence on job satisfaction; they are not identical (cf., Cranny et al., 1992). AET proposes that affective reactions and job satisfaction have different outcomes: affective reactions precede affect-driven behavior, and job satisfaction precedes judgment-driven behavior.

Affective reactions in AET are influenced by work events and dispositions—suggesting that what happens in the work environment (along with one's traits) is integral to affective responses and attitude formation. Relatedly, a focus on time is fundamental to AET, which recognizes fluctuations in affective reactions over time as work events occur. As such, AET has influenced the use of the experience sampling method (ESM) to examine the unfolding of affective reactions in response to work events that influence job satisfaction. AET has been integral to the advancement of job satisfaction theory, given its successes in integrating several perspectives from the preceding decades: the affective approach, the dispositional approach, and the cognitive approach. Just as the study of job satisfaction has benefitted from intensive study over the last century, so has the conceptualization and operationalization of job satisfaction. In the following sections, we will discuss how job satisfaction (and its facets) has been defined, as well as how job satisfaction as a construct has been operationalized.

## What is Job Satisfaction?

Although definitions and forms of job satisfaction have changed over the years (cf. Cranny et al., 1992), job satisfaction can be defined as an overall, evaluative judgment of one's job ranging from positive to negative (Judge & Kammeyer-Mueller, 2012; Judge et al., 2017; Weiss, 2002). Following the tripartite model of attitudes, job satisfaction contains *cognitive* (beliefs or judgments about the job), *affective* (feelings that the job arouses), and *behavioral* (how the individual tends to behave toward the job) aspects (Rosenberg & Hovland, 1960; Schleicher, Hansen, & Fox, 2011). Although not all three components apply to every type of job attitude (Hulin & Judge, 2003), job satisfaction is typically seen as being comprised of all three components (Schleicher et al., 2011).

The cognitive and affective components are both particularly challenging to separate (Adolphs & Damasio, 2001) and appear to be intimately related as contributors to job satisfaction (Judge & Kammeyer-Mueller, 2012). Although research and measurement of job satisfaction once eschewed the affective component in favor of the cognitive (Judge & Kammeyer-Mueller, 2012), recent work on job satisfaction has ushered in a new era, focusing on the affective component (Judge, Hulin, & Dalal, 2012; Judge et al., 2017). For example, work on the emotional drivers of job satisfaction and well-being differentiates between hedonic (i.e., enjoyment and pleasure) and eudaimonic (i.e., meaning and purpose fulfillment) emotional content (Rothausen & Henderson, 2019). Given job satisfaction's categorization as a job attitude, it can be directed toward several job-relevant targets, such as pay or supervision. (Judge & Kammeyer-Mueller, 2012). This has led researchers to study job satisfaction either as directed toward several job-relevant targets or as directed toward the job as a whole.

## Job Satisfaction Dimensionality and Facets

At the broadest level, job satisfaction is often represented as a manifestation of a higher-order job attitudes factor (Harrison, Newman, & Roth, 2006; Newman, Joseph, & Hulin, 2010; Webster, Adams, & Beehr, 2014). At more specific levels, job satisfaction can be represented by various facets, often differentiated by common targets of job satisfaction, such as pay or supervision

(Judge & Kammeyer-Mueller, 2012). At a greater level of specificity, facets of job satisfaction, such as pay, have been broken down into sub-facets (e.g., raises, benefits, etc.; Heneman & Schwab, 1985). As another example, supervisor satisfaction has been broken down into supervisor competence and supervisor human relations (Weiss et al., 1967). Notably, these sub-facets can take different forms depending upon the types of employees making the judgments (e.g., white- vs. blue-collar; Hu, Kaplan, & Dalal, 2010; Williams, McDaniel, & Ford, 2007). Despite sub-facets traditionally emerging in the study of pay satisfaction and supervisor satisfaction, we believe that additional sub-facets may emerge for other facets in a similar fashion and call on future research to examine these potential sub-facets. For example, it is reasonable to believe that satisfaction with co-workers (a facet of the JDI; Ironson et al., 1989) could be broken down into competence and relations, much like supervisor satisfaction.

Research has demonstrated that the global conceptualization of job satisfaction is empirically distinct from an additive composition of separate facet satisfactions (Highhouse & Becker, 1993; Ironson et al., 1989). Furthermore, there appears to be a dispositional component of facet job satisfaction, with both traits, positive and negative affect, significantly predicting satisfaction toward a number of job facets (Bowling, Hendricks, & Wagner, 2008). Overall, the focus on general vs. facet-level conceptualizations of job satisfaction ultimately depends on the research question being asked, or to the specific practical need that's being addressed (Harrison et al., 2006; Schleicher et al., 2011). Depending upon the question or need, it may be appropriate to focus on specific facets of job satisfaction. For example, a compensation analyst surveying employee satisfaction in an organization may very well be more interested in satisfaction with pay (or benefits or raises) than with satisfaction in general.

Furthermore, a number of job satisfaction researchers (Fisher, 1980; Harrison et al., 2006; Newman et al., 2010) have drawn on the *compatibility principle* (Ajzen & Fishbein, 1977) to suggest that general conceptualizations of job satisfaction should be more strongly related to behavioral criteria that are more general in breadth (e.g., "the favorableness or unfavorableness of an individual's total set of work-related behaviors"; Fisher, 1980, p. 607). This suggests that global job satisfaction should be more strongly related to global criteria (as opposed to narrow criteria). As such, job satisfaction researchers and practitioners need to ensure that the breadth of the predictor domain is aligned with the breadth of criterion domain. In the next section, we discuss more of the issues surrounding the selection of *global* vs. *facet* measures of job satisfaction, along with several other measurement considerations.

## Job Satisfaction Measurement

With each passing year, managers increasingly realize the importance of measuring job satisfaction. Indeed, one report found that nearly half (49%) of organizations assessed job satisfaction within the last year (Society for Human Resource Management, 2015). However, the question of *how* to measure job satisfaction is complex. To illustrate, a number of job satisfaction measures have been introduced over the last century, which all differ by response format (e.g., survey), target (e.g., pay), valence (e.g., affective or cognitive), and specificity (e.g., event-based or the job in general; Judge et al., 2012; Judge et al., 2017; Judge & Kammeyer-Mueller, 2012; Kaplan et al., 2009). Taking these features into account, we argue that job satisfaction measure selection should be purpose-driven (Guion, 2011), although one may perhaps derive the most usefulness out of using multi-faceted, multi-item scales (Judge et al., 2017). In this section, we discuss commonly used job satisfaction measures (examples of which can be found in Table 9.1) as well as design considerations.

### *Job Satisfaction Measures*

One primary issue in job satisfaction measurement is whether to use global or multi-faceted job attitudes measures. Global measures elicit overall reactions or judgments regarding job satisfaction, or all aspects of their jobs in general (Judge & Kammeyer-Mueller, 2012). Examples of global measures include single-item scales (see, for example, Fisher, Matthews, & Gibbons, 2016; or the "Faces" scale, which prompts the respondent to select the face which best corresponds to their feelings toward their job, Kunin, 1998) as well as multi-item scales such as the Overall Job Satisfaction (OJS) scale (Brayfield & Rothe, 1951), the general satisfaction scale from the Job Diagnostic Survey (JDS; Hackman & Oldham, 1974, 1975, 1976), the satisfaction scale from the Michigan Organizational Assessment (Bowling & Hammond, 2008; University of Michigan, 1975), the Global Job Satisfaction Scale (Warr, Cook, & Wall, 1979), and the Job in General scale that accompanies the Job Descriptive Index (JDI; Ironson et al., 1989; Russell et al., 2004; Stanton et al., 2002). Some of these measures, such as the Brayfield and Rothe (1951), have since been adapted for experience-sampling designs (Ilies & Judge, 2004; see Table 9.1).

Global measures are limited as they may fall short of capturing the underlying structure of attitudes, and they may tend to be less reliable (Judge et al., 2017). Regardless, many have opted for using single-item job satisfaction measures for practical reasons, as they may be easier to complete, less time-intensive, less expensive, more face valid, and more flexible than multi-faceted measures (Nagy, 2002). Indeed, prior work suggests that single-item, global job satisfaction measures correspond well with their multi-item counterparts and have acceptable validity and reliability evidence (Fisher et al., 2016; Nagy, 2002; Wanous & Hudy, 2001; Wanous, Reichers, & Hudy, 1997).

Multi-faceted measures, on the other hand, are targeted towards several aspects of the job (see Table 9.1). Some examples of multi-faceted job satisfaction measures include the Minnesota Satisfaction Questionnaire (MSQ; Weiss et al., 1967), the JDI (Balzer et al., 1997; Smith et al., 1969), the JDS (Hackman

& Oldham, 1974, 1975, 1976), the Index of Organizational Reactions (IOR; Dunham, Smith, & Blackburn, 1977), and the Job Satisfaction Survey (JSS; Spector, 1985). Multi-faceted measures have been used quite frequently over time, and a large body of evidence has amassed to support these measures, particularly the JDI and the MSQ (Judge et al., 2017; Kinicki et al., 2002). Indeed, multi-faceted measures have generally been preferred given that factor analysis can be used to assess their dimensionality and structural validity, and they

*Table 9.1* Sample Job Satisfaction Measures

| Measure Type | Measure Name | Scaling | Facet | Item |
|---|---|---|---|---|
| Global, Single Item Measure | Global Job Satisfaction Measure (Fisher, Matthews, & Gibbons, 2016) | 7-point Likert-type scale (1 = *Strongly Disagree* to 7 = *Strongly Agree*) | N/A | 1. Overall, I am satisfied with my job. |
| Global, Multiple Item Measure | General Satisfaction (from the Michigan Organizational Assessment; Institute for Social Research, 1975) | 7-point Likert-type scale (1 = *Strongly Disagree* to 7 = *Strongly Agree*) | N/A | 1. All in all, I am satisfied with my job. 2. In general, I like working here. 3. In general, I don't like my job. |
| Global, Multiple Item Measure (Experience-Sampled Form) | Experience-Sampled Job Satisfaction (Ilies & Judge, 2004; Judge et al., 1998) | 7-point Likert-type scale (1 = *Strongly Disagree* to 7 = *Strongly Agree*) | N/A | 1. At the moment, I feel fairly satisfied with my job. 2. At the moment, I am enthusiastic about my work. 3. At the moment, each minute at work seems like it will never end. 4. At the moment, I am finding real enjoyment in my work. 5. At the moment, I consider my job rather unpleasant. |

*(continued)*

*Table 9.1* (Cont.)

| Measure Type | Measure Name | Scaling | Facet | Item |
|---|---|---|---|---|
| Multi-Faceted, Multiple Item Measure | Job Diagnostic Survey (JDS; Hackman & Oldham, 1974) | 7-point Likert-type scale (1 = *Extremely Dissatisfied* to 7 = *Extremely Satisfied*) | | *How satisfied are you with this aspect of your job?* |
| | | | Job Security | 1. The amount of job security I have. |
| | | | | 2. How secure things look for me in the future in this organization. |
| | | | Peers and Coworkers | 3. The people I talk to and work with at my job. |
| | | | | 4. The chance to get to know other people while on the job. |
| | | | | 5. The chance to help other people while at work. |
| | | | Supervision | 6. The degree of respect and fair treatment I receive from my boss. |
| | | | | 7. The amount of support and guidance I receive from my supervisor. |
| | | | | 8. The overall quality of the supervision I receive in my work. |
| | | | Pay and Other Compensation | 9. The amount of pay and fringe benefits I receive. |
| | | | | 10. The degree to which I am fairly paid for what I contribute to this organization. |
| | | | Opportunity for Personal Growth and Development on the Job | 11. The amount of personal growth and development I get in doing my job. |

214

*Table 9.1* (Cont.)

| Measure Type | Measure Name | Scaling | Facet | Item |
|---|---|---|---|---|
| | | | | 12. The feeling of worthwhile accomplishment I get from doing my job. |
| | | | | 13. The amount of independent thought and action I can exercise in my job. |
| | | | | 14. The amount of challenge in my job. |

tend to be more reliable than global, single-item measures (Judge et al., 2017). However, some limitations to multi-faceted measures include how composites of sub-facets might not capture what is important to each respondent, how they fail to capture the complex psychological process through which employees form overall attitudes about their jobs (Judge et al., 2017), and how they use non-parallel items. One newer measure, The Facet Satisfaction Scale (FSS; Beehr et al., 2006; Bowling, Wagner, & Beehr, 2018), attempts to address some of these limitations by more directly including affective content and through using parallel items. Reconciling the two, past research has shown that global measures correspond most closely with sub-facets from measures that assess satisfaction with the work itself (Judge & Kammeyer-Mueller, 2012).

### *Job Satisfaction Measurement Considerations*

There are several issues to consider when approaching the measurement of job satisfaction. For example, research in recent years has sought to determine whether workers from various backgrounds differ on job satisfaction, or otherwise perceive job satisfaction items and respond to them similarly. For example, when using the "faces" scale discussed earlier, women differ in their judgment of faces when compared with men (e.g., they tend to judge neutral faces as "sad" more often than men; Elfering & Grebner, 2011). Meta-analytic reviews in recent years have uncovered that temporary workers tend to be less satisfied with their jobs than permanent employees and contractors (Wilkin, 2013) and that Black employees in the U.S., particularly those in complex jobs, tend to feel less satisfied than White employees (Koh, Shen, & Lee, 2016). These groups may tend to feel less satisfied because of systematic disadvantages (e.g., fewer resources and a lack of opportunities). Furthermore, with regards to cultural differences, cross-cultural measurement equivalence studies suggest that job

215

satisfaction surveys may be perceived similarly across cultures as well as bilingual and native respondents (Liu, Borg, & Spector, 2004; Mueller, Hattrup, & Straatmann, 2011).

Research on the effect of job satisfaction change (i.e., "systematic improvement or decline in job satisfaction over time"; Chen et al., 2011, p. 116) has suggested change in job satisfaction over time can be used to predict turnover intentions. As such, longitudinal issues in job satisfaction measurement have become more salient to those wishing to explore the effect of job satisfaction change on organizational outcomes. Similarly, some research has explored whether measures should be altered to more precisely and unobtrusively measure job satisfaction within-persons (Grube et al., 2008; Ilies & Judge, 2004). Aside from the modification of existing scales to assess momentary job satisfaction, other researchers have employed the event reconstruction method to more precisely triangulate on specific events that might influence job satisfaction evaluations (Grube et al., 2008). Using this technique, participants recall the last occurrence of a typical work event (e.g., interacting with a customer), describe the event in detail (i.e., event reconstruction), and then rate their job satisfaction during the event.

Beyond group differences and the measurement of change, several other aspects of job satisfaction measurement have been addressed, including characteristics of job satisfaction measures. For instance, some work has forwarded a clear distinction between job *satisfaction* and job *dissatisfaction*, with satisfaction predicting positive outcomes and OCBs more strongly, and dissatisfaction predicting negative outcomes and CWBs more strongly (Credé et al., 2009). As such, researchers may need to be more precise in their approach toward job (dis)satisfaction measurement. However, recent work suggests that these differences may be due in part to careless responding and acquiescence (Kam & Meyer, 2015). Second, with regard to the response model, some work using the JDI suggests that the work satisfaction scale (and perhaps global job satisfaction measures) tends to follow an ideal-point, rather than a dominance response model (Carter & Dalal, 2010). This suggests that there may be more precise ways of scoring job satisfaction that do not assume that higher magnitude ratings reflect larger levels of satisfaction. Third, drawing on research on attitude strength (Fazio, 1995), researchers have found that relationships between job satisfaction and criteria are larger when employees' evaluations are strong, rather than weak (Schleicher et al., 2015). This suggests that one property of job satisfaction (the strength of the attitude) may moderate relationships between job satisfaction and criteria. As a final measurement consideration, one could either take a manifest or latent approach to the modeling of multi-faceted job satisfaction measures (Judge & Kammeyer-Mueller, 2012). However, as mentioned earlier, researchers should be clear at the outset regarding their treatment of the job satisfaction construct and use measures that align with their conceptualization of job satisfaction and with the purpose of the assessment.

# Antecedents of Job Satisfaction

The theory and measurement of job satisfaction have steadily developed over the last century. Now that we have established this foundation, we review the antecedents of job satisfaction as well as its consequences in the following section. As can be seen in Figure 9.1, there are a number of antecedents that predict job satisfaction, which we group into three categories: dispositional, contextual, and event-based. We believe that categorizing the antecedents in this way appropriately reflects the influence of the person (i.e., disposition), the situation (i.e., context), and events (i.e., temporal influences and states).

## *Dispositional Antecedents*

Once the dispositional basis of job satisfaction was established (Arvey et al., 1989; Staw & Ross, 1985; Staw et al., 1986), researchers' attention focused on specific dispositions as antecedents of job satisfaction. First, Watson and Slack (1993) found that trait positive affect (PA) and negative affect (NA) were significantly related to job satisfaction two years later. Later, meta-analyses further substantiated this relationship, confirming that both PA and NA had a moderate relationship with job satisfaction (Thoresen et al., 2003).

Second, research on specific dispositions has focused on the relationship between the Big Five (Goldberg, 1990), one of the most widely used personality frameworks, and job satisfaction. Meta-analytic research on this relationship has observed a multiple correlation of .41 between job satisfaction and the Big Five traits (Judge, Heller, & Mount, 2002). Except for the low predictive power of Agreeableness and Openness to Experience, the traits of Neuroticism, Extraversion, and Conscientiousness all had moderate correlations with job satisfaction. Taking this personality-satisfaction relationship to the organization-level, Oh, Kim, and Van Iddekinge (2015) found that personality-based human capital resources (i.e., organization-level mean emotional stability, extraversion, and conscientiousness) are positively related to organization-level managerial job satisfaction.

Third, more narrowly defined personality traits have been examined as predictors of job satisfaction. For example, proactive personality, which reflects individuals' dispositional tendency to take personal initiative to influence their environment, was found to improve employees' job satisfaction by helping them establish a high-quality exchange relationship with their supervisors (Li, Liang, & Crant, 2010).

Fourth, and finally, researchers have examined the extent to which core self-evaluations (CSE) affect job satisfaction. Judge, Locke, and Durham (1997) introduced CSE, which represents fundamental beliefs individuals hold about themselves and their self-worth. CSE is a latent construct that comprises four dispositional traits: (a) self-esteem, (b) generalized self-efficacy, (c) neuroticism, and (d) locus of control (Judge et al., 2003). CSE has been successfully linked

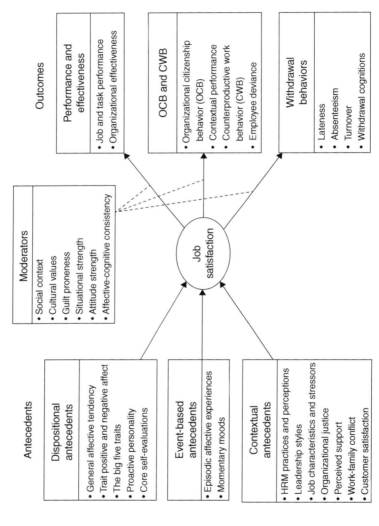

*Figure 9.1* The Nomological Network of Job Satisfaction.

to job satisfaction, and a meta-analysis found that the composite measure of the four traits has a correlation of 0.37 with job satisfaction (Judge & Bono, 2001). Judge, Heller, and Klinger (2008) compared the validity of the three dispositional typologies—the five-factor model, PA/NA, and CSE in predicting job satisfaction and found that when all three typologies were examined in tandem, only CSE was significantly related to job satisfaction. Although CSE is typically conceptualized as a stable personality metatrait that influences job satisfaction, recent research has begun to examine reciprocal relationships between CSE and job satisfaction (Wu & Griffin, 2012). Using longitudinal data spanning 10 years, Wu and Griffin (2012) found that individuals' CSE both shapes and is shaped by experiences in their work environment (i.e., job satisfaction).

## Contextual Antecedents

As we have alluded to earlier, research on the contextual antecedents of job attitudes predominated in the 1960s and 1970s and has continued to grow since then. A summary of the early studies indicates that factors such as work conditions, pay, career opportunities, coworkers, and supervisors are important factors influencing job satisfaction (Locke, 1976). Researchers have continued to study the contextual antecedents of job satisfaction, and we review a number of these below.

### Job Design Characteristics

Work-related characteristics have been one of the most researched antecedents of job satisfaction. The prominent role played by job characteristics in impacting individual work attitudes has long been recognized in the job design literature (e.g., Hackman & Oldham, 1975, 1976) and the effects of five core characteristics (task identity, task significance, skill variety, autonomy, and feedback) on job satisfaction have received considerable empirical support (Fried & Ferris, 1987; Loher et al., 1985). However, in most of those studies, both the task characteristics and job attitudes data were collected via self-reported surveys, making it difficult to distinguish the influence of task characteristics from that of dispositions because personalities such as CSE are likely to influence perceptions of job characteristics. To address this issue, Judge, Bono, and Locke (2000) studied self-report and analysis-based job characteristics concurrently and found that subjective perceptions of job characteristics are more closely related to job satisfaction than objective indicators.

Given the prevalence of stressful work demands, various work stressors have also been examined with respect to their detrimental effects on job satisfaction. However, the two-dimensional work stressor framework (challenge vs. hindrance stressors) suggests that two types of stressors are differentially related to employee job attitudes (Boswell, Olson-Buchanan, & LePine, 2004).

Challenge stressors refer to job demands that may create opportunities for personal growth and achievement, including high levels of workload and time pressure. In contrast, hindrance stressors refer to job demands that may thwart personal development and task accomplishment, including role ambiguity and organizational politics (Boswell et al., 2004).

A meta-analysis of work stressors' effects on job satisfaction further confirmed this distinction (Podsakoff, LePine, & LePine, 2007). This meta-analysis found that hindrance stressors were negatively related to job satisfaction, while challenge stressors were positively related to job satisfaction. Extending the static role stressors-job satisfaction relationship, Ritter et al. (2016) employed a longitudinal research design and examined relationships between role stressors and job satisfaction over time. Their findings largely supported adaption theory, which refers to "the psychological process by which people become accustomed to a positive or negative stimulus, such that the emotional effects of that stimulus are attenuated over time" (Lyubomirsky, 2011, p. 201). Specifically, they found that although role clarity was positively related to job satisfaction initially, over time, employees grew accustomed to role clarity, and their level of job satisfaction decreased to a preexisting level. In contrast, role conflict caused an immediate reduction in job satisfaction, but over time, employees adjusted to this stressor, and their job satisfaction returned to a more positive level.

Another job stressor that has caught numerous researchers' attention is job insecurity, which refers to individuals' concern about the future continuity of their jobs (van Vuuren & Klandermans, 1990). A meta-analysis of the relationship between job insecurity and job satisfaction found a correlation of -.43 (Cheng & Chan, 2008). As job insecurity is becoming a globally relevant phenomenon, a recent study employed a cross-cultural perspective and examined the generalizability of job insecurity across 24 countries (Debus et al., 2012). This study found that two country-level moderators (enacted uncertainty avoidance and the social safety net) buffer the negative relationships between job insecurity and job satisfaction. Countries with high enacted uncertainty avoidance have extensive norms, rules, and procedures to alleviate the uncertainty brought by job insecurity and social safety nets such as social insurance programs provide essential resources to buffer employees from economic shocks.

## Social Environment Characteristics

Research on job-related characteristics can help us understand how the work itself can impact individual job attitudes. However, other features of the workplace, such as relationships with supervisors, coworkers, and customers, may also have significant influences. For example, Morgeson and Humphrey (2006) found that perceived social support from others in the workplace is significantly related to individual work satisfaction, even when the effects of motivational work characteristics were controlled. A comprehensive meta-analysis of coworker effects on job satisfaction found that both the positive (support) and negative (antagonism) coworker predictors have a significant impact on job satisfaction (Chiaburu & Harrison, 2008). This meta-analysis also found that affective coworker support has a stronger relationship with job satisfaction than instrumental support and that coworker support has a stronger relationship with job satisfaction than coworker antagonism.

Another frequently studied social environment characteristic is conflict in work teams. A meta-analysis showed that relationship conflict ($\rho = -.48$) has a more negative effect than task conflict ($\rho = -.27$) on team member satisfaction (De Dreu & Weingart, 2003). Although conflict has been found to be generally negatively related to job satisfaction, a recent study found that mild task conflict can *improve* job satisfaction through increased employee information acquisition and subsequent positive active emotions (Todorova, Bear, & Weingart, 2014). This unexpected finding demonstrates the importance of considering conflict intensity when examining the effects of conflict on employee job satisfaction.

Most of the studies on the relationship between social environment characteristics and job satisfaction focus on factors internal to an organization. However, factors external to an organization such as the work-family interface and customer attitudes may also have a close relationship with job satisfaction. For example, a meta-analysis showed that work-to-family conflict has a correlation of -.25 with job satisfaction, while family-to-work conflict has a correlation of -.14 with job satisfaction (Shockley & Singla, 2011).

## *Organizational Justice*

A large amount of research has focused on the effects of organizational characteristics on job satisfaction. Among all the organizational characteristics, organizational justice has drawn the most attention. A recent meta-analysis of this line of research found that pay satisfaction has a substantial relationship with distributive justice ($\rho = .79$) and procedural justice ($\rho = 0.42$; Williams, McDaniel, & Nguyen, 2006). Besides pay satisfaction, overall job satisfaction has also been examined as an important outcome of the four dimensions of justice, including distributive justice ($\rho = .56$), procedural justice ($\rho = .62$), interpersonal justice ($\rho = .35$), and informational justice ($\rho = .43$; Colquitt et al., 2001). These findings show that compared with procedural justice, distributive justice has a stronger relationship with pay satisfaction and a weaker relationship with overall job satisfaction. The results are consistent with prior findings by Sweeney and McFarlin (1993), which suggest that procedural justice would exert greater influence on more general evaluations of systems (e.g., overall job satisfaction) while distributive justice would exert greater influence on more specific person-referenced outcomes (e.g., pay satisfaction).

## *Human Resource Management Practices and Perceptions*

Another large body of research in organizational practices concerns the influence of human resource management practices on employee job satisfaction. This line of research involves multilevel studies in which human resources practices are examined at the group or organizational level and job satisfaction at the individual level. For example, Takeuchi, Chen, and Lepak (2009) found that unit-level high-performance work systems are positively related to individual job satisfaction through the mediating role of unit-level concern for employees' climate. Besides the influences of general HR practices, the effects of specific HR practices on job satisfaction have also been investigated. For example, a meta-analysis found that service-oriented HR practices are positively related to job satisfaction, and this relationship is mediated by employees' perceptions of service climate (Hong et al., 2013). Research has also found that changes in employees' HR system perceptions are related to changes in their job satisfaction and that the effect of HR system perceptions on job satisfaction gradually declines over time (Piening, Baluch, & Salge, 2013). These findings suggest that there is an adaption effect, in which HR inducements reduce employees' attitudinal responses to similar inducements in the future because employees adapt their expectations to such stimuli.

## *Leadership*

The importance of the effect of leadership on job satisfaction cannot be emphasized enough, given the power and influence leaders have over employees in organizations. In fact, more than one meta-analysis confirmed the significant impact of leadership on job satisfaction. For example, Judge, Piccolo, and Ilies (2004) found that the two classic dimensions of leadership behavior, consideration ($\rho = .46$) and initiating structure ($\rho = .22$), are effective predictors of job satisfaction. Two other meta-analyses have also found significant relationships between widely studied positive leadership styles such as transformational leadership (Judge & Piccolo, 2004) and ethical leadership (Ng & Feldman, 2015) and employees' job or supervisor satisfaction.

Compared with a large amount of research examining the link between positive leader behaviors and job satisfaction, fewer studies have examined how the dark side of leadership may affect job satisfaction. This line of research is especially important, given that negative contextual stimuli are more salient than positive in influencing individual attitudes (Baumeister et al., 2001). Existing studies have found that negative leadership behaviors such as abusive supervision (Tepper et al., 2004) and supervisor aggression (Hershcovis & Barling, 2010) lead to decreased job satisfaction.

Another widely studied antecedent of job satisfaction is the relationship quality within a supervisor-subordinate dyad, or leader-member exchange

(LMX, Dienesch & Liden, 1986), which has been found to be consistently related to job satisfaction (Dulebohn et al., 2012). Recent research has taken a multi-level perspective and examined the mediating role of empowerment in the relationship between LMX and job satisfaction (Zhou et al., 2012). LMX has also been examined as an important mediator linking distal predictors to job satisfaction. For example, employees with stronger mastery orientations can establish higher-quality exchanges with their supervisors, which in turn improves their job satisfaction (Janssen & Van Yperen, 2004). Mastery orientations are a type of goal orientation that focuses on learning and developing mastery of a task, as opposed to performance orientations, which focus on avoiding failure or proving competence (Dweck, 1999). Other studies have also found support for the reciprocal relationships between job satisfaction and LMX (Volmer et al., 2011), suggesting that satisfied employees may reciprocate the high-quality relationship with supervisors by increasing work efforts and engaging in more positive behaviors.

### *Event-Based Antecedents*

As we noted earlier, job satisfaction is comprised of affective, cognitive, and behavioral components (Hersey, 1932; George & Brief, 1992; Rosenburg & Hovland, 1960). Although job attitudes have an affective or emotional component, AET (Weiss & Cropanzano, 1996) posits that job attitudes (and their affective components) are conceptually distinct from affective reactions and states. AET also emphasizes how affective events precede emotional reactions, which in turn lead to the development of work attitudes such as job satisfaction. Given the episodic and fleeting nature of affective reactions, researchers have used ESM to capture the unfolding of emotions and moods within an individual as well as the events triggering such moods. Findings in this line of research show that a substantial proportion of job satisfaction variance is within-person (Podsakoff, Spoelma, Chawla, & Gabriel, 2019) and that job satisfaction is preceded by daily affective events and moods (e.g., Weiss, Nicholas, & Daus, 1999).

Using a diary study that lasted for 16 workdays, Weiss and colleagues (1999) found that episodic affective experiences, as represented by average levels of pleasant mood, predicted overall job satisfaction over and above cognitive beliefs. A meta-analysis further demonstrated that state positive affect is positively associated with job satisfaction, and state negative affect is negatively associated with job satisfaction (Thoresen et al., 2003). However, this meta-analysis did not find significant differences between trait and state affect as predictors of job satisfaction. Thoresen et al. (2003) suggested this was because individuals with high trait PA and NA are more prone to experience positive and negative momentary moods, which in turn influence their job satisfaction. Evidence for the mediating role of momentary moods in affect-job satisfaction relations can also be found in other studies (e.g., Nemanick & Munz, 1997; Watson & Clark, 1997).

## Outcomes of Job Satisfaction

Just as researchers have been trying to determine what causes or leads to changes in job satisfaction (as discussed in the previous section), there has been similar interest in determining the impact of job satisfaction on job-relevant outcomes (especially considering the financial and practical implications of satisfaction). In the current review, we focused mainly on three categories of outcomes: performance and effectiveness, OCB and CWB, and withdrawal. We grouped the outcomes in this way in order to align with earlier work on behavioral engagement, which found empirical support for a behavioral engagement factor, which included performance, OCB, and withdrawal (Harrison et al., 2006; Newman et al., 2010). Although they were unable to test the inclusion of CWB due to a lack of studies at the time (Harrison et al., 2006), we grouped this category with OCB. Furthermore, we also included organizational effectiveness with performance in order to catalog research that has examined the effect of job satisfaction on organizational productivity and effectiveness.

### *Job Performance and Effectiveness*

#### *Job Performance*

The relationship between job satisfaction and performance has often been called the "Holy Grail" of industrial psychology (Landy, 1989) and great efforts have been made to help us gain a thorough understanding of this relationship (e.g., Harter, Schmidt, & Hayes, 2002; Judge et al., 2001). As research on the job satisfaction-performance relationship expanded, Judge and colleagues (2001) performed a meta-analysis of the growing literature and found a moderate positive relationship between job satisfaction and job performance ($\rho = .30$). However, the cross-sectional nature of studies in this meta-analysis makes it challenging to determine the causal direction of the relationship between job satisfaction and job performance. To address this issue, Riketta (2008) conducted a meta-analysis of 16 predictive validation studies and concluded that job satisfaction is more likely to influence performance than vice versa.

#### *Moderators of the Job Satisfaction-Job Performance Relationship*

Despite the substantial relationship between job satisfaction and job performance, magnitudes of these effect sizes vary greatly (Judge et al., 2001), and researchers have thus tried to examine moderators of this relationship. For example, Schleicher, Watt, and Greguras (2004) found that affective-cognitive consistency, which reflects the extent to which individuals' general affective attitudes toward a job and their cognitive evaluations of a job are consistent with one another, strengthen the relationship between job satisfaction and job performance. Moreover, validating the pivotal role played by situations in constraining individuals' behavioral alternatives, a meta-analysis found that the constraints facet of situational strength, as measured by items describing various work characteristics from the online database O*NET, weakened the relationship between job satisfaction and job performance (Bowling et al., 2015).

As studies on the job satisfaction-job performance relationship perpetuated across different countries and cultures, questions about the universality of this relationship arose. A subsequent meta-analysis of studies conducted in different countries found significant moderating effects of cultural values in this linkage (Ng, Sorensen, & Yim, 2009). Specifically, this study found that in cultures that emphasize high individualism, low power distance, low uncertainty-avoidance, and/or high masculinity, job satisfaction is likely to have a stronger relationship with job performance. They also found that the moderating effects were weaker for contextual performance compared to task performance, because the latter is prescribed stronger behavioral norms by the culture and is traditionally attached more importance than the former.

*Organizational Effectiveness*

Just as the link between job satisfaction and job performance has been deemed the "holy grail" by academics, the potential linkage between job satisfaction and organizational effectiveness has also caught the eye of organizational practitioners. For example, in their book *The Enthusiastic Employee*, David Sirota laid out the business case for improving employee job satisfaction drawing on evidence from over 13 million employees in over 800 companies (Sirota & Klein, 2014; Sirota, Mischkind, & Meltzer, 2005). Studying this relationship at the business-unit level is critical because business-unit level performance is directly relevant to most organizations and is a significant concern of practitioners.

As studies on the relationship between job satisfaction and performance at the individual level burgeoned, researchers also noticed neglect of scientific research at the organizational level of analysis (Heneman & Judge, 2000). Echoing the call for more job satisfaction research at the business-unit level, Harter and colleagues (2002) conducted a meta-analysis of data collected from 7,939 business units in 36 companies using the Gallup Workplace Audit, which included a single-item measure of workers' overall job satisfaction. They found a substantial relation between unit-level employee satisfaction and business-unit outcomes such as productivity and profit (Harter et al., 2002).

To further determine the causal direction in the relationship between job satisfaction and job performance, subsequent research explored the causal ordering using lagged analyses (Schneider et al. , 2003). This study found that organizational financial and market performance predicted overall job satisfaction and satisfaction with security more strongly than its converse. In contrast, pay satisfaction has a more reciprocal relationship with organizational financial and market performance. A more holistic meta-analysis on the relationship between collective job satisfaction and macro-level outcomes was conducted later (Whitman, Van Rooy, & Viswesvaran, 2010). Results show that unit-level satisfaction has significant relationships with strategically focused criteria, including unit-level productivity and financial/sales performance, unit-level customer satisfaction, unit-level OCBs, and unit-level withdrawal.

### Organizational Citizenship Behavior and Counterproductive Work Behavior

#### Organizational Citizenship Behavior

OCBs (and their closely related counterpart, contextual performance) refer to discretionary and cooperative behaviors exhibited by organizational members that go beyond formal role expectations (Organ, 1988, 1997). It has been suggested that employees' job satisfaction is one of the most robust predictors of OCB (Kinicki et al., 2002) as the most salient mode of reciprocation occurs when employees are satisfied with their job and feel the need to reciprocate (Bateman & Organ, 1983). One meta-analysis showed that different facets of job satisfaction, including pay, co-workers, work, and supervision satisfaction, all had significant correlations with OCBs (Kinicki et al. 2002). Substantiating the important role played by the supervisor, supervisor satisfaction has been found to have a stronger relationship ($\rho = .45$) with OCB than the other facets of satisfaction (pay, $\rho = .23$; coworker, $\rho = .23$; work, $\rho = .16$). The predictive strength of job satisfaction on OCB was confirmed in later meta-analyses (Ilies et al., 2009), which also found that job satisfaction mediated the relationship between the personality traits of agreeableness and conscientiousness and OCB.

#### Counterproductive Work Behavior

CWBs (and their closely related counterpart, deviance) are volitional acts that may violate the interests of or do harm to the organization or its stakeholders (Sackett & DeVore, 2001). Job satisfaction's effect on CWB is presumed to operate similarly to that of OCB: as a mechanism for social exchange (Credé et al., 2007). Notably, job satisfaction appears to have a *stronger* effect on CWB ($\rho = -.37$) than it does on OCB ($\rho = .16$, Dalal, 2005). Indeed, prior research has shown that dissatisfaction can lead to an increase in deviant or counterproductive behaviors, including theft, substance abuse, and privilege abuse (Bolin & Heatherly, 2001). Furthermore, one study of customer service employees suggested that disagreeable employees tend to engage in more

CWBs because they are more likely to be dissatisfied with their jobs (Mount, Ilies, & Johnson, 2006). Furthermore, using an ESM design, Judge, Scott, & Ilies (2006) found evidence for the relationship between job satisfaction and CWBs within-person, suggesting that the experience of interpersonal mistreatment can lead one to become dissatisfied, which in turn leads to CWBs (providing support for AET).

## *Withdrawal*

Researchers have examined the effect of job satisfaction on two families of withdrawal behaviors: work withdrawal and job withdrawal. Work withdrawal constitutes behaviors that attempt to avoid performing one's tasks (e.g., absenteeism, taking extended breaks) while job withdrawal behaviors reflect one's intentions to leave the organization (e.g., turnover and retirement intentions; Hanisch & Hulin, 1990). Job satisfaction has also been proposed as the most intuitive attitudinal antecedent to withdrawal behaviors such as turnover and absenteeism because it is individuals' natural behavioral response to stay away from or leave environments they dislike (Hackett & Guion, 1985; Sagie, 1998). A meta-analysis demonstrated that job satisfaction and turnover have a corrected correlation of -.27 (Tett & Meyer, 1993). Turning to facets of satisfaction, the relationship between four relatively distinct dimensions of work, pay, promotions, and supervision satisfaction were all significantly related to turnover in a meta-analysis (Kinicki et al., 2002). Examining the relationship between job satisfaction change and turnover, Chen, Ployhart, Thomas, Anderson, and Bliese (2011) found that job satisfaction change accounts for the change in employees' turnover intentions, even when the influence of average levels of job satisfaction were controlled.

Meta-analyses also revealed a negative and moderate relationship between job satisfaction and absenteeism, ranging from .21 to .23 (Harrison et al., 2006). Extending the satisfaction-absenteeism relationship to the team level, Dineen et al. (2007) examined how team absenteeism was predicted by mean and dispersion levels of two satisfaction foci: internally focused satisfaction, which refers to individuals' satisfaction with others on their teams and externally focused satisfaction, which reflects members' satisfaction with their jobs. This study found that when the internally focused satisfaction mean and dispersion were both low, team absenteeism was highest. However, team absenteeism was lowest when the externally focused satisfaction mean and dispersion were both low. Inspired by developments in the moral emotions literature, Schaumberg and Flynn (2017) found that guilt-proneness, which reflects an individual's tendency to feel guilty when committing transgressions, mitigated the relationship between job satisfaction and absenteeism. They argue that this is because guilt is a kind of moral affectivity that regulates individuals' self-interested behaviors. Guilt-proneness motivates employees to think more about others and adhere to collective standards of worthy behaviors.

## Discussion

Throughout the work we have discussed, research on job satisfaction has seemingly oscillated between various approaches, as work on job satisfaction shifted from humanistic and cognitive approaches toward dispositional and affective approaches. We argue that these various epochs have made their own unique contributions to the study of job satisfaction (and even sparked interest in topics and questions that were important to earlier epochs; Judge et al., 2017). Yet, we also see several promising ways in which the study of job satisfaction can be refined or improved. First, as argued in earlier work, progress may be made by integrating various approaches to job satisfaction to address compelling research questions, such as the mutual influence of the person and situation on job satisfaction (Judge et al., 2017). The debates that surround different approaches to job satisfaction are not inherently a zero-sum game—the study of job satisfaction can move forward through recognition of the need to reconcile and integrate.

We also argue that job satisfaction research can move forward by employing abductive inference (Mathieu, 2016) and theory elaboration (Fisher & Aguinis, 2017). Taking this approach, one shifts from a process of theory development and validation toward one in which theories are pruned and elaborated based on empirical observation. For example, Ohly and Schmitt (2015) started with a simple question geared toward one of the tenants of AET (i.e., events at work cause the affective reactions which influence attitude formation): "what makes us enthusiastic, angry, … or worried [at work]?" To answer this question and contribute to the elaboration of AET, they developed a taxonomy of work events from a diary study that produced nearly 1,000 work events. The taxonomy they developed appeared to cluster around the personal values of agency and communion, suggesting the work events in AET signal threats to agency and communion values. We argue that although a validation approach has its merits, so does an approach that focuses on discovery and theory-building (Fisher & Aguinis, 2017). In general, the field can move forward through not only the integration of distinct paradigms and approaches to job satisfaction but also through a dual validation and discovery approach to studying job satisfaction.

### *Implications for Practice*

Research on job satisfaction suggests that it is related to a plethora of important organizational criteria. Job satisfaction appears to be reliably related to not just employee performance but also to organizational effectiveness and employee turnover, two metrics intimately tied to organizations' bottom lines. The influence of job satisfaction, however, moves beyond improving metrics. As one executive noted, "a satisfied employee is not just a retained employee but an ambassador for the brand, internally and externally." (Bathena, 2018, p. 1). Job satisfaction is invaluable to organizations not just for its potential to enhance the bottom line, but also because satisfied employees are more likely to serve as ambassadors, champions, and advocates of the organization beyond the task performance context.

Given what we know about the importance of job satisfaction, are employees satisfied with their jobs? Although current surveys of job satisfaction suggest that employees are generally satisfied with their jobs (89%) and that the number is increasing annually (3% since 2014), this by no means indicates that organizations should disregard job satisfaction (Lee, Esen, & DiNicola, 2017). Indeed, failing to attempt to improve employee job satisfaction would be a missed opportunity. What can managers do to improve job satisfaction? Our review suggests that employee perceptions of justice are a powerful influence on job satisfaction. According to a recent job satisfaction survey, the three most significant contributors to job satisfaction all involve organizational justice (e.g., respectful treatment, fair pay, and manager-subordinate trust). These are also areas in which employees experience the biggest gaps between their own satisfaction and what is important to them (Lee et al., 2017). In order to improve job satisfaction, managers are encouraged to foster transparency and fairness in compensation, to build trust amongst their teams, and to forge a climate where people treat each other with respect.

## *Future Research Directions*

The centrality of affect and emotion in job satisfaction research has been emphasized in previous work and characterizes the most recent epoch in job satisfaction research (Judge & Kammeyer-Mueller, 2012; Judge et al., 2012). As such, our recommendations for future research focus mainly on the affective components of job satisfaction. First, progress has been made in terms of examining episodic affective experiences as sources of within-person variance of job satisfaction using ESM (Thoresen et al., 2003; Weiss et al., 1999). However, a more nuanced treatment of affect in job satisfaction is needed to help us gain a better understanding of this burgeoning research area. For example, the causal direction is still not clearly explicated, as job satisfaction can also be a source of individuals' positive mood/emotions. Thus, more longitudinal research is needed to determine the nature and directions of relationships between the experience of moods/emotions and how they influence job satisfaction. A longitudinal research design involves repeated measurements during a certain period, therefore it would be necessary to determine how long these processes take to unfold. This is important because we may fail to fully capture the causal effects if the time lags are not appropriate (Spector & Meier, 2014). In order to uncover just what these time lags may be, future research should seek to identify the "optimal time lag" (Dormann & Griffin, 2015) between job satisfaction and criteria (as well as with its event-based antecedents)—extant research in this area suggests that this optimal time lag might be shorter than expected (Ilies & Judge, 2004; Judge et al., 2006).

Second, although the roles of emotion valance and arousal level, discrete emotions, affective changes, and events have all been emphasized in the AET framework (cf. Weiss & Beal, 2005), much less research has been conducted in areas such as emotional arousal level and discrete emotions than PA/NA. Future research may explore the specific relationships between job satisfaction and discrete emotions such as anger, guilt, sadness, calm, and excitement, which differ in terms of valance, activation level, and self-other orientation.

Third, besides examining how the focal person's affect may influence his or her own job satisfaction, future research may explore how a focal employee's job satisfaction may be influenced by the emotions exhibited by his or her co-worker, supervisor, or customer. Moreover, focal employee's interpretations of others' emotions may be incorporated in this process to understand the consequences of emotional contagion fully. Examination of employees' cognitive processes such as appraisals and attributions in the emotional processes can also better reflect the entangled relationships between emotions and cognitions (Lazarus & Folkman, 1984).

Fourth, the experience of discrete emotions or moods may play moderating roles in job satisfaction research (despite primarily being studied as main effects). For example, guilt-proneness is found to weaken the relationship between job satisfaction and withdrawal behavior (Schaumberg & Flynn, 2017). Future research may consider the moderating role of other specific affective dispositions such as trait gratitude (Emmons & McCullough, 2004) in relationships between job satisfaction and various outcomes.

Lastly, although emotions have been examined mostly as fleeting and short-lived, recent research has shown that it is theoretically meaningful to study emotions at the organizational level (Knight, Menges, & Bruch, 2018). Ashkanasy (2003) proposed a multilevel framework of emotions that suggests that emotions can be examined at the micro- (within- and between-person variability), meso- (dyadic and teams), and macro- (organization-wide) levels. Thus, it may be a promising future research direction to study how organizational or team level affective tone may influence unit level job satisfaction (Parke & Seo, 2017). In sum, we hope the above suggestions may offer fresh perspectives for studying the roles played by emotions in job satisfaction research and help us gain a deeper understanding of the affective components of job satisfaction.

## Conclusion

Job satisfaction research has grown greatly, both theoretically and methodologically, since its inception. Such developments, as noted by Judge et al. (2017), showed a cyclical pattern, in which new theories in each generation emerge by introducing explanations for experiences not sufficiently characterized by previous theories. This pattern of paradigm revision cuts across our reviews of the conceptualization, operationalization, antecedents, and consequences of job satisfaction. Our review also reveals some of the most recent developments in job satisfaction research. For example, researchers have begun exploring the affective and dynamic nature of job satisfaction (Chen et al., 2011; Ritter et al., 2016). We suggest that to ensure the continued development of the current epoch in job satisfaction research, a more nuanced approach should be taken to unpack the affective components of job satisfaction. At the same time, we suggest that advancements in job satisfaction research across epochs can be made through integration, synthesis, and a greater emphasis on theory elaboration.

# References

Adler, S. & Weiss, H.M. (1988). Recent developments in the study of personality and organizational behavior. In C.L. Cooper & I. Robertson (Eds.), *International Review of Industrial and Organizational Psychology* (pp. 307–330). New York, NY: Wiley.

Adolphs, R. & Damasio, A.R. (2001). The interaction of affect and cognition: A neurobiological perspective. In J.P. Forgas (Ed.), *Handbook of Affect and Social Cognition* (pp. 27–49). Mahwah, NJ: Lawrence Erlbaum.

Ajzen, I. & Fishbein, M. (1977). Attitude-behavior relations: A theoretical analysis and review of empirical research. *Psychological Bulletin, 84*(5), 888–918. doi.org/10.1037/0033-2909.84.5.888

Arvey, R.D., Bouchard, T.J., Segal, N.L., & Abraham, L.M. (1989). Job satisfaction: Environmental and genetic components. *Journal of Applied Psychology, 74*, 187–192. doi:10.1037/0021-9010.74.2.187

Ashkanasy, N.M. (2003). Emotions in organizations: a multilevel perspective. In F. Dansereau, & F.J. Yammarino (Eds.), *Research in Multi-Level Issues: Multi-Level Issues in Organizational Behavior and Strategy* (Vol. 2, pp. 9–54). Oxford, U.K.: Elsevier Science.

Balzer, W.K., Kihm, J.A., Smith, P.C., Irwin, J.L., Bachiochi, P.D., Robie, C., ... Parra, L.F. (1997). *Users' Manual for the Job Descriptive Index (JDI; 1997 Revision) and the Job in General Scales*. Bowling Green, OH: Bowling Green State University.

Bateman, T.S. & Organ, D.W. (1983). Job satisfaction and the good soldier: The relationship between affect and employee "citizenship." *Academy of Management Journal, 26*, 587–595. doi.org/10.5465/255908

Bathena, Z. (2018, March). Why job satisfaction is an important phenomenon of the vicious circle? *Entrepreneur,* www.entrepreneur.com/article/310608

Baumeister, R.F., Bratslavsky, E., Finkenauer, C., & Vohs, K.D. (2001). Bad is stronger than good. *Review of General Psychology, 5*(4), 323–370. doi.org/10.1037/1089-2680.5.4.323

Beehr, T.A., Glaser, K.M., Beehr, M.J., Beehr, D.E., Wallwey, D.A., Erofeev, D., & Canali, K.G. (2006). The nature of satisfaction with subordinates: Its predictors and importance to supervisors. *Journal of Applied Social Psychology, 36*(6), 1523–1547. doi.org/10/bcv6xk

Bolin, A. & Heatherly, L. (2001). Predictors of employee deviance: The relationship between bad attitudes and bad behavior. *Journal of Business and Psychology*, *15*(3), 405–418. doi.org/10.1023/A:1007818616389

Boswell, W.R., Olson-Buchanan, J.B., & LePine, M.A. (2004). Relations between stress and work outcomes: The role of felt challenge, job control, and psychological strain. *Journal of Vocational Behavior*, *64*(1), 165–181. doi.org/10.1016/S0001-8791(03)00049-6

Bowling, N.A. & Hammond, G.D. (2008). A meta-analytic examination of the construct validity of the Michigan Organizational Assessment Questionnaire Job Satisfaction Subscale. *Journal of Vocational Behavior*, *73*(1), 63–77. doi.org/10/fnmqf8

Bowling, N.A. Hendricks, E.A., & Wagner, S.H. (2008). Positive and negative affectivity and facet satisfaction: a meta-analysis. *Journal of Business and Psychology*, *23*(3–4), 115–125. doi.org/10.1007/s10869-008-9082-0

Bowling, N.A., Khazon, S., Meyer, R.D., & Burrus, C.J. (2015). Situational strength as a moderator of the relationship between job satisfaction and job performance: A meta-analytic examination. *Journal of Business and Psychology*, *30*(1), 89–104. doi.org/10.1007/s10869-013-9340-7

Bowling, N.A., Wagner, S.H., & Beehr, T.A. (2018). The Facet Satisfaction Scale: An Effective Affective Measure of Job Satisfaction Facets. *Journal of Business and Psychology*, *33*(3), 383–403. doi.org/10/gckfns

Brayfield, A.H. & Crockett, W.H. (1955). Employee attitudes and employee performance. *Psychological Bulletin*, *52*, 396–424. dx.doi.org/10.1037/h0045899

Brayfield, A.H. & Rothe, H.F. (1951). An index of job satisfaction. *Journal of Applied Psychology*, *35*(5), 307–311. doi.org/10/gdr

Carter, N.T. & Dalal, D.K. (2010). An ideal point account of the JDI Work satisfaction scale. *Personality and Individual Differences*, *49*(7), 743–748. doi.org/10/c79zzp

Chen, G., Ployhart, R.E., Thomas, H.C., Anderson, N., & Bliese, P.D. (2011). The power of momentum: A new model of dynamic relationships between job satisfaction change and turnover intentions. *Academy of Management Journal*, *54*(1), 159–181. doi.org/10.5465/amj.2011.59215089

Cheng, G.H.L. & Chan, D.K.S. (2008). Who suffers more from job insecurity? A meta-analytic review. *Applied Psychology*, *57*(2), 272–303. doi.org/10.1111/j.1464-0597.2007.00312.x

Chiaburu, D.S. & Harrison, D.A. (2008). Do peers make the place? Conceptual synthesis and meta-analysis of coworker effects on perceptions, attitudes, OCBs, and performance. *Journal of Applied Psychology*, *93*(5), 1082–1103. doi:10.1037/0021-9010.93.5.1082

Colquitt, J.A., Conlon, D.E., Wesson, M.J., Porter, C.O.L.H., & Ng, K.Y. (2001). Justice at the millennium: A meta-analytic review of 25 years of organizational justice research. *Journal of Applied Psychology*, *86*(3), 425–445. doi:10.1037/0021-9010.86.3.425

Cranny, C.J., Smith, P.C., & Stone, E.F. (1992). *Job Satisfaction: Advances in Research and Applications*. New York, NY: The Free Press.

Credé, M., Chernyshenko, O.S., Bagraim, J., & Sully, M. (2009). Contextual Performance and the Job Satisfaction–Dissatisfaction Distinction: Examining Artifacts and Utility. *Human Performance*, *22*(3), 246–272. doi.org/10/fgs55w

Credé, M., Chernyshenko, O.S., Stark, S., Dalal, R.S., & Bashshur, M. (2007). Job satisfaction as mediator: An assessment of job satisfaction's position within the nomological network. *Journal of Occupational and Organizational Psychology, 80*(3), 515–538. doi.org/10.1348/096317906X136180

Dalal, R.S. (2005). A meta-analysis of the relationship between organizational citizenship behavior and counterproductive work behavior. *Journal of Applied Psychology, 90*(6), 1241–1255. doi.org/10.1037/0021-9010.90.6.1241

Debus, M.E., Probst, T.M., König, C.J., & Kleinmann, M. (2012). Catch me if I fall! Enacted uncertainty avoidance and the social safety net as country-level moderators in the job insecurity–job attitudes link. *Journal of Applied Psychology, 97*(3), 690–698. dx.doi.org/10.1037/a0027832

De Dreu, C.K.W. & Weingart, L.R. (2003). Task versus relationship conflict, team performance, and team member satisfaction: A meta-analysis. Journal of Applied Psychology, 88(4), 741–749. doi.org/10.1037/0021-9010.88.4.741

Dweck, C.S. (1999). *Self Theories: Their Role in Motivation, Personality, and Development.* Philadelphia: Psychology Press.

Dienesch, R.M. & Liden, R.C. (1986). Leader-member exchange model of leadership: A critique and further development. *Academy of Management Review, 11*(3), 618–634. doi.org/10.5465/amr.1986.4306242

Digman, J.M. (1990). Personality structure: Emergence of the five-factor model. *Annual Review of Psychology, 41*, 417–440. dx.doi.org/10.1146/annurev.ps.41.020190.002221

Dineen, B.R., Noe, R.A., Shaw, J.D., Duffy, M.K., & Wiethoff, C. (2007). Level and dispersion of satisfaction in teams: Using foci and social context to explain the satisfaction-absenteeism relationship. *Academy of Management Journal, 50*(3), 623–643. doi.org/10.5465/amj.2007.25525987

Dormann, C. & Griffin, M.A. (2015). Optimal time lags in panel studies. *Psychological Methods, 20*(4), 489–505. doi.org/10.1037/met0000041

Dulebohn, J.H., Bommer, W.H., Liden, R.C., Brouer, R.L., & Ferris, G.R. (2012). A meta-analysis of antecedents and consequences of leader-member exchange: Integrating the past with an eye toward the future. *Journal of Management, 38*(6), 1715–1759. doi.org/10.1177/0149206311415280

Dunham, R.B., Smith, F.J., & Blackburn, R.S. (1977). Validation of the index of organizational reaction with the JDI, the MSQ, and faces scales. *Academy of Management Journal, 20*(3), 420–432. doi.org/10/bpt6gd

Elfering, A. & Grebner, S. (2011). On the Intra- and interindividual differences in the meaning of smileys. *Swiss Journal of Psychology, 70*(1), 13–23. doi.org/10.1024/1421-0185/a000034

Emmons, R.A. & McCullough, M.E. (2004). *The Psychology of Gratitude.* New York: Oxford University Press.

Ewen, R.B. (1964). Some determinants of job satisfaction: A study of the generality of Herzberg's theory. *Journal of Applied Psychology, 48*, 161–163. dx.doi.org/10.1037/h0048383

Fazio, R.H. (1995). Attitudes as object-evaluation associations: Determinants, consequences, and correlates of attitude accessibility. In R. Petty & J. Krosnick (Eds.), *Attitude strength: Antecedents and Consequences* (pp. 247–282). Hillsdale, NJ: Erlbaum.

Fisher, C.D. (1980). On the dubious wisdom of expecting job satisfaction to correlate with performance. *Academy of Management Review, 5*(4), 607. doi.org/10.2307/257468

Fisher, G. & Aguinis, H. (2017). Using theory elaboration to make theoretical advancements. *Organizational Research Methods, 20*(3), 438–464. doi.org/10.1177/1094428116689707

Fisher, G.G., Matthews, R.A., & Gibbons, A.M. (2016). Developing and investigating the use of single-item measures in organizational research. *Journal of Occupational Health Psychology, 21*(1), 3–23. doi.org/10/f77jgg

Fisher, V.E. & Hanna, J.V. (1931). *The Dissatisfied Worker*. New York, NY: Macmillan. dx.doi.org/10.1037/10719-000

Fried, Y. & Ferris, G.R. (1987). The validity of the job characteristics model: A review and meta-analysis. *Personnel Psychology, 40*, 287–322.

George, J.M. & Brief, A.P. (1992). Feeling good-doing good: A conceptual analysis of the mood at work-organizational spontaneity relationship. *Psychological Bulletin, 112*(2), 310–329. doi:10.1037/0033-2909.112.2.310

Goldberg, L.R. (1990). An alternative "description of personality": The Big-Five factor structure. *Journal of Personality and Social Psychology, 59*(6), 1216–1229. dx.doi.org/10.1037/0022-3514.59.6.1216

Grube, A., Schroer, J., Hentzschel, C., & Hertel, G. (2008). The event reconstruction method: An efficient measure of experience-based job satisfaction. *Journal of Occupational and Organizational Psychology, 81*(4), 669–689. doi.org/10/bx9nw2

Guion, R.M. (2011). *Assessment, Measurement, and Prediction for Personnel Decisions* (2nd ed.). New York, NY: Lawrence Erlbaum.

Hackett, R.D. & Guion, R.M. (1985). A reevaluation of the absenteeism-job satisfaction relationship. *Organizational Behavior and Human Decision Processes, 35*(3), 340–381. doi.org/10.1016/0749-5978(85)90028-7

Hackman, J.R. & Oldham, G.R. (1974). *The Job Diagnostic Survey: An Instrument for the Diagnosis of Jobs and the Evaluation of Job Redesign Projects* (No. 4; pp. 1–87). New Haven, CT: Yale University.

Hackman, J.R. & Oldham, G.R. (1975). Development of the job diagnostic survey. *Journal of Applied Psychology, 60*(2), 159–170. doi.org/10/chz

Hackman, J.R. & Oldham, G.R. (1976). Motivation through the design of work: Test of a theory. *Organizational Behavior and Human Performance, 16*(2), 250–279. doi.org/10/hbs

Hanisch, K.A. & Hulin, C.L. (1990). Job attitudes and organizational withdrawal: An examination of retirement and other voluntary withdrawal behaviors. *Journal of Vocational Behavior, 37*(1), 60–78. doi.org/10.1016/0001-8791(90)90007-O

Harrison, D.A., Newman, D.A., & Roth, P.L. (2006). How important are job attitudes? Meta-analytic comparisons of integrative behavioral outcomes and time sequences. *Academy of Management Journal, 49*(2), 305–325. doi.org/10.5465/amj.2006.20786077

Harter, J.K., Schmidt, F.L., & Hayes, T.L. (2002). Business-unit-level relationship between employee satisfaction, employee engagement, and business outcomes: A meta-analysis. *Journal of Applied Psychology, 87*(2), 268–279. doi:10.1037/0021-9010.87.2.268

Heneman, H.G. III & Judge, T.A. (2000). Compensation attitudes. In S.L. Rynes & B. Gerhart (Eds.), *Compensation in Organizations: Current Research and Practice* (pp. 61–103). San Francisco, CA: Jossey-Bass.

Heneman, H.G. & Schwab, D.P. (1985). Pay satisfaction: Its multidimensional nature and measurement. *International Journal of Psychology, 20*(1), 129–141. doi.org/10.1080/00207598508247727

Hersey, R.B. (1932). *Workers' Emotions in Shop and Home: A Study of Individual Workers from the Psychological and Physiological Standpoint*. Oxford, England: University of Pennsylvania Press.

Hershcovis, M.S. & Barling, J. (2010). Towards a multi-foci approach to workplace aggression: A meta-analytic review of outcomes from different perpetrators. *Journal of Organizational Behavior, 31*(1), 24–44. doi.org/10.1002/job.621

Herzberg, F., Mausner, B., & Snyderman, B.B. (1959). *The Motivation to Work* (2nd ed.). New York, NY: Wiley.

Highhouse, S. & Becker, A.S. (1993). Facet Measures and Global Job Satisfaction. *Journal of Business and Psychology, 8*(1), 117–127. doi.org/10/d8thkn

Hong, Y., Liao, H., Hu, J., & Jiang, K. (2013). Missing link in the service profit chain: A meta-analytic review of the antecedents, consequences, and moderators of service climate. *Journal of Applied Psychology, 98*(2), 237–267. dx.doi.org/10.1037/a0031666

House, R.J. & Wigdor, L.A. (1967). Herzberg's dual-factor theory of job satisfaction and motivation: A review of the evidence and a criticism. *Personnel Psychology, 20*, 369–389. dx.doi.org/10.1111/j.1744-6570.1967.tb02440.x

Hu, X., Kaplan, S., & Dalal, R.S. (2010). An examination of blue- versus white-collar workers' conceptualizations of job satisfaction facets. *Journal of Vocational Behavior, 76*(2), 317–325. doi.org/10.1016/j.jvb.2009.10.014

Hulin, C.L. & Judge, T.A. (2003). Job Attitudes. In I.B. Weiner (Ed.), *Handbook of Psychology* (pp. 255–276). doi.org/10.1002/0471264385.wei1211

Hulin, C.L. & Smith, P.C. (1964). Sex differences in job satisfaction. *Journal of Applied Psychology, 48*, 88–92. dx.doi.org/10.1037/h0040811

Ilies, R., Fulmer, I.S., Spitzmuller, M., & Johnson, M.D. (2009). Personality and citizenship behavior: The mediating role of job satisfaction. *Journal of Applied Psychology, 94*(4), 945–959. doi.org/10.1037/a0013329

Ilies, R. & Judge, T.A. (2004). An experience-sampling measure of job satisfaction and its relationships with affectivity, mood at work, job beliefs, and general job satisfaction. *European Journal of Work and Organizational Psychology, 13*(3), 367–389. doi.org/10/cnc34h

Ironson, G.H., Brannick, M.T., Smith, P.C., Gibson, W.M., & Paul, K.B. (1989). Construction of a job in general scale: A comparison of global, composite, and specific measures. *Journal of Applied Psychology, 74*(2), 193–200. doi.org/10/b4293n

Janssen, O. & Van Yperen, N.W. (2004). Employees' goal orientations, the quality of leader-member exchange, and the outcomes of job performance and job satisfaction. *Academy of Management Journal, 47*(3), 368–384. doi.org/10.5465/20159587

Judge, T.A. & Bono, J.E. (2001). Relationship of core self-evaluations traits—Self-esteem, generalized self-efficacy, locus of control, and emotional stability—With job satisfaction and job performance: A meta-analysis. *Journal of Applied Psychology, 86*, 80–92. dx.doi.org/ 10.1037/0021-9010.86.1.80

Judge, T.A., Bono, J.E., & Locke, E.A. (2000). Personality and job satisfaction: The mediating role of job characteristics. *Journal of Applied Psychology, 85*(2), 237–249. doi.org/10.1037/0021-9010.85.2.237

Judge, T.A., Erez, A., Bono, J.E. & Thoresen, C.J. (2003). The core self-evaluations scale: Development of a measure. *Personnel Psychology, 56*(2), 303–331. doi.org/10.1111/j.1744-6570.2003.tb00152.x

Judge, T.A., Heller, D., & Klinger, R. (2008). The dispositional sources of job satisfaction: A comparative test. *Applied Psychology, 57*(3), 361–372. doi.org/10.1111/j.1464-0597.2007.00318.x

Judge, T.A., Heller, D., & Mount, M.K. (2002). Five-factor model of personality and job satisfaction: A meta-analysis. *Journal of Applied Psychology*, *87*(3), 530–541. dx.doi. org/10.1037/0021-9010.87.3.530

Judge, T.A., Hulin, C.L., & Dalal, R.S. (2012). Job satisfaction and job affect. In S.W.J. Kozlowski (Ed.), *The Oxford Handbook of Organizational Psychology* (Vol. 1, pp. 496–525). doi.org/10.1093/oxfordhb/9780199928309.013.0015

Judge, T.A. & Kammeyer-Mueller, J.D. (2012). Job attitudes. *Annual Review of Psychology*, *63*(1), 341–367. doi.org/10/fg5gvs

Judge T.A., Locke, E.A., & Durham, C.C. (1997). The dispositional causes of job satisfaction: a core evaluations approach. *Research in Organizational Behavior*, 19, 151–188.

Judge, T.A., Locke, E.A., Durham, C.C., & Kluger, A.N. (1998). Dispositional effects on job and life satisfaction: The role of core evaluations. *Journal of Applied Psychology*, *83*, 17–34. dx.doi.org/10.1037/0021-9010.83.1.17

Judge, T.A. & Piccolo, R.F. (2004). Transformational and transactional leadership: A meta-analytic test of their relative validity. *Journal of Applied Psychology*, *89*(5), 755–768. dx.doi.org/10.1037/0021-9010.89.5.755

Judge, T.A., Piccolo, R.F., & Ilies, R. (2004). The forgotten ones? The validity of consideration and initiating structure in leadership research. *Journal of Applied Psychology*, *89*(1), 36–51. dx.doi.org/10.1037/0021-9010.89.1.36

Judge, T.A., Scott, B.A., & Ilies, R. (2006). Hostility, job attitudes, and workplace deviance: Test of a multilevel model. *Journal of Applied Psychology*, *91*(1), 126–138. doi. org/10.1037/0021-9010.91.1.126

Judge, T.A., Thoresen, C.J., Bono, J.E., & Patton, G.K. (2001). The job satisfaction–job performance relationship: A qualitative and quantitative review. *Psychological Bulletin*, *127*(3), 376–407. dx.doi.org/10.1037/0033-2909.127.3.376

Judge, T.A., Weiss, H.M., Kammeyer-Mueller, J.D., & Hulin, C.L. (2017). Job attitudes, job satisfaction, and job affect: A century of continuity and of change. *Journal of Applied Psychology*, *102*(3), 356–374. doi.org/10/f9zrh6

Kam, C.C.S. & Meyer, J.P. (2015). How careless responding and acquiescence response bias can influence construct dimensionality: The case of job satisfaction. *Organizational Research Methods*, *18*(3), 512–541. doi.org/10/f7frc6

Kaplan, S.A., Warren, C.R., Barsky, A.P., & Thoresen, C.J. (2009). A note on the relationship between affect(ivity) and differing conceptualizations of job satisfaction: Some unexpected meta-analytic findings. *European Journal of Work and Organizational Psychology*, *18*(1), 29–54. doi.org/10/bqdf34

Kinicki, A.J., McKee-Ryan, F.M., Schriesheim, C.A., & Carson, K.P. (2002). Assessing the construct validity of the Job Descriptive Index: A review and meta-analysis. *Journal of Applied Psychology*, *87*(1), 14–32. doi.org/10/fjzwzx

Knight, A.P., Menges, J.I., & Bruch, H. (2018). Organizational affective tone: A meso perspective on the origins and effects of consistent affect in organizations. *Academy of Management Journal*, *61*(1), 191–219.

Koh, C.W., Shen, W., & Lee, T. (2016). Black–White mean differences in job satisfaction: A meta-analysis. *Journal of Vocational Behavior*, *94*, 131–143. doi.org/10/gfz5jb

Kunin, T. (1955). The construction of a new type of attitude measure. *Personnel Psychology*, *8*, 65–77. dx.doi.org/10.1111/j.1744–6570.1955.tb01189.x

Kunin, T. (1998). The construction of a new type of attitude measure. *Personnel Psychology*, *51*, 823–824. doi.org/10/dck728

Landy, F.J. (1989). *Psychology of Work Behavior*. Pacific Grove, CA: Brooks/Cole.

Lazarus, R.S. & Folkman, S. (1984). *Stress, Appraisal, and Coping.* New York: Springer Publishing.

Lee, C., Esen, E., & DiNicola, S. (2017). *Employee Job Satisfaction and Engagement: The Doors of Opportunity are Open.* Alexandria, VA: Society for Human Resource Management.

Li, N., Liang, J., & Crant, J.M. (2010). The role of proactive personality in job satisfaction and organizational citizenship behavior: A relational perspective. *Journal of Applied Psychology, 95*(2), 395–404. dx.doi.org/10.1037/a0018079

Liu, C., Borg, I., & Spector, P.E. (2004). Measurement equivalence of the German job satisfaction survey used in a multinational organization: Implications of Schwartz's culture model. *Journal of Applied Psychology, 89*(6), 1070–1082. doi.org/10/fhqckc

Locke, E.A. (1969). What is job satisfaction? *Organizational Behavior and Human Performance, 4*, 309–336. dx.doi.org/10.1016/0030-5073(69)90013-0

Locke, E.A. (1976). The nature and causes of job satisfaction. In M.D. Dunnette (Ed.), *Handbook of Industrial and Organizational Psychology* (pp. 1297–1349). Chicago, IL: Rand McNally.

Loher, B.T., Noe, R.A., Moeller, N.L., & Fitzgerald, M.P. (1985). A meta-analysis of the relation of job characteristics to job satisfaction. *Journal of Applied Psychology, 70*(2), 280–289. dx.doi.org/10.1037/0021-9010.70.2.280

Lyubomirsky, S. (2011). Hedonic adaptation to positive and negative experiences. In S. Folkman (Ed.), *The Oxford Handbook of Stress, Health, and Coping* (pp. 200–224). New York, NY: Oxford University Press.

Mathieu, J.E. (2016). The problem with [in] management theory. *Journal of Organizational Behavior, 37*(8), 1132–1141. doi.org/10.1002/job.2114

McGregor, D. (1960). *The Human Side of Enterprise.* New York, NY: McGraw-Hill.

Morgeson, F.P. & Humphrey, S.E. (2006). The work design questionnaire (WDQ): Developing and validating a comprehensive measure for assessing job design and the nature of work. *Journal of Applied Psychology, 91*(6), 1321–1339. dx.doi.org/10.1037/0021-9010.91.6.1321

Morse, N.C. (1953). *Satisfactions in the White-Collar Job.* Oxford, England: Survey Research Center.

Mount, M., Ilies, R., & Johnson, E. (2006). Relationship of personality traits and counterproductive work behaviors: The mediating effects of job satisfaction. *Personnel Psychology, 59*(3), 591–622. doi.org/10.1111/j.1744-6570.2006.00048.x

Mueller, K., Hattrup, K., & Straatmann, T. (2011). Globally surveying in English: Investigation of the measurement equivalence of a job satisfaction measure across bilingual and native English speakers. *Journal of Occupational and Organizational Psychology, 84*, 618–624. doi.org/10.1348/096317910X493585

Nagy, M.S. (2002). Using a single-item approach to measure facet job satisfaction. *Journal of Occupational and Organizational Psychology, 75*(1), 77–86. doi.org/10/dk3hkd

Nemanick, R.C., Jr. & Munz, D.C. (1997). Extraversion and neuroticism, trait mood, and state affect: A hierarchical relationship? *Journal of Social Behavior and Personality, 12*, 1079–1092.

Newman, D.A., Joseph, D.L., & Hulin, C.L. (2010). Job attitudes and employee engagement: considering the attitude "A-factor." In S. Albrecht (Ed.), *Handbook of Employee Engagement.* Northampton, MA: Edward Elgar. doi.org/10.4337/9781849806374

Ng, T.W.H. & Feldman, D.C. (2015). Ethical leadership: Meta-analytic evidence of criterion-related and incremental validity. *Journal of Applied Psychology, 100*(3), 948–965. dx.doi.org/10.1037/a0038246

Ng, T.W.H., Sorensen, K.L., & Yim, F.H. (2009). Does the job satisfaction—job performance relationship vary across cultures?. *Journal of Cross-Cultural Psychology, 40*(5), 761–796. doi.org/10.1177/0022022109339208

Oh, I.S., Kim, S., & Van Iddekinge, C.H. (2015). Taking it to another level: Do personality-based human capital resources matter to firm performance?. *Journal of Applied Psychology, 100*(3), 935–947. dx.doi.org/10.1037/a0039052

Ohly, S. & Schmitt, A. (2015). What makes us enthusiastic, angry, feeling at rest or worried? Development and validation of an affective work events taxonomy using concept mapping methodology. *Journal of Business and Psychology, 30*(1), 15–35. doi.org/10.1007/s10869-013-9328-3

Organ, D.W. (1988). *Organizational Citizenship Behavior: The Good Solider Syndrome.* Lexington, MA: Lexington Books.

Organ, D.W. (1997). Organizational citizenship behavior: It's construct clean-up time. *Human Performance, 10*, 85–97.

Organ, D.W. & Near, J.P. (1985). Cognition vs. affect in measures of job satisfaction. *International Journal of Psychology, 20*, 241–253. dx.doi.org/10.1080/00207598508246751

Parke, M.R. & Seo, M.G. (2017). The role of affect climate in organizational effectiveness. *Academy of Management Review, 42*(2), 334–360. doi.org/10.5465/amr.2014.0424

Piening, E.P., Baluch, A.M., & Salge, T.O. (2013). The relationship between employees' perceptions of human resource systems and organizational performance: Examining mediating mechanisms and temporal dynamics. *Journal of Applied Psychology, 98*(6), 926–947. dx.doi.org/10.1037/a0033925

Podsakoff, N.P., LePine, J.A., & LePine, M.A. (2007). Differential challenge stressor-hindrance stressor relationships with job attitudes, turnover intentions, turnover, and withdrawal behavior: A meta-analysis. *Journal of Applied Psychology, 92*(2), 438–454. dx.doi.org/10.1037/0021-9010.92.2.438

Podsakoff, N.P., Spoelma, T.M., Chawla, N., & Gabriel, A. S. (2019). What predicts within-person variance in applied psychology constructs? An empirical examination. *Journal of Applied Psychology, 104*(6), 727–754. dx.doi.org/10.1037/apl0000374

Riketta, M. (2008). The causal relation between job attitudes and performance: A meta-analysis of panel studies. *Journal of Applied Psychology, 93*(2), 472–481. dx.doi.org/10.1037/0021-9010.93.2.472

Ritter, K.-J., Matthews, R.A., Ford, M.T., & Henderson, A.A. (2016). Understanding role stressors and job satisfaction over time using adaptation theory. *Journal of Applied Psychology, 101*(12), 1655–1669. dx.doi.org/10.1037/apl0000152

Rosenberg, M.J. & Hovland, C.I. (1960). Cognitive, affective and behavioral components of attitudes. In M.J. Rosenberg & C.I. Hovland (Eds.), *Attitude Organization and Change: An Analysis of Consistency among Attitude Components* (pp. 1–14). New Haven, CT: Yale University Press.

Rothausen, T.J. & Henderson, K.E. (2019). Meaning-based job-related well-being: exploring a meaningful work conceptualization of job satisfaction. *Journal of Business and Psychology, 34*(3), 357–376. doi.org/10.1007/s10869-018-9545x

Russell, S.S., Spitzmueller, C., Lin, L.F., Stanton, J.M., Smith, P.C., & Ironson, G.H. (2004). Shorter can also be better: The abridged job in general scale. *Educational and Psychological Measurement, 64*(5), 878–893. doi.org/10/b9cjzk

Sackett, P.R. & DeVore, C.J. (2001). Counterproductive behaviors at work. In N. Anderson, D.S. Ones, H.K., Sinangil, & C. Viswesvaran (Eds.), *Handbook of Industrial, Work, and Organizational Psychology* (Vol. 1, pp. 145–164). London: Sage.

Sagie, A. (1998). Employee absenteeism, organizational commitment, and job satisfaction: Another look. *Journal of Vocational Behavior, 52*(2), 156–171. doi.org/10.1006/jvbe.1997.1581

Schaffer, R.H. (1953). Job satisfaction as related to need satisfaction in work. *Psychological Monographs, 67*, 1–29. dx.doi.org/10.1037/h0093658

Schaumberg, R.L. & Flynn, F.J. (2017). Clarifying the link between job satisfaction and absenteeism: The role of guilt proneness. *Journal of Applied Psychology, 102*(6), 982–992. dx.doi.org/10.1037/apl0000208

Schleicher, D.J., Hansen, S.D., & Fox, K.E. (2011). Job attitudes and work values. In S. Zedeck (Ed.), *APA Handbook of Industrial and Organizational Psychology* (Vol. 3, pp. 137–189). doi.org/10.1037/12171-004

Schleicher, D.J., Smith, T.A., Casper, W.J., Watt, J.D., & Greguras, G.J. (2015). It's all in the attitude: The role of job attitude strength in job attitude–outcome relationships. *Journal of Applied Psychology*, 100(4), 1259–1274. dx.doi.org/10.1037/a0038664

Schleicher, D.J., Watt, J.D., & Greguras, G.J. (2004). Reexamining the job satisfaction-performance relationship: The complexity of attitudes. *Journal of Applied Psychology, 89*(1), 165–177. dx.doi.org/10.1037/0021-9010.89.1.165

Schneider, B., Hanges, P.J., Smith, D.B., & Salvaggio, A.N. (2003). Which comes first: Employee attitudes or organizational financial and market performance? *Journal of Applied Psychology, 88*(5), 836–851. dx.doi.org/10.1037/0021-9010.88.5.836

Shockley, K.M. & Singla, N. (2011). Reconsidering work—family interactions and satisfaction: A meta-analysis. *Journal of Management, 37*(3), 861–886. doi.org/10.1177/0149206310394864

Sirota, D. & Klein, D.A. (2014). *The Enthusiastic Employee: How Companies Profit by Giving Workers What They Want* (2nd ed.). Upper Saddle River, NJ: Pearson.

Sirota, D., Mischkind, L.A., & Meltzer, M.I. (2005). *The Enthusiastic Employee: How Companies Profit by Giving Workers What They Want* (1st ed.). Upper Saddle River, NJ: Prentice Hall.

Smith, P.C., Kendall, L.M., & Hulin, C.L. (1969). *The Measurement of Satisfaction in Work and Retirement*. Chicago, IL: Rand McNally.

Society for Human Resource Management. (2015). *Employee Job Satisfaction and Engagement: Optimizing Organizational Culture for Success* (No. 15–0133). Alexandria, VA.

Spector, P.E. (1985). Measurement of human service staff satisfaction: Development of the job satisfaction survey. *American Journal of Community Psychology, 13*(6), 693–713. doi.org/10/c4f8v6

Spector, P.E. & Meier, L.L. (2014). Methodologies for the study of organizational behavior processes: How to find your keys in the dark. *Journal of Organizational Behavior, 35*(8), 1109–1119. doi.org/10.1002/job.1966

Stanton, J.M., Sinar, E.F., Balzer, W.K., Julian, A.L., Thoresen, P., Aziz, S., … Smith, P.C. (2002). Development of a compact measure of job satisfaction: The abridged job descriptive index. *Educational and Psychological Measurement, 62*(1), 173–191. doi.org/10/gdkxzg

Staw, B.M., Bell, N.E., & Clausen, J.A. (1986). The dispositional approach to job attitudes: A lifetime longitudinal test. *Administrative Science Quarterly, 31*, 56–77.

Staw, B.M. & Ross, J. (1985). Stability in the midst of change: A dispositional approach to job attitudes. *Journal of Applied Psychology*, *70*, 469–480. dx.doi.org/10.1037/0021-9010.70.3.469

Sweeney, P.D. & McFarlin, D.B. (1993). Workers' evaluations of the "ends" and the" means": An examination of four models of distributive and procedural justice. *Organizational Behavior and Human Decision Processes*, *55*(1), 23–40. doi.org/10.1006/obhd.1993.1022

Takeuchi, R., Chen, G., & Lepak, D.P. (2009). Through the looking glass of a social system: cross-level effects of high-performance work systems on employees' attitudes. *Personnel Psychology*, *62*(1), 1–29. doi.org/10.1111/j.1744-6570.2008.01127.x

Tepper, B.J., Duffy, M.K., Hoobler, J., & Ensley, M.D. (2004). Moderators of the relationships between coworkers' organizational citizenship behavior and fellow employees' attitudes. *Journal of Applied Psychology*, *89*(3), 455–465. dx.doi.org/10.1037/0021-9010.89.3.455

Tett, R.P. & Meyer, J.P. (1993). Job satisfaction, organizational commitment, turnover intention, and turnover: path analyses based on meta-analytic findings. *Personnel Psychology*, *46*(2), 259–293. doi.org/10.1111/j.1744–6570.1993.tb00874.x

Thoresen, C.J., Kaplan, S.A., Barsky, A.P., Warren, C.R., & de Chermont, K. (2003). The affective underpinnings of job perceptions and attitudes: A meta-analytic review and integration. *Psychological Bulletin*, *129*, 914–945.

Todorova, G., Bear, J.B., & Weingart, L.R. (2014). Can conflict be energizing? A study of task conflict, positive emotions, and job satisfaction. *Journal of Applied Psychology*, *99*(3), 451–467. dx.doi.org/10.1037/a0035134

University of Michigan. (1975). *Michigan Organizational Assessment Package: Progress Report II* (p. 244). Ann Arbor, MI.

Volmer, J., Niessen, C., Spurk, D., Linz, A., & Abele, A.E. (2011). Reciprocal relationships between leader–member exchange (LMX) and job satisfaction: A cross-lagged analysis. *Applied Psychology*, *60*(4), 522–545. doi.org/10.1111/j.1464-0597.2011.00446.x

Wanous, J.P. & Hudy, M.J. (2001). Single-item reliability: A replication and extension. *Organizational Research Methods*, *4*(4), 361–375. doi.org/10/fqxg5v

Wanous, J.P., Reichers, A.E., & Hudy, M.J. (1997). Overall job satisfaction: How good are single-item measures? *Journal of Applied Psychology*, *82*(2), 247–252. doi.org/10/fgjq9z

Warr, P., Cook, J., & Wall, T. (1979). Scales for the measurement of some work attitudes and aspects of psychological well-being. *Journal of Occupational Psychology*, *52*(2), 129–148. doi.org/10.1111/j.2044–8325.1979.tb00448.x

Watson, D. & Clark, L.A. (1997). Extraversion and its positive emotional core. In R. Hogan, J.J. Johnson, & S. Briggs (Eds.), *Handbook of Personality Psychology* (pp. 767–793). San Diego, CA: Academic Press.

Watson, D. & Slack, A.K. (1993). General factors of affective temperament and their relation to job satisfaction over time. *Organizational Behavior and Human Decision Processes*, *54*(2), 181–202.

Webster, J.R., Adams, G.A., & Beehr, T.A. (2014). Core work evaluation: The viability of a higher-order work attitude construct. *Journal of Vocational Behavior*, *85*(1), 27–38. doi.org/10.1016/j.jvb.2014.03.008

Weiss, D.J., Dawis, R.V., England, G.W., & Lofquist, L.H. (1967). *Manual for the Minnesota Satisfaction Questionnaire*. Vol. 22, Minnesota Studies in Vocational Rehabilitation. Minneapolis: University of Minnesota, Industrial Relations Center.

Weiss, H.M. (2002). Deconstructing job satisfaction. *Human Resource Management Review*, *12*(2), 173–194. doi.org/10.1016/S1053-4822(02)00045-1

Weiss, H.M. & Beal, D.J. (2005). Reflections on affective events theory. In N.M. Ashkanasy, W.J. Zerbe, & C.E.J. Härtel (Eds.), *The effect of affect in organizational settings* (Vol. 1, pp. 1–21). San Diego, CA: Emerald.

Weiss, H.M. & Cropanzano, R. (1996). Affective events theory: A theoretical discussion of the structure, causes and consequences of affective experiences at work. *Research in Organizational Behavior*, *18*, 1–74.

Weiss, H.M., Nicholas, J.P., & Daus, C.S. (1999). An examination of the joint effects of affective experiences and job beliefs on job satisfaction and variations in affective experiences over time. *Organizational Behavior and Human Decision Processes*, *78*(1), 1–24. doi.org/10.1006/obhd.1999.2824

Weitz, J. & Nuckols, R.C. (1955). Job satisfaction and job survival. *Journal of Applied Psychology*, *39*, 294–300. dx.doi.org/10.1037/h0044736

Whitman, D.S., Van Rooy, D.L., & Viswesvaran, C. (2010). Satisfaction, citizenship behaviors, and performance in work units: A meta-analysis of collective construct relations. *Personnel Psychology*, *63*(1), 41–81. doi.org/10.1111/j.1744-6570.2009.01162.x

Wilkin, C.L. (2013). I can't get no job satisfaction: Meta-analysis comparing permanent and contingent workers. *Journal of Organizational Behavior*, *34*(1), 47–64. doi.org/10/cf8v

Williams, M.L., McDaniel, M.A., & Ford, L.R. (2007). Understanding multiple dimensions of compensation satisfaction. *Journal of Business and Psychology*, *21*(3), 429–459. doi.org/10.1007/s10869-006-9036-3

Williams, M.L., McDaniel, M.A., & Nguyen, N.T. (2006). A meta-analysis of the antecedents and consequences of pay level satisfaction. *Journal of Applied Psychology*, *91*(2), 392–413. dx.doi.org/10.1037/0021-9010.91.2.392

Wu, C.-H. & Griffin, M.A. (2012). Longitudinal relationships between core self-evaluations and job satisfaction. *Journal of Applied Psychology*, *97*(2), 331–342. dx.doi.org/10.1037/a0025673

Van Vuuren, C.V. & Klandermans, P.G. (1990). Individual reactions to job insecurity: An integrated model. In P.J.D. Drenth, J.A. Sergeant, & R.J. Takens (Eds.), *European Perspectives in Psychology, Vol. 3. Work and Organizational, Social and Economic, Cross-Cultural* (pp. 133–146). Oxford, England: John Wiley & Sons.

Zhou, L., Wang, M., Chen, G., & Shi, J. (2012). Supervisors' upward exchange relationships and subordinate outcomes: Testing the multilevel mediation role of empowerment. *Journal of Applied Psychology*, *97*(3), 668–680. dx.doi.org/10.1037/a0026305

# 10

# EMPLOYEE ENGAGEMENT

*Alan M. Saks and Jamie A. Gruman*

For almost two decades, employee engagement has received a considerable amount of attention from academics, practitioners, organizations, and in the popular press. A concept rarely captures so much attention from academics and non-academics at the same time and for so long, but such is the case with employee engagement. In just 15 years, there has been an explosion of research and review articles as well as select journal issues devoted to engagement, several meta-analyses, and numerous books on the subject.

Several factors explain the continued interest in and research on this topic. First, most surveys of employee engagement indicate that only a small percentage of employees are "actively engaged," and most employees across the globe are actually disengaged (Albrecht et al., 2015; Kowalski, 2003). It has also been estimated that disengaged employees cost U.S. businesses billions of dollars a year in lost productivity (Johnson, 2004).

Second, employee engagement has been shown to be strongly related to employee work outcomes such as job performance, organizational citizenship behavior, turnover intentions, and job attitudes such as job satisfaction and organizational commitment, as well as general employee health, stress, burnout, and well-being (Bailey et al., 2017; Crawford, LePine, & Rich, 2010; Halbesleben, 2010; Saks, 2006).

Third, employee engagement has also been linked to organizational performance. For example, a meta-analysis by Harter, Schmidt, and Hayes (2002) that included close to 8,000 business units in 36 organizations found significant positive correlations between employee engagement and several business outcomes (customer satisfaction, profitability, productivity, retention, and safety). More recently, Schneider et al. (2018) examined workforce engagement in a sample of 102 publicly traded organizations from a variety of industries. They found that workforce engagement was positively related to financial (ROA and Net Margin) and customer metrics (The American Customer Satisfaction Index, The Harris Reputation Quotient).

In this chapter, we provide an overview and critical analysis of research on employee engagement in which we discuss the meaning of employee engagement, provide a brief history of engagement research, review the main theories of employee engagement, discuss the instruments that have been developed to measure employee engagement, review the antecedents and consequences of engagement, note some cultural and global issues of engagement, and provide a critique of the engagement literature and suggestions for future research and practice.

## Definitions of Employee Engagement

Several definitions of employee engagement can be found in the literature. In this section, we discuss the two most common and frequently cited definitions along with some extensions of these definitions.

### *Kahn's (1990) Definition of Personal Engagement*

According to Kahn (1990), personal engagement refers to "the harnessing of organization members' selves to their work roles; in engagement, people employ and express themselves physically, cognitively, and emotionally during role performances" (p.694). By comparison, personal disengagement involves "the uncoupling of selves from work roles; in disengagement, people withdraw and defend themselves physically, cognitively, or emotionally during role performances" (p.694). Thus, Kahn's (1990) definition of engagement involves three dimensions that correspond to being physically, cognitively, and emotionally engaged. He also notes that engagement involves the "simultaneous employment and expression of a person's 'preferred self' in task behaviors that promote connections to work and to others, personal presence (physical, cognitive, and emotional), and active, full role performance" (p.700).

There are two important components to Kahn's (1990) definition of engagement: self-in-role and psychological presence. Self-in-role has to do with the extent to which people draw on themselves in the performance of their roles. When people are personally engaged, they keep their true selves within the role they are performing; when people are disengaged, they remove their true selves from the performance of their role (i.e., their actual thoughts and feelings; this is different from organizational or job withdrawal, which tends to involve more visible actions such as turnover and absenteeism which might be outcomes of disengagement). Further, when people are engaged, they are psychologically present when occupying and performing a role (Kahn, 1990, 1992). Psychological presence involves being attentive, connected, integrated, and focused when performing a role (Kahn, 1992).

### *Schaufeli et al.'s (2002) Definition of Work Engagement*

The second most popular definition of engagement refers specifically to "work" engagement and considers engagement to be the opposite or positive antithesis of burnout (Maslach, Schaufeli, & Leiter, 2001). According to

Schaufeli et al. (2002), work engagement is "a positive, fulfilling, work-related state of mind that is characterized by vigor, dedication, and absorption" (p.74). *Vigor* involves high levels of energy and mental resilience while working; *dedication* refers to being strongly involved in one's work and experiencing a sense of significance, enthusiasm, and challenge; and *absorption* refers to being fully concentrated and engrossed in one's work. Further, engagement is not a momentary and specific state, but rather, it is "a more persistent and pervasive affective-cognitive state that is not focused on any particular object, event, individual, or behavior" (p.74).

### Other Definitions of Employee Engagement

Several authors have extended the definition of engagement. For example, Christian, Garza, and Slaughter (2011) noted three common characteristics of engagement. First, engagement involves a psychological connection with the performance of work tasks. Second, it involves the self-investment of personal resources at work, and third, it is a "state" rather than a "trait." Christian et al. (2011) distinguish engagement from other constructs (i.e., job satisfaction, organizational commitment, job involvement) by noting that engagement is a broader construct that involves a holistic investment of the entire self, focuses on work performed at a job, and involves a willingness to dedicate physical, cognitive, and emotional resources to one's job. They define engagement "as a relatively enduring state of mind referring to the simultaneous investment of personal energies in the experience or performance of work" (p.95).

According to Rich, Lepine, and Crawford (2010), engagement is a more complete representation of the self than other constructs such as job satisfaction and job involvement, which represent much narrower aspects of the self. They note that "job engagement is best described as a multidimensional motivational concept reflecting the simultaneous investment of an individual's physical, cognitive, and emotional energy in active, full work performance" (p.619).

### Summary

In summary, although numerous definitions of employee engagement can be found in the literature, they all suggest that employee engagement is a multidimensional motivational state that involves the simultaneous investment of an individual's full self and personal resources in the performance of a role and one's work. Thus, it is a more holistic and complete representation of the self and not merely a repackaging of other constructs such as job satisfaction and organizational commitment, or what has been referred to as the "Jangle Fallacy" (Macey & Schneider, 2008). Although the Kahn (1990) and Schaufeli et al. (2002) definitions differ in that the latter is focused on work engagement while Kahn's (1990) is more of a role-specific construct, both definitions involve three similar dimensions such that absorption, vigor, and dedication correspond to Kahn's (1990) cognitive, physical, and emotional dimensions (Bakker & Demerouti, 2008).

## A Brief History of Employee Engagement

Although Kahn (1990) conducted the first significant study on employee engagement, the concept was popularized by consulting firms before the academic community began to show any interest in the construct in the early 2000s. However, for consulting firms, the focus of employee engagement has been the organization rather than work or the job (Schneider et al., 2018). In fact, as noted by Schneider et al. (2018), the measurement of employee engagement by consulting firms often includes items that refer to having pride in and satisfaction with the organization and speaking positively about the organization. Such measures are similar to organizational commitment and suggest that the "Jangle Fallacy" is perhaps operating in some cases within the consulting world.

The earliest studies on employee engagement in the academic literature originated from three sources: Kahn's ethnographic study, research on burnout and engagement, and Britt's (1999) research on the Triangle Model of responsibility.

### Kahn's Ethnographic Study

The first major study on employee engagement was Kahn's (1990) ethnographic study in which he was a participant and observer at a summer camp and an observer at an architecture firm. Using a variety of qualitative methods (e.g., observation and in-depth interviews), Kahn (1990) studied moments of engagement and disengagement and the reasons why participants personally engaged or disengaged. Based on ratings of the experiences of the participants, Kahn (1990) found that people were more personally engaged in situations characterized by psychological meaningfulness (a feeling that one is receiving a return on investments of oneself), psychological safety (a feeling that one is able to show and employ one's self without fear of negative consequences to self-image, status, or career), and psychological availability (the sense of having the physical, emotional, or psychological resources to engage in a particular moment personally). In addition, Kahn (1990) also identified the factors that influenced psychological meaningfulness (e.g., task characteristics), psychological safety (e.g., interpersonal relationships), and psychological availability (e.g., physical and emotional energy).

### Research on Burnout and Engagement

The emergence of the engagement construct can also be traced to research on burnout. Maslach et al. (2001) considered job engagement to be an expansion of and the opposite of burnout, and Maslach and Leiter (2008) referred to the burnout-engagement continuum with the negative experience of burnout at one end of the continuum and the positive experience of engagement at the other end of the continuum. In fact, early research on engagement assessed engagement using the Maslach-Burnout Inventory (MBI). Engagement was indicated by the opposite pattern of scores on the three dimensions of burnout (exhaustion-energy, cynicism-involvement, and inefficacy-efficacy; Maslach & Leiter, 2008).

According to Maslach et al. (2001), job burnout and engagement are the results of mismatches or matches in six critical areas of organizational life (workload, control, rewards and recognition, community and social support, perceived fairness, and values). Burnout occurs when there is a gap or mismatch between the person and these six areas, while engagement results when there is a match or fit between a person and these six areas of organizational life.

Schaufeli et al. (2002) also consider engagement to be the positive antithesis of burnout; however, they argued that engagement is not adequately measured by the opposite profile of MBI scores, but rather should be measured independently from burnout using a different instrument. Thus, as discussed later, they developed a measure of work engagement that consists of three dimensions (vigor, dedication, and absorption).

## *Britt's (1999) Research on the Triangle Model of Responsibility*

Britt (1999) studied the effects of engagement in a sample of U.S. Army soldiers. He used Schlenker's (1997) Triangle Model of responsibility to argue that the more responsible an individual feels for a given event, the more engaged the individual will be in the event. Britt (1999) found that soldiers were most engaged when the rules for their performance were clear (event-prescription link), performance was relevant to their training (identity-prescription link), and they had personal control for their performance (identity-event link). He also found that unit differences in engagement were due to differences in the linkages of the responsibility model. In addition, work-related experiences (e.g., work stress) were more strongly related to the psychological health (e.g., well-being) of soldiers when they were more engaged in their jobs. In a subsequent study, Britt (2003) found that the three components of the Triangle Model predicted engagement in voting, and engagement in voting mediated the relationship between the components of the Triangle Model and voting behavior. As stated by Britt (1999), "individuals who were engaged in voting were not only more likely to vote, but were also more likely to be emotionally invested in the outcome of the election" (p.355).

## *Summary*

In summary, most of the research on employee engagement can be traced back to Kahn's (1990) ethnographic study and the burnout literature

(Maslach et al., 2001; Schaufeli et al., 2002). Britt's (1999, 2003) research on engagement and the Triangle Model of responsibility has not received as much attention.

## Theories and Models of Employee Engagement

Several theories and models of employee engagement have been used to explain the employee engagement process and the relationship between antecedents and consequences of engagement. In this section, we describe several engagement theories and models, including Kahn's (1990) theory of psychological presence, the job demands-resources (JD-R) model, social exchange theory, and the multidimensional model.

### *Kahn's Theory of Psychological Presence*

Kahn (1992) developed a theory of psychological presence and personal engagement that is based in part on job design research on the relationship between workers and the characteristics of their tasks. His theory involves three psychological conditions (psychological meaningfulness, safety, and availability) that influence psychological presence and the extent to which people become engaged in a role. The three psychological conditions are influenced by work, organization, and individual factors. Psychological presence is an experiential state that accompanies engagement in role performances.

According to Kahn (1992), there are four dimensions of psychological presence: attentiveness (being open rather than closed), connected (feeling related to some aspect of one's situation), integration (a sense of wholeness in a situation), and focus (staying within the boundaries of a work role, situation, and relationship). The three psychological conditions drive psychological presence, which leads to personal engagement, and personal engagement results in various outcomes. Thus, the experience of the three psychological conditions influences the extent to which individuals are psychologically present and engaged in a work situation. A number of studies have investigated the relationship between the three psychological conditions and engagement (e.g., May, Gilson, & Harter, 2004); however, less attention has been given to the prediction and consequences of psychological presence.

### *The Job Demands-Resources (JD-R) Model*

The most researched theory of employee engagement is the Job Demands-Resources (JD-R) model (Bakker & Demerouti, 2007). The JD-R model divides working conditions into job demands and job resources. Job demands refer to physical, psychological, social, or organizational features of a job that require sustained physical, mental, and/or psychological effort from an employee that can result in physiological and/or psychological costs. Job demands include work overload, job insecurity, role ambiguity, time pressure, and role conflict. Job resources refer to physical, psychological, social, or organizational features of a job that are functional in that they help achieve work goals, reduce job demands, and stimulate personal growth, learning, and development. Job resources can come from the organization (e.g., pay, career opportunities, job security), interpersonal and social relations (e.g., supervisor and coworker support, team climate), the organization of work (e.g., role clarity, participation in decision making), and from the task itself (e.g., skill variety, task identity, task significance, autonomy, performance feedback; Bakker & Demerouti, 2007).

Job resources play an intrinsic and extrinsic motivational role. They can be intrinsic because they satisfy and facilitate basic psychological needs such as growth, learning, and development. They can be extrinsic because they are instrumental in achieving work-related goals (Bakker & Demerouti, 2007). Job resources also help employees cope with job demands because they buffer the negative effect of job demands on job strain and burnout (Bakker & Demerouti, 2007). This is an essential function of job resources because high job demands can exhaust employees' physical and mental resources and lead to a depletion of energy and increased stress that can cause disengagement, burnout, and health problems (Bakker & Demerouti, 2007, 2008).

### *Social Exchange Theory*

Social exchange theory is a key conceptual paradigm in organizational behavior (Cropanzano & Mitchell, 2005) which suggests that parties in a relationship will abide by certain exchange rules such as the norm of reciprocity. Social exchange theory has been used to explain the employee engagement process. According to Saks (2006), employees choose to engage themselves in their jobs based on the resources they receive from their organization. When employees receive valued resources from their organizations (e.g., rewards and recognition), it creates a sense of obligation, and employees will reciprocate or repay their organization with higher levels of engagement, or they will withdraw their engagement if they do not receive sufficient resources. In a review of 214 studies on employee engagement, Bailey et al. (2017) found that social exchange theory is the second most widely used theory in engagement research.

### *The Multidimensional Model*

A final model of employee engagement is the multidimensional model, which suggests that employee engagement can be separated into two distinct targets of engagement: job engagement and organization engagement (Shuck, 2011). The basis for the multidimensional model is that engagement is a role-specific construct and refers to the extent to which an individual is psychologically present and engaged in a particular role, and the two main roles for most employees is their work role and their role as a member of their organization (Saks, 2006). In support of the multidimensional model, Saks (2006) found that although job and organization engagement are positively related, participants reported significantly higher job engagement than organization engagement, and there were some differences in the antecedents and consequences of job and organization engagement. Thus, job and organization engagement are related but distinct constructs.

## The Measurement of Employee Engagement

The measurement of employee engagement has been one of the most pressing concerns in the engagement literature. With so many different measures, it is not yet clear which ones are the most valid. Most measures are based on either Kahn's (1990) or Schaufeli et al.'s (2002) definitions of engagement. However, most measures suffer from at least one of three problems.

### *Overlap with Other Constructs*

First, some measures include items that overlap with other constructs. For example, Britt's (1999) five-item scale includes an item that refers to commitment (e.g., "*I am committed to my job*"). Stumpf, Tymon, and van Dam (2013) developed a two-dimensional measure of engagement for professionals in technically-oriented workgroups that includes five items that measure felt engagement and nine items that measure behavioral engagement. The item, "*The work I do is very satisfying to me*," overlaps with job satisfaction. Shuck, Adelson, and Reio (2017a) developed a 12-item employee engagement scale (EES) with three dimensions (cognitive, emotional, and behavioral). They argue that their scale is the first to measure employee engagement, given that other scales measure job, work, or organization engagement. However, the behavioral engagement item, "*I care about the future of my company*," is similar to items that measure organizational identification.

### *Overlap with Antecedents*

Second, some measures include items that are more like antecedents of engagement. For example, the 12-item Gallup Workplace Audit (GWA) measure used by Harter et al. (2002) includes items that have to do with having a friend at work and receiving recognition and praise. As noted by Harter et al. (2002), the GWA items are "antecedents of personal job satisfaction and other affective constructs" (p.269). Similarly, the Utrecht Work Engagement Scale (UWES) (Schaufeli et al., 2002) includes the item, "*To me, my job is challenging*," which is more like a job characteristic than engagement.

### *Overlap with Outcomes*

The third problem is that some measures include items that are similar to outcomes of engagement. For example, the Stumpf et al. (2013) scale includes the items, "*I often take extra initiative to get things done*" and "*My work performance goes beyond expectations*," which are both similar to performance outcomes. Soane et al. (2012) developed a scale of employee engagement known as the Intellectual, Social, and Affective Engagement Scale (ISA Engagement Scale) to be used by human resource development (HRD) scholars and practitioners. The nine-item scale consists of three facets (intellectual, social, and affective engagement). One of the items for social engagement, however, refers to work attitudes ("*I share the same work attitudes as my colleagues*").

### *Implications of Overlap*

Engagement measures that overlap with other measures are likely to produce results that are misleading and inflated. For example, if an engagement measure includes items that are similar to other constructs (e.g., organizational commitment), this will inflate the relationship between engagement and those constructs, and it also means that the engagement measure is susceptible to the "old wine in a new bottle" criticism. If an engagement measure includes antecedents of engagement, then certain antecedents will be more strongly related to engagement, and when an engagement measure includes outcomes of engagement, then engagement will be more strongly related to those outcomes. Thus, the results of engagement studies that use measures that include items that overlap with other variables are likely to be inflated, inaccurate, and misleading.

### *The UWES*

Most research on employee engagement has used the UWES, which is the most popular measure of employee engagement (Bailey et al., 2017). As shown in Table 10.1, the UWES consists of 17 items that measure three dimensions of engagement: vigor (five items), dedication (six items), and absorption dimensions (six items). There is also a nine-item short form of the UWES (the UWES-9) (Schaufeli, Bakker, & Salanova, 2006), and a three-item version (UWES-3) with one item for vigor ("*At my work, I feel bursting with energy*"), dedication ("*I am enthusiastic about my job*"), and absorption ("*I am immersed in my work*") (Schaufeli et al., 2019).

The UWES has been validated in numerous countries, and there is some support for a three-factor structure (Bakker, Albrecht, & Leiter, 2011). However, the three-factor structure of the long and short form of the scale has not always been supported, and many studies simply combine the three dimensions into one overall factor (Saks & Gruman, 2014). Furthermore, there has also been considerable concern about the construct validity of the UWES due to its

*Table 10.1* The Utrecht Work Engagement Scale (UWES)

Vigor

1. When I get up in the morning, I feel like going to work.
2. At my work, I feel bursting with energy.
3. At my work, I always persevere, even when things do not go well.
4. I can continue working for very long periods at a time.
5. At my job, I am very resilient, mentally.
6. At my job, I feel strong and vigorous.

Dedication

1. To me, my job is challenging.
2. My job inspires me.
3. I am enthusiastic about my job.
4. I am proud of the work that I do.
5. I find the work that I do full of meaning and purpose.

Absorption

1. When I am working, I forget everything else around me.
2. Time flies when I am working.
3. I get carried away when I am working.
4. It is difficult to detach myself from my job.
5. I am immersed in my work.
6. I feel happy when I am working intensely.

*Source*: Schaufeli et al. (2002).

*Notes*: All items use a 7-point scale with anchors of 0=Never, 1=Almost never/a few times a year or less, 2=Rarely/Once a month or less, 3=Sometimes/A few times a month, 4=Often/Once a week, 5=Very often/A few times a week, 6=Always/Every day.

high correlations to job attitude measures (Byrne, Peters, & Weston, 2016) and overlap of item content with the MBI measure of burnout (Cole et al., 2012). According to Cole et al. (2012), the UWES is empirically redundant with the MBI. They advised researchers to "avoid treating the UWES as if it were tapping a distinct, independent phenomenon" (p.1576). Thus, there appears to be considerable overlap between the UWES and measures of burnout and job attitudes.

### *Measures Based on Kahn's Theory*

Two scales have been developed that measure Kahn's (1990) three dimensions of engagement (cognitive, physical, emotional). May et al. (2004) developed a 13-item scale based on the three components of Kahn's (1990) definition of engagement (i.e., people employ and express themselves physically, cognitively, and emotionally). Their measure includes four items to measure cognitive engagement (e.g., "*Performing my job is so absorbing that I forget about everything else*"), four items to measure emotional engagement (e.g., "*I really put my heart into my job*"), and five items to measure physical engagement (e.g., "*I exert a lot of energy*

251

*performing my job*"). However, the results of an exploratory factor analysis did not support three separate and reliable factors.

The most often used measure of engagement based on Kahn's (1990) definition of engagement is the Job Engagement Scale (JES) by Rich et al. (2010). The 18-item scale consists of three sets of six items to measure physical engagement (e.g., "*I work with intensity on my job*"), emotional engagement (e.g., "*I am enthusiastic in my job*"), and cognitive engagement (e.g., "*At work, my mind is focused on my job*"). Rich et al. (2010) found support for three first-order factors that load on a second-order factor. Byrne et al. (2016) found that although the JES and UWES are correlated, they are not interchangeable, and they measure different aspects of engagement. In addition, they found that the UWES overlaps more with job attitudes than the JES.

### Multidimensional Measures of Engagement

Several other scales are worth noting because they measure different targets of engagement. For example, Rothbard (2001) developed two nine-item scales to measure work engagement and family engagement that focus on *attention* devoted to and *absorption* in work and family. Each scale consists of four items that measure attention (e.g., "*I spend a lot of time thinking about my work/family*") and five items that measure absorption (e.g., "*When I am working/When I am focused on my family, I often lose track of time*"). Although this scale has seldom been used in engagement research, it is unique in that it can easily be used to measure engagement in any role simply by inserting the relevant role in each item (e.g., "I spend a lot of time thinking about my work/family/organization/department/team").

Saks (2006) developed two separate scales to measure two targets of engagement: job engagement (e.g., "*I really 'throw' myself into my job*") and organization engagement (e.g., "*Being a member of this organization is very captivating*"). This is the only scale that includes a measure of organization engagement (see Table 10.2). In a subsequent paper, Saks (2019) found that single items to measure job engagement ("*I am highly engaged in this job*") and organization engagement ("*I am highly engaged in this organization*") operate similarly to the complete scales. The single items were more discriminating when predicting job-related versus organization-related consequences of engagement. These scales can be used to examine the multidimensional model of engagement and are relatively short compared to other measures of engagement.

### Summary

In summary, there are numerous measures of employee engagement that have been developed and used in engagement research. The main problem with most measures is that they include items that overlap with other constructs (e.g., organizational commitment), antecedents of engagement (e.g., job challenge), and consequences of engagement (e.g., organizational citizenship

*Table 10.2* Job and Organization Engagement Scales. Saks (2006)

Job Engagement
1. I really "throw" myself into my job.
2. Sometimes I am so into my job that I lose track of time.
3. This job is all consuming; I am totally into it.
4. My mind often wanders and I think of other things when doing my job. (reverse scored)
5. I am highly engaged in this job.

Organization Engagement
1. Being a member of this organization is very captivating.
2. One of the most exciting things for me is getting involved with things happening in this organization.
3. I am really not into the "goings-on" in this organization. (reverse scored)
4. Being a member of this organization make me come "alive."
5. Being a member of this organization is exhilarating for me.
6. I am highly engaged in this organization.

*Source*: Saks (2006).

*Note*: All items use a 5-point scale with anchors of 1=Strongly disagree to 5=Strongly agree.

behavior). Although the UWES is the most popular and frequently used measure of engagement, it has received the most criticism. In general, measures of employee engagement tend to be multidimensional (e.g., vigor, dedication, absorption), focus on a particular target (e.g., job engagement, work engagement, organization engagement), or general measures of employee engagement (e.g., Shuck et al., 2017a, Employee Engagement Scale). While most of the scales overlap in terms of the items or dimensions they measure, they are not interchangeable and are likely to produce different research results (Byrne et al., 2016; Viljevac, Cooper-Thomas, and Saks, 2012).

## Nomological Network of Employee Engagement

The nomological network of employee engagement remains underspecified because the antecedents and consequences of engagement have not been subject to thorough theoretical or empirical scrutiny (Christian et al., 2011; Macey & Schneider, 2008). That said, in line with the JD-R model, which grounds over half of the empirical research on this topic (Crawford et al., 2010), numerous demands and resources have been shown to serve as antecedents of engagement.

### *Antecedents of Engagement*

Crawford et al. (2014) note that the majority of the resources that serve as drivers of engagement fit within Kahn's (1990) antecedent conditions, which

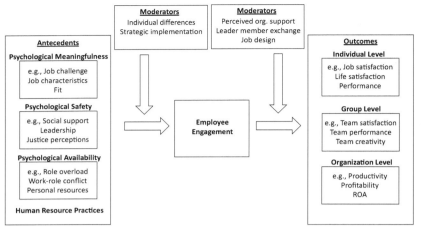

*Figure 10.1* The Nomological Network of Employee Engagement.

were empirically confirmed by May et al. (2004). For instance, job challenges, job characteristics, and fit with the work environment satisfy the condition of psychological meaningfulness. Social support, transformational leadership, and justice perceptions fulfill the need for psychological safety; and role overload, work-role conflict, and personal resources influence psychological availability (see Figure 10.1).

### Resources Affecting Psychological Meaningfulness

In line with the notion of resources as a driver of engagement, a meta-analysis by Christian et al. (2011) found that a number of job characteristics that promote psychological meaningfulness are positively associated with engagement. These characteristics include task variety, task significance, autonomy, feedback, problem-solving, and job complexity. Resources in the form of working conditions have also been shown to serve as antecedents of engagement. For example, opportunities for development, rewards and recognition, and work-role fit are associated with higher levels of engagement (Crawford et al., 2010).

### Resources Affecting Psychological Safety

Several meta-analyses have shown that engagement is associated with social support (e.g., Halbesleben, 2010), transformational leadership, leader-member exchange (Christian et al., 2011), and a positive work climate (Crawford et al., 2010). In addition, perceived learning climate (Eldor & Harpaz, 2016) and justice perceptions (Haynie, Mossholder, & Harris, 2016) have also been found to be positively related to engagement.

*Resources Affecting Psychological Availability*

A number of job demands have been identified that compromise the degree to which employees are available to engage in their roles. Meta-analytic results suggest that job demands, such as situational constraints, role ambiguity, and role overload, are negatively related to engagement (Crawford et al., 2010).

However, job demands have demonstrated an inconsistent relationship with engagement. In an earlier review, Mauno et al. (2010) suggested that the available evidence is consistent with the JD-R prediction that high job demands produce decreases in engagement. However, this conclusion is qualified by two meta-analyses that have demonstrated that whereas hindrance demands—demands that can interfere with goal attainment—are negatively associated with engagement, challenge demands—demands that can promote mastery—generally show a positive relationship (Crawford et al., 2010; Goering et al., 2017). Further, job resources have been shown to diminish the negative effects of job demands on engagement and are most important for work engagement when job demands are high (Bakker et al., 2007).

Individual differences, such as self-efficacy, resilience, and optimism, that serve as personal resources can also satisfy the need for psychological availability and promote engagement (Bakker & Demerouti, 2008; Halbesleben, 2010). All of the "Big Five" personality factors have been found to be associated with engagement, but the personality characteristics that show the strongest associations with engagement are positive affectivity, proactive personality, conscientiousness, and extraversion (Young et al., 2018).

Individual differences can also mediate the relationship between job resources and engagement. For instance, Xanthopoulou et al. (2007) found that the personal resources of self-efficacy, organizational-based self-esteem, and optimism partially mediated the relationships between job resources (e.g., autonomy, social support) and engagement. However, this mediating effect has not been reliably observed (Xanthopoulou et al., 2008).

*Human Resource Practices*

Human resource (HR) practices have also been found to be important for engagement. For example, Zhong, Wayne, and Liden (2016) found that high-performance HR practices (e.g., selective staffing, extensive training) were directly and positively related to job engagement and indirectly related through perceived organizational support. Bal and De Lange (2015) found that the availability of flexible HR practices was positively related to engagement, and engagement mediated the relationship between flexible HR practices and job performance. HR practices that enhance employees' skills, motivation, and opportunities may foster engagement by providing them with resources that allow them to satisfy Kahn's (1990) antecedent conditions and successfully perform their roles (Saks & Gruman, 2017).

## *Job Crafting*

Engagement can also be influenced by employees themselves when they engage in job crafting behaviors. Job crafting involves initiating changes in job design by making changes to the level of job demands and job resources to achieve a better balance with one's personal abilities and needs (Tims, Bakker, & Derks, 2012, 2013). Tims et al. (2012) identified four dimensions of job crafting: increasing structural job resources, increasing social job resources, decreasing hindering job demands, and increasing challenging job demands. They found that increasing structural and social job resources and increasing challenging job demands were positively related to work engagement. Tims et al. (2013) found that employees who crafted structural and social job resources increased their job resources, and an increase in job resources was positively related to work engagement. They also found that increasing challenging job demands was positively related to increased work engagement. In addition, a meta-analysis of job crafting found that overall job crafting was positively related to work engagement (Rudolph et al., 2017).

## **Contextual Issues**

As implied above, as the resources that satisfy the antecedent conditions change, engagement levels also change. For instance, Schaufeli, Bakker, and Van Rhenen (2009) found that when the job resources of job control, feedback, social support, and opportunities for learning increased over the course of a year, engagement also increased. However, the relationship among resources, both job and personal, and engagement is complicated because there is evidence that they are reciprocal (Xanthopoulou et al., 2009a).

In a relative importance analysis (Tonidandel & LeBreton, 2011), Cooper-Thomas, Xu, and Saks (2018) found that learning and development and vision and purpose were particularly important resources in generating engagement. More research is needed on the relative importance of various resources in producing engagement and on whether the relative importance changes depending on the way engagement is operationalized.

A small number of studies has demonstrated that the relationship between antecedents and engagement is moderated by other variables. For example, Zhu, Avolio, and Walumbwa (2009) found that transformational leadership had a stronger effect on follower work engagement when followers were higher in positive characteristics involving independence and innovation. Similarly, Rudolph and Baltes (2017) found that the relationship between flexible work arrangements and work engagement was strongest among objectively younger, and both subjectively younger and older, employees who enjoyed better relative health. Barrick et al. (2015) found that the relationship between organizational resources and collective engagement was moderated by the degree to which top management established and monitored progress towards strategic objectives.

More research is needed on the unique and interactive effects of the factors associated with engagement (Crawford et al., 2014).

## Outcomes of Engagement

Employee engagement has been found to be related to individual-, group-, and organization-level outcomes.

### Individual-Level Outcomes

As noted earlier, engagement has been shown to relate to numerous work attitudes and behaviors. At the individual level, engagement is positively associated with work attitudes such as job satisfaction and organizational commitment, in addition to well-being indicators such as life satisfaction and health. It has also been shown to be negatively related to stress and burnout, turnover intentions, and absenteeism, and positively related to both task and contextual performance (Bailey et al., 2017; Christian et al., 2011; Cole et al., 2012; Hakanen & Schaufeli, 2012; Schaufeli et al., 2009). Engagement has also repeatedly been shown to mediate the relationship between antecedents and outcomes. For example, Shantz et al. (2013) found that engagement fully mediated the effect of job design variables on task performance, organizational citizenship behaviors, and deviance, and Eldor and Harpaz (2016) found that employee engagement mediated the relationship between learning climate and extra-role behaviors. Meta-analytic results provide further support for the idea that engagement at least partially mediates the relationship between various antecedents and both task and contextual performance (Christian et al., 2011).

### Group-Level Outcomes

Although a nascent area of investigation, some research has examined the effect of engagement at the group level. Individual and team engagement is associated with perceived team performance (Mäkikangas et al., 2016), and team engagement is associated with objective team performance (Costa, Passos, & Bakker, 2015). Team engagement is also positively related to team satisfaction (Guchait, 2016) and team task creativity (Rodríguez-Sánchez et al., 2016). Additionally, engagement has been found to mediate the relationship between a learning organization culture and team performance improvement (Song et al., 2014).

### Organization-Level Outcomes

A few studies have also shown that engagement is associated with organization-level outcomes. For example, Harter et al. (2002) found that engagement was associated with customer satisfaction, productivity, and profitability in a sample of 36 companies from a variety of industries. Similarly, Schneider et al. (2018) found that engagement predicted return on assets and net margins one year later in a sample of publicly-traded organizations. Collective organizational engagement has also been shown to mediate the relationship between organizational resources, such as CEO transformational leadership, and firm performance (Barrick et al., 2015). However, this research must be interpreted with caution because although there are exceptions (Barrick et al., 2015; Xanthopoulou et al., 2009b), as noted by Schaufeli (2014), the operationalization of engagement in organization-level research tends to overlap with established constructs such as organizational commitment, or measure antecedents of engagement as opposed to engagement itself.

## More Contextual Issues

The relationship between engagement and outcomes has been shown to be moderated by other variables. Alfes et al. (2013) found that the negative relationship between engagement and turnover intentions was moderated by perceived organizational support (POS), and the positive relationship between engagement and organizational citizenship behaviors was moderated by POS and leader-member exchange (LMX). Shantz and Alfes (2015) observed that the negative relationship between engagement and voluntary absence was moderated by organizational trust, LMX, and job design. Mäkikangas et al. (2016) found that the association between engagement and perceived team performance was moderated by shared job crafting. The fact that some of these moderators can also be considered antecedents of engagement underscores the interactive and contextual nature of the factors that produce engagement.

## Measurement and the Nomological Network

As indicated earlier, measures of engagement are not interchangeable, and the way in which engagement is operationalized has important implications for understanding the nomological net of the construct. This is because the relationships among the antecedents and outcomes of engagement can vary depending on how it is measured.

In a series of studies comparing the nomological net of engagement assessed with the UWES (Schaufeli et al., 2002) and the JES (Rich et al., 2010), Byrne et al. (2016) demonstrated that the two operationalizations have different relationships with the antecedents of perceived stress, psychological availability, and psychological meaningfulness, and the outcomes of job performance, job commitment, physical strains, and burnout. Additionally, the UWES and JES differ with respect to whether or not they mediate the relationships between particular antecedents and outcomes. Byrne et al. (2016) concluded that their "results demonstrate the UWES and JES do not relate similarly to variables within the engagement nomological network" (p. 15). Advancements in understanding the nomological network of engagement will accelerate if and when agreement on its definition and operationalization occurs.

## Diversity and Global Issues

There is some evidence to suggest that the relevance and meaning of engagement might differ across cultures and countries, and the drivers of engagement might vary across the globe and between cultural groups.

### *The Meaning of the Self*

As noted earlier, Kahn's (1990) conceptualization of engagement involves bringing one's full self to one's role. However, perceptions of the self and how one brings oneself to a role differ across the globe. For instance, the primary feature of Western notions of the self is that people are separate from others, whereas Eastern notions of the self place a greater emphasis on connections to others within significant social relationships (Kitayama et al., 1997). Therefore, one's self-concept and what it means to bring one's full self to a role can differ internationally and have implications for employee engagement. Along similar lines, self-concept differentiation refers to the degree to which people manifest different identities in different social roles (Donahue et al., 1993). Garczynski et al. (2013) found that Indian employees demonstrated less self-concept differentiation than American employees and that high levels of differentiation were associated with less engagement, but only in the American subsample.

### *Engagement Around the Globe*

Most of the research on employee engagement has been conducted in countries that share the characteristics of having democratic governments, an economic system of private ownership, and an emphasis on individualism, raising questions about whether the findings from this body of research generalize to other countries and cultures (Rothmann, 2014).

The UWES was developed and validated using samples from mostly Western nations (e.g., Schaufeli et al., 2002; Schaufeli, Bakker, & Salanova, 2006). It has been claimed that the factor structure of the UWES is stable, does not differ between countries, and that total scores are a reliable indicator of work engagement (Shimazu, Miyanaka, & Schaufeli, 2010). However, Klassen et al. (2012) demonstrated variability in the factor structure of the UWES when comparing Western and non-Western groups of teachers and concluded that the factor structure of the scale should be tested in particular cross-cultural contexts because its stability cannot be assumed.

Garczynski et al. (2013) found that, compared to American employees, Indian employees scored significantly higher on the UWES, and Shimazu et al. (2010) showed that Japanese employees scored much lower than employees from any other country, possibly due to their reluctance to endorse items reflecting positive affect. Using the ultra-short version of the UWES, Schaufeli (2018) found engagement scores varied among a sample of European countries with the highest scores in the Netherlands (4.22) and the lowest in Serbia (3.54). These results may reflect differences in engagement levels across countries but may also reveal differences in the ways people from different regions and cultures interpret and endorse engagement scale items (Rothmann, 2014).

## The Drivers of Engagement

Schaufeli (2018) found that across European countries, the cultural values of individualism and indulgence were positively related to engagement, whereas power distance and uncertainty avoidance were negatively related. He also found that engagement demonstrated a relationship with measures of a country's governance, and a positive, curvilinear relationship with economic activity. However, when economic, governance, and culture variables were considered simultaneously, only productivity emerged as a significant predictor. This highlights the importance of research on how cultural and non-cultural factors interact in producing engagement in different settings (Gelfand, Leslie, & Fehr, 2008).

As noted earlier, the JD-R model underlies much of the research on engagement. There is some evidence that the JD-R model generalizes across countries and cultures. For example, job crafting that increases employees' challenging job demands and job resources are positively associated with engagement in the Netherlands (Tims et al., 2012) and Japan (Sakuraya et al., 2017). However, there is also evidence of cross-cultural variation. Using an industry-developed measure, Sanchez and McCauley (2006) reported that the resources that produce engagement differ across nations with, for example, growth and development opportunities important in the U.S., but not in the U.K. or China, and regular feedback on performance demonstrating the opposite pattern. Farndale and Murrer (2015) found that financial rewards and team climate were more strongly related to engagement in Mexico and the U.S. compared to the Netherlands. Brough et al. (2013) found that work hours were a positive predictor of engagement in an Australian sample and a negative predictor in a Chinese sample. Further, three African studies (Oliver & Rothmann, 2007; Rothmann & Rothmann, 2010; Rothmann & Welsh, 2013) were unable to obtain satisfactory internal consistency for measures of psychological safety, an established driver of engagement in Western contexts (Kahn, 1990). Together, these results suggest that the drivers of engagement and the way those drivers are construed may vary across the globe and between cultural groups.

## *Summary*

In summary, research reveals that the engagement construct may not be internationally invariant. There are a number of questions about the degree to which the measurement and drivers of engagement across geographic and cultural groups are equivalent, free from bias, and allow valid global and cross-cultural comparisons to be made (Rothmann, 2014).

# Criticisms of Employee Engagement

Engagement has been the subject of consistent criticism. Among these are charges of construct redundancy, construct confusion, and weak research methods.

## *Construct Redundancy*

The main criticism leveled against the engagement construct is that it conceptually overlaps with traditional job attitudes and states and is thus a redundant construct representing "old wine in a new bottle" (Cole et al., 2012; Newman & Harrison, 2008). For example, in their meta-analysis, Cole et al. (2012) concluded that engagement conceptualized as vigor, dedication, and absorption and operationalized using the UWES is redundant with the MBI, the most common measure of burnout. However, based on construct-level analyses using different measures, Byrne et al. (2016) found that the two constructs are distinct, with engagement and burnout demonstrating a small to moderate negative relationship. Similarly, in their meta-analytic investigation, Goering et al. (2017) found that burnout and engagement demonstrated dissimilar associations with resources and outcomes. The distinction between engagement and burnout remains an unresolved issue (Schaufeli, 2014). One potential resolution has been proposed by Sonnentag (2017), who argues that engagement is best conceptualized as a dynamic state that varies throughout the day in response to task characteristics, whereas burnout is best viewed as a chronic, stable condition.

With respect to the confluence of engagement and job attitudes, Rich et al. (2010) found that when job engagement, job involvement, job satisfaction, and intrinsic motivation were analyzed in tandem, job engagement emerged as the only significant predictor of task performance and organizational citizenship behavior, supporting the distinctiveness of the engagement construct. Similarly, Mackay, Allen, and Landis (2017) found that employee engagement offered small to medium incremental prediction of employee effectiveness over and above individual job attitudes; however, this effect was reduced when a higher-order job attitude construct was employed. Shuck, Nimon, and Zigarmi (2017b) found that a substantial percentage of the variance in employee engagement remained unexplained after taking job satisfaction, organizational commitment, and job involvement into account. In their meta-analysis, Christian et al. (2011) concluded that engagement exhibits discriminant validity from, and offers incremental prediction of task and contextual performance, over job attitudes. Employing a multivariate importance analysis, Dalal et al. (2012) found that engagement was the most important job attitude predicting a multivariate job performance criterion comprised of task performance, organizational citizenship behavior, and counterproductive work behavior. Dalal et al. (2012) concluded that their results extend those of Christian et al. (2011), providing evidence that new constructs such as employee engagement offer additional explanatory power over traditional job attitudes. Although Viljevac et al. (2012) found that two engagement scales demonstrated overlap with job satisfaction, the available research suggests that the criticism that engagement is merely old wine in new a bottle is overstated.

## *Construct Confusion*

Ultimately, whether or not engagement is redundant with existing constructs depends on the way engagement is defined and measured. This represents another criticism of engagement research. There are enduring disagreements about the theoretical meaning of engagement (Cole et al., 2012), and it continues to be conceptualized and operationalized in several ways (Bailey et al., 2017; Shuck et al., 2017c). This is important because, as suggested earlier, the various measures of engagement are not equivalent, and research results can differ depending on the way engagement is operationalized (Byrne et al., 2016; Christian et al., 2011).[1] The UWES is the most commonly used measure of engagement in academic research (Schaufeli, 2014), but it overlaps with traditional organizational variables to a greater extent than other measures of engagement (Byrne et al., 2016). As noted earlier, engagement is a holistic construct (Christian et al., 2011) that involves a more extensive representation of the self than other job-related variables (Rich et al., 2010). Properly studying engagement requires using a measure that effectively captures this feature, which some have suggested is best achieved with scales based on Kahn's (1990) inclusive definition of engagement (e.g., Rich et al., 2010) as opposed to the UWES (Cole et al., 2012; Saks & Gruman, 2014). Progress on this topic will intensify when an agreed-upon conceptualization and measure of engagement is achieved.

## *Weak Research Methods*

One final criticism is that most studies on engagement have been cross-sectional and have used self-report data to measure engagement as well as its antecedents and consequences (Bailey et al., 2017). As a result, the relationships between engagement and other variables might be inflated due to common method bias. Further, one has to be cautious in drawing conclusions about the causes and consequences of engagement as well as the direction of causality until more longitudinal and experimental studies are conducted and additional sources of data besides self-report become more common.

# Future Engagement Research

In this section, we discuss several areas that would benefit from further research, including employee engagement interventions, Kahn's (1990) model of engagement, targets of employee engagement, and changes in employee' engagement over time.

## *Employee Engagement Interventions*

One area of research that needs more attention is experimental research that tests the effects of interventions for increasing employee engagement. Knight, Patterson, and Dawson (2017) conducted a meta-analysis of 20 work engagement interventions that they categorized into four types of interventions: personal resource building, job resource building, leadership training, and health promotion. They found an overall small but positive effect on work engagement and a medium to large effect for group interventions. As noted by the authors, there is a need for research on more work engagement interventions. Ideally, this research would examine the extent to which the effects of interventions are maintained over time (e.g., months or years).

One type of intervention that might be particularly worth exploring is a job crafting intervention that instructs employees on how to perform different job crafting behaviors. Another potentially worthwhile intervention is to improve employees' psychological capital, a multidimensional construct comprised of hope, optimism, self-efficacy, and resiliency (Luthans, Youssef, & Avolio, 2007). Both of these interventions have the potential to be effective means of improving employee engagement, given that both job crafting (Tims et al., 2012, 2013) and psychological capital (Thompson, Lemmon, & Walter, 2015) are positively related to work engagement. A third type of intervention might focus on enhancing the three psychological conditions of Kahn's (1990) engagement theory. In fact, there is already some evidence that a meaningfulness intervention can improve meaningfulness in and at work as well as job and organization engagement (Fletcher & Schofield, 2019). Given that so few studies have examined engagement interventions, this represents a significant gap in the literature. More research is needed to identify what interventions have the greatest effect on improving engagement and under what conditions (Bailey et al., 2017).

## *Kahn's (1990) Model of Engagement*

A second area in need of research concerns the two important components of Kahn's (1990) model of engagement: self-in-role and psychological presence. Although numerous measures of engagement have been developed, none of them assess Kahn's (1990) notion of self-in-role or the idea that when an individual is engaged, they bring their true and complete selves into the performance of a role. In addition, although psychological presence (attentiveness, connected, integrated, focus) is the most immediate precursor of personal engagement in Kahn's (1992) recursive model of psychological presence, we are not aware of any studies that have measured psychological presence. Therefore, future research is required to more thoroughly test Kahn's (1990, 1992) theory of engagement by measuring self-in-role and psychological presence.

### Targets of Employee Engagement

Although employees perform multiple roles in organizations (Rothbard, 2001), most research on employee engagement has been on the work role or job engagement. As indicated earlier, the multidimensional model of employee engagement suggests that engagement is a role-specific construct and involves the extent to which an individual is psychologically present and engaged in a particular role. Thus, future research is needed on engagement in other roles besides the work role (e.g., organization role, group role). In particular, research is needed on the antecedents and consequences of different targets of engagement as well as the extent to which engagement in one role is influenced by and influences engagement in other roles.

### Changes in Employee Engagement

A final area in need of research is on changes in employee engagement over time, how engagement changes, and why it changes. Saks and Gruman (2018) introduced the notion of work engagement maintenance curves, noting that employee engagement can slowly or rapidly increase or decrease or it can remain stable. Research is needed to learn more about work engagement maintenance curves, the factors that are most important for increasing engagement, as well as when to intervene to prevent a decline in engagement and to facilitate an increase. Thus, future research is needed to examine how, why, and when employee engagement changes and fluctuates over time (Christian et al., 2011).

## Practical Implications for Organizations

In terms of practice, there is a great deal that organizations can do to increase the engagement of their employees. Based on the existing research, organizations should provide employees with resources to effectively perform their jobs and minimize job demands that can be stressful and harmful to employees. Although the research suggests that some of the most important resources for driving engagement are social support, job characteristics, and opportunities for learning and development, the most important resources for improving engagement will probably depend to some degree on employee needs and the nature of the job. Therefore, organizations should first perform an engagement audit to determine levels of employee engagement across the organization and employee perceptions of the existence and importance of various job resources and demands. This will help to identify areas of an organization where employees are disengaged and what resources are lacking and need to be provided, and what demands need to be reduced. In addition, organizations should provide employees with opportunities to craft their own jobs (Tims et al., 2013).

## Conclusion

Employee engagement has become one of the most important topics in organizational behavior for researchers, practitioners, and organizations. We have learned a great deal about what drives employee engagement, its consequences for employees and organizations, and how to measure it. However, there is still much to learn, particularly when it comes to interventions to increase engagement, how and why engagement changes over time, different targets of employee engagement, and the role that context and culture play in the engagement process.

Given the potential benefits of engagement for employees and organizations, we suspect that employee engagement will continue to be on top of the agenda for researchers and practitioners for years to come. We hope that this chapter will contribute to the further development, evolution, and science of employee engagement.

## Note

1 We note that research results can also vary depending on how the other variables in an engagement study are operationalized. For instance, a conceptual paper comparing engagement and job involvement (e.g., Newman & Harrison, 2008) will find overlap if the latter is conceptualized and measured using Lodahl and Kejner's (1965) expansive scale versus Kanungo's (1982) more focused scale. Similarly, empirical research on engagement will be strongly influenced by the other scales included in the study.

## References

Albrecht, S.L., Bakker, A.B., Gruman, J.A., Macey, W.H., & Saks, A.M. (2015). Employee engagement, human resource management practices and competitive advantage: An integrated approach. *Journal of Organizational Effectiveness: People and Performance, 2*(1), 7–35.

Alfes, K., Shantz, A.D., Truss, C., & Soane, E.C. (2013). The link between perceived human resource management practices, engagement and employee behavior: A moderated mediation model. *The International Journal of Human Resource Management, 24,* 330–351.

Bailey, C., Madden, A., Alfes, K., & Fletcher, L. (2017). The meaning, antecedents and outcomes of employee engagement: A narrative synthesis. *International Journal of Management Reviews, 19,* 31–53.

Bakker, A.B., Albrecht, S.L., & Leiter, M.P. (2011). Key questions regarding work engagement. *European Journal of Work and Organizational Psychology, 20*, 4–28.

Bakker, A.B. & Demerouti, E. (2007). The job demands-resources model: State of the art. *Journal of Managerial Psychology, 22*, 309–328.

Bakker, A.B. & Demerouti, E. (2008). Towards a model of work engagement. *Career Development International, 13*, 209–223.

Bakker, A.B., Hakanen, J.J., Demerouti, E., & Xanthopoulou, D. (2007). Job resources boost work engagement, particularly when job demands are high. *Journal of Educational Psychology, 99*, 274–284.

Bal, P.M. & De Lange, A.H. (2015). From flexibility human resource management to employee engagement and perceived job performance across the lifespan: A multi-sample study. *Journal of Occupational and Organizational Psychology, 88*, 126–154.

Barrick, M.R., Thurgood, G.R., Smith, T.A., & Courtright, S.H. (2015). Collective organizational engagement: linking motivational antecedents, strategic implementation, and firm performance. *Academy of Management Journal, 58*, 111–135.

Britt, T.W. (1999). Engaging the self in the field: Testing the triangle model of responsibility. *Personality and Social Psychology Bulletin, 25*, 696–706.

Britt, T.W. (2003). Motivational and emotional consequences of self-engagement: Voting in the 2000 U.S. presidential election. *Motivation and Emotion, 27*, 339–358.

Brough, P., Timms, C., Siu, O., Kalliath, T., O'Driscoll, M.P., & Sit, C.H.P. (2013). Validation of the Job Demands-Resources model in cross-national samples: Cross-sectional and longitudinal predictions of psychological strain and work engagement. *Human Relations, 66*, 1311–1335.

Byrne, Z.S., Peters, J.M., & Weston, J.W. (2016). The struggle with employee engagement: Measures and construct clarification using five samples. *Journal of Applied Psychology, 101*, 1201–1227.

Christian, M.S., Garza, A.S., & Slaughter, J.E. (2011). Work engagement: A quantitative review and test of its relations with task and contextual performance. *Personnel Psychology, 64*, 89–136.

Cole, M.S., Walter, F., Bedeian, A.G., & O'Boyle, E.H. (2012). Job burnout and employee engagement: A meta-analytic examination of construct proliferation. *Journal of Management, 38*, 1550–1581.

Cooper-Thomas, H.D., Xu, J., & Saks, A.M. (2018). The differential value of resources in predicting employee engagement. *Journal of Managerial Psychology, 33*, 326–344.

Costa, P., Passos, A.M., & Bakker, A.B. (2014). Team work engagement: A model of emergence. *Journal of Occupational and Organizational Psychology, 87*, 414–436.

Costa, P., Passos, A.M., & Bakker, A.B. (2015). Direct and contextual influence of team conflict on team resources, team work engagement, and team performance. *Negotiation and Conflict Management Research, 8*, 211–227.

Crawford, E.R., LePine, J.A., & Rich, B.L. (2010). Linking job demands and resources to employee engagement and burnout: A theoretical extension and meta-analytic test. *Journal of Applied Psychology, 95*, 834–848.

Crawford, E.R., Rich, B.L., Buckman, B., & Bergeron, J. (2014). The antecedents and drivers of employee engagement. In C. Truss, R. Delbridge, K. Alfes, A. Shantz, & E. Soane (Eds.), *Employee engagement in theory and practice* (pp. 57–81). New York, NY: Routledge.

Cropanzano, R. & Mitchell, M.S. (2005). Social exchange theory: An interdisciplinary review. *Journal of Management, 31*, 1–27.

Dalal, R.S., Baysinger, M., Brummel, B.J., & LeBreton, J.M. (2012). The relative importance of employee engagement, other job attitudes, and trait affect as predictors of job performance. *Journal of Applied Social Psychology*, *42*, E295–E325.

Donahue, E.M., Robins, R.W., Roberts, B.W., & John, O.P. (1993). The divided self: Concurrent and longitudinal effects of psychological adjustment and social roles on self-concept differentiation. *Journal of Personality and Social Psychology*, *64*, 834–846.

Eldor, L. & Harpaz, I. (2016). A process model of employee engagement: The learning climate and its relationship with extra-role performance behaviors. *Journal of Organizational Behavior*, *37*, 213–235.

Farndale, E. & Murrer, I. (2015). Job resources and employee engagement: A cross-national study. *Journal of Managerial Psychology*, *30*, 610–626.

Fletcher, L. & Schofield, K. (2019). Facilitating meaningfulness in the workplace: A field intervention study. *International Journal of Human Resource Management*.

Garczynski, A.M., Waldrop, J.S., Rupprecht E.A., & Grawitch, M.J. (2013). Differentiation between work and nonwork self-aspects as a predictor of presenteeism and engagement: Cross-cultural differences. *Journal of Occupational Health Psychology*, *18*, 417–429.

Gelfand, M.J., Leslie, L.L., & Fehr, R. (2008). To prosper, organizational psychology should… adopt a global perspective. *Journal of Organizational Behavior*, *29*, 493–517.

Goering, D.D., Shimazu, A., Zhou, F., Wada, T., & Sakai, R. (2017). Not if, but how they differ: A meta-analytic test of the nomological networks of burnout and engagement. *Burnout Research*, *5*, 21–34.

Guchait, P. (2016). The mediating effect of team engagement between team cognitions and team outcomes in service-management teams. *Journal of Hospitality & Tourism Research*, *40*, 139–161.

Hakanen, J.J. & Schaufeli, W.B. (2012). Do burnout and work engagement predict depressive symptoms and life satisfaction? A three-wave seven-year prospective study. *Journal of Affective Disorders*, *141*, 415–424.

Halbesleben, J.R.B. (2010). A meta-analysis of work engagement: Relationships with burnout, demands, resources, and consequences. In A.B. Bakker and M.P. Leiter (Eds.), *Work engagement: A handbook of essential theory and research* (pp.102–117). Hove, East Sussex: Psychology Press.

Harter, J.K., Schmidt, F.L., & Hayes, T.L. (2002). Business-unit level relationship between employee satisfaction, employee engagement, and business outcomes: A meta-analysis, *Journal of Applied Psychology*, *87*, 268–279.

Haynie, J.J., Mossholder, K.W., & Harris, S.G. (2016). Justice and job engagement: The role of senior management trust. *Journal of Organizational Behavior*, *37*, 889–910.

Johnson, G. (2004). Otherwise engaged. *Training*, *41*(10), 4.

Kahn, W.A. (1990). Psychological conditions of personal engagement and disengagement at work, *Academy of Management Journal*, *33*, 692–724.

Kahn, W.A. (1992). To be full there: Psychological presence at work, *Human Relations*, *45*, 321–349.

Kanungo, R.N. (1982). Measurement of job and work involvement. *Journal of Applied Psychology*, *67*(3), 341–349.

Kitayama, S., Markus, H.R., Matsumoto, H., & Norasakkunkit, V. (1997). Individual and collective processes in the construction of the self: self-enhancement in the United States and self-criticism in Japan. *Journal of Personality and Social Psychology*, *72*, 1245–1267.

Klassen, R.M., Aldhafri, S., Mansfield, C.F., Purwanto, E., Siu, A.F.Y., Wong, M.W., & Woods-McConney, A. (2012). Teachers' engagement at work: An international validation study. *The Journal of Experimental Education, 80*, 317–337.

Knight, C., Patterson, M., & Dawson, J. (2017). Building work engagement: A systematic review and meta-analysis investigating the effectiveness of work engagement interventions. *Journal of Organizational Behavior, 38*, 792–812.

Kowalski, B. (2003). The engagement gap. *Training, 40*(4), 62.

Lodahl, T.M. & Kejner, M. (1965). The definition and measurement of job involvement. *Journal of Applied Psychology, 49*, 24–33.

Luthans, F., Youssef, C.M., & Avolio, B.J. (2007). *Psychological capital: Developing the human competitive edge*. New York, NY: Oxford University Press.

Macey, W.H. & Schneider, B. (2008). The meaning of employee engagement. *Industrial and Organizational Psychology, 1*, 3–30.

Mackay, M.M., Allen, J.A., & Landis, R.S. (2017). Investigating the incremental validity of employee engagement in the prediction of employee effectiveness: A meta-analytic path analysis. *Human Resource Management Review, 27*, 108–120.

Mäkikangas, A., Aunola, K., Seppälä, P., & Hakanen, J. (2016). Work engagement—team performance relationship: shared job crafting as a moderator. *Journal of Occupational and Organizational Psychology, 89*, 772–790.

Maslach, C. & Leiter, M.P. (2008). Early predictors of job burnout and engagement. *Journal of Applied Psychology, 93*, 498–512.

Maslach, C., Schaufeli, W.B., & Leiter, M.P. (2001). Job Burnout. *Annual Review of Psychology, 52*, 397–422.

Mauno, S., Kinnunen, U., Mäkikangas, A., & Feldt, T. (2010). Job demands and resources as antecedents of work engagement: A qualitative review and directions for future research. In S. Albrecht (Ed.), *Handbook of Employee Engagement: Perspectives, Issues, Research and Practice* (pp. 111–128). Cheltenham, UK: Edward Elgar.

May, D.R., Gilson, R.L., & Harter, L.M. (2004). The psychological conditions of meaningfulness, safety and availability and the engagement of the human spirit at work, *Journal of Occupational and Organizational Psychology, 77*, 11–37.

Newman, D.A. & Harrison, D.A. (2008). Been there, bottled that: Are state and behavioral work engagement new and useful construct "wine"? *Industrial and Organizational Psychology, 1*, 31–35.

Oliver, A. & Rothmann, S. (2007). Antecedents of work engagement in a multinational oil company. *SA Journal of Industrial Psychology, 33*, 49–56.

Rich, B.L., Lepine, J.A., & Crawford, E.R. (2010). Job engagement: antecedents and effects of job performance. *Academy of Management Journal, 53*, 617–635.

Rodríguez-Sánchez, A.M., Devloo, T., Rico, R., Salanova, M., & Anseel, F. (2016). What makes creative teams tick? Cohesion, engagement, and performance across creativity tasks: A three-wave study. *Group & Organization Management, 42*, 521–547.

Rothbard, N.P. (2001). Enriching or depleting: The dynamics of engagement in work and family roles. *Administrative Science Quarterly, 46*, 655–684.

Rothmann, S. (2014). Employee engagement in a cultural context. In C. Truss, R. Delbridge, K. Alfes, A. Shantz, & E. Soane (Eds.), *Employee engagement in theory and practice* (pp. 163–179). New York, NY: Routledge.

Rothmann, S. & Rothmann, S., Jr. (2010). Factors associated with employee engagement in South Africa. *SA Journal of Industrial Psychology, 36*. doi: 10.4102/sajip.v36i2.925

Rothmann, S. & Welsh, C. (2013). Employee engagement: The role of psychological conditions. *Management Dynamics, 22*, 14–25.

Rudolph, C.W. & Baltes, B.B. (2017). Age and health jointly moderate the influence of flexible work arrangements on work engagement: Evidence from two empirical studies. *Journal of Occupational Health Psychology, 22*, 40–58.

Rudolph, C.W., Katz, I.M., Lavigne, K.N., & Zacher, H. (2017). Job crafting: A meta-analysis of relationships with individual differences, job characteristics, and work outcomes. *Journal of Vocational Behavior, 102*, 112–138.

Sakuraya, A., Shimazu, A., Eguchi, H., Kamiyama, K., Hara, Y., Namba, K., & Kawakami, N. (2017). Job crafting, work engagement, and psychological distress among Japanese employees: a cross-sectional study. *BioPsychoSocial Medicine, 11*. doi. org/10.1186/s13030-017-0091-y

Sanchez, P. & McCauley, D. (2006). Measuring and managing engagement in a cross-cultural workforce: New insights for global companies. *Global Business and Organizational Excellence, 26*, 41–50.

Saks, A.M. (2006). Antecedents and consequences of employee engagement. *Journal of Managerial Psychology, 21*, 600–619.

Saks, A.M. (2019). Antecedents and consequences of employee engagement revisited. *Journal of Organizational Effectiveness: People and Performance, 6*, 19–38.

Saks, A.M. & Gruman, J.A. (2014). What do we really know about employee engagement? *Human Resource Development Quarterly, 25*, 155–182.

Saks, A.M. & Gruman, J.A. (2017). Human resource management and employee engagement. In P. Sparrow & C.L. Cooper (Eds.), *A research agenda for human resource management* (pp. 95–113). Northampton, MA: Edward Elgar Publishing Limited.

Saks, A.M. & Gruman, J.A. (2018). Socialization resources theory and newcomers' work engagement: A new pathway to newcomer socialization. *Career Development International, 23*, 12–32.

Schaufeli, W.B. (2014). What is engagement? In C. Truss, R. Delbridge, K. Alfes, A. Shantz, & E. Soane (Eds.), *Employee engagement in theory and practice* (pp. 15–35). New York, NY: Routledge.

Schaufeli, W.B. (2018). Work engagement in Europe: Relations with national economy, governance, and culture. *Organizational Dynamics, 47*, 99–106.

Schaufeli, W.B., Bakker, A.B., & Van Rhenen, W. (2009). How changes in job demands ad resources predict burnout, work engagement, and sickness absenteeism. *Journal of Organizational Behavior, 30*, 893–917.

Schaufeli, W.B., Bakker, A.B., & Salanova, M. (2006). The measurement of work engagement with a short questionnaire: A cross-national study. *Educational and Psychological Measurement, 66*, 701–716.

Schaufeli, W.B., Salanova, M., Gonzalez-Roma, V., & Bakker, A.B. (2002). The measurement of engagement and burnout: A two sample confirmatory factor analytic approach, *Journal of Happiness Studies, 3*, 71–92.

Schaufeli, W.B., Shimazu, A., Hakanen, J., Salanova, M., & De Witte, H. (2019). An ultra-short measure for work engagement: The UWES-3 validation across five countries. *European Journal of Psychological Assessment, 35*, 577–591.

Schlenker, B.R. (1997). Personal responsibility: Applications of the Triangle Model. In B.M. Staw & L.L. Cummings (Eds.), *Research in organizational behavior* (Vol.19, pp.241–301). Greenwich, CT: JAI Press.

Schneider, B., Yost, A.B., Kropp, A., Kind, C., & Lam, H. (2018). Workforce engagement: What it is, what drives it, and why it matters for organizational performance. *Journal of Organizational Behavior, 39*, 462–480.

Shantz, A. & Alfes, K. (2015). Work engagement and voluntary absence: The moderating role of job resources. *European Journal of Work and Organizational Psychology, 24*, 530–543.

Shantz, A., Alfes, K., Truss, C., & Soane E. (2013). The role of employee engagement in the relationship between job design and tusk performance, citizenship and deviant behaviors. *The International Journal of Human Resource Management, 24*, 2608–2627.

Shimazu, A., Miyanaka, D., & Schaufeli, W.B. (2010). Work engagement from a cultural perspective. In S. Albrecht (Ed.), *Handbook of Employee Engagement: Perspectives, Issues, Research and Practice* (pp. 364–372). Cheltenham, UK: Edward Elgar.

Shuck, B. (2011). Four emerging perspectives of employee engagement: An integrative literature review. *Human Resource Development Review, 10*, 304–328.

Shuck, B., Adelson, J.L., & Reio, Jr. T.G. (2017a). The employee engagement scale: Initial evidence for construct validity and implications for theory and practice. *Human Resource Management, 56*, 953–977.

Shuck, B., Nimon, K., & Zigarmi, D. (2017b). Untangling the predictive nomological validity of employee engagement: Partitioning variance in employee engagement using job attitude measures. *Group & Organization Management, 42*, 79–112.

Shuck, B., Osam, K., Zigarmi, D., & Nimon, K. (2017c). Definitional and conceptual muddling: Identifying the positionality of employee engagement and defining the construct. *Human Resource Development Review, 16*, 263–293.

Soane, E., Truss, C., Alfes, K., Shantz, A., Rees, C., & Gatenby, M. (2012). Development and application of a new measure of employee engagement: The ISA Engagement Scale. *Human Resource Development International, 15*, 529–547.

Song, J.H., Lim, D.H., Kang, I.G., & Kim, W. (2014). Team performance in learning organizations: Mediating effect of employee engagement. *The Learning Organization, 21*, 290–309.

Sonnentag, S. (2017). A task-level perspective on work engagement: A new approach that helps to differentiate the concepts of engagement and burnout. *Burnout Research, 5*, 12–20.

Stumpf, S.A., Tymon, W.G. Jr., & van Dam, N.H.M. (2013). Felt and behavioral engagement in workgroups of professionals. *Journal of Vocational Behavior, 83*, 255–264.

Thompson, K.R., Lemmon, G., & Walter, T.J. (2015). Employee engagement and positive psychological capital. *Organizational Dynamics, 44*, 185–195.

Tims, M., Bakker, A.B., & Derks, D. (2012). Development and validation of the job crafting scale. *Journal of Vocational Behavior, 80*, 173–186.

Tims, M., Bakker, A.B., & Derks, D. (2013). The impact of job crafting on job demands, job resources, and well-being. *Journal of Occupational Health Psychology, 18*, 230–240.

Tonidandel, S. & LeBreton, J.M. (2011). Relative importance analysis: A useful supplement to regression analysis. *Journal of Business and Psychology, 26*, 1–9.

Viljevac, A., Cooper-Thomas, H.D., & Saks, A.M. (2012). An investigation into the validity of two measures of work engagement. *The International Journal of Human Resource Management, 23*, 3692–3709.

Xanthopoulou, D., Bakker, A.B., Demerouti, E., & Schaufeli, W.B. (2007). The role of personal resources in the Job Demands-Resources Model. *International Journal of Stress Management, 14*, 121–141.

Xanthopoulou, D., Bakker, A.B., Demerouti, E., & Schaufeli, W.B. (2009a). Reciprocal relationships between job resources, personal resources, and work engagement. *Journal of Vocational Behavior, 74*, 235–244.

Xanthopoulou, D., Bakker, A.B., Demerouti, E., & Schaufeli, W.B. (2009b). Work engagement and financial returns: A diary study on the role of job and personal resources. *Journal of Occupational and Organizational Psychology, 82*, 183–200.

Xanthopoulou, D., Bakker, A.B., Heuven, E., Demerouti, E., & Schaufeli, W.B. (2008). Working in the sky: A diary study on work engagement among flight attendants. *Journal of Occupational Health Psychology, 13*, 345–356.

Young, H.R., Glerum, D.R., Wang, W., & Joseph, D.L. (2018). Who are the most engaged at work? A meta-analysis of personality and employee engagement. *Journal of Organizational Behavior, 39*, 1330–1346.

Zhong, L., Wayne, S.J., & Liden, R.C. (2016). Job engagement, perceived organizational support, high-performance human resource practices, and cultural value orientations: A cross-level investigation. *Journal of Organizational Behavior, 37*, 823–844.

Zhu, W., Avolio, B.J., & Walumbwa, F.O. (2009). Moderating role of follower characteristics with transformational leadership and follower work engagement. *Group & Organization Management, 34*, 590–619.

# 11

# TEAM-RELATED WORK ATTITUDES

*Natalie J. Allen*

Among organizational scholars, there is a strong interest in work-related psychological constructs, including attitudes, beliefs, and reactions. Indeed, this volume is a testament to this. Much of this research has focused on how workers perceive and respond to their jobs, occupations/professions, or organizations.

Given the ubiquity and criticality of teams in the workplace, however, it is not surprising that scholars, from various disciplines, are turning increasing attention to understanding how people react to teams and teamwork, the bases of these "team attitudes," and their potential behavioral consequences. Also unsurprising is the considerable interest in team attitudes and related constructs that is expressed by practitioners who work in, manage, or train teams.

Accordingly, the goal of this chapter is to provide an overview of the body of research in which attitudes toward teams and teamwork are assessed within *work-relevant* contexts and to sketch out the beginnings of a nomological network involving these constructs. I begin by describing how teams—or "work groups"—are typically defined. This is followed by a review of various ways in which researchers have approached the conceptualization and assessment of *team-related attitudes* in *work-relevant settings*. In doing so, I examine evidence relevant to the construct validity associated with particular measures by drawing from empirical research that examines the reliability and correlates of each measure, and, where available, summarize what research suggests about the "development," and "outcomes," deemed to be associated with the underlying construct. Finally, I discuss ways in which existing team attitude research might be used to inform practice in organizational settings that rely on teams, and I suggest research directions in which the field might head so as to enhance both practitioner and research goals.

## What Is a Team?

Formal definitions of "teams" abound (e.g., Hackman, 2002; Mathieu, Hollenbeck, van Knippenberg, & Ilgen, 2017; Sundstrom, DeMeuse, & Futrell, 1990). Common to all, however, is the notion that a team includes *two or more people* who work *interdependently* in order to achieve *a shared goal*.

Beyond this, of course, teams vary in numerous ways. Within our particular domain of interest—the workplace—the team may be large or small. The team's "shared goal" may be one that is achieved once or repeatedly, and under similar or quite different conditions. The activity in which the members of a given team engage may be lengthy or quite brief. The team may include members who either regularly or only occasionally work together. Team interaction can take place among co-located members who work "face-to-face" or among members whose interaction is virtual. Needless to say, team tasks also vary considerably. A flight crew that shuttles its passengers from Toronto to New York is a team. A cross-national group of software developers charged with coming up with the "next best thing" is a team. The crew staffing a restaurant during the dinner shift is a team. Engineering students working together on a project intended to demonstrate their collective knowledge of fundamental design principles are a team. In short, work-relevant teams come in many forms.

Teams are also exceedingly common within most workplaces. Indeed, in both the research and practitioner literature, we are told some version of the "teams are everywhere" claim (e.g., Salas, Shuffler, Thayer, Bedwell, & Lazzara, 2014), that teams have "become the basic building block of modern organizations" (Killumets, D'Innocenzo, Maynard, & Mathieu, 2015, p. 228) and, hence, that teams are considered essential in many workplaces (e.g., Devaraj & Jiang, 2019; Shuffler, Diazgranados, Maynard, & Salas, 2018). Not surprisingly, therefore, mastering teamwork is seen as a vital workplace skill (Loughry, Ohland, & Woehr, 2014) and those who are both capable *and* enthused "team players" are considered to offer particular value to their organizations (e.g., Calanca, Sayfullina, Minkus, Wagner, & Malmi, 2019; Hirschfeld, Jordan, Feild, Giles, & Armenakis, 2006; Lencioni, 2002, 2016). Similar assumptions are made about those members who have positive attitudes toward particular *types* of teams or to the *specific team* to which they belong. For all these reasons, there is considerable interest among both scholars (see Mathieu et al., 2017) and practitioners (DesMarais, 2017; Kokemuller (n.d.); TRISOFT, 2017) in understanding and enhancing how positively people feel about working in teams.

## "Situating" Team Attitude Scholarship

Both researchers and practitioners from various disciplines, professions, and workplaces have an interest in understanding group or team effectiveness. While models that specify the ordering and positioning of particular variables may differ, scholars from these disciplines and areas of inquiry all emphasize the critical role that members' team-related "attitudes" play in shaping how—and how well—work groups or teams perform.

Among social scientists, formal interest in team-related attitudes has a reasonably long, but relatively straightforward, history. In the well-established "input-process-output" model of groups forwarded by McGrath (1964), both performance *and* attitude variables (e.g., team member satisfaction, team cohesion) were considered "output" variables. Both sets of variables, it was argued, serve to sustain the *viability* of the team, something that is particularly important for teams that have difficult and/or long-term performance challenges to meet and, hence, require membership stability. Subsequent scholars followed suit, with Hackman (1983) describing "growth and personal well-being of team members" (p. 7) as a key dimension of group effectiveness, and Gladstein (1984), Sundstrom et al., (1990), Campion, Medsker, and Higgs (1993), and Guzzo and Dickson (1996) highlighting the role of team member satisfaction in a similar fashion.

This increased interest in team-related attitudes was prescient as, throughout the 1990s, and due to a combination of factors (increased work complexity, the need for greater collaboration, and a recognition of the value of enhanced employee connectedness) team-based structures began to permeate work organizations. Despite the challenges associated with the design and management of teams (Hackman, 1990; Lencioni, 2002; Turner, 2001) and debates regarding the performance capacity of entire teams relative to "solo" workers (e.g., Allen & Hecht, 2004a,b; Larson, 2010; Staw & Epstein, 2000; West, Brodbeck, & Richter, 2004), it was clear that by the beginning of the 21st century, teams had become firmly entrenched in the broad organizational landscape.

It is not surprising, therefore, that discussions of and research examining numerous "team-related attitudes" have made their way into contemporary scholarly work conducted in various social scientific and professional disciplines. Indeed, there appears to be a robust interest in such constructs. What follows describes various ways in which these constructs have been conceptualized, examines the measurement strategies that empirical team researchers have used to assess the constructs, and explores the relevance of such measures for practice. Based on this theoretical and empirical work, I attempt to integrate these constructs into a nomological net, illustrated in Figure 11.1, that outlines their proposed interrelations and their respective antecedents and consequences.

## Examining the Team Attitude Literature

At its core, an attitude is a psychological construct directed toward some focal entity and to which the person expresses a degree of favor or disfavor (Eagly & Chaiken, 1993). The degree to which one has a favorable or unfavorable evaluation of the entity manifests itself in terms of an *affective/emotional reaction* to the entity in question, *thoughts* about the entity, and *behaviors* of relevance to the entity.

Researchers who are interested in what I will refer to as team-related attitudes have focused attention in three directions—or attitudinal targets—with some researchers examining attitudes to the *idea of teamwork*, others to specific *features of teams*, and still others to the *particular team* to which a member belongs.

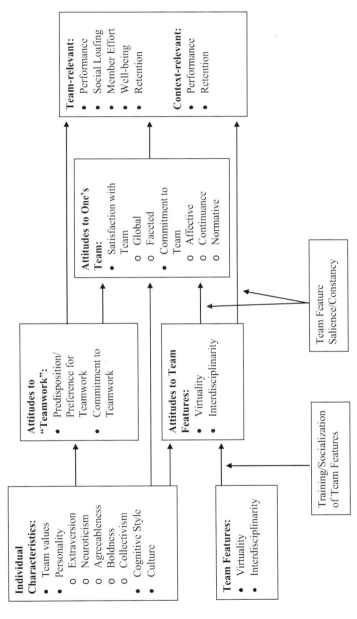

*Figure 11.1* The Nomological Network of Team-Related Work Attitudes.

Across this wide-ranging research literature and, somewhat consistent with attitudes toward other work-related foci examined by organizational scholars, these team-related "attitude" constructs vary considerably in terms of how closely they conform to the classic tripartite conceptualization of an attitude referred to above. Arguably, however, each can be considered to be *somewhat* reflective of the extent to which the individual sees the focal entity in a favorable light—and feels, thinks, and behaves accordingly.

Thus, for example, individuals who react positively to *teamwork* and/or prefer team activity over solo work would be expected to enjoy working in teams, to choose team-based work whenever possible, and to more strongly endorse—and behave in accordance with—team-based principles and best practices. Similarly, those expressing a more positive attitude to a key *team feature*, such as virtuality or interdisciplinarity, would be expected to enjoy working in teams that had that particular feature. In addition, such individuals might be expected to consider more carefully and more strongly endorse the principles associated with the feature in question. Further, they would be likely to work more diligently to support such features and grapple with any challenges that maintaining such features might present. Finally, team members expressing a positive attitude (e.g., satisfaction, commitment) to the *particular team* to which they belonged would be likely to feel positively toward key aspects of their team (e.g., its goals, practices, members), desire to maintain membership in their team, and behave in accordance with what they believed to be best for the team by working hard in the service of its goals.

## Team-Related Attitudes: Toward a Nomological Net

Across fairly widespread and multi-disciplinary research literature, scholars have developed various measures of these team-related attitudes and conducted research examining some of their potential precursors and consequences. Based on this body of construct measurement research, substantive research involving these measures, and inferences based on the wider "attitude-behavior" literature, I propose a nomological net that encompasses the team-related attitude constructs outlined above, and the hypothesized linkages among them and their antecedents and consequences.

To "set the stage," I begin by providing an overview of the relevant measure/construct literature. Although the empirical study of attitudes arguably has its origins within psychology, scholarship focusing on the assessment of *team-related attitudes* is widespread. In addition to psychology, relevant contemporary work is found in sociology and organizational behavior, and within the scholarly work associated with those professions in which team-based work is particularly critical. Thus, in considering this body of knowledge, I examined *empirical* research, conducted over the past 20+ years, in which some measurement strategy was used to assess what people believe, feel, or think about some aspect of teamwork and teams.

Subsequently, in keeping with the goal of this volume, the focus of this chapter narrowed so as to consider only research that examined team members in *actual workplace* or *professional* settings, or in settings that could be considered *analogous* to those in which such teams operate. Perhaps the best example of the latter are those studies in which post-secondary students—typically within professional programs such as business, engineering, medicine, or pharmacy—work together in teams for course/professional credit. Excluded from this review, therefore, is research that was conducted with *non-work* teams (e.g., recreational sports teams, teams of community volunteers) and research conducted with "teams" of research participants that were assembled solely for examination in short-term experimental/laboratory studies.

Further, the focus narrowed to include only those studies that empirically assessed *team-related* attitudes toward one or more of the three attitudinal targets, or foci, outlined above: (1) the general *idea* of "teamwork," (2) particular *features* associated with teams, and (3) the *particular team* to which a team member belongs. Accordingly, excluded from the review are discussions of measures that were designed primarily to evaluate behaviors, strategies used, or the performance achieved in a given team or type of team. With this as an organizing framework, I focused most attention on research areas in which these three types of team-related attitude *constructs* were clearly articulated and where the *measures* used to assess them were described in enough detail, and/ or had been administered to members of workplace-relevant teams frequently enough that they provided readers with a useful resource and/or food for thought.

Not surprisingly, this body of research is wide-ranging in its scholarly goals, disciplinary bases, and methodological approaches to measure development/ validation, and, inevitably, one cannot do justice to it all. To the extent possible, however, I sought to review this work in such a way that the reader might learn something about the nomological net in which these various attitude constructs are embedded. Accordingly, in addition to outlining *how* the various constructs are assessed, I examined research that reported relations among the various attitude measures and research that provided what might be considered evidence regarding the development, and consequences, of these attitudes.

As shown in Figure 11.1, the proposed nomological net outlines hypothesized links among variables that are considered antecedents of the three sets of team-related attitudes, the attitudes themselves, and their consequences for behavior. Broadly, it is proposed that both individual characteristics (e.g., team member personality traits) and the presence of team features (e.g., virtuality) shape individuals' attitudes/reactions to *the idea of teamwork* and *team features*, respectively. These latter constructs will, in turn, influence how *satisfied* members feel toward their teams and the strength of their *commitment* to these teams. Further, as indicated in Figure 11.1, the effects involving team features are moderated by the extent to which emphasis is placed on the feature in question (training/socialization regarding the feature; the constancy of the feature). Finally, it is proposed that team members' satisfaction with, and commitment to, their *own teams* will influence their well-being, likelihood of remaining on their teams, and a variety of performance-related variables (e.g., effort, social loafing, task performance).

In what follows, I turn my attention to the various measures of team-related attitudes that form the primary focus of this chapter and that, as depicted in Figure 11.1, are hypothesized to have consequences for various team-relevant behavior and team outcomes. As outlined above, these measures relate to the three sets of team foci to which an individual team member is likely to form an "attitude": (1) the *idea* of "teamwork," (2) particular *features* associated with teams, and (3) the *particular team* to which the team member belongs.

## Team-Related Attitudes 1: The Idea of Teamwork

### *The Team Player Inventory*

In 1999, Kline developed The Team Player Inventory (TPI). This 10-item self-report measure, shown in Appendix 11.A, was designed to assess "the degree to which individuals are positively predisposed to working on teams" (Kline, 1999a, p. 62). Arguably, therefore, the construct underlying this measure corresponds reasonably well to classic conceptualizations of an "attitude." It is important to note, however, that the focus here is on "teamwork" rather than on any *particular* team to which one might belong. Thus, as depicted in Figure 11.1, this predisposition toward working in teams might well be considered antecedent to individuals' attitudes to their *own* teams.

In describing the "team player" construct, Kline (1999a,b) referred to it as a *general orientation* toward engaging in team activity that will predispose high TPI scorers toward such activity, but not necessarily ensure positive reactions to every team to which such individuals belong. *Somewhat* consistent with this view are two sets of TPI findings. First, TPI scores have been shown to correlate with particular personality traits in the expected direction. These include positive relations with both extraversion and agreeableness (Ilarda & Findlay, 2006; Kline & O'Grady, 2009), and negative relations with neuroticism (Ilarda & Findlay, 2006). Further, Neo, Sellbom, Smith, and Lilienfeld (2018) added to the nomological net regarding this measure by establishing an interesting linkage between TPI scores and the three traits associated with the triarchic model of psychopathy (disinhibition, meanness, and boldness). As predicted, they noted that TPI scores were positively associated with one of these—employee boldness—a trait that some argue is particularly helpful in group activities. Second, as foreshadowed above, the evidence linking TPI scores to individuals' reactions to a *particular* team is also somewhat mixed. Some studies (MacDonnell, O'Neill, Kline, & Hambley, 2009; O'Neill & Kline, 2008), but not all (French & Kottke, 2013), report that those with high TPI scores react more positively to, and are more engaged with their work in, team-based environments.

Overall, therefore, there appears to be *modest* evidence that TPI scores are related to personality traits in a manner consistent with theoretical expectations regarding both the antecedents and consequences of the construct. Further, high TPI scorers are more likely than low scorers to express interest and engage in team activity. Thus, as depicted in Figure 11.1, particular personality traits are related to this predisposition toward working in teams, which, in turn, might well be considered antecedent to individuals' attitudes to their own teams and, subsequently, to team-relevant behavior.

### The Preference for Group Work Scale

Drawing from theory and measurement work examining the well-established individualism-collectivism personality dimension (e.g., Erez & Earley, 1987; Wagner, 1995), Shaw, Duffy, and Stark (2000) developed the Preference for Group Work Scale. As its name suggests, this 7-item scale, shown in Appendix 11.A, assesses the degree to which individuals favor *group-based work* over that which is done when one *works alone*. The original measure, and/or minor variations thereof, has been used in a small body of empirical studies (e.g., Decker, Calo, Yao, & Weer, 2015; Hendry et al., 2005; Stark, Shaw, & Duffy, 2007). Taken together, this research reports satisfactory scale reliability coefficients, ranging across studies from .83 to .89, and provides some evidence consistent with theoretical predictions. For example, preference for group work is positively associated with satisfaction with one's current group/team, negatively related to social loafing behavior within the team (Shaw et al., 2000; Stark et al., 2007), and positively related to helping others and to a concern about what others think (Decker et al., 2015).

As depicted in Figure 11.1, it seems reasonable to conceptualize each of the "Attitudes to Teamwork" constructs as having both direct effects on team-relevant behaviors (e.g., work performance, social loafing) and indirect effects on such behaviors that are mediated by attitudes (satisfaction; affective commitment) towards one's team. In addition, members with a strong preference for group work would be likely to perform better and engage in less "social loafing" than those who preferred solo work. Further, these individuals would be more likely to stay in their team and experience greater well-being. All else being equal, it is also likely that teams comprising members who share a strong preference for group work are likely to create a more positive team environment and to behave in a manner that is consistent with a positive attitude toward teams.

## The Team Commitment Scale

Foote and Tang (2008) took a somewhat similar approach, in their study of self-directed teams in the manufacturing sector, to the development of what they refer to as a "team commitment scale." As can be seen in Appendix 11.A, the attitudinal focus of this 10-item measure is "the team concept," *not* the specific team to which respondents belonged. Thus, respondents with high scores on this measure might best be considered those who find *teamwork* compelling, and hence are "committed" to that work style, not those who feel a strong commitment to their particular team. Needless to say, this distinction is rather important. Disappointingly, however, as indicated by the way in which Foote and Tang's oft-cited and interesting work is *sometimes* described, it appears, in this regard, to have been somewhat misunderstood. This issue aside, it seems reasonable to expect personality traits similar to those proposed as antecedents of the constructs associated with the Team Player Inventory and the Preference for Group Work Scale will play a similar role in shaping "team commitment." Although construct validation work to date has been somewhat limited, for those researchers who are interested in assessing an individual's general orientation to, or appreciation of, team-based work, this measure appears to have some promise.

Finally, as depicted in Figure 11.1, it seems reasonable to conceptualize each of these attitudes toward the "*idea of teamwork*" as having both direct effects on team-relevant behaviors and indirect effects that are mediated by attitudes (satisfaction; affective commitment) toward the particular team to which the individual belongs. I turn now to a consideration of those team-related constructs that focus on attitudes to "*team features*".

## Team-Related Attitudes II: Team Features

Some team scholars focus their "team attitude" attention more narrowly. Rather than assessing how respondents feel about the *general idea of teamwork*, as outlined above, this second line of research examines team members' psychological reactions to, or preferences for, particular team *features*. Not surprisingly, perhaps, such research is somewhat unevenly distributed with respect to which team features have received the most attention, the purposes for which such measures are used and the extent to which measure development and validation work has been undertaken. Below I describe two features, team virtuality and team interdisciplinarity, that have received particular attention. Also examined are members' attitudes toward key "team concepts."

As depicted in Figure 11.1, team member reactions to a given "team feature" are conceptualized as a predictor of the members' attitude to their particular team; further, it is argued that this relation is moderated by *salience* and/or *constancy* of the team feature. For example, in teams in which *all* aspects of the work are done virtually, and few team members have met in person, the links between team members' attitudes toward team virtuality and team satisfaction with their team might be particularly strong.

## Team Virtuality

### Preference for Virtual Teams

Luse, McElroy, Townsend, and DeMarie (2013) developed two 4-item measures (shown in Appendix 11.B), examining respondents' psychological reactions to *virtual teams*. Each measure is described as assessing two independent facets of this construct—one assessing respondents' preference for working in virtual teams over solo work, and the other assessing their preference for working in virtual teams over traditional, face-to-face teams. Both measures exhibited adequate internal consistency reliability (>.80), and, arguably, somewhat rare among what might be considered a "niche" aspect of team attitude research, these researchers tested theoretically driven predictions regarding respondent personality traits, thus providing some construct validation support for the new measures. Specifically, consistent with theoretical expectations, they reported that higher Openness to Experiences scores characterized those who preferred virtual teams over face-to-face teams. Although promising, the measure has received little subsequent empirical attention. Theoretically, however, one would expect those with a stronger preference for virtual teams would be more open to working in such teams and would feel stronger satisfaction and affective commitment to such teams.

### Commitment to Virtual Teams

In some cases, of course, more "standard" work attitude measures can be modified to suit a *team*'s focus. For example, in a study of teams comprising graduate-level commerce students from three countries, Powell, Galvin, and Piccoli (2006) examined and compared team member commitment to virtual teams *and* to collocated teams using modified versions of the items that appear in two well-established organizational commitment scales—one that assesses affective commitment and one that assesses normative commitment. The two modified scales exhibited adequate reliability, both in excess of .85, and appear to be related to team member process measures in accordance with the researchers' theorizing. Other researchers interested in team virtuality have taken a similar approach to modifying existing commitment measures (e.g., Johnson, Bettenhausen, & Gibbons, 2009).

## Team Interdisciplinarity

Several scholars have examined team members' attitudes toward interdisciplinary and/or inter-professional teams and team activity. While critical to the accomplishment of many complex tasks, such teams are challenging as members from different backgrounds, and with differing content knowledge and "understandings," grapple with communicating and working effectively together. Not surprisingly, this issue attracts considerable attention in health-care/human service contexts, as well as in aviation and broad-scale emergency management. In each of these contexts, the use of interdisciplinary or interprofessional teams is extensive in both professional training and practice. Below, I discuss a measure that is widely used in healthcare settings to assess team members' beliefs in the value of such teams.

### *Teamwork, Roles, and Responsibilities Scale*

The Interprofessional Attitude Scale (IPAS) was developed to assess the attitudes of *trainees* in health/human services programs (Norris et al., 2015) and comprises five sub-scales. Of particular relevance here is the 9-item "Teamwork, Roles, and Responsibilities Scale" (TRR) subscale, shown in Appendix 11.B. Items focus on respondents' beliefs that trainees/students in healthcare and human service professions will benefit from the collaborative "shared learning" that those in interprofessional groups will experience. Thus, the underlying construct here is the *value* that respondents place on interprofessional teamwork, with high scorers seeing such teamwork in a positive light. Norris et al. (2015) reported that the TRR has a reliability of .91. Although TRR scores are modestly correlated with scores on the other IPAS subscales, confirmatory factor analysis generally supports the independence of the TRR. More recently, Mishoe et al. (2018) administered the TRR before and after a half-day "inter-professional co-curricular learning experience" offered to healthcare students from various sub-disciplines. Scale reliabilities for the first and second administration of the measure were described, perhaps overly enthusiastically, as "acceptable" (.68, .81) and, consistent with expectations, participants' post-training TRR scores exceeded their pre-training scores, thus providing some additional evidence regarding the construct validity of the measure.

### Teamwork "Core Concepts"

Arguably, in order to work successfully in teams, individuals *must endorse and feel positively toward* the core principles, beliefs, and associated behaviors that are deemed to underlie effective teamwork. This premise is reiterated in much practitioner-oriented work that is aimed at those who seek to develop their own capacity for teamwork and those who train such individuals. One of the measures that is used most widely in order to evaluate such initiatives is described below.

## *TeamSTEPPS: T-TAQ*

The Teamwork Attitude Questionnaire (T-TAQ) was developed by Baker, Amodeo, Krokos, Slonim, and Herrera (2010) as part of the broader TeamSTEPPS™ initiative launched several years ago by the US Department of Defense and the Agency for Healthcare Research Quality. The goal of this initiative was to integrate teamwork into healthcare more fully and, in so doing, to improve various healthcare performance indicators. At the time the T-TAQ was developed, there were no existing measures that assessed "*attitudes* towards what research suggests are the *core concepts of teamwork*" (italics mine; Baker et al., 2010, p. 2). Given this rationale, it is perhaps not surprising that each of the 30 scale items assesses the degree to which the respondent expresses *agreement with*, or *endorsement of*, what might be considered aspects of good teamwork or team member practice. Structurally, the T-TAQ is made of five subscales (e.g., monitoring/backup behavior; team leadership). As seen in Appendix 11.B, some T-TAQ items appear to assess preferences, others reflect beliefs, and still others refer to behavioral intentions. Collectively, therefore, this measure appears to capture what is considered the key elements of an "attitude."

The measure has been used in numerous studies, and this research has been cited extensively in both academic and professional outlets. Overall, the reported reliabilities associated with each of the subscales fall within an acceptable range, and the measure is described as having "strong content validity" (Havyer et al., 2013, p. 902). Moreover, there is evidence linking T-TAQ scores to some theoretically relevant variables. For researchers interested in the development, structure, and consequences of these constructs, or as a means by which teamwork training can be assessed, the T-TAQ would appear to have much to offer. Perhaps not surprisingly, therefore, it has been used as an outcome measure in studies examined in meta-evaluative work of healthcare team training initiatives (Hughes et al., 2016; Vertino, 2014). Such studies, typically involving students in professional healthcare programs, are described as providing evidence of the anticipated improvement in team-related attitudes that occurs with teamwork training and/or experience.

## Team Team-Related Attitudes III: Attitudes toward "My Team"

Finally, attention turns to the assessment of individual attitudes toward the *team in which one is a member*. Perhaps not surprisingly, both conceptual work and research conducted to develop and evaluate such measures most closely parallel the larger body of psychological research that examines employees' attitudes, beliefs, and opinions about other commonly examined work foci such as the job, occupation, or organization. Further, this body of work aligns most closely with classic conceptualizations of "attitudes."

Accordingly, as with these other foci, most measures that assess attitudes to "my team" are used to assess one of two key work attitudes: the *satisfaction* that members feel with respect to their team and the *commitment* they have to their team. Further, as in the broader work attitude literature, some of this team-related research is designed to assess either the *development* among individuals who work in teams of a particular team-related attitude, or the potential *outcomes* that may be associated with the team-related attitude. Still others use team attitude scores as "outcome measures" in order to evaluate training/ development programs that are designed to enhance how members feel toward their teams.

The remainder of this review, therefore, focuses on the measurement strategies and related research that has been used to examine team members' *satisfaction* with their work team and team members' *commitment* to their work team. For the most part, I have reported few empirical findings from the studies cited, except as they relate to the construct validity of the measures under consideration and to the nomological net in which these constructs are embedded.

## Team Satisfaction

Over a decade ago, Gevers and Peeters (2009) noted that "team member satisfaction presents itself as an essential aspect of team effectiveness and an important outcome variable for team research" (p. 380). In contrast to the more extensive body of *job satisfaction* research, however, one could certainly argue that efforts to develop team satisfaction measures and to establish their construct validity have been considerably less vigorous, with many researchers using a small set of items that appear to be written for their particular study and context. Also in contrast to job satisfaction literature, little formal attention appears to have been given to what one might refer to as the "structure" of team satisfaction and, hence, to the exploration of whether global or faceted approaches are more compelling, a point I return to later. Nonetheless, dozens of studies have examined members' levels of satisfaction with their teams, and various measures have been used. Across this body of work, most researchers rely, unsurprisingly, on fairly straightforward self-report measures that, typically, are administered to each member of each team. The key approaches that researchers have taken are described below.

### Global Team Satisfaction

*Global* team satisfaction measures are frequently used in team research literature. That said, no particular global measure appears to have established itself as most commonly used or more useful in predicting team member reactions or behavior. This may reflect the fact that differences across these simple measures are slight and that the work associated with developing such measures is relatively straightforward. Most global team satisfaction measures are designed to assess the degree to which team members feel positively about the team to which they belong, considered in its totality; thus, these measures typically focus on the team in general and have very few items. For example, Cronin, Bezrukova, Weingart, and Tinsley (2011) took a particularly streamlined approach, simply asking, "Overall, how satisfied are you with being on this team?" (p. 838), and Gardner and Pierce (2016) asked team members to rate their satisfaction with "The way in which my work group works as a team" (p. 399). Finally, and not surprisingly, most such measures use traditional numeric rating scales on which respondents indicate the extent which they agree with each item (de la Torre-Ruiz, Ferrón-Vilchez, & Ortiz-de-Mandojana, 2014; Medina, 2016; Medina & Srivastava, 2016; Peeters, Rutte, van Tuijl, & Reymen, 2006). Interestingly, however, some researchers who have taken a global satisfaction approach have relied on the classic Kunin Faces (Kunin, 1955) as response anchors (e.g., Cronin et al., 2011; Lloyd & Härtel, 2010).

## "Facets" of Team Satisfaction

Other researchers assess team satisfaction by asking team members about specific aspects, or "facets" of the team (e.g., "my teammates," "the team's task," "the team's performance"). In a few such studies, these are then treated as items on a single scale, thus forming a composite team satisfaction measure (e.g., Lourenço, Dimas, & Rebelo, 2014; Nguyen, Seers, & Hartman, 2007; Van der Vegt, Emans, & Van de Vliert, 2001). More typically, however, researchers treat each facet as reflecting a separate construct, thus providing more precise, or nuanced, information that is likely to be more useful in practice. For example, in their study of engineering students working in project teams over a 13-week period, Gevers and Peeters (2009) administered two separate measures: one, a 3-item measure assessing team members' satisfaction with the team and the other, a 2-item measure assessing member satisfaction with the team project.

As noted earlier, however, relative to the broader job satisfaction literature, the assessment of team satisfaction facets has been given little formal attention. Possibly, this simply reflects the fact that few attempts have been made to delineate what these "team facets" actually might be. Alternatively, it might reflect that the phenomenological experience of teamwork is quite simple and one that aligns particularly well with a global approach to team satisfaction. Accordingly, such a measure might explain as much variance in relevant criteria as any facet-based measure would. On the other hand, it may be, as some work team members might well attest, that it is one or more of the "little things"—that irritate or delight—that garner team member attention and that support a multidimensional view of team satisfaction (Cameron & Allen, 2017). In this regard, qualitative work examining how those who regularly work in teams construe the "team construct," with respect to all its possible facets, would likely be of considerable value in mapping out the bases on which members experience team satisfaction.

Overall, one could argue that no particular measure, or set of measures, emerging from the large body of team satisfaction research appears to be most useful in predicting team member reactions or behavior. That said, a close examination of the various measurement strategies referred to above suggests that each seems conceptually and psychometrically defensible. Finally, formal discussion of the nomological net in which team satisfaction constructs are embedded remains limited. As the linkages summarized in Figure 11.1 depict, however, it seems reasonable to suggest that individual traits (e.g., extraversion; collectivism) may play an important role in shaping satisfaction to one's team. Also reasonable is the suggestion that individuals' reactions to a particular team feature (e.g., virtual vs. face-to-face) would influence their satisfaction with, and affective commitment to, a team with said feature. Team satisfaction, in turn, has implications for the team member behaviors and outcomes depicted in Figure 11.1.

## Team Commitment

Commitment to one's team has also received a fair amount of research attention. Although there is some diversity in the approaches that researchers have taken, most rely on adaptations of measures designed to assess commitment to other work foci—most commonly, the organization. Typically, this is accomplished simply by changing the referent in each item from "my organization" to "my team" and making necessary wording changes to suit the new focus of the construct. Below, I describe the two conceptualizations of "team commitment," and its measurement, that are used in most of the relevant research literature.

### The "OCQ" Approach

Some team commitment research relies on modified versions of the Organizational Commitment Questionnaire (OCQ) developed by Mowday, Steers, and Porter (1979). The 15-item OCQ, for which construct validity is strong, is based on a widely accepted unidimensional "affective" view of commitment characterized by the degree to which an employee accepts the organization's values, is willing to exert effort on behalf of the organization, and desires to remain with the organization. Perhaps not surprisingly, this view of commitment can also be applied to one's team and, indeed, this has been demonstrated using the 8-item measure developed by Bishop and colleagues (Bishop & Scott, 2000; Bishop, Scott & Burroughs, 2000). In this work, the researchers showed that respondents saw clear distinctions between team commitment and other conceptually related attitudes (organizational commitment, satisfaction with coworkers, satisfaction with supervision). Further, they reported relations, consistent with theory, between their team commitment measure and various forms of conflict (Bishop & Scott, 2000) and perceived support (Bishop et al., 2000).

Additionally, in a multi-sample study, Bishop, Scott, Goldsby, and Cropanzano (2005) reported evidence supporting the distinctiveness of their team commitment measure from measures of some other related constructs (e.g., perceived organization support). In this research, and the numerous other studies that have administered this team commitment measure to individual team members (e.g., Lee, Kwon, Shin, Kim, & Park, 2018; Li, Rubenstein, Lin, Wang, & Chen, 2018; Neininger, Lehmann-Willenbrock, Kauffeld, & Henschel, 2010; Rousseau & Aube, 2014) researchers have reported acceptable scale reliabilities, ranging from .79 to .92, and relations between the measures are in general accordance with predictions. The reliable 8-item team-adapted version of the "OCQ-inspired" team commitment measure is shown in Appendix 11.C.

## The Three-Component Model Approach

Other researchers have opted to assess team commitment through the lens of the three-component model (TCM) of commitment. Initially forwarded as a conceptualization of employee commitment to the *organization* (Allen & Meyer, 1990; Meyer & Allen, 1991, 1997), the TCM has been extended to numerous other work foci, including the occupation, organizational change, and one's team. Specifically, the model proposes that commitment to a focal entity is best conceptualized as having three distinct components. Affective commitment refers to one's *desire* to remain with the focal entity, continuance commitment is based on the *costs* associated with leaving the entity, and normative commitment refers to one's *feelings of obligation* to remain. All three are considered to predict the strength of the individual's intention to stay with the entity and to contribute to its success. TCM theorizing further suggests, however, that the three components are best considered in concert, as a profile, the form of which will have implications for the individual's reactions and behavior with respect to the focal entity (Meyer, Stanley & Parfyonova, 2012).

As with the "OCQ-inspired" approach to team commitment assessment described above, numerous researchers have modified one or more of the organization-focused TCM-based commitment measures to suit the team/ group focus. For example, Stinglhamber and colleagues (Bentein, Stinglhamber, & Vandenberghe, 2002; Stinglhamber, Bentein, & Vandenberghe, 2002) developed reliable TCM-based measures assessing affective, continuance, and normative commitment to various foci, including the workgroup. The settings and types of teams in which these measures have been administered include teams in the US military (O'Shea, Goodwin, Driskell, Salas, & Ardison, 2009) and workgroups in a French iron and steel company (Bentein et al., 2002). Studies in which researchers made team-referent modifications to one or more of the three TCM measures reported acceptable scale reliabilities. Further, theoretically relevant links among key variables were observed. For example, in accordance with hypothesizing, Bentein et al. (2002) reported that links between affective commitment to the workgroup and citizenship behavior were target-specific: workgroup commitment was correlated with OCBs directed to the workgroup, but not to OCBs directed to the organization or supervisor.

## Implications and Future Directions for Research and Practice

Over the past several years, as illustrated above, researchers have turned considerable attention to the assessment of team-related attitudes. Arguably, the examination of this interesting line of conceptual and measurement work requires some academic "treasure-hunting" as relevant work is spread across disciplines and professions and, most certainly, is conducted with varying scholarly and practitioner goals in mind.

As noted above and depicted in Figure 11.1, there appear to be three distinguishable, but arguably interrelated, sets of team attitude constructs—those that focus on the *idea* of "teamwork," particular *features* associated with teams, and the *particular team* to which a member belongs. Below, I draw from each line of research in order to discuss its potential implications for practice, and, where relevant, I identify areas that would benefit from more research attention, with respect to both the conceptual articulation and measurement of key attitudes constructs and the assessment of relations embedded in the proposed nomological net.

### The "Idea" of Teamwork

Based on the research summarized above, it appears that individuals differ somewhat with respect to their general orientation toward or preferences for *teamwork* and that these constructs have links to relevant behavior. All else being equal, teams comprising members who share a preference for group work (over solo work) are likely to create a more positive team environment and to perform accordingly. Along with the myriad of other attributes deemed important when selecting for and/or assembling a team (West & Allen, 1997), therefore, human resource practitioners might well try to evaluate how individuals feel about "the idea of teamwork" and, during selection, favor those who have positive attitudes. In this regard, some of the measures noted above (e.g., Team Player Inventory; Preference for Group Work Scale) might be useful additions to an organization's human resource management information system.

It is worth noting that—in comparison to many other individual difference constructs—very little is known about the relative *malleability* (or stability) of one's orientation to or preference for teamwork. Indeed, it may be that, with training, support from one's colleagues, and appropriate attention paid to key team design features, the *idea* of working in teams can be made comfortable for a wide range of employees, even those with little initial attraction to teamwork. Accordingly, practitioners might find the measures noted above to be useful as part of an evaluation of team training, socialization, and job design initiatives.

## Team Features

Within the past decade or so, researchers have begun to examine how people react, attitudinally, to particular *features* associated with teams. Thus far, as outlined above, there is a small body of work examining the assessment of attitudes toward virtual teams, interdisciplinary teams, and the "core concepts" of teamwork. Although less is known about the *antecedents* of these attitudes, suggesting some interesting questions for team researchers to pursue, the attitudes do vary across individuals. Arguably, individuals will contribute more to and will remain longer with a team that has a feature they prefer. Relatedly, it is hypothesized that the presence and/or constancy of virtuality and interdisciplinarity in members' teams will moderate the relations between individuals' attitudes toward these features and both team attitudes (satisfaction; commitment) and team-relevant behavior. Further, as depicted in Figure 11.1, in teams with either of these features, members will likely express more positive attitudes to the feature in question to the extent that they have received some form of briefing, training, or socialization relevant to the feature. Accordingly, organizations that rely on either of these types of teams might explore such developmental possibilities and, in so doing, make use of the relevant measures to assess attitudinal outcomes.

In addition, it seems likely that those who feel positively toward a particular team feature will feel more satisfied with and/or committed to their teams. Potentially, such individuals will also contribute more to their team than will those who find such features unappealing. As shown in Figure 11.1, these effects of attitudes toward team features, on either performance or retention, are hypothesized as being *mediated* by attitudes toward the team and *moderated* by the salience of the team feature and/or the degree to which it is a constant feature of the team. For example, team members with little enthusiasm for virtuality are likely to feel less positively toward their team to the extent that team member interaction is always (vs. only occasionally) virtual. In light of this, organizations might take such preferences into account when selecting members for teams with these particular features. Alternatively, as suggested above, it is possible that well-designed feature-specific team training—and the support necessary to sustain its effects—will pay dividends.

## One's Own Team

Turning to the third line of research reviewed here, there seems little doubt that individuals' attitudes to the *specific* team to which they belong can vary considerably, and that these are shaped by a range of individual, team, and organizational characteristics. Much of this draws directly from research examining *job* satisfaction and *organizational* commitment. In order to conduct credible work examining how any of these team-related attitudes develop, and under what conditions changes take place, researchers and practitioners must have access to valid and reliable attitude measures. In this regard, some of the measures reviewed here may play key roles. Worth noting, of course, is that the process of evaluating construct validity is never really over and that any measurement choice that a researcher or practitioner makes should be made with as much relevant psychometric information as possible. Indeed, if one were to express concern about the "state of play" with respect to measure development strategies used in this sub-field, it might be that the items in some team-related attitude measures appear to be merely modest rewrites of items found in measures assessing other foci (e.g., switching "my organization" to "my team"). The implications for this with respect to construct validity may be non-trivial and might well deserve some research attention.

Further, although detailed commentary on this is beyond the scope of this chapter, some mention of the levels of analysis issue, broadly conceived, seems warranted. Clearly, in order to address the goals that many researchers or practitioners have, an *individual-level* approach to attitude assessment and analysis will be most appropriate and informative, and, indeed whether it has focused on attitudes toward teamwork, attitudes toward specific team features, or attitudes toward the team to which one belongs, *most* of the research referred to here has been conceptualized and conducted at the individual level of analysis. Some team attitude researchers, however, will have *team-level* team composition questions in mind. It might be of interest, for example, to learn whether teams whose members, on average, have a strong commitment to the particular team perform differently than "weak commitment" teams, or there may be interest in learning whether variation in average team-level satisfaction will foreshadow differential rates of team member retention across teams. Alternatively, researchers may choose to study whether all a team needs to doom its ability to perform well is *one* member who dislikes or is dissatisfied with the idea of teamwork, a particular feature of the team, or the team itself. Accordingly, it will be important to use the theoretically appropriate strategy for aggregating individual attitude scores to the group level, and to examine the resultant "group-level attitude" in relation to group-level variables of interest.

## Some Concluding Thoughts and Future Considerations

It is clear that there is considerable interest among researchers and practitioners in understanding and shaping positive team-related attitudes, and, as noted above, there is considerable practitioner value in this body of research. Arguably, however, this literature could be described as somewhat scattered—or perhaps eclectic—and, as such, is challenging to synthesize. Further, although attitudes toward teams, and team-related features, have received a fair amount of research attention, the measurement standards in this body of work in no way appear to rival, or even come close to, those that characterize research that examines attitudes to other work foci such as the job, organization, or profession/occupation. Indeed, many team-related attitude studies appear to rely on measures that have received relatively little construct development work. Needless to say, such work is important and cannot be accomplished on the fly. Even when dealing with attitude constructs that allow for almost seamless substitution of "team" where "job," "organization," or "occupation" might have appeared in the items of established scales, construct validation work seems critical.

That said, this broad, albeit "messier," area of measurement inquiry would seem to have much promise. First, evidence provided by such research can highlight concerns that team members may be feeling and, if acted upon, have the potential to reduce team member dissatisfaction, or team-level conflict, and their numerous attendant sequelae. Given the documented challenges associated with inspiring superior team performance and the links between attitudes, retention, and performance, such information may be useful, even if collected under anonymous conditions from team members, as would be likely. Second, and relatedly, such measures can be used to evaluate the impact that changes in team policies or complex team procedures might have on key team-related attitudes. In this regard, there seems merit in periodic assessment of such constructs, perhaps as part of a broader organization survey that is administered on a regular basis. Third, several of the team-related attitude measures described above are likely useful as part of a more extensive evaluation of team training and other developmental initiatives. Overall, it is reasonable to describe research that examines team-related attitudes as providing valuable information that could help practitioners tailor socialization, training, and team development initiatives.

It appears that the emphasis placed on workplace teams over a quarter-century ago was no "flash in the pan" and that teams are likely to remain a key part of the workplace landscape. Hence, it seems critically important that we understand how team-related attitudes are shaped and how they might shape subsequent behavior. Arguably, however, it is only through research employing clearly articulated constructs and the right measures that this can be achieved.

## References

Allen, N.J. & Hecht, T.D. (2004a). The "romance of teams": Toward an understanding of its psychological underpinnings and implications. *Journal of Occupational and Organizational Psychology, 77*, 439–462.

Allen, N.J. & Hecht, T.D. (2004b). Further thoughts on the romance of teams: A reaction to the commentaries. *Journal of Occupational and Organizational Psychology, 77*, 485–493.

Allen, N.J. & Meyer, J.P. (1990). The measurement and antecedents of affective, continuance and normative commitment to the organization. *Journal of Occupational and Organizational Psychology, 63*, 1–18.

Baker, D.P., Amodeo, A.M., Krokos, K.J., Slonim, A., & Herrera, H. (2010). Assessing teamwork attitudes in healthcare: Development of the TeamSTEPPS teamwork attitudes questionnaire. *Quality & Safety in Health Care, 19*, e49.

Bentein, K., Stinglhamber, F., & Vandenberghe, C. (2002). Organization-, supervisor-, and workgroup-directed commitments and citizenship behaviours: A comparison of models. *European Journal of Work and Organizational Psychology, 11*, 341–362

Bishop, J.W. & Scott, K.D. (2000). An examination of organizational and team commitment in a self-directed team environment. *Journal of Applied Psychology, 85*, 439–450.

Bishop, J.W., Scott, K.D., & Burroughs, S.M. (2000). Support, commitment, and employee outcomes in a team environment. *Journal of Management, 26*, 1113–1132.

Bishop, J.W., Scott, K.D., Goldsby, M.G., & Cropanzano, R. (2005). A construct validity study of commitment and perceived support variables. *Group & Organization Management, 30*, 153–180

Calanca, F., Sayfullina, L., Minkus, L., Wagner, C. & Malmi, E. (2019). Responsible team players wanted: An analysis of soft skill requirements in job advertisements. *EPI Data Science, 8:13*, 8–20.

Cameron, K.A. & Allen, N.J. (2017, July). Revisiting the multidimensional measurement of team member satisfaction. Poster session presented at the meeting of the Interdisciplinary Network for Group Research (InGroup), St. Louis, MO.

Campion, M.A., Medsker, G.J., & Higgs, A.C. (1993). Relations between work group characteristics and effectiveness: Implications for designing effective work groups. *Personnel Psychology, 26*, 823–850.

Cronin, M.A., Bezrukova, K., Weingart, L.R., & Tinsley, C.H. (2011). Subgroups within a team: The role of cognitive and affective integration. *Journal of Organizational Behavior, 32*, 831–849.

de la Torre-Ruiz, J.M., Ferrón-Vilchez, V., & Ortiz-de-Mandojana, N. (2014). Team decision making and individual satisfaction with the team. *Small Group Research, 45*, 198–216.

Decker, W.H., Calo, T.J., Yao, H., & Weer, C.H. (2015). Preference for group work in China and the US. *Cross Cultural Management, 22*, 90–115.

DesMarais, C. (2017). 5 easy ways to improve your team's attitude right now. *Inc.com*. Retrieved from www.inc.com/christina-desmarais/5-easy-ways-to-improve-your-teams-attitude-right-now.html

Devaraj, S. & Jiang, K. (2019). It's about time: A longitudinal adaptation model of high-performance work teams. *Journal of Applied Psychology, 104*, 433–447.

Eagly, A.H. & Chaiken, S. (1993). *The psychology of attitudes*. Fort Worth, TX: Harcourt Brace Jovanovich.

Erez, M. & Earley, P.C. (1987). Comparative analysis of goal-setting strategies across cultures. *Journal of Applied Psychology, 72*, 658–665.

Foote, D.A. & Tang, T.L-P. (2008). Job satisfaction and organizational citizenship: Does commitment make a difference in self-directed teams? *Management Decision, 46*, 933–947.

French, K.A. & Kottke, J.L. (2013). Teamwork satisfaction: Exploring the multilevel interaction of teamwork interest and group extraversion. *Active Learning in Higher Education, 14*, 189–200.

Gardner, D.G. & Pierce, J.L. (2016). Organization-based self-esteem in work teams. *Group Processes & Intergroup Relations, 19*, 394–408.

Gevers, J.M.P. & Peeters, M.A.G. (2009). A pleasure working together? The effects of dissimilarity in team member conscientiousness on team temporal processes and individual satisfaction. *Journal of Organizational Behavior, 30*, 379–400.

Gladstein, D.L. (1984). Groups in context: A model of task group effectiveness. *Administrative Science Quarterly, 29*, 499–517.

Guzzo, R.A. & Dickson, M.W. (1996). Teams in organizations: Recent research on performance and effectiveness. *Annual Review of Psychology, 47*, 307–338.

Hackman, J.R. (1983, November). *A normative model of work team effectiveness*. Technical Report #2: Research Program on Group Effectiveness. New Haven: Yale School of Organization and Management.

Hackman, J.R. (1990). *Groups that work (and those that don't): Creating conditions for effective teamwork*. San Francisco, CA: Jossey-Bass.

Hackman, J.R. (2002). *Leading teams: Setting the stage for great performances*. Boston, MA: Harvard Business School Press.

Havyer, R.D., Wingo, M.T., Comfere, N.I., Nelson, D.R., Halvorsen, A.J., McDonald, F.S., & Reed, D.A. (2013). Teamwork assessment in internal medicine: A systematic review of validity evidence and outcomes. *Journal of General Internal Medicine, 29*, 894–910.

Hendry, G.D., Heinrich, P., Lyon, P.M., Barratt, A.L., Simpson, J.M., Hyde, S.J., Gonsalkorale, S., Hyde, M., & Mgaieth, S. (2005). Helping students understand their learning styles: Effects on study self-efficacy, preference for group work, and group climate. *Educational Psychology, 25*, 395–407.

Hirschfeld, R.R., Jordan, M.H., Feild, H.S., Giles, W.F., & Armenakis, A.A. (2006). Becoming team players: Team members' mastery of teamwork knowledge as a predictor of team task proficiency and observed teamwork effectiveness. *Journal of Applied Psychology, 91*, 467–474.

Hughes, A.M., Gregory, M.E., Joseph, D.L., Sonesh, S.C., Marlow, S.L., Lacerenza, C.N., Benishek, L.E., King, H.B., & Salas, E. (2016). Saving lives: A meta-analysis of team training in healthcare. *Journal of Applied Psychology, 101*, 1266–1304.

Ilarda, E. & Findlay, B.M. (2006). Emotional intelligence and propensity to be a team-player. *E-Journal of Applied Psychology: Emotional Intelligence, 2*, 19–29.

Johnson, S.K., Bettenhausen, K., & Gibbons, E. (2009). Realities of working in virtual teams: Affective and attitudinal outcomes if using computer-mediated communication. *Small Group Research, 40*, 623–649.

Killumets, E., D'Innocenzo, L.D., Maynard, M.T., & Mathieu, J.E. (2015). A multi-level examination of the impact of team interpersonal processes. *Small Group Research, 46*, 227–259.

Kline, T.J.B. (1999a). *Remaking teams: The revolutionary research-based guide that puts theory into practice*. San Francisco, CA: Jossey-Bass Pfeiffer.

Kline, T.J.B. (1999b). The Team Player Inventory: Reliability and validity of a measure of predisposition toward organizational team-working environments. *Journal for Specialists in Group Work, 24*, 102–112.

Kline, T.J.B. & O'Grady, J.K. (2009). Team member personality, team processes and outcome: Relationships within a graduate student team sample. *North American Journal of Psychology, 11*, 369–382.

Kokemuller, N. The effects of team commitment. *Chron.com*. Retrieved from smallbusiness.chron.com/effects-team-commitment-42028.html

Kunin, T. (1955). The construction of a new type of attitude measure. *Personnel Psychology, 8*, 65–77.

Larson, J.R. (2010). *In search of synergy in small group performance.* New York: Psychology Press.

Lee, S., Kwon, S., Shin., S.J., Kim, M., & Park, I. (2018). How team-level and individual-level conflict influences team commitment: A multilevel investigation. *Frontiers in Psychology, 8*, 2365.

Lencioni, P.M. (2002). *The five dysfunctions of a team: A leadership fable.* Jossey-Bass: Hoboken, NJ.

Lencioni, P.M. (2016). *The ideal team player: How to recognize and cultivate the three essential values.* Jossey-Bass: Hoboken, NJ.

Li, G., Rubenstein, A.L., Lin, W., Wang, M., & Chen, X. (2018). The curvilinear effect of benevolent leadership on team performance: The mediating role of team action processes and the moderating role of team commitment. *Personnel Psychology, 71*, 369–397.

Lloyd, S. & Härtel, C. (2010). Intercultural competencies for culturally diverse work teams. *Journal of Managerial Psychology, 25*, 845–875.

Loughry, M.L., Ohland, M.W., & Woehr, D.J. (2014). Assessing teamwork skills for assurance of learning using CATME team tools. *Journal of Marketing Education, 36*, 5–19.

Lourenço, P.R., Dimas, I.D., & Rebelo, T. (2014). Effective workgroups: The role of diversity and culture. *Revista de Psicología del Trabajo y de las Organizaciones, 30*(3), 123–132.

Luse, A., McElroy, J.C., Townsend, A.M., & DeMarie, S. (2013). Personality and cognitive style as predictors of preference for working in virtual teams. *Computers in Human Behavior, 29*, 1825–1832.

MacDonnell, R., O'Neill, T., Kline, T., & Hambley, L. (2009). Bringing group-level personality to the electronic realm: A comparison of face-to-face and virtual contexts. *The Psychology-Manager Journal, 12*, 1–24.

Mathieu, J., Hollenbeck, J.R., van Knippenberg, D., & Ilgen, D.R. (2017). A century of work teams in the Journal of Applied Psychology. *Journal of Applied Psychology, 102*, 452–467.

McGrath, J.E. (1964). *Social psychology: A brief introduction.* New York, NY: Holt, Rinehart and Winston.

Medina, M.N. (2016). Conflict, individual satisfaction with team, and training motivation. *Team Performance Management, 22*, 223–239.

Medina, M.N. & Srivastava, S. (2016). The role of extraversion and communication methods on an individual's satisfaction with the team. *Journal of Organizational Psychology, 16*, 78–92.

Meyer, J.P. & Allen, N.J. (1991). A three-component conceptualization of organizational commitment. *Human Resource Management Review, 1*, 61–89.

Meyer, J.P. & Allen, N.J. (1997). *Commitment in the workplace: Theory, research, and application.* Thousand Oaks, CA: Sage Publications.

Meyer, J.P., Stanley, L.J., & Parfyonova, N.M. (2012). Employee commitment in contexts: The nature and implication of commitment profiles. *Journal of Vocational Behavior, 80*, 1–16.

Mishoe, S. C., Tufts, K. A., Diggs, L. A., Blando, J. D., Claiborne, D. M., Hoch, J., & Walker, M. L. (2018). Health professions students' attitudes toward teamwork before and after an interprofessional education co-curricular experience. *Journal of Research in Interprofessional Practice and Education, 8*, 1–16.

Mowday, R.T., Steers, R.M., & Porter, L.W. (1979). The measurement of organizational commitment. *Journal of Vocational Behavior, 14*, 224–247

Neininger, A., Lehmann-Willenbrock, N., Kauffeld, S., & Henschel, A. (2010). Effects of team and organizational commitment–A longitudinal study. *Journal of Vocational Behavior, 76*, 567–579.

Neo, B., Sellbom, M., Smith, S. F., & Lilienfeld, S. O. (2018). Of boldness and badness: Insights into workplace malfeasance from a triarchic psychopathy model perspective. *Journal of Business Ethics, 149*, 187–205.

Norris, J., Carpenter, J.G., Eaton, J., Guo, J., Lassche, M., Pett, M. & Blumenthal, D.K. (2015). The development and validation of the Interprofessional Attitudes Scale: Assessing the Interprofessional attitudes of students in the health professions. *Academic Medicine, 90*, 1394–1400.

Nguyen, N.T., Seers, A., & Hartman, N.S. (2007). Putting a good face on impression management: Team citizenship and team satisfaction. *Journal of Behavioral & Applied Management, 9*, 148–168.

O'Neill, T.A. & Kline, T.J.B. (2008). Personality as a predictor of teamwork: A business simulator study. *North American Journal of Psychology, 10*, 65–77.

O'Shea, P.G., Goodwin, G.F., Driskell, J.E., Salas, E., & Ardison, S. (2009). The many faces of commitment: Facet-level links to performance in military contexts. *Military Psychology, 21*, 5–23.

Peeters, M.A., Rutte, C.G., van Tuijl, H.F., & Reymen, I.M. (2006). The big five personality traits and individual satisfaction with the team. *Small Group Research, 37*, 187–211.

Powell, A., Galvin, J., & Piccoli, G. (2006). Antecedents to team member commitment from near and far: A comparison between collocated and virtual teams. *Information Technology & People, 19*, 299–322.

Rousseau, V. & Aube, C. (2014). The reward-performance relationship in work teams: The role of leaders behaviors and team commitment. *Group Processes & Intergroup Relations, 17*, 645–662.

Salas, E., Shuffler, M.L., Thayer, A.L., Bedwell, W.L., & Lazzara, E.H. (2014). Understanding and improving teamwork in organizations: A scientifically based practical guide. *Human Resource Management, 54*, 599–622.

Shaw, J.D., Duffy, M.K., & Stark, E.M. (2000). Interdependence and preference for group work: Main and congruence effects on the satisfaction and performance of group members. *Journal of Management, 26*, 259–279.

Shuffler, M.L., Diazgranados, D., Maynard, M.T., & Salas, E. (2018). Developing, sustaining, and maximizing team effectiveness: An integrative, dynamic perspective of team development interventions. *Academy of Management Annals, 12*, 688–724.

Stark, E.M., Shaw, J.D., & Duffy, M.K. (2007). Preference for group work, winning orientation, and social loafing behavior in groups. *Group & Organization Management, 32*, 699–723.

Staw, B.M. & Epstein, L.D. (2000). What bandwagons bring: Effects of popular management techniques on corporate performance, reputation, and CEO pay. *Administrative Science Quarterly, 45*, 523–556.

Stinglhamber, F., Bentein, K., & Vandenberghe, C. (2002). Extension of the three-component model of commitment to five foci. *European Journal of Psychological Assessment, 18,* 123–138.

Sundstrom, E., De Meuse, K.P., & Futrell, D. (1990). Work teams: Applications and effectiveness. *American Psychologist, 45,* 120–133.

TRISOFT. (2017). 7 Things You Can Do To Improve Your Team's Attitude. Retrieved from medium.com/remote-symfony-team/7-things-you-can-do-to-improve-your-teams-attitude-d9edfca4b30a

Turner, M.E. (Ed.) (2001). *Groups at work: Theory and research.* Erlbaum: Mahwah, NJ.

Van der Vegt, G.S., Emans, B.J.M., & Van de Vliert, E. (2001). Patterns of interdependence in work teams: A two-level investigation of the relations with job and team satisfaction. *Personnel Psychology, 54,* 51–69.

Vertino, K.A. (2014). Evaluation of a TeamSTEPPS initiative on staff attitudes toward teamwork. *Journal of Nursing Administration, 44,* 97–102.

Wagner, J.A. (1995). Studies of individualism-collectivism: Effects on cooperation in groups. *Academy of Management Journal, 38,* 152–172.

West, M.A. & Allen, N.J. (1997). Selecting for team work. In N. Anderson & P. Herriot (Eds.), *International handbook of selection and assessment* (pp. 493–506). Chichester, UK: Wiley.

West, M.A., Brodbeck, F.C., & Richter, A.W. (2004). Does the "romance of teams" exist? The effectiveness of teams in experimental and field settings. *Journal of Occupational and Organizational Psychology, 63,* 467–474.

# APPENDIX 11.A
# MEASURES ASSESSING REACTIONS
# TO THE IDEA OF TEAMWORK

### A-1 TPI: Team Player Inventory (Kline, 1999)

| |
|---|
| 1. I enjoy working on team/group projects. |
| 2. Team/group work easily allows others to not "pull their weight." (R) |
| 3. Work that is done as a team/group is better than the work done individually. |
| 4. I do my best work alone rather than in a team/group. |
| 5. Team/group work is overrated in terms of the actual results produced. (R) |
| 6. Working in a team/group gets me to think more creatively. |
| 7. Teams/groups are used too often, when individual work would be more effective. (R) |
| 8. My own work is enhanced when I am in a team/group situation. |
| 9. My experiences working in a team/group have been primarily negative. (R) |
| 10. More solutions/ideas are generated when working in a team/group situation than when working alone. |

Item response scale: 1 (disagree completely) to 5 (agree completely). Items drawn from Kline (1999b). The Team Player Inventory: Reliability and validity of a measure of predisposition toward organizational team-working environments. *Journal for Specialists in Group Work, 24,* 102–112.

### A-2 Preference for Group Work Scale
### (Shaw, Duffy, & Stark, 2000)

| |
|---|
| 1. When I have a choice, I try to work in a group instead of by myself |
| 2. I prefer to work on a team rather than on individual tasks |
| 3. Working in a group is better than working alone |
| 4. Given the choice, I would rather do a job where I can work alone rather than do a job where I have to work with others in a group (R) |
| 5. I prefer to do my own work and let others do theirs (R) |
| 6. I like to interact with others when working on projects |
| 7. I personally enjoy working with others |

Item response scale: 1 (strongly disagree) to 7 (strongly agree). Items drawn from Shaw et al. (2000).

## A-3 Team Commitment Scale (Foote & Tang, 2008)

| |
|---|
| 1.  I am proud to tell others that my company uses the team concept |
| 2.  I am extremely glad our company chose the team concept over other ideas |
| 3.  This company's decision to implement the team concept was a definite mistake (R) |
| 4.  In the long run, there is not much to be gained by using the team concept (R) |
| 5.  I talk up the team concept to my peers as a positive change for our company |
| 6.  The team concept really inspires the best in me in the way of job performance |
| 7.  I really care about the success of the team concept |
| 8.  I am willing to put in a great deal of effort beyond that normally expected in order to help the team concept be successful |
| 9.  It would take very little change in my present circumstances to cause me to give up on the team concept (R) |
| 10.  I feel very little loyalty to the team concept (R) |

*Source*: Items drawn from Foote & Tang, 2008.

*Note*: Item response scale: 1 (disagree completely) to 7 (agree completely).

# APPENDIX 11.B
# MEASURES ASSESSING REACTIONS TO TEAM TYPES, FEATURES, AND CONTEXTS

## B-1 Preference for Working in Virtual Teams
### (Luse et al., 2013)*

| |
|---|
| 1. When I have a choice, I would rather work in virtual teams than by myself |
| 2. I prefer to work on a virtual team task than on an individual task |
| 3. Working in a virtual group is better than working alone |
| 4. Given the choice, I would rather do a job where I can work alone rather than do a job where I have to work with others in a virtual team (R) |
| 5. I would be as comfortable working on a virtual team as I would a face-to-face team |
| 6. If given the appropriate technology, I can be just as effective working on a virtual team as I can on a face-to-face team |
| 7. I could not feel a part of a team that did not meet face-to-face (R) |
| 8. I would participate as easily on a team that used chat rooms, e-mail, and conference calls to communicate with my fellow team members as I could in face-to-face discussions |

*Source*: Items drawn from Luse et al. (2013).

*Notes*: Item response scale:1 (disagree completely) to 5 (agree completely).
* First four items adapted from Shaw et al. (2000) with referent changed.

## B-2 Interprofessional Attitudes Scale: Teamwork, Roles & Responsibilities Sub-scale (Norris et al., 2015)

| |
|---|
| 1. Shared learning before graduation will help me become a better team worker. |
| 2. Shared learning will help me think positively about other professionals. |
| 3. Learning with other students will help me become a more effective member of a health care team. |
| 4. Shared learning with other health sciences students will increase my ability to understand clinical problems. |
| 5. Patients would ultimately benefit if health sciences students worked together to solve patient problems. |
| 6. Shared learning with other health sciences students will help me communicate better with patients and other professionals. |

| 7. I would welcome the opportunity to work on small-group projects with other health sciences students. |
| 8. It is not necessary for health sciences students to learn together. |
| 9. Shared learning will help me understand my own limitations. |

*Source*: Items drawn from Norris et al. (2015).

*Note*: Item response scale: 1 (strongly disagree) to 5 (strongly agree).

## B-3 TEAMSTEPPS: *Teamwork Attitude Questionnaire (T-TAQ)* (Baker et al., 2010)

| **Team Structure** |
| 1. It is important to ask patients and their families for feedback regarding patient care. |
| 2. Patients are a critical component of the care team. |
| 3. This facility's administration influences the success of direct care teams. |
| 4. A team's mission is of greater value than the goals of individual team members. |
| 5. Effective team members can anticipate the needs of other team members. |
| 6. High performing teams in health care share common characteristics with high performing teams in other industries. |
| **Leadership** |
| 7. It is important for leaders to share information with team members. |
| 8. Leaders should create informal opportunities for team members to share information. |
| 9. Effective leaders view honest mistakes as meaningful learning opportunities. |
| 10. It is a leader's responsibility to model appropriate team behavior. |
| 11. It is important for leaders to take time to discuss with their team members plans for each patient. |
| 12. Team leaders should ensure that team members help each other out when necessary. |
| **Situation Monitoring** |
| 13. Individuals can be taught how to scan the environment for important situational cues. |
| 14. Monitoring patients provides an important contribution to effective team performance. |
| 15. Even individuals who are not part of the direct care team should be encouraged to scan for and report changes in patient status. |
| 16. It is important to monitor the emotional and physical status of other team members. |
| 17. It is appropriate for one team member to offer assistance to another who may be too tired or stressed to perform a task. |

| | |
|---|---|
| 18. | Team members who monitor their emotional and physical status on the job are more effective. |
| **Mutual Support** | |
| 19. | To be effective, team members should understand the work of their fellow team members. |
| 20. | Asking for assistance from a team member is a sign that an individual does not know how to do his/her job effectively. |
| 21. | Providing assistance to team members is a sign that an individual does not have enough work to do. |
| 22. | Offering to help a fellow team member with his/her individual work tasks is an effective tool for improving team performance. |
| 23. | It is appropriate to continue to assert a patient safety concern until you are certain that it has been heard. |
| 24. | Personal conflicts between team members do not affect patient safety. |
| **Communication** | |
| 25. | Teams that do not communicate effectively significantly increase their risk of committing errors. |
| 26. | Poor communication is the most common cause of reported errors. |
| 27. | Adverse events may be reduced by maintaining an information exchange with patients and their families. |
| 28. | I prefer to work with team members who ask questions about information I provide. |
| 29. | It is important to have a standardized method for sharing information when handing off patients. |
| 30. | It is nearly impossible to train individuals how to be better communicators. |

*Source*: Reprinted with permission from Baker et al. (2010).

*Note*: Item response scale: Strongly disagree (SD) = 0; Moderately disagree (MD) = 1; Somewhat disagree (SWD) = 2; Somewhat agree (SA) = 3; Moderately agree (MA) = 4; Strongly agree (SA) = 5.

# APPENDIX 11.C
# MEASURES ASSESSING
# ATTITUDES TO "MY TEAM"

## C-1 Team Satisfaction Measures (various)

### *Single-item measures:*

"Overall, how satisfied are you with being on this team?"

The 5 "Kunin Faces" (Kunin, 1955) were used as response anchors. From Cronin et al. (2011).

"The way in which my work group works as a team"

Item response scale: 1= very dissatisfied; 5= very satisfied. From Gardner and Pierce (2016).

### *Multiple-item measures*

| Satisfaction with the Team Scale |
| --- |
| 1. Taken as a whole, I was satisfied with the composition of our design team. |
| 2. Taken as a whole, things went pleasantly within our design team. |
| 3. If I ever had to participate in a similar project again, I would like to do it with this team. |

*Source*: Reprinted with permission from Peeters et al. (2006).

*Note*: Item response scale: 1 = very dissatisfied; 5 = very satisfied.

## C-2 Team Commitment Measures

### *Team Commitment Scales*

| |
| --- |
| 1. I talk up (brag about) this team to my friends as a great team to work on. |
| 2. I would accept almost any job in order to keep working with this team. |
| 3. I find that my values and the team's values are very similar. |
| 4. I am proud to tell others that I am part of this team. |
| 5. This team really inspires the very best in me in the way of job performance. |
| 6. I am extremely glad that I chose this team to work with over other teams. |
| 7. I really care about the fate of this team. |
| 8. For me this is the best of all possible teams with which to work. |

*Source*: Reprinted with permission from Bishop and Scott (2000).

*Note*: Item response scale: 1 (strongly disagree) to 6 (strongly agree).

## *Affective Commitment to My Team*

| |
|---|
| 1.  I would be very happy to spend the rest of my career with this work group |
| 2.  I enjoy discussing my work group with people outside it |
| 3.  I do not feel like "part of the family" with my work group (R) |
| 4.  I do not feel "emotionally attached" to this work group (R) |
| 5.  This work group has a great deal of personal meaning for me |
| 6.  I do not feel a *strong* sense of belonging to my work group (R) |

*Source*: Reprinted with permission from Johnson et al. (2009).

*Note*: Item response scale: 1 (strongly disagree) to 5 (strongly agree).

## *Normative Commitment to "my team"*

| |
|---|
| 1.  Even if it had been to my advantage, I do not feel it would have been right to leave my team. |
| 2.  I would feel guilty if I left my team |
| 3.  My team deserved my loyalty |
| 4.  I would not have left my team during the project because I had a sense of obligation to the people in it |

*Source*: Reprinted with permission from Powell et al. (2006).

*Note*: Item response scale: 0 (best) to 6 (worst).

# Part III

# CONCLUSION

# 12

# CRITICAL EVALUATION OF THE LITERATURE AND A CALL FOR FUTURE RESEARCH

*Nathan A. Bowling, Valerie I. Sessa, and Catrina Notari*

As is apparent from the previous chapters, organizational researchers have studied a variety of job attitudes, opinions, and beliefs. Although this research has led to considerable scientific progress within each attitude, the previous chapters noted that more research is needed. In this final chapter, we critically evaluate the existing literature as a whole, and we discuss areas that require further research. We focus our attention here on themes that cut across the many constructs examined earlier in this book. Our ability to evaluate the job attitude literature from this "macro" perspective was aided by the organization of the previous chapters: Chapters 3 through 11 each used a similar structure to summarize the research on their respective construct. The inclusion of parallel content across the chapters assisted us in understanding the literature in its entirety, in comparing and contrasting constructs, and in recognizing general themes that are present throughout the job attitude literature. We divide the current chapter into four main sections: (a) What are the constructs that we are interested in?, (b) How are we measuring these constructs?, (c) Generally ignored substantive questions, and (d) Organizational uses and interventions.

## What Are the Constructs of Interest?

In this section, we address the following issues: (a) Defining our constructs and relating them to relevant literature, (b) Fitting constructs together, and (c) Addressing construct proliferation and redundancy.

### *Defining Our Constructs and Relating Them to Relevant Literature*

#### *Is "Job Attitude" the Correct Term?*

We used competency 7 from SIOP's Guidelines for Education and Training in Industrial-Organizational Psychology (Society for Industrial and Organizational Psychology, Inc, 2016), titled "Attitude Theory, Measurement, and Change" as the basis for developing this book. This book includes the topics suggested in the competency (engagement, global and facet job satisfaction, job involvement, organizational commitment, and perceptions of support and fairness), two additional topics, as suggested by our reviewers (organizational identification and job embeddedness) and team-level attitudes. In addition, as suggested by the competency, we included a chapter reviewing the basics of the larger social psychology literature on attitude theory.

As this book and the subsequent topic chapters written by experts in the field unfolded, we quickly realized that the term "job attitudes" has often been used by organizational researchers as a catch-all phrase for a number of workplace psychological constructs. We found that our chapter experts used the terms "perceptions" (Chapters 3 and 4 on Organizational Justice and Perceptions of Organizational Support), "identity" (Chapters 5 and 6 on Organizational Identity and Job Involvement), "bonds" (Chapters 7 and 8 on Workplace Commitment and Job Embeddedness), and "motivational state" (Chapter 10 on Employee Engagement) with only Chapter 9 on Job Satisfaction using the term "attitude."

We believe that referring to these psychological constructs as "attitudes" (even if we know or suspect that they are not, in fact, attitudes) may be hindering our understanding and the development of the constructs, limiting our due diligence in keeping up with related literature in social psychology and narrowing our understanding of how these constructs might relate to each other. A future book on these topics, therefore, might include not just a primer on attitudes, but also ones on perception, identity, bonds, and states.

### Is "Job Attitude" the Correct Term

As seen in this book, "job attitudes" include a number of targets other than "the job." Although some constructs do focus on an employee's current position, others focus on their work, other people in the organization, on their organization as a whole, or on the employee themselves. In addition, for some constructs, the target is not necessarily clear. Job satisfaction, for example, often includes satisfaction with daily duties (jobs), satisfaction with direct managers and team members (other people), as well as satisfaction with higher-level administration and organizational policies (organizational level; see chapter 9). Similarly, the engagement literature uses the terms job engagement as well as employee engagement (see chapter 10). We suggest that referring to these psychological constructs without being clear about the target can also limit our understanding of the construct, how the constructs fit together, and how we measure the construct. Chapter 7, which focuses on Workplace Commitments, addresses this directly by suggesting we carefully consider each target separately.

### Research on These Constructs Should Draw More from Social Psychology Literature

Much can be gained by considering the intersection between social psychology and industrial-organizational psychology. Such an interdisciplinary approach is particularly relevant to the study of job attitudes and other constructs. Social psychology offers a rich literature, not just on attitudes, but also on perceptions, identity, bonds, and psychological states. Indeed, there are already several examples of organizational researchers borrowing concepts from attitude theory and research. Research has found, for instance, that two important concepts from social psychology—attitude strength (Schleicher, Smith, Casper, Watt, & Greguras, 2015) and situational strength (Bowling, Khazon, Meyer, & Burrus, 2015)—moderate job satisfaction's relationship with job performance.

We offer a few additional ideas here, but acknowledge that we cannot do justice to the social psychology literature and its connections with the constructs in this book. Research on event perception (see, for example, Zacks, 2020) might be useful for researchers interested in perceived organizational justice and perceived organizational support. Understanding how people partition ongoing organizational experiences into segments, how they structure those segments, how segments are remembered and linked, and outcomes of those memories might advance our understanding of perception development and outcomes of perceptions in organizations. Research on self and social identity (see Ellemers, Spears, & Doosje, 2002) might help organizational researchers better understand how identities are activated and their influence on their perceptual, affective, and behavioral responses. Research on attachment theory (see, for example, Mikulincer & Shaver, 2003) suggests that adults attach or form bonds not just with individuals (including supervisors and co-workers), but also with teams and organizations. Furthermore, there may be more than one sort of bond ranging from acquiescence or bonding with someone or some entity because there is no other alternative to identity or merging of oneself with the attachment target (Klein, Molloy, & Brinsfield, 2012). While there are many possible linkages between the attachment literature and the organizational literature, it might be interesting to better understand the link between proximity seeking as a strategy of the attachment behavioral system when a person has a need for support (Bowlby, 1982/1969) and organizational research on withdrawal behaviors.

Importantly, organizational researchers might not just use the literature to inform the development of specific constructs and their relationships to outcomes of interest, but they can also extend the social psychological literature. Basic social psychological research is often designed to expand our fundamental knowledge about the world around us; organizational research, on the other hand, is often designed to find solutions to real-world problems. Social psychology researchers in the area of attitudes and attitude change, for example, are often interested in better understanding the components of attitudes, how attitudes develop and change. That is, they are interested in understanding attitudes themselves. While it is useful for organizational researchers to understand this research and literature, we can contribute to the understanding of that construct by understanding how people use attitudes in their everyday life, such as at work.

Based on the above three issues, we recommend refining the Job Attitude competency and our own language to be more accurate and encompassing. Perhaps a better term is "Workplace Psychological Constructs." We will be using this new term throughout the remainder of this chapter. Further, we suggest that the SIOP competency should be modified to read as follows:

> Workplace psychological constructs, including perceptions, identities, commitments, and other bonds, attitudes, and motivational states are important for quality of work life, for diagnosing problems in organizations, and in regards to their relation to behavioral intentions and behaviors at work. Some of the workplace psychological constructs typically studied by I-O psychologists include, but are not limited to, perceptions of justice and support, organizational identity, job involvement, workplace commitments, job embeddedness, satisfaction (general and facets), and engagement.
>
> I-O psychologists should also be aware of the extensive social psychological literature connected to these constructs in areas such as perception, identity, bonds, attitudes, and motivational states. In particular, I-O psychologists must know how these constructs are formed and changed and how they relate to behaviors of interest in organizations.

### Fitting Workplace Psychological Constructs together

A side effect of focusing on a single workplace psychological construct within a given study is that we know surprisingly little about how various psychological constructs relate to each other. Although global job satisfaction and affective organizational commitment are strongly correlated (Meyer, Stanley, Herscovitch, & Topolnytsky, 2002), for example, the causal nature of the relationship is unclear. Does satisfaction cause commitment? Does commitment cause satisfaction? Or is their relationship the result of satisfaction and commitment sharing many of the same causes?

Based on the information in the chapters, in particular the nomological network figures, we offer one suggested model to begin the conversation (see Figure 12.1). Most of the nomological networks in this book include organizational factors or perceptions of organizational factors on the antecedent side of their models. Our model begins with these as antecedents. According to Klein et al. (2012), identity, commitment, and instrumental bonds are on a continuum of types of bonds from defining oneself in terms of the job or organization (identity) to embracement of the bond (commitment) to acceptance of the bond (job embeddedness). According to the nomological networks, these bonds are stimulated by perceptions; thus, Organizational Identity, Job Involvement, Workplace Commitments, and Job Embeddedness are in the middle of the model. Many of the nomological networks place job satisfaction and employee

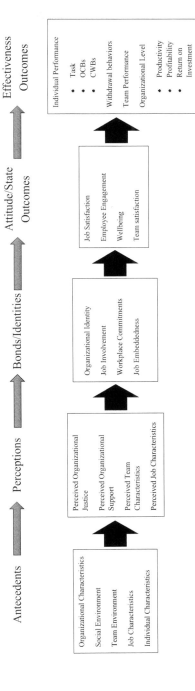

*Figure 12.1* Suggested Nomological Network of Workplace Psychological Constructs.

engagement on the consequence side of their models. Interestingly, few of the nomological networks suggest moderated relationships or other more complex relationships with other workplace psychological constructs, so we have not included them in our model. Much more theory and research is needed to better understand how these constructs are interrelated.

Another option might be to distinguish between constructs based on their objects and develop separate (but related) models. Indeed, the object at which the construct is directed is a fundamental means of categorizing the construct (see Bohner & Dickel, 2011). This suggests, for example, that psychological constructs targeting one's job can be placed into one construct category, while constructs directed at one's employer can be placed in a separate construct category.

### Construct Redundancy and Proliferation

On a related topic, we need to ask the question, what are the constructs we are interested in and are we including too few or too many? When looking at the constructs, definitions, and measures, two issues become apparent. First, in considering the field as a whole, are we missing any constructs? Our proposal reviewers, for example, suggested we add organizational identity and job embeddedness to our original list of chapters. And Allen, this volume, suggested that we add work team psychological constructs into our field as well. Should additional constructs be included as workplace psychological constructs?

Second, it is important to consider whether it is necessary to retain all of the constructs described in the earlier chapters of this book. That is, might the literature include too many construct distinctions, thus understating construct similarity? This problem, which is commonly referred to as the "jangle fallacy" (see, for example, Shuck, Ghosh, Zigarmi, & Nimon, 2013), is indeed common across various other organizational research topics. Construct proliferation, for instance, has been identified within workplace aggression (Hershcovis, 2011), leadership (Shaffer, DeGeest, & Li, 2016) and employee personality (Judge, Erez, Bono, & Thoresen, 2002) literatures. Drawing unnecessary construct distinctions is problematic because it needlessly complicates the literature and makes it difficult for researchers to build off of previous findings from other researchers. Excessive definitional overlap undermines our understanding of these concepts and makes it difficult to determine whether the instruments researchers have developed actually measure the constructs they were designed to assess.

Many of the previous chapters do suggest the necessity of additional definitional work to clarify and come to consensus on what exactly the construct is and what it is not. Indeed, there are conceptual and empirical bases supporting the lack of distinctiveness of many of the constructs reviewed in the previous chapters. Consider, for example, three ostensibly distinct workplace psychological constructs: perceived organizational support (Eisenberger,

Huntington, Hutchison, & Sowa, 1986), organizational identification (Mael & Tetrick, 1992), and affective organizational commitment (Allen & Meyer, 1990). Theoretically, social exchange theory and social enhancement processes suggest that perceived organizational support should lead to organizational identity and organizational commitment (see Stinglhamber & Caesans, Chapter 4). In addition, others have suggested that commitment and identity can both be considered a type of bond (see Klein et al., 2012). Furthermore, each of these constructs is directed at the same object—the participant's employer. Thus, there is a theoretical basis for expecting a strong relationship between these variables. Meta-analyses have found that affective organizational commitment is strongly related to both perceived organizational support ($\rho = .73$; Rhoades & Eisenberger, 2002) and organizational identification ($\rho = .78$; Riketta, 2005) and that perceived organizational support is strongly related to organizational identification ($\rho = .55$, Kurtessis et al., 2015). Little research addresses why these constructs are related. They may be related as suggested by theory, because those taking the instruments are unable to distinguish between the concepts, or because there is content overlap within the instruments.

To examine the possibility of overlap between measures, we informally reviewed the way these three constructs have been measured and found a close connection between the affective commitment measure (Allen & Meyer, 1990) and organizational identification using the OIQ (Cheney, 1982, 1983, as cited in Wu et al., Chapter 5, p. 111). Wu et al. (Chapter 5) states that the OIQ (Cheney, 1982, 1983) is the second most common organizational identification instrument used. We did not see as much direct overlap between affective commitment items and other organizational identification measures, although there were items that were similar. See Table 12.1.

*Table 12.1* Similar Items within the Affective Commitment Scale (Allen & Meyer, 1990) and the Organizational Identification Questionnaire (Cheney, 1982)

| *Affective Commitment Scale (8 item scale)* | *OIQ (25 item scale)* |
| --- | --- |
| I would be happy to spend the rest of my career with this organization. | I would be quite willing to spend the rest of my career with [Organization X]. |
| I enjoy discussing my organization with people outside it. | I talk up [Organization X] to my friends as a great company to work for. |
| I really feel as if this organization's problems are my own. | In general, I view [Organization X]'s problems as my problems. |
| I do not feel like "part of the family" at my organization (R). | I would describe [Organization X] as a large "family" in which most members feel a sense of belonging. |
| I do not feel "emotionally attached" to this organization (R). | I have warm feelings toward [Organization X] as a place to work. |

We found little item overlap between the POS scale (Eisenberger et al., 1986) and affective commitment (Allen & Meyer, 1990). However, there were some similar items between the POS scale and the OIQ scale (for example, POS—"The organization shows very little concern for me"(R) and OIQ—"I feel that [Organization X] cares about me"). In addition, Saks and Gruman (Chapter 10) and Diefendorff et al. (Chapter 6) discuss the overlap between various measures of engagement and organizational identity, job involvement, commitment, and job satisfaction. Considering the field as a whole should help clarify both definitional and measurement issues. This will help scholars draw clearer distinctions and boundaries between the constructs.

## Dealing with Construct Proliferation

How should researchers resolve the possible overabundance of workplace psychological constructs? We offer two suggestions. First, researchers could use item sorting tasks (e.g., Anderson & Gerbing, 1991) to examine the extent to which workers can consistently assign items to their corresponding construct category. This approach requires researchers first to create construct definitions that are easily understood by participants. After providing participants with these construct definitions, researchers can then ask participants to assign each item to one—and only one—of the constructs. Item sorting tasks typically provide participants with a minimum of two constructs to which to assign each item, and they include items drawn from a minimum of two ostensibly distinct scales. If participants are unable to consistently assign a given item to its "correct" construct (i.e., the construct that the researcher intended the item to assess), then it may indicate one of two things: (a) that constructs are not as conceptually distinct as previously thought or (b) that the scales include content that fails to reflect real differences between constructs adequately.

A second approach to assessing the extent to which construct proliferation is a problem involves first developing distinct nomological networks for each ostensibly distinct workplace psychological construct (see Cronbach & Meehl, 1955). Researchers could then test whether ostensibly distinct constructs relate to external variables in a pattern that is consistent with those described in the nomological network. To examine the distinctiveness of organizational commitment and perceived organizational support, for instance, researchers would need to develop nomological networks that identify differences in the external variables that relate to these two focal constructs. Collectively, the previous chapters suggest that the nomological networks for various constructs are quite similar to each other. More work is thus needed to identify differences in the nomological networks of similar constructs.

## Measurement Issues

In the previous section we discussed problems in how various workplace psychological constructs have been conceptualized. We now discuss three measurement-related issues: (a) the failure to use conventional scale development procedures, (b) the problem of constructs being confounded with a particular scale, and (c) over-reliance on self-report measures.

### *Failure to Use Conventional Scale Development Procedures*

Developing a valid psychological measure requires considerable effort. Fortunately, guidelines exist to help researchers create psychometrically sound measures (see DeVellis, 2012; Hinkin, 1998; Spector, 1991). In short, this process involves (a) developing a clear definition of the construct of interest, (b) writing several items that correspond to the construct definition, (c) conducting pilot testing aimed at improving the quality of those items, (d) using item analyses to identify the most effective items, and (e) examining the reliability and validity of the resulting scales (for example articles that have used these procedures, see Bowling et al., 2017; Ferris, Brown, Berry, & Lian, 2008; Judge, Erez, Bono, & Thoresen, 2003).

Because scientific progress in any research area depends upon effective measurement, the creation of valid measures of a given construct should precede substantive research on that construct. Unfortunately, however, it appears that substantive research on a given workplace psychological construct has sometimes preceded any systematic scale development effort. Spector and Jex (1998), in fact, described a similar state of affairs within occupational stress literature:

> Many scales are introduced to the field in an empirical paper in which the scale was used. Other researchers looking for a measure of that construct will begin to use the scale, despite only limited information about psychometric properties.
>
> (p. 365)

An informal review of scales described in the previous chapters suggests that some were, in fact, developed in a manner that was mostly consistent with conventional scale development procedures (e.g., the scale by Colquitt, 2001 and Salanova, Gonzalez-Roma, & Bakker, 2002); others, however, were developed in a manner that makes only partial use of those procedures (e.g., the scales by Cammann, Fichman, Jenkins, & Klesh, 1979 and Peeters, Rutte, van Tuijl, & Reymen, 2006). Does this imply that the latter scales are invalid? Not necessarily. In fact, subsequent research may find support for the validity of an existing measure that was created without the use of conventional scale development methods. Bowling and Hammond (2008), for instance, used meta-analysis to summarize construct validity evidence for the MOAQ job satisfaction subscale nearly 30 years after Cammann et al. (1979) first introduced the scale. Despite the potential usefulness of this post hoc approach, we encourage researchers to use standard scale development procedures to guide the creation of any new workplace psychological construct scale. Applying these procedures will maximize the validity of a new scale, thus enhancing the quality of any subsequent substantive research that uses it. It may also be worthwhile to reevaluate the validity of existing scales that weren't developed using conventional scale development procedures.

### *Workplace Psychological Constructs Are often Confounded with a Particular Scale*

Some of the workplace psychological constructs described in the prior chapters are virtually synonymous with a particular measure. Perceived organizational support, for instance, is almost always assessed using Eisenberger et al.'s (1986) scale. This raises an important question: Is it a problem to confound a construct with a particular scale? We believe that it is. It is possible that the idiosyncrasies of a given measure may produce results that would differ from those of alternative measures of the same construct. And indeed, alternative measures of a given construct often do yield different results. Riketta (2005), for example, found that the two most commonly used measures of organizational identification—the Mael and Tetrick (1992) scale and the Organizational Identification Questionnaire (Cheney, 1982, 1983)—often yield distinct results. Differences in results obtained from ostensibly interchangeable measures may occur because of seemingly trivial differences in item content written by different research teams, or because different research teams define a given construct differently from each other (e.g., they may disagree about the dimensions that should be included within a given construct). We thus encourage researchers to create alternative measures of any workplace psychological construct that is currently dominated by a single scale. Doing so will help ensure that the findings attributed to a given construct aren't, in fact, attributable to a particular scale.

We should note, however, that not all of the constructs examined in the previous chapters are confounded with a particular scale. Global job satisfaction, for instance, is assessed using a variety of different measures, including the Overall Job Satisfaction Scale (Brayfield & Rothe, 1951), the Michigan Organizational Assessment Questionnaire (Cammann et al., 1979), and the Job In General Scale (Ironson, Smith, Brannick, Gibson, & Paul, 1989). Given this, it is unlikely that the results observed within the global job satisfaction literature are the product of the idiosyncrasies of a given measure.

## *Reliance on Self-Report Measures*

As is apparent from the previous chapters, workplace psychological constructs have almost always been assessed using self-report measures (for exceptions, see Judge, Locke, Durham, & Kluger, 1998; Leavitt, Fong, & Greenwald, 2011). Reliance on self-report measures should not be surprising: Psychological constructs are internal; therefore, self-reports represent a rather direct, face-valid assessment strategy. Given this, reliance on self-report measures is not necessarily a problem, but we do believe that self-reports could be supplemented by alternative means of assessing psychological constructs.

These alternative measures could include (a) informant-reports and (b) indirect, implicit measures of psychological constructs. Informant-reports provide a useful means of assessing other psychological constructs, particularly employee personality traits (e.g., Connelly & Ones, 2010). Informant-reports offer two potential advantages. First, it may be less contaminated by various response biases (e.g., impression management and self-deception; Paulhus, 1984) than are self-reports. Informant data, therefore, may offer advantages over self-reports when measuring social sensitive workplace psychological constructs (e.g., satisfaction with one's direct supervisor). Second, the use of informant data creates the possibility that multiple sources can be used to assess the construct of interest. Of course, when researchers rely on self-reports, the data necessarily come from a single source—the participant. Computing composite scores across multiple informants minimizes the effects of idiosyncrasies of any single source, thus leveraging the principle of aggregation (Rushton, Brainerd, & Pressley, 1983). For this reason, composite predictor scores often yield higher reliability and better prediction of criterion variables than is possible when single-source predictor data are used (for an example from the personality literature see Connelly & Ones, 2010).

Implicit measures represent a second alternative means of assessing workplace psychological constructs. These measures come in a variety of forms, including implicit association tests, word-fragment tasks, and conditional reasoning tests (for a discussion of the use of implicit measures within organizational research, see the special issue of *Human Resource Management Review* edited by Bowling & Johnson, 2013). Rather than ask participants to report their experiences directly, these measures indirectly assess constructs by measuring implicit (unconscious) content. Similar to other-reports, implicit measures may be resistant to the effects of impression management and self-deception (see LeBreton, Barksdale, Robin, & James, 2007). Furthermore, implicit measures may assess a component of attitudes that is largely ignored by self-report measures—the implicit, unconscientious aspect of employees' attitudes. This is a potentially important feature of indirect measures because direct (i.e., explicit) and indirect (i.e., implicit) measures of the same construct generally yield modest relationships to each other (Hofmann, Gawronski, Gschwendner, Le, & Schmitt, 2005).

# Generally Ignored Substantive Questions

In this section, we discuss several generally ignored research questions related to the study of workplace psychological constructs, including four research topics discussed by the chapter authors as needing more attention, interactions between the constructs, and the relationship between non-traditional work arrangements and workplace psychological constructs.

## *Common Research Areas Mentioned across Chapters*

In this section, we highlight four areas that a number of the chapter authors mention as meriting additional attention. These include focusing on the dark side or adverse effects of workplace psychological constructs, exploring the stability or fluidity of these constructs via longitudinal studies, understanding these constructs at different levels of analysis, and considering these constructs in the global arena. We touch on these areas here, although various chapters discuss the issues in regards to their workplace psychological construct in more detail.

### *The Dark Side*

Researchers have largely assumed that high levels of a given workplace psychological construct are preferable to low levels. In addition, most studies examining the hypothesized effects of these constructs have focused on linear effects in line with these beliefs. This assumption, for instance, is implied when researchers treat job satisfaction as an indicator of employee well-being, as a cause of desirable work-related criteria (e.g., job performance), or when they use low job satisfaction scores to diagnose organizational dysfunction (see Spector, 1997). The potential adverse effects of high levels of workplace psychological constructs, however, are often overlooked. Many previous chapters in this book, in fact, have cited possible adverse effects of high levels of each workplace psychological construct as leading to increased stress, burnout, and possible risky or unethical behaviors. Further research into the dark side of workplace psychological constructs can help to find and strike the necessary balance to achieve the desired performance benefits without the risk of adverse side effects. We, as well as the chapter authors, encourage future studies to examine various non-linear relationships.

### *Stability vs Fluidity*

Several workplace psychological constructs were originally believed to be stable. In addition, much of the research on these constructs has been cross-sectional. However, authors of the previous chapters have noted that this assumption is increasingly being questioned. Questions to be further explored include whether these constructs are stable or fluid, and if fluid, what causes changes, how much time elapses before a change occurs, and what is the impact of changing levels of these constructs on variables of interest. We, as well as the chapter authors suggest conducting more longitudinal research to help better understand these issues.

### Levels of Analysis

Workplace psychological constructs are often considered and measured at the individual level of analysis; however, research is beginning to demonstrate that team- and organizational-levels of these constructs are also important to consider, as well as the effects between levels. More theory and research is needed beyond the micro-level to also include both meso- and macro-levels.

### Global Issues

The majority of industrial-organizational psychology research has been conducted within the US, and because of this, a common theme within the chapters of this book is the need for more global research on workplace psychological constructs. There is little research on the effects of different cultures on workplace psychological constructs and any possible dualities that may come from working in a multi-national corporation or having multiple cultural identities. This is especially relevant today, given that more and more companies are expanding internationally, including the global transfer of employees from one location to another. Much of the research thus far has widely left out these employees, so additional global research is needed to bridge this gap.

## Interactions between Various Workplace Psychological Constructs

In addition to recurring themes that were identified by our chapter authors, we have identified additional themes that should be addressed in future research. First, studies have often focused on the effects of a single workplace psychological construct. As a result, little is known about how these psychological constructs relate or interact with each other to affect various criterion variables. There are at least two mutually exclusive types of interactions, which we refer to as (a) the magnification effect and (b) the compensation effect. The former suggests that the effects of one workplace psychological construct (e.g., job satisfaction) on an outcome variable (e.g., job performance) become progressively *stronger* at higher levels of a second construct (e.g., organizational commitment); the latter suggests that the effects of one workplace psychological construct on an outcome variable become progressively *weaker* at higher levels of a second workplace psychological construct.

In terms of job satisfaction, for example, the magnification effect may occur to the extent that employees are more fixated on attitude objects toward which they have a negative rather than a positive attitude (see Baumeister, Bratslavsky, Finkenauer, & Vohs, 2001). Employees who are low in affective organizational commitment, for instance, may be highly preoccupied with their negative attitude toward their employer. As a result of this fixation, their attitude toward their job (i.e., global job satisfaction) may become less salient and thus unlikely to relate to performance criteria. Global job satisfaction levels of employees who are high in affective organizational commitment, on the other hand, may be relatively salient because those employees are not preoccupied with a negative attitude toward their employer. As a result, a relatively strong positive job satisfaction-job performance relationship may be present among these workers.

The compensation effect, on the other hand, suggests that various workplace psychological constructs can serve as substitutes for each other. Sticking with the previous example, employees' commitment toward their organization may serve as a functional substitute for their attitude toward their job. Likewise, their attitudes toward their job may serve as a functional substitute for their commitment to their organization. The compensation effect, therefore, suggests that the presence of just one positive workplace psychological construct is sufficient to produce effective job performance. As a result, the effects of one employee attitude (e.g., global job satisfaction) on job performance become weaker at high levels of a second workplace psychological construct (e.g., organizational commitment).

### *Non-Traditional Work Arrangements*

A final area that we would like to address is workplace psychological constructs in non-traditional work arrangements. Most studies cited in this book are based on core workers with traditional ties to their employer, with traditional work arrangements, and who are treated as though they have a stake in the company (Belous, 1990). In recent years, these core employees are increasingly experiencing non-traditional work arrangements such as flextime, telecommuting, and part-time schedules. In addition, the use of independent contributors, on-call workers, temporary or seasonal workers, temp agency workers, and workers employed through labor market platforms (such as Upwork and TaskRabbit) is growing, representing about 10% of the workforce (16 million workers, Nunn & O'Donnell, 2020). Finally, even organizations are increasingly complex, with such arrangements as joint ventures, virtual structures, and placing employees in client organizations. We cannot assume that the findings developed on traditional core employees will transfer to workers in these work arrangements. Current instruments measuring various workplace psychological constructs may not work. Industrial-organizational thought leaders need to extend or develop theory and conduct research on these populations for the same reasons that we do so with the traditional core employees: Understanding the workplace psychological constructs of these populations is valuable in its own right. If we are to address the betterment of society, these workers are important too. This research is needed especially in light of the fact that they earn less, have lower rates of health insurance, and experience larger and more frequent changes in weekly hours (Nunn & O'Donnell, 2020). How are these workers perceiving the organization (and what organization are they perceiving?); how is this influencing their identities towards (multiple and temporary) organizations and their jobs; how is this influencing their (multiple and temporary) bonds, attitudes, and engagement? At what level should improvements and interventions be enacted (organizational- or societal-level), and how does one measure the relevant outcomes? And, finally, what influence are these work arrangements having on bottom-line organizational outcomes as mediated by workplace psychological constructs of workers in these non-traditional arrangements?

## Practical Implications of Workplace Psychological Constructs

As we stated in the first chapter, workplace psychological constructs are important for four reasons. First, they are inherently valuable in their own right. Most adults spend much of their waking hours at work. A majority of adults work for an organization or identify with an organization (even if they are an independent contractor, as even tenuous connections lead to identification, such as Amway distributors and Uber drivers; Pratt, 2000, Rogers, Corley, & Ashforth, 2016). Second, measures of these constructs provide organizations with diagnostic information regarding how employees perceive the organization and the impacts of those perceptions. These diagnostic measures can help organizations obtain useful information regarding what is working and what needs to be changed. Similarly, they can be used for assessing the effectiveness of organizational interventions. Finally, workplace psychological constructs, as seen in the research reported in these chapters, are potential causes of key organizational outcomes. Each of the chapter authors offered practical advice based on the research and findings regarding the psychological construct targeted in their chapter. Here, we take a bird's eye view drawing information from all the chapters together.

Perceptions are key. According to the chapters in this book, employees want to work for reputable organizations that they can be proud of, they want to be treated fairly, and they want to feel valued and supported. Employees base their perceptions of these issues on organizational variables such as how the organization is perceived in the wider community, how the organization is led and managed, organizational culture, HR, and other practices. Second, employees want meaningful jobs, and they want the resources to get those jobs done. Here they consider the characteristics of their jobs, their workload, and other stressors, as well as the resources they have available to accomplish their jobs. Employees want to work with others in an efficient and friendly manner. They consider their supervisors and peer support as well as the teams they work in. Finally, employees exist in a setting beyond the workplace. They have family and live in a community which both impacts and is impacted by their work. When employees perceive that they work for a great organization that treats them fairly, that values and supports them, that they have meaningful jobs and the resources to do them, and that they work with others in an efficient and friendly manner, they reciprocate. They bond with the organization by committing to the organization, people (supervisors, peers, team members), and the job, and identifying with them. They are satisfied and motivated. Bonds, attitudes, and motivations have teeth, they matter. Employees perform their jobs, they go beyond what is expected, they are less likely to engage in counterproductive behaviors, and they show up on time and regularly and continue with the organization. Research demonstrates that this has an impact not just on individual employee behaviors but also on the organizational bottom line (Sirota & Klein, 2014).

The most lucrative place for the organization to intervene, then, is through creating organizational direction, structure, policies, practices, procedures, systems, etc. while keeping ideas of justice, support, achievement (including meaningful jobs and the resources to do them), and friendly and efficient work arrangements in mind, as well as communicating the reasoning of why they are creating or changing any of these. Communications should include regular feedback from the employees—how are they perceiving the organization?—which can lead to information regarding what is working and what needs to be changed.

## Summary

Job attitudes, perceptions, bonds, and motivational states—what we collectively referred to in this chapter as "Workplace Psychological Constructs"—have long played an important role in the organizational research literature. The importance of these constructs should not be surprising since they help to diagnose organizational problems, are potential predictors of important work-related outcomes (e.g., job performance), and are valued in their own right as indicators of employee well-being. The current chapter has critically evaluated the literature on these constructs and has identified several future research directions as well as made a few practical implications. Most importantly, we showed that the various workplace psychological constructs have much in common with each other and that much is to be gained by studying them together.

## References

Allen, N.J. & Meyer, J.P. (1990). The measurement and antecedents of affective, continuance and normative commitment to the organization. *Journal of Occupational Psychology, 63*, 1–18.

Anderson, J.C. & Gerbing, D.W. (1991). Predicting the performance of measures in a confirmatory factor analysis with a pretest assessment of their substantive validities. *Journal of Applied Psychology, 76*, 732–740.

Baumeister, R.F., Bratslavsky, E., Finkenauer, C., & Vohs, K.D. (2001). Bad is stronger than good. *Review of General Psychology, 5*(4), 323–370.

Belous, R.S. (1990). Flexible employment: The employer's point of view. In P. B. Doeringer (Ed.), *Bridges to retirement: Older workers in a changing labor market* (pp. 111–129). Ithaca, NY: Cornell University.

Bohner, G. & Dickel, N. (2011). Attitudes and attitude change. *Annual Review of Psychology, 62*, 391–417.

Bowlby, J. (1982/1969). *Attachment and loss: Vol. 1. Attachment* (2nd ed.). New York: Basic Books.

Bowling, N.A. & Hammond, G.D. (2008). A meta-analytic examination of the construct validity of the Michigan Organizational Assessment Questionnaire Job Satisfaction Subscale. *Journal of Vocational Behavior, 73*, 63–77.

Bowling, N.A. & Johnson, R.E. (2013). Measuring implicit content and processes at work: A new frontier within the organizational sciences. *Human Resource Management Review, 23*, 203–204.

Bowling, N.A., Khazon, S., Alarcon, G.M., Blackmore, C.E., Bragg, C.B., Hoepf, M.R., & Li, H. (2017). Building better measures of role ambiguity and role conflict: The validation of new role stressor scales. *Work & Stress, 31*, 1–23.

Bowling, N.A., Khazon, S., Meyer, R.D., & Burrus, C.J. (2015). Situational strength as a moderator of the relationship between job satisfaction and job performance: A meta-analytic examination. *Journal of Business and Psychology, 30*, 89–104.

Brayfield, A.H. & Rothe, H.F. (1951). An index of job satisfaction. *Journal of Applied Psychology, 35*, 307–311.

Cammann, C., Fichman, M., Jenkins, D., & Klesh, J. (1979). The Michigan Organizational Assessment Questionnaire (Unpublished manuscript). University of Michigan, Ann Arbor, MI.

Cheney, G. (1982). Organization identification as a process and product: A field study. Unpublished master's thesis, Purdue University, West Lafayette, IN.

Cheney, G. (1983). On the various and changing meanings of organizational membership: A field study of organizational identification. *Communication Monographs, 50*, 343–362.

Colquitt, J.A. (2001). On the dimensionality of organizational justice: A construct validation of a measure. *Journal of Applied Psychology, 86*(3), 386–400.

Connelly, B.S. & Ones, D.S. (2010). An other perspective on personality: Meta-analytic integration of observers' accuracy and predictive validity. *Psychological Bulletin, 136*, 1092–1122.

Cronbach, L.J. & Meehl, P.E. (1955). Construct validity in psychological tests. *Psychological Bulletin, 52*(4), 281–302.

DeVellis, R.F. (2012). *Scale Development: Theory and Applications.* Thousand Oaks, CA: Sage.

Eisenberger, R., Huntington, R., Hutchison, S., & Sowa, D. (1986). Perceived organizational support. *Journal of Applied Psychology, 71*, 500–507.

Ellemers, N., Spears, R., & Doosje, B. (2002). Self and social identity. Annual Review of Psychology, 53(1), 161–186. doi:10.1146/annurev.psych.53.100901.135228

Ferris, D.L., Brown, D.J., Berry, J.W., & Lian, H. (2008). The development and validation of the Workplace Ostracism Scale. *Journal of Applied Psychology, 93*, 1348–1366.

Harrison, D.A., Newman, D.A., & Roth, P.L. (2006). How important are job attitudes? Meta- analytic comparisons of integrative behavioral outcomes and time sequences. *Academy of Management Journal, 49*, 305–325.

Hershcovis, M.S. (2011). "Incivility, social undermining, bullying… oh my!": A call to reconcile constructs within workplace aggression research. *Journal of Organizational Behavior 32*, 499–519.

Hinkin, T.R. (1998). A brief tutorial on the development of measures for use in survey questionnaires. *Organizational Research Methods, 1*, 104–121.

Hofmann, W., Gawronski, B., Gschwendner, T., Le, H., & Schmitt, M. (2005). A meta-analysis on the correlation between the Implicit Association Test and explicit self-report measures. *Personality and Social Psychology Bulletin, 31*(10), 1369–1385.

Ironson, G.H., Smith, P.C., Brannick, M.T., Gibson, W.M., & Paul, K.B. (1989). Construction of a job in general scale: A comparison of global, composite, and specific measures. *Journal of Applied Psychology, 74*, 193–200.

Judge, T.A., Erez, A., Bono, J.E., & Thoresen, C.J. (2002). Are measures of self-esteem, neuroticism, locus of control, and generalized self-efficacy indicators of a common core construct? *Journal of Personality and Social Psychology, 83*, 693–710.

Judge, T.A., Erez, A., Bono, J.E., & Thoresen, C.J. (2003). The core self-evaluations scale: Development of a measure. *Personnel Psychology, 56*, 303–331.

Judge, T.A., Locke, E.A., Durham, C.C., & Kluger, A.N. (1998). Dispositional effects on job and life satisfaction: The role of core evaluations. *Journal of Applied Psychology, 83*, 17–34.

Klein, H.J., Molloy, J.C., & Brinsfield, C.T. (2012). Reconceptualizing workplace commitment to redress a stretched construct: Revisiting assumptions and removing confounds. *Academy of Management Review, 37*(1), 130–151.

Kurtessis, J.N., Eisenberger, R., Ford, M.T., Buffardi, L.C., Stewart, K.A., & Adis, C.S. (2015). Perceived organizational support: A meta-analytic evaluation of organizational support theory. Journal of Management, 43(6), 1854–1884. doi:10.1177/0149206315575554

Leavitt, K., Fong, C.T., & Greenwald, A.G. (2011). Asking about well-being gets you half an answer: Intra-individual processes of implicit and explicit job attitudes. *Journal of Organizational Behavior, 32*, 672–687.

LeBreton, J.M., Barksdale, C.D., Robin, J., & James, L.R. (2007). Measurement issues associated with conditional reasoning tests: Indirect measurement and test faking. *Journal of Applied Psychology, 92*(1), 1–16.

Levin, I. & Stokes, J.P. (1989). Dispositional approach to job satisfaction: Role of negative affectivity. *Journal of Applied Psychology, 74*, 752–758.

Mael, F.A., & Tetrick, L.E. (1992). Identifying organizational identification. *Educational and Psychological Measurement, 52*, 813–824.

Meyer, J.P., Stanley, D.J., Herscovitch, L., & Topolnytsky, L. (2002). Affective, continuance, and normative commitment to the organization: A meta-analysis of antecedents, correlates, and consequences. *Journal of Vocational Behavior, 61*, 20–52.

Mikulincer, M. & Shaver, P.R. (2003). The attachment behavioral system in adulthood: Activation, psychodynamics, and interpersonal processes. Advances in Experimental Social Psychology, 53–152. doi:10.1016/s0065-2601(03)01002-5

Nunn, R. & O'Donnell, J. (May 7, 2020). The labor market experiences of workers in alternative work arrangements. *The Hamilton Project. Brookings.* (www.brookings.edu/research/the-labor-market-experiences-of-workers-in-alternative-work-arrangements/).

Paulhus, D.L. (1984). Two-component models of socially desirable responding. *Journal of Personality and Social Psychology, 46*, 598–609.

Peeters, M.A., Rutte, C.G., van Tuijl, H.F., & Reymen, I.M. (2006). The big five personality traits and individual satisfaction with the team. *Small Group Research, 37*, 187–211.

Pratt, M.G. (2000). The good, the bad, and the ambivalent: Managing identification among Amway distributors. *Administrative Science Quarterly, 45(3)*, 456–493.

Rhoades, L. & Eisenberger, R. (2002). Perceived organizational support: A review of the literature. *Journal of Applied Psychology, 87*, 698–714.

Richardson, K.M. & Rothstein, H.R. (2008). Effects of occupational stress management intervention programs: A meta-analysis. *Journal of Occupational Health Psychology, 13*, 69–93.

Riketta, M. (2005). Organizational identification: A meta-analysis. *Journal of Vocational Behavior, 66*, 358–384.

Rogers, K.M., Corley, H.G., & Ashforth, B.E. (2016). Seeing more than orange: Organizational respect and positive identity transformation in a prison context. *Administrative Science Quarterly, 62(2)*, 219–269.

Rushton, J.P., Brainerd, C.J., & Pressley, M. (1983). Behavioral development and construct validity: The principle of aggregation. *Psychological Bulletin, 94*, 18–38.

Salanova, M., Gonzalez-Roma, V., & Bakker, A.B. (2002). The measurement of engagement and burnout: A two sample confirmatory factor analytic approach. *Journal of Happiness Studies, 3*, 71–92.

Schleicher, D.J., Smith, T.A., Casper, W.J., Watt, J.D., & Greguras, G.J. (2015). It's all in the attitude: The role of job attitude strength in job attitude–outcome relationships. *Journal of Applied Psychology, 100*, 1259–1274.

Shaffer, J.A., DeGeest, D., & Li, A. (2016). Tackling the problem of construct proliferation: A guide to assessing the discriminant validity of conceptually related constructs. *Organizational Research Methods, 19*, 80–110.

Shuck, B., Ghosh, R., Zigarmi, D. & Nimon, K. (2013) The jingle jangle of employee engagement. *Human Resource Development Review, 12*, 11–35.

Sirota, D. & Klein, D. A. (2014). *The Enthusiastic Employee: How Companies Profit by Giving Workers What They Want* (2nd ed.). Upper Saddle River, NJ: Pearson.

Spector, P.E. (1991). *Summated rating scale construction: An introduction.* Newbury Park, CA: Sage.

Spector, P.E. (1997). *Job Satisfaction: Applications, Assessment, Causes and Consequences.* Thousand Oaks, CA: Sage.

Spector, P.E. & Jex, S.M. (1998). Development of four self-report measures of job stressors and strain: interpersonal conflict at work scale, organizational constraints scale, quantitative workload inventory, and physical symptoms inventory. *Journal of Occupational Health Psychology, 3*, 356–367.

Whitman, D.S., Van Rooy, D.L., & Viswesvaran, C. (2010). Satisfaction, citizenship behaviors, and performance in work units: A meta-analysis of collective construct relations. *Personnel Psychology, 63*, 41–81.

Zacks, J.M. (2020). Event perception and memory. Annual Review of Psychology, 71(1), 165–191. doi:10.1146/annurev-psych-010419-051101

# INDEX

Made in United States
Orlando, FL
09 August 2022

20757532R00200